The United Nations and Nuclear Non-Proliferation

The United Nations
Blue Books Series, Volume III

The United Nations and

Nuclear WITHDRAWN

Non-Proliferation

**With an introduction by
Boutros Boutros-Ghali,
Secretary-General of the United Nations**

Department of Public Information
United Nations, New York

Published by the United Nations
Department of Public Information
New York, NY 10017

Editor's note:

This book focuses on the Nuclear Non-Proliferation Treaty and Regime. Each of the United Nations documents and other materials reproduced herein ("Texts of documents", pages 45-189) has been assigned a number (e.g. Document 1, Document 2, etc.). This number is used throughout the Introduction and other parts of this book to guide readers to the document texts. For other documents mentioned in the book but not reproduced, the United Nations document symbol (e.g.A/49/436) is provided. With this symbol, such documents can be consulted at the Dag Hammarskjöld Library at United Nations Headquarters in New York, at other libraries in the United Nations system or at libraries around the world which have been designated as depository libraries for United Nations documents.

Copyright © 1995 United Nations

The United Nations and Nuclear Non-Proliferation
The United Nations Blue Books Series
Volume III
ISBN 92-1-100557-4

United Nations Publication
Sales No. E. 95.I.17 (Soft)

Printed by the United Nations Reproduction Section
New York, NY

Contents

Section One
Introduction

I   Overview

1   Fifty years have passed since the world entered the nuclear age. The scientific and technological achievement of splitting the atom remains a source of both inspiration and consternation. Harnessing the energy released from a controlled series of nuclear explosions provides a possible solution to many countries' energy requirements. At the same time, the awesome lethal destruction of a nuclear weapon, which results from the non-controlled release of an atomic explosion, continues to haunt humanity. Guaranteeing that the benefits of the peaceful application of nuclear energy are universally recognized while simultaneously ensuring that nuclear weapons are never again used is a tremendous challenge to world peace and prosperity. The Treaty on the Non-Proliferation of Nuclear Weapons (commonly known as the Non-Proliferation Treaty, or NPT)[1] represents the single most important effort of the international community to meet this challenge.

1/Document 11
See page 59

2   The Treaty spells out numerous obligations that nuclear-weapon States (NWS) and non-nuclear-weapon States (NNWS) agree to undertake regarding nuclear weapons, nuclear explosive devices and nuclear energy. All parties to the Treaty are to be able to benefit from the peaceful applications of nuclear energy. As the proliferation of nuclear weapons is seen to undermine international security, non-nuclear weapon States parties agree not to develop or obtain nuclear weapons, and nuclear-weapon States parties agree to pursue nuclear disarmament. All parties to the Treaty pledge to work towards general and complete disarmament.

3   Opened for signature in 1968, the Treaty entered into force in 1970. Today there are 171 parties to the Treaty. The fact that more countries have ratified the NPT than any other arms limitation and disarmament agreement attests to the Treaty's pre-eminent significance. Conditions should be created that will encourage universal membership. We cannot rest until this goal is attained.

4   The NPT's importance cannot be overemphasized. The critical importance of nuclear non-proliferation and disarmament was clearly stated in the Final Document[2] that the United Nations General Assembly adopted in 1978, at the conclusion of its first special session devoted entirely to the question of disarmament. The Final Document stated: "... it is imperative to remove the threat of nuclear weapons, to halt and reverse the nuclear arms race until the total elimination of nuclear weapons and their delivery systems has been achieved, and to prevent the proliferation of nuclear weapons."

2/Document 25
See page 124

3/Document 38
See page 168

5   More recently, in January 1992, members of the United Nations Security Council, meeting at the level of Heads of State and Government, issued a statement[3] declaring that the proliferation of nuclear weapons and other weapons of mass destruction (including chemical and biological weapons) posed a threat to international peace and security. They stressed that the NPT played a fundamental role in addressing that threat.

6   The NPT, together with other measures that comprise the nuclear non-proliferation regime, has succeeded in stemming the proliferation of nuclear weapons and in reducing the existing nuclear arsenals. While the NPT was being negotiated there was much concern that failure to create a treaty would result in significant nuclear proliferation. Even after the NPT entered into force, sceptics warned that there could be 20 to 30 nuclear-weapon States by the 1980s. That this has not occurred is not simply good luck. A cause-and-effect relationship is discernible.

7   Today, more than ever, the NPT remains the vital instrument it has always been. For the nuclear non-proliferation regime to remain effective, the Treaty must remain in force. Ensuring the Treaty's continued existence and further strengthening its effectiveness, therefore, provides the international community with an opportunity to move forward in a crucial area of preventive diplomacy. On a number of occasions and in various forums,[4] I have stressed the importance of this Treaty for international peace and security.

4/Document 40
See page 170;
Document 43
See page 174;
Document 44
See page 176;
Document 47
See page 184

8   On the eve of the 1995 NPT Conference, I welcome the opportunity to discuss the Treaty's unique importance. This Introduction, which comprises Section One of this volume, first reviews the multilateral diplomatic efforts to prevent the proliferation of nuclear weapons and to promote nuclear disarmament that preceded the Treaty and then discusses the nuclear non-proliferation regime. Section Two contains a chronological account of events in the creation of the nuclear non-proliferation regime, the texts of important agreements, declarations and resolutions, and a list of other documents of interest. With respect to the United Nations documents that are cited but not reproduced or that are excerpted, the full texts are available at United Nations information centres and depository libraries throughout the world.

II Treaty on the Non-Proliferation of Nuclear Weapons

9   In the immediate aftermath of the Second World War, rebuilding war-torn economies and competition for ideological and political alliances were of paramount concern. Mistrust and national security considerations explain why some countries put greater emphasis on developing their own nuclear capabilities than on promoting the need for total nuclear disarmament. By 1964, five countries — China, France, the Union of Soviet Socialist Republics (USSR), the United Kingdom of Great Britain and Northern Ireland and the United States of America — had both tested and developed nuclear weapons.

10   Early multilateral diplomacy in this area led to the adoption of a number of resolutions[5] in the United Nations General Assembly, culminating in the unanimous adoption in 1961 of resolution 1665 (XVI)[6] — commonly referred to as the "Irish resolution" in recognition of the Irish initiative and leadership in the matter. By that resolution, the General Assembly: "[*Called*] upon all States, and in particular upon the States at present possessing nuclear weapons, to use their best endeavours to secure the conclusion of an international agreement containing provisions under which the nuclear States would undertake to refrain from relinquishing control of nuclear weapons and from transmitting the information necessary for their manufacture to States not possessing such weapons, and provisions under which States not possessing nuclear weapons would undertake not to manufacture or otherwise acquire control of such weapons".

5/Document 1
See page 45;
Document 2
See page 45;
Document 3
See page 46

6/Document 4
See page 48

11   Efforts to prevent proliferation continued. In its resolution 2028(XX) of 19 November 1965,[7] the General Assembly spelled out more concretely what the Member States wanted. "Convinced that the proliferation of nuclear weapons would endanger the security of all States and make more difficult the achievement of general and complete disarmament under effective international control," the Assembly called upon the Eighteen-Nation Committee on Disarmament to give urgent consideration to the question of the non-proliferation of nuclear weapons, and to commence negotiations on an international treaty for that purpose. The Assembly stipulated that:

7/Document 5
See page 47

(*a*) The treaty should be void of any loopholes which might permit nuclear or non-nuclear Powers to proliferate, directly or indirectly, nuclear weapons in any form;

(*b*) The treaty should embody an acceptable balance of mutual responsibilities and obligations of the nuclear and non-nuclear Powers;

(*c*) The treaty should be a step towards the achievement of general and complete disarmament and, more particularly, nuclear disarmament;

(*d*) There should be acceptable and workable provisions to ensure the effectiveness of the treaty;

(*e*) Nothing in the treaty should adversely affect the right of any group of States to conclude regional treaties in order to ensure the total absence of nuclear weapons in their respective territories.

12   Various versions of draft treaties were subsequently submitted by the United States and the Soviet Union to the General Assembly and to the Eighteen-Nation Committee on Disarmament, and the Assembly adopted further resolutions[8] in which it reiterated the urgency of concluding the treaty. My predecessors also conveyed to the General Assembly, in their reports on the work of the Organization,[9] their views on the importance of non-proliferation. In the course of 1967 the Committee made steady progress in its negotiations and in early 1968 it submitted a draft treaty to the General Assembly. After further discussion and revision, the Assembly adopted resolution 2373 (XXII),[10] by which it commended the Treaty, the text of which was annexed to the resolution, and expressed the hope for the widest possible adherence to it.

13   The Treaty was opened for signature on 1 July 1968 at London, Moscow and Washington. According to article IX, paragraph 3, the Treaty would enter into force when the Governments of the three designated depositaries and at least 40 other signatory States had ratified it. The three designated depositaries, as provided in article IX, paragraph 2, were the Governments of the United Kingdom of Great Britain and Northern Ireland, the United States of America and the Union of Soviet Socialist Republics. The condition in article IX, paragraph 3, was met on 5 March 1970.

8/Document 7
See page 49;
Document 8
See page 49;
Document 10
See page 59

9/Document 6
See page 48;
Document 14
See page 75

10/Document 11
See page 59

The NPT: General principles

14   The Treaty on the Non-Proliferation of Nuclear Weapons incorporates faithfully the five principles enunciated in General Assembly resolution 2028 (XX). It is an agreement freely entered into between nuclear-weapon States and non-nuclear-weapon States as to how best to take advantage of nuclear energy's peaceful applications while taking pains not to undermine international peace and security.

15   Under article IX, paragraph 3, of the Treaty, a "nuclear-weapon State" is defined as one "which has manufactured and exploded a nuclear weapon or other nuclear explosive device prior to 1 January

1967." There were five States that fitted this definition: China, France, the USSR, the United Kingdom and the United States. While two of them initially chose not to ratify the Treaty, all five are now States parties.

16   The NPT is not a coercive attempt to force some countries into subservient positions. The Treaty neither created nuclear weapons nor sanctioned their existence. It should be seen for what it is: a cooperative effort to address a potentially destabilizing factor.

17   Two principles in particular are of fundamental importance in understanding the Treaty. One is that the peaceful application of nuclear energy should be made universally available. In the preamble to the Treaty, the States parties: "[Affirm] the principle that the benefits of peaceful applications of nuclear technology, including any technological by-products which may be derived by nuclear-weapon States from the development of nuclear explosive devices, should be available for peaceful purposes to all Parties to the Treaty, whether nuclear-weapon or non-nuclear-weapon States". A second overriding principle is that the spread of nuclear weapons undermines international peace and security. According to the preamble, the States parties believe that "the proliferation of nuclear weapons would seriously enhance the danger of nuclear war" and, in conformity with resolutions of the General Assembly, call for "the conclusion of an agreement on the prevention of wider dissemination of nuclear weapons".

18   Towards these ends, the Treaty in its preamble and 11 articles spells out a number of obligations that the parties to the NPT agree to undertake. Some of these obligations pertain only to nuclear-weapon States parties, others pertain only to non-nuclear-weapon States parties, and others pertain to all parties to the Treaty.

Obligations pertaining to nuclear-weapon States parties to the Treaty

19   Under article I, NWS parties to the Treaty agree to refrain from transferring nuclear weapons or nuclear explosive devices to any recipient. They are also prohibited from transferring control over such weapons or such devices. NWS parties are thus permitted to deploy nuclear weapons in areas outside their territory that are not otherwise prohibited under international agreements. The deployment of any nuclear weapons, however, would have to remain under the direct command and control of the nuclear-weapon State. The United States and the Soviet Union were the only nuclear-weapon States parties to deploy nuclear weapons beyond their territories. The 1987 Treaty between the United States and the Soviet Union on the Elimination of Their Interme-

diate-Range and Shorter-Range Missiles (the INF Treaty) resulted in the removal of many of these weapons.

20   When the Russian Federation replaced the Soviet Union as a designated depositary of the Treaty in December 1991, nuclear weapons under its direct control remained in lands outside its territory. The Russian Federation inherited the nuclear weapons deployed in what are now the independent States of Belarus, Kazakhstan and Ukraine. All three nations have renounced their intentions to become nuclear-weapon States, and all three have since adhered to the Treaty as non-nuclear-weapon States.

21   Furthermore, article VII states that "nothing in this Treaty affects the right of any group of States to conclude regional treaties in order to assure the total absence of nuclear weapons in their respective territories." Two groups of Member States have concluded such regional treaties and created what are known as "nuclear-weapon-free zones". The 1967 Treaty of Tlatelolco[11] covers a vast territory throughout Latin America and the Caribbean, and the 1985 Treaty of Rarotonga[12] covers a vast territory in the South Pacific. The text of a treaty establishing an African nuclear-weapon-free zone is expected to be finalized in 1995.

11/Document 9
See page 50

12/Document 32
See page 138

22   Article V provides for measures to ensure that NWS parties make available to NNWS parties potential benefits from any peaceful applications of nuclear explosions "on a non-discriminatory basis and that the charge to such Parties for the explosive devices used will be as low as possible and exclude any charge for research and development".

23   Under article VI, NWS parties agree "to pursue negotiations in good faith on effective measures relating to cessation of the nuclear arms race at an early date and to nuclear disarmament". The preamble also addresses NWS parties' obligation to disarm, stating that parties to the Treaty "[declare] their intention to achieve at the earliest possible date the cessation of the nuclear arms race and to undertake effective measures in the direction of nuclear disarmament". Initial measures that NWS parties undertook were ineffective in curtailing the nuclear arms race ("qualitative" proliferation) and did not halt the growth of nuclear arsenals ("quantitative" proliferation). These measures did, however, provide important and necessary confidence- and security-building measures. Recently, however, the two NWS parties with the greatest nuclear arsenals have begun to implement their stated intentions. Nuclear disarmament has begun in reality.

Obligations pertaining to non-nuclear-weapon States parties to the Treaty

24   As for obligations pertaining solely to NNWS parties to the Treaty, each non-nuclear-weapon State party undertakes, under article II, not to receive or control any nuclear weapons or other nuclear explosive devices and not to seek or receive any assistance in manufacturing such weapons or devices. As a confidence- and security-building measure, article III, paragraph 1, of the Treaty obliges NNWS parties to accept the safeguards of the International Atomic Energy Agency (IAEA) "with a view to preventing diversion of nuclear energy from peaceful uses to nuclear weapons or other nuclear explosive devices." Article III, paragraph 4, stipulates the time-frame in which such agreements are to be carried out.

Obligations pertaining to both NWS and NNWS parties to the Treaty

25   Many obligations pertain to both NWS and NNWS parties. Under article III, paragraph 2, "each State Party to the Treaty undertakes not to provide: (*a*) source or special fissionable material, or (*b*) equipment or material especially designed or prepared for the processing, use or production of special fissionable material, to any non-nuclear-weapon State for peaceful purposes, unless the source or special fissionable material shall be subject to the safeguards required by this article."

26   Under article IV, paragraph 2, "all the Parties to the Treaty undertake to facilitate, and have the right to participate in, the fullest possible exchange of equipment, materials and scientific and technological information for the peaceful uses of nuclear energy. Parties to the Treaty in a position to do so shall also cooperate in contributing alone or together with other States or international organizations to the further development of the applications of nuclear energy for peaceful purposes, especially in the territories of non-nuclear-weapon States Party to the Treaty, with due consideration for the needs of the developing areas of the world."

27   The often-repeated selective quotation of article VI has led to some misunderstanding. As discussed above, article VI reiterates the goal stated in the preamble to the Treaty that effective measures should be taken towards nuclear disarmament. The full text of article VI, however, addresses *all* States parties to the Treaty and does not limit itself to nuclear disarmament matters. The full text reads as follows: "Each of the Parties to the Treaty undertakes to pursue negotiations in good faith on effective measures relating to cessation of the nuclear arms race at an early date and to nuclear disarmament, and on a treaty on general and complete disarmament under strict and effective international control."

The NPT: 1970-1995 and beyond

13/Document 18
See page 93

28   Article VIII, paragraph 3, states that five years after the Treaty enters into force, a conference of parties to the Treaty is to be held. The intention of such a conference was to review the operation of the Treaty with a view to assuring that the purposes of the preamble and the provisions of the articles were being realized. Accordingly, the first NPT Review Conference was held at Geneva in 1975.[13] Article VIII, paragraph 3, also stipulates that a majority of the parties to the Treaty can propose the convening of additional review conferences at five-year intervals. A majority of States parties have been so inclined, and subsequent Review Conferences were held at Geneva in 1980, 1985[14] and 1990. On each occasion, the Secretary-General of the United Nations and the Director General of IAEA reiterated the importance of the NPT for international peace and security.[15]

14/Document 35
See page 150

15/Document 16
See page 90;
Document 17
See page 92;
Document 27
See page 131;
Document 28
See page 132;
Document 33
See page 145;
Document 34
See page 146;
Document 36
See page 162;
Document 37
See page 163

29   The Treaty also calls upon parties to convene a conference 25 years after its entry into force to discuss the terms by which it will be extended. This conference is not a continuation of the review conference mechanism established in article VIII, paragraph 3, discussed above. Article X, paragraph 2, of the Treaty stipulates the conditions clearly. The entire text reads as follows: "Twenty-five years after the entry into force of the Treaty, a conference shall be convened to decide whether the Treaty shall continue in force indefinitely, or shall be extended for an additional fixed period or periods. This decision shall be taken by a majority of the Parties to the Treaty." The Conference will be convened in New York from 17 April to 12 May 1995. The 171 parties to the Treaty have a unique opportunity to consolidate what has become the centre-piece of the world's efforts to confront the threat of nuclear proliferation.

Importance of the universality of the NPT

30   Apart from the five nuclear-weapon States, no other State has been officially declared to be a nuclear-weapon State. In 1974, India, after detonating a nuclear device, declared that it had done so for peaceful purposes and that it had no intention of developing nuclear weapons. Over the years, however, considerable concern has developed among the States parties to the NPT that some non-nuclear-weapon States might have acquired the capability to develop nuclear-weapon programmes. This concern was expressed particularly in connection with the so-called "threshold" States that were not covered by existing non-proliferation arrangements. Consequently, on different occasions and in various contexts, States parties to the NPT have repeatedly called for universal adherence to the Treaty as a means of strengthening the nuclear non-proliferation regime and thus contribute to enhanced international security and stability.

31   Developments during the last few years have further under-lined the need for the universality of the NPT. In 1993, South Africa provided an official account of its past nuclear-weapon programme. It stated that at one stage it had developed a limited nuclear-fission deter-rent capability; by the end of the 1980s, however, a nuclear deterrent had become not only superfluous, but an obstacle to the development of its international relations. This prompted South Africa to accede to the NPT in July 1991.

32   Some very recent developments have given rise to new con-cerns on the part of the international community, since they involve parties to the NPT and their non-compliance with the Treaty's provisions on the one hand, and related safeguards agreements on the other. The first case stemmed from information that Iraq had, over the years, engaged in activities inconsistent with its Treaty obligations under article III. The second case involved the controversy over compliance with safeguards obligations by the Democratic People's Republic of Korea.

33   Following revelations after the 1991 Gulf war—based on reports in the hands of Member States—that Iraq had attempted to acquire material for a nuclear-weapon programme contrary to its obliga-tions under the NPT, the Security Council took specific corrective action. This was initiated in Council resolution 687 (1991) and subsequently elaborated in resolutions 707 (1991) and 715 (1991). Since the adoption of resolution 687 (1991), the IAEA, with the assistance and cooperation of the United Nations Special Commission established for the purpose, has been engaged in the implementation of its relevant provisions. Pro-gress has been made. By late 1993, Iraq had acknowledged its obligations under the various resolutions. It has committed itself publicly to cooper-ate with the Special Commission and the IAEA in the implementation of ongoing monitoring and verification and to respect their rights and privileges in doing so.

34   Regarding the case of the Democratic People's Republic of Korea, after prolonged discussion and negotiation in October 1994, an "Agreed Framework" was concluded between the United States and the Democratic People's Republic of Korea, providing for a set of phased measures ultimately permitting the IAEA to conduct full-scope safe-

guards activities in the latter country. It is generally believed that, with conclusion of that agreement, the dispute has been largely resolved, reaffirming the duty of parties to the NPT to comply with the obligations assumed under the Treaty.

35 Although a number of problematic situations have thus been successfully resolved, calls for universal adherence to the NPT are being made more forcefully than ever before. This sense of urgency is largely related to fears that several other States that remain outside the framework of the Treaty and whose nuclear facilities are not subject to international safeguards may have developed a nuclear-weapon capability or may be advancing towards acquiring such a capability. Some of the non-nuclear-weapon States parties to the NPT are expressing unwillingness to support the indefinite extension of the Treaty unless a satisfactory solution to this problem is found. The question of the universality of the NPT will clearly remain high on the agenda of the States parties to the Treaty.

III The nuclear non-proliferation regime

36   The intrinsic worth of the NPT is enhanced even further by additional efforts that have been undertaken to thwart the proliferation of nuclear weapons. These agreements — whether in the form of treaties or resolutions, or concluded unilaterally, bilaterally or multilaterally — together form what is known as the nuclear non-proliferation regime. The system incorporates measures intended to make the acquisition of nuclear weapons less attractive and more difficult.

37   Because the NPT guarantees non-nuclear-weapon States access to the peaceful uses of nuclear energy, the regime includes several mechanisms to ensure that this provision does not help create additional nuclear-weapon States. Towards this end, non-nuclear-weapon States parties to the NPT have undertaken to accept safeguards on all source or special fissionable material in all peaceful nuclear activities within their territories, under their jurisdiction or control. Not all countermeasures result from an agreement voluntarily reached between a supplier and a recipient, however. Export controls on equipment deemed to be sensitive and potentially destabilizing to the maintenance of international peace and security have also been established.

38   These actions, which address concerns over the supply of material and technology used to make nuclear weapons, comprise important parts of the regime. However, as mentioned below, there are problems concerning the manner in which some of the mechanisms are implemented.

39   Just as important are measures that confront the potential demand for material and technology to make nuclear weapons. Providing for the security of non-nuclear-weapon States so that they do not feel compelled to attempt to procure nuclear weapons for their defence represents another aspect of the nuclear non-proliferation regime. Both the security assurances issued by the nuclear-weapon States and the creation of nuclear-weapon-free zones address this question of demand. They have the potential to provide significant disincentives to procuring nuclear weapons, and thus serve to buttress efforts to curtail horizontal proliferation.

Safeguards

40   In the 1950s, nuclear technologies and natural resources intended for the production of nuclear energy and other peaceful purposes were exported under national guidelines. The various controls under which this equipment and material were sold or transferred proved to be either haphazardly applied or ineffective. The IAEA was created in 1957 to help to achieve the twin objectives of promoting the peaceful uses of nuclear energy and ensuring that assistance provided by the Agency, at its request or under its supervision or control would, in accordance with article II of the IAEA Statute, not be used in such a way as to further any military purpose. The second objective was to be achieved through the establishment of a safeguards system based, *inter alia*, on nuclear material accounting, containment and surveillance measures, and on-site inspections.

41   The European Atomic Energy Community (EURATOM), the Agency for the Prohibition of Nuclear Weapons in Latin America and the Caribbean (OPANAL) and the Brazilian-Argentine Agency for Accounting and Control of Nuclear Materials (ABACC) — established in 1957, 1967 and 1991, respectively — all represent important regional initiatives to promote the peaceful uses of nuclear energy and provide important confidence- and security-building measures that complement the work of the IAEA.

The International Atomic Energy Agency

42   The IAEA, which began its operations in 1957, now has 122 member States. As an autonomous intergovernmental organization with cooperative links with the United Nations and its relevant organs, the IAEA reports annually on its operations to the United Nations General Assembly. It also works closely with other parts of the United Nations system on the management of radioactive waste and other environmental concerns.

43   According to the Agency's Statute, the IAEA is to promote and develop the contributions that nuclear energy can make towards world peace, health and prosperity. In the debate about nuclear proliferation, it is important to remember that besides the benefits from nuclear energy, nuclear physics has many other beneficial applications in agriculture and medicine. The IAEA's Statute makes it clear, however, that its assistance in these efforts must not further any military purpose.

44   To carry out its mandate, the IAEA has developed safeguards to ensure that material is not diverted from peaceful uses to build nuclear weapons or nuclear explosive devices. All IAEA safeguards procedures require the relevant State to submit to IAEA review: (1) Design information about its nuclear facilities, existing or planned; (2) Full and accurate accounting reports relating to nuclear materials subject to safeguards; (3) Special reports in the unusual or unexpected circumstances specified in the safeguards agreement. The requirement that States with comprehensive safeguards agreements establish national systems of accounting and control of nuclear material is very important. It obliges facility operators submitting reports through the State to adhere to IAEA reporting requirements. Furthermore, it has been instrumental in promoting national legislation concerning nuclear material and its accountability. Another aspect that is common to all IAEA safeguards is the requirement that the plant be accessible to IAEA officials for the purposes of inspections.

45   The political objectives of NPT safeguards are to assure the international community that a State party to the Treaty is complying with its peaceful-use undertakings and to deter, through the risk of early detection, the diversion from peaceful uses or the misuse of nuclear materials and facilities. The technical objectives of IAEA safeguards under NPT agreements are to ensure that the IAEA is able to detect, in a timely manner, a diversion of nuclear material from a State's peaceful nuclear activities and to ensure that all nuclear material subject to safeguards in a State is declared to the Agency. Safeguards are a form of internationalized nuclear transparency and are applied to create the added confidence that is attained through verification.

46   The initial safeguards system that the IAEA developed was set out in a document that has been expanded twice and is known as INFCIRC/66/Rev.2.[16] As originally designed, the document was intended to apply to individual plants, which might only comprise one aspect in the production of material that could be used in nuclear weapons. By contrast, the safeguards agreement developed for the NPT[17] is truly comprehensive, and covers the entire fuel cycle of the non-nuclear-weapon States concerned. Known as IAEA document INFCIRC/153, it represents the combined efforts of 45 States that participated in drafting the safeguards agreement.

47   There are in total 199 IAEA safeguards agreements in force with 118 States, covering some 800 facilities. These include 102 comprehensive safeguards agreements pursuant to the NPT. Thus, the IAEA plays an essential role in the implementation of the nuclear non-proliferation regime.

16/Document 13
See page 64

17/Document 15
See page 76

International Convention on Nuclear Safety

48   The adoption of the International Convention on Nuclear Safety signals States' recognition of the need to be more open about their

nuclear programmes. The Convention, which is the first legal instrument that directly addresses the issue of the safety of nuclear power plants, was opened for signature at Vienna on 20 September 1994. By the end of 1994, 54 States had signed it. It will enter into force after the depositary — the IAEA — receives instruments of ratification from 22 States, including 17 States having at least one operating nuclear power plant. The Convention applies to land-based civil nuclear power plants and obliges contracting parties, *inter alia*, to establish and maintain proper legislative and regulatory frameworks to govern safety. Of equal significance is the provision that States must commit themselves to apply fundamental safety principles to their nuclear installations and agree to participate in periodic "peer" review meetings and to submit national reports on the implementation of their obligations.

49   Addressing concerns about the safety of nuclear power plants will also influence, where applicable, the States parties' procedures at other nuclear installations, pending the adoption of an instrument on the safety of waste management. This effort will also address environmental concerns and promote the security of nuclear material.

Convention on the Physical Protection of Nuclear Material

50   Besides the IAEA safeguards agreements and those of the other regional agencies, and the International Convention on Nuclear Safety, there is another very important instrument designed specifically to prevent the illegal diversion of nuclear material. The Convention on the Physical Protection of Nuclear Material obliges the parties to ensure that international transport of nuclear material is protected at an agreed level. The parties also agree not to export or import nuclear material unless they receive assurances that it will be sufficiently protected throughout all the stages of its shipment. Should something go awry during the transport of the nuclear material, parties to the Convention agree to share information on the incident so as to facilitate recovery. The Convention calls for the enactment of national legislation that would make attempts to undermine such shipments punishable offences. The Director General of the IAEA is the depositary of the Convention, which was signed on 3 March 1980 and entered into force in 1987.

Export controls

51   It will be recalled that article III, paragraph 2, of the NPT requires parties not to provide the means to process, use or produce fissionable material unless the recipient agrees to submit to IAEA safe-

guards. This raised the question of what technologies were to be restricted under the article's description of "equipment or material especially designed or prepared for the processing, use or production of special fissionable material".

The Zangger Committee

52   In 1971, many parties that were in a position to provide such equipment and materials undertook a series of meetings to address this question. The Nuclear Exporters Committee, as the informal group was initially called, attempted to agree upon a uniform interpretation of the terms "equipment or material especially designed or prepared for the processing, use or production of special fissionable material" (article III, paragraph 2). The Committee has since been known by the name of its first Chairman, a Swiss professor named Claude Zangger. The Zangger Committee interpreted article III (2) as requiring exporting countries to ensure that an importer places safeguards on specified material that relates to the manufacture of nuclear power or research installations. The Committee exchanges information among its members on relevant export licences that have been granted and those that have been refused. The Committee informs the IAEA of its actions.

The Nuclear Suppliers Group

53   In 1975, another effort was undertaken to protect nuclear material from being diverted from peaceful purposes. An informal group of nuclear supplier States, which had been meeting from 1975 to 1977 in London and was later known as the Nuclear Suppliers Group, established a list of materials, equipment and technology for export that would require recipients to provide adequate protection and pledge not to use them for other than peaceful purposes. Peaceful nuclear explosions were not permitted. Known as the London Guidelines for Nuclear Transfers,[18] the agreed list and terms for implementing the guidelines were adopted in 1977 and revised in 1993.[19]

18/Document 19
See page 116

54   At the conclusion of a meeting in Poland in April 1992, the Nuclear Suppliers Group adopted additional measures that extended the scope of their existing guidelines. The Group formally created a list of dual-use equipment, material and related technology — subsequently known as the Warsaw Guidelines[20] — whose transfer its members would restrict through national export legislation. They also agreed to export such items only to States that were parties to the NPT or that had accepted comprehensive IAEA safeguards. In addition, a consultative forum was created to review requests for export licence applications. The intention of this mechanism was to prevent States or companies that had

19/Document 41
See page 171

20/Document 39
See page 169

been refused export licences for restricted equipment to bypass the regulations as the result of an oversight by a member State of the Nuclear Suppliers Group, which is composed of 30 States with advanced nuclear capabilities.

The Missile Technology Control Regime

55   To ensure that efforts to prevent the proliferation of nuclear weapons and other weapons of mass destruction are as effective as possible, it is necessary also to confront the proliferation of the means to deliver such weapons. In April 1987, seven industrialized nations created the Missile Technology Control Regime and established guidelines for sensitive missile-relevant transfers. Eighteen other developed countries have since joined the Regime.

56   Under the Regime, participating States agree to cease exporting technologies and equipment that could be used to produce missiles with a range beyond 300 kilometres (187 miles) and a payload in excess of 500 kilograms (1,102 pounds). In July 1992, the guidelines were amended to cover also any missile capable of delivering chemical and biological weapons, in recognition of the threat that these other weapons of mass destruction pose to international peace and security.

*

57   Restricting exports of material and technology is an important part of the nuclear non-proliferation regime. A problem exists, however, in the manner in which the presently agreed restrictions are being implemented. For it is not the supply of material and technology that necessarily undermines international peace and security but rather the manner in which some of the equipment and resources may be employed.

58   Some countries state that current restrictions unduly harm their economic growth and well-being. Article IV, paragraph 2, of the NPT provides that "all the Parties to the Treaty undertake to facilitate, and have the right to participate in, the fullest possible exchange of equipment, materials and scientific and technological information for the peaceful uses of nuclear energy." Any technology, it is argued, should be made available to another country provided there is a reliable verification mechanism that would allow any concerns regarding its possible misuse to be quickly allayed.

Security assurances

59   Efforts to diminish the appeal nuclear weapons may possess for a non-nuclear-weapon State include the giving of security assurances by nuclear-weapon States. Declarations that nuclear-weapon States will

come to the assistance of any non-nuclear-weapon State threatened with nuclear weapons are known as "positive assurances". Nuclear-weapon States' guarantees that they will refrain from using their nuclear weapons against non-nuclear-weapon States are known as "negative assurances".

Positive security assurances

60   The NPT does not provide for either type of guarantee. When the Treaty was concluded, however, the USSR, the United Kingdom and the United States made identical formal declarations to the effect that they, as permanent members of the Security Council, would have to act immediately through the Council to take the measures necessary to counter aggression with nuclear weapons or the threat of such aggression against a non-nuclear-weapon State. They also submitted a draft resolution on the subject to the Security Council. The Council adopted it on 19 June 1968 — two weeks before the Treaty was opened for signature — as resolution 255 (1968).[21] The resolution reads as follows:

21/Document 12
See page 63

"*The Security Council . . .*

"1. *Recognizes* that aggression with nuclear weapons or the threat of such aggression against a non-nuclear-weapon State would create a situation in which the Security Council, and above all its nuclear-weapon State permanent members, would have to act immediately in accordance with their obligations under the United Nations Charter;

"2. *Welcomes* the intention expressed by certain States that they will provide or support immediate assistance, in accordance with the Charter, to any non-nuclear-weapon State Party to the Treaty on the Non-Proliferation of Nuclear Weapons that is a victim of an act or an object of a threat of aggression in which nuclear weapons are used".

22/Document 20
See page 122;
Document 21
See page 123;
Document 22
See page 123;
Document 23
See page 123;
Document 24
See page 123;
Document 26
See page 131;
Document 29
See page 137;
Document 30
See page 137;
Document 31
See page 137;
Document 42
See page 174

Negative security assurances

61   All five nuclear-weapon States parties to the Treaty have issued negative assurances.[22] While non-nuclear-weapon States welcome such guarantees, they would prefer that they be reiterated and reissued in a formal treaty containing unconditional and absolute negative security assurances. The unilateral declarations made by the nuclear-weapon States are not uniform. They are as follows:

(*a*) China delivered a letter to the Secretary-General of the United Nations on 28 April 1982, stating: "As is known to all, the Chinese Government has long declared on its own initiative and unilaterally that at no time and under no circumstances will China be the first to use nuclear weapons, and that it undertakes unconditionally not to use or threaten to use nuclear weapons against non-nuclear countries and nuclear-free zones."

(*b*) The French Foreign Minister declared before the United Nations General Assembly on 11 June 1982 that: "For its part, [France] states that it will not use nuclear arms against a State that does not have them and that has pledged not to seek them, except if an act of aggression is carried out in association or alliance with a nuclear-weapon State against France or against a State with which France has a security commitment."

(*c*) The Russian Federation submitted the following declaration to the Conference on Disarmament on 17 August 1993: "The Russian Federation will not use nuclear weapons against any non-nuclear-weapon State party to the Treaty on the Non-Proliferation of Nuclear Weapons, except in the event of an attack on the Russian Federation, its territory, armed forces or allies conducted by a State of this kind that is linked by an agreement or association with a nuclear-weapon State or that acts together with, or with the support of a nuclear-weapon State in carrying out such an attack."

(*d*) The representative of the United Kingdom to the United Nations General Assembly made the following declaration on 28 June 1978: "I accordingly give the following assurance, on behalf of my Government, to non-nuclear-weapon States which are parties to the Treaty on the Non-Proliferation of Nuclear Weapons and to other internationally binding commitments not to manufacture or acquire nuclear explosive devices: Britain undertakes not to use nuclear weapons against such States except in the case of an attack on the United Kingdom, its dependent territories, its armed forces or its allies by such a State in association or alliance with a nuclear-weapon State."

(*e*) A letter citing a United States Presidential Declaration was delivered to the First Committee of the United Nations General Assembly on 17 November 1978 stating: "The United States will not use nuclear weapons against any non-nuclear-weapon State Party to the Treaty on the Non-Proliferation of Nuclear Weapons or any comparable internationally binding commitment not to acquire nuclear explosive devices, except in the case of an attack on the United States, its territories or armed forces, or its allies, by such a State allied to a nuclear-weapon State or associated with a nuclear-weapon State in carrying out or sustaining the attack."

62   An Ad Hoc Committee on Effective International Arrangements to Assure Non-Nuclear-Weapon States against the Use or Threat of Use of Nuclear Weapons has been addressing this issue at the Conference on Disarmament for many years.

Nuclear-weapon-free zones

63   Nuclear-weapon-free zones (NWFZs) provide another means of addressing non-nuclear-weapon States' security concerns and thus strengthening their decision to refrain from obtaining nuclear weapons. NWFZs function as important confidence- and security-building measures. In 1975, the General Assembly, in its resolution 3472 B (XXX) of 11 December, defined the concept of a nuclear-weapon-free zone as follows: "A 'nuclear-weapon-free zone' shall, as a general rule, be deemed to be any zone, recognized as such by the General Assembly of the United Nations, which any group of States, in the free exercise of their sovereignty, has established by virtue of a treaty or convention whereby: (*a*) the statute of total absence of nuclear weapons to which the zone shall be subject, including the procedure for the delimitation of the zone, is defined; and (*b*) an international system of verification and control is established to guarantee compliance with the obligations derived from that statute."

64   Several regional groups of States have taken it upon themselves to create nuclear-weapon-free zones. Their efforts underline the important role that regional organizations and arrangements can play in promoting and maintaining international peace and security. Two regional groups have already concluded treaties, and a third is in the process of finalizing a draft treaty. In addition, proposals have been put forward for such zones in South Asia and in the Middle East.

The Treaty of Tlatelolco

65   The Treaty for the Prohibition of Nuclear Weapons in Latin America and the Caribbean, also known as the Treaty of Tlatelolco,[23] was signed at Mexico City on 14 February 1967 and entered into force on 22 April 1968. Of the 33 States in the region, 29 have ratified the Treaty and become full parties. Of the four that remain, all have either signed the Treaty and are in the process of ratifying their accession, or have stated their intention to do so. The Treaty prohibits the testing, use, manufacture, production or acquisition by any means, as well as the receipt, storage, installation, deployment and any form of possession, of any nuclear weapons by Latin American and Caribbean countries.

66   Under Additional Protocol I, the four States situated outside the Treaty's region of application that have international responsibility for territories within the region — France, the Netherlands, the United Kingdom and the United States — are called upon to respect the conditions laid down in the Treaty. Under the terms of Protocol II, all nuclear-weapon States parties to the NPT agree to recognize the nuclear-

23/Document 9
See page 50

weapon-free zone in question and undertake not to use or threaten to use nuclear weapons against the States parties to the Treaty.

67   The Treaty also created a regional organization, the Agency for the Prohibition of Nuclear Weapons in Latin America and the Caribbean (known by its Spanish acronym OPANAL), to ensure that parties complied with the various provisions. In 1992, the Treaty was amended to give the IAEA sole responsibility for conducting special inspections. OPANAL continues to carry out its other responsibilities effectively, with the full support of the parties.

The Treaty of Rarotonga

24/Document 32
See page 138

68   The South Pacific Nuclear Free Zone Treaty, also known as the Treaty of Rarotonga,[24] was signed at Rarotonga, Cook Islands, on 6 August 1985 and entered into force on 11 December 1986. The Treaty prohibits the manufacture or acquisition by other means of any nuclear explosive device, as well as the possession of or control over such device by the parties anywhere inside or outside its zone. It also bans the dumping of radioactive matter at sea and prohibits the possession and testing of nuclear explosive devices for peaceful purposes. The Treaty allows the parties to make an exception for nuclear weapons that may be on board foreign ships visiting their ports.

An African nuclear-weapon-free zone

69   Ever since the Organization of African Unity (OAU) convened its first ordinary session in 1964, African countries have expressed their support for their continent to become a nuclear-weapon-free zone. When South Africa acceded to the NPT as a non-nuclear-weapon State party on 10 July 1991, the last remaining obstacle to the creation of an African nuclear-weapon-free zone was removed. A Group of Experts to Draw up a Draft Treaty on the Denuclearization of Africa, established jointly by the OAU and the United Nations, has nearly completed its task. At its forty-ninth session, the General Assembly adopted a resolution (49/138) that encouraged African States to continue their efforts towards finalizing the draft and requested that the text of the treaty be submitted to the General Assembly at its next session. This would be a most welcome way to commemorate the Fiftieth Anniversary of the United Nations.

The Antarctic Treaty

70   Given the immense territory covered, the agreement to demilitarize the entire continent of Antarctica represents a most significant accomplishment. The Antarctic Treaty was signed on 1 December 1959

and entered into force on 23 June 1961. It establishes the entire continent as a demilitarized zone to be used for peaceful purposes only. All weapons — nuclear as well as non-nuclear — military manoeuvres and military installations are prohibited. Nuclear explosions and the disposal of radioactive waste are similarly banned. Observers of the 12 original parties to the Treaty have the right to conduct aerial reconnaissance and enjoy unobstructed access to any area or installation. No violations of the Treaty have ever been reported. As of 31 July 1994, there were 42 States parties to the Treaty.

The Outer Space Treaty

71   The Treaty on Principles Governing the Activities of States in the Exploration and Use of Outer Space, including the Moon and Other Celestial Bodies, was signed on 27 January 1967 and entered into force on 10 October of the same year. Also known as the Outer Space Treaty, the Treaty prohibits the placing into orbit around the earth of any objects carrying nuclear weapons or any other kinds of weapons of mass destruction, the installation of such weapons on celestial bodies or the stationing of them in outer space in any other manner. As of 31 July 1994, there were 93 parties to the Treaty.

The Moon Agreement

72   On 18 December 1979, in the presence of the Secretary-General of the United Nations — the designated depositary — the Agreement Governing the Activities of States on the Moon and Other Celestial Bodies was opened for signature. Known as the Moon Agreement, it complements the Outer Space Treaty by establishing that the moon may be used for peaceful purposes only. It prohibits the use of force on the moon, the planting of any weapons on it or in orbit around it and any kind of militarization of it or of other celestial bodies. The Moon Agreement entered into force on 11 July 1984; there were nine parties to it as of 31 July 1994.

The Seabed Treaty

73   The Treaty on the Prohibition of the Emplacement of Nuclear Weapons and Other Weapons of Mass Destruction on the Seabed and the Ocean Floor and in the Subsoil Thereof also restricts the deployment of nuclear (as well as biological and chemical) weapons. Negotiations began in 1969 in the Eighteen-Nation Committee on Disarmament, and continued at the Conference of the Committee on Disarmament, which succeeded the Eighteen-Nation Committee. The Treaty was signed on

11 February 1971 and entered into force on 18 May 1972. The full name of the Treaty, which is also known as the Seabed Treaty, accurately reflects its main precepts. It also prohibits the emplacement of launching installations or any other facilities specifically designed for storing, testing or using the weapons in question. The zone of application is the area beyond a 12-nautical-mile territorial limit measured from the coastline. As of 31 July 1994, there were 89 parties to the Treaty.

Nuclear-test-ban treaties

74   Besides restricting deployment, some of these treaties also ban the testing of nuclear weapons or nuclear explosive devices. Prohibiting tests of nuclear weapons represents a major impediment to their proliferation. Though current technology enables nuclear explosive devices and nuclear weapons to be developed and manufactured without testing, their reliability would be suspect and this would make them less desirable. A comprehensive ban on testing would inhibit the introduction of new weapons and thus curtail sharply the qualitative development of nuclear weapons.

The Partial Test Ban Treaty

75   On 5 August 1963, a convention was signed at Moscow that prohibited certain types of nuclear tests. The Treaty Banning Nuclear Weapon Tests in the Atmosphere, in Outer Space and under Water represented a major accomplishment. Also known as the Partial Test Ban Treaty (PTBT), it prohibits nuclear-weapon-test explosions as well as "any other" nuclear explosions in three environments: the atmosphere; outer space; and under water. The Treaty, of unlimited duration, entered into force on 10 October 1963. As of 31 July 1994, there were 123 States parties to the PTBT.

76   Besides providing an important confidence-building measure, the PTBT also represents progress towards respecting the environment and reducing potentially deleterious health effects associated with radioactive fallout. Two nuclear-weapon States that have not formally signed the Treaty have nevertheless agreed to refrain from conducting atmospheric nuclear tests.

The Threshold Test Ban Treaty

77   A subsequent bilateral treaty, concluded between the United States and the Soviet Union, placed restrictions on tests underground — an environment that the PTBT did not address. The Treaty on the

Limitation of Underground Nuclear Weapon Tests was opened for signature on 3 July 1974. Also known as the Threshold Test Ban Treaty (TTBT), it established a limit of 150 kilotons on the amount of energy that might be released by an underground explosion. The two parties signed the Treaty and pledged to restrict the number of tests as well. The United Kingdom, though not a signatory to the Treaty, subsequently pledged to abide by its provisions. The TTBT entered into force on 11 December 1990 following the conclusion of a protocol on verification.

The Peaceful Nuclear Explosions Treaty

78   The bilateral Treaty on Underground Nuclear Explosions for Peaceful Purposes provided for the same restrictions and conditions established under the TTBT to apply to nuclear explosions for peaceful purposes as well. Also known as the Peaceful Nuclear Explosions Treaty, the United States and the Soviet Union signed it on 28 May 1976.

A comprehensive test ban

79   While all of the above nuclear test ban treaties are important for the reasons mentioned, they are still insufficient. The nuclear-weapon States have long declared their intention to reach a comprehensive nuclear test ban. Article I of the PTBT states in part that the parties undertake to conclude "a treaty resulting in the permanent banning of all nuclear test explosions". In the preamble to the PTBT, the "Original Parties" to the Treaty (the Soviet Union, the United Kingdom and the United States) describe themselves as "seeking to achieve the discontinuance of all test explosions of nuclear weapons for all time, determined to continue negotiations to this end, and desiring to put an end to the contamination of man's environment by radioactive substances".

80   The "Original Parties" to the Partial Test Ban Treaty had initiated tripartite negotiations to conclude a comprehensive test ban in 1958 at the Conference on the Discontinuance of Nuclear Weapon Tests. The Conference adjourned in 1962 and further discussions on the subject were held in the Eighteen-Nation Committee on Disarmament. Political and technical considerations did not permit the parties to reach a comprehensive agreement at that time. Concerted efforts by the same three States to finalize a comprehensive test-ban treaty resumed after the Peaceful Nuclear Explosions Treaty was concluded in 1976. The trilateral talks that began in 1977 and lasted until 1980 saw progress on a number of controversial issues, but several questions remained to be resolved.

81   Multilateral discussions relating to a comprehensive test ban continued in the Conference on Disarmament, a later successor to the

Eighteen-Nation Committee on Disarmament. The Ad Hoc Group of Scientific Experts, created in 1976, proceeded in its efforts to develop measures to record seismic activity in order to identify nuclear explosions. The General Assembly adopted resolutions in 1986 (resolution 41/59 N) and 1987 (resolution 42/38 C) requesting Member States to notify the United Nations of any information they had on nuclear explosions. The Secretary-General was requested to make this information available and to submit a register of such information annually to the General Assembly.

82   The General Assembly also adopted resolutions in the latter half of the 1980s recommending that Member States that were parties to the PTBT should take advantage of existing provisions of the Treaty and hold a conference to convert the partial ban into a total ban. An Amendment Conference was subsequently convened in January 1991 but could not arrive at a substantive decision on conversion or agree on the suitability of that Conference as a forum for achieving a comprehensive test ban. However, the President of the Conference, at its request, continued to conduct consultations on the matter.

83   A more promising prospect for attaining this goal lies in ongoing developments in the Conference on Disarmament, which in 1993 gave its Ad Hoc Committee on a Nuclear Test Ban a mandate to negotiate a comprehensive test ban treaty. On 16 December of that year, the General Assembly adopted unanimously resolution 48/70, in which it called upon all States to support the multilateral negotiations in the Conference on Disarmament as a means to reach the desired goal. This provides the Conference on Disarmament with strong political support to undertake this most important endeavour. Such a treaty will have a significant impact on nuclear disarmament and, consequently, on the enhancement of international peace and security.

IV   Nuclear disarmament

84   The various mechanisms of the nuclear non-proliferation regime have succeeded in addressing the threat of the horizontal proliferation of nuclear weapons. The nuclear-weapon States parties to the NPT have also agreed to pursue negotiations in good faith to cease the nuclear arms race and to commence nuclear disarmament. Several agreements have established important confidence-building measures that implicitly were effective in slowing the pace of vertical proliferation. This was not an insignificant accomplishment, given the tensions that prevailed between the two major nuclear Powers during the cold war. However, limiting the rate of nuclear proliferation was not in itself sufficient to eliminate the nuclear danger. Progress was needed with respect to actual measures of nuclear disarmament.

85   At the tenth special session of the General Assembly — the first special session devoted to disarmament — held in May-June 1978, the Assembly noted the connection between a continuation of the nuclear arms race and the increased threat of nuclear proliferation. The Final Document of the Tenth Special Session[25] states that "failure of efforts to halt and reverse the arms race, in particular the nuclear arms race, increases the danger of proliferation of nuclear weapons". The Strategic Arms Limitation Talks between the United States and the Soviet Union in the 1970s addressed the creation of ceilings they wanted to attain. However, the numerous efforts undertaken over the last 30 years began to reach fruition only in the late 1980s. Today, vertical proliferation has been largely curtailed and the stockpiles of nuclear weapons are being reduced significantly.

25/Document 25
See page 124

The INF Treaty

86   The Treaty between the United States of America and the Union of Soviet Socialist Republics on the Elimination of Their Intermediate-Range and Shorter-Range Missiles (also known as the INF Treaty) represented a significant departure from previous practice. The INF Treaty, which was signed at Washington on 8 December 1987 and entered into force on 1 June 1988, eliminates the two parties' ground-launched ballistic and cruise missiles with ranges between 500 and 5,500 kilometres. More than 2,500 missiles with nuclear warheads together with their launching systems were destroyed within the designated three-year period. The Treaty established a Special Verification Commission that continues to carry out its functions successfully.

The START I Treaty

87 Negotiations between the same two countries to reduce their strategic nuclear arsenals were held simultaneously with the INF talks. On 31 July 1991, the United States and the Soviet Union successfully concluded their Strategic Arms Reduction Talks, which they had begun nine years earlier. The Treaty between the United States of America and the Union of Soviet Socialist Republics on the Reduction and Limitation of Strategic Offensive Arms, subsequently known as START I, provides for a significant reduction of the two parties' nuclear stockpiles in three phases over a seven-year period. The Treaty also places numerous restrictions on their strategic nuclear arsenals, including the number of warheads and delivery systems.

The Lisbon Protocol

88 The dissolution of the Soviet Union in December 1991 complicated — but did not derail — the implementation of START I. The Russian Federation maintained full responsibility for the rights and obligations of the USSR under the Charter of the United Nations and continued to honour its commitments deriving from treaties concluded by the USSR. Subsequently, at Lisbon on 23 May 1992, Belarus, Kazakhstan, the Russian Federation and Ukraine — as "successor States" of the Soviet Union in connection with the Treaty — and the United States signed the Lisbon Protocol to the START I Treaty. In accordance with its terms, Belarus, Kazakhstan and Ukraine have acceded to the NPT as "non-nuclear-weapon States" and have undertaken to implement the restrictions and limitations set out in START I with respect to the nuclear weapons that remain on their territories.

The START II Treaty

89 The delay in the entry into force of START I has not proven to be disruptive. A second accord, the Treaty between the United States of America and the Russian Federation on the Further Reduction and Limitation of Strategic Offensive Arms (known as START II), was concluded two years later, in January 1993. It calls for significant reductions beyond those envisaged under START I, requiring each of the parties to reduce their deployed strategic nuclear warheads to between 3,000 and 3,500 by the year 2003.

90 As the United States and the Russian Federation have the largest nuclear arsenals of the five nuclear-weapon States, the bilateral agreements concluded between them represent a particularly important accomplishment. It is expected that China, France and the United Kingdom will join in at an appropriate moment.

V   Conclusion

Recognizing new challenges

91   The commitment of the United States and the Russian Federation to reduce their nuclear arsenals by some 70 per cent under the START agreements is being implemented. Each party has begun to dismantle and destroy almost 2,000 warheads a year.

92   The rapid pace of the present disarmament process is a welcome change from the previous inertia, but it has brought to the fore several issues that need to be addressed. To store securely the components of nuclear weapons — especially enriched uranium and plutonium — requires that numerous logistical, administrative, legislative and technical challenges be met.

93   A number of incidents involving the smuggling or attempted smuggling of nuclear and other radioactive material have been reported in Europe. Although the incidents have not proved to be very serious, the collective effect has been to raise fears that weapons grade material might fall into the wrong hands. All evidence to date is that the persons arrested or charged have been inspired by profit rather than a political motive. Nevertheless, these incidents give credence to concerns already expressed about standards of protection and the accounting of material in some States with nuclear facilities. There are also concerns about the potential hazard to individuals and the environment.

94   While the States themselves are primarily responsible for the control of illicit trafficking, the IAEA maintains safeguards on their nuclear materials and assists them with guidelines and standards for other radioactive materials. The Director General of the IAEA and I have been in close contact since this issue emerged. The Agency has taken initiatives to intensify its assistance to States, to develop a database on illicit trafficking and to collaborate with States and international organizations in combating this threat. For my part, I have established a Working Group within the Secretariat to follow the situation and have asked an eminent personality to serve informally as an adviser on this issue.

Indispensability of the NPT to the nuclear non-proliferation regime

95   The Treaty on the Non-Proliferation of Nuclear Weapons and the nuclear non-proliferation regime continue to serve the international community well. Lack of security, real or perceived, and expanding energy needs are the root causes of concerns about proliferation. This dual challenge of peace and prosperity necessitates an integrated approach to disarmament, collective security and economic and scientific cooperation. States parties to the Treaty that have renounced the intention to develop nuclear weapons consider that they should participate fully in the technological, commercial and developmental benefits of nuclear energy. The non-nuclear-weapon States parties to the NPT or comparable treaties also consider that they should receive satisfactory security assurances from nuclear-weapon States. It is widely agreed that a comprehensive nuclear test ban, one of the highest-priority objectives of the international community in the field of disarmament and non-proliferation, should be concluded as soon as possible.

96   Efforts that promote means to achieve these ends are worthwhile and should be supported. Threatening to withhold support for a measure that is clearly beneficial in an effort to hasten progress elsewhere is not, I believe, helpful. The NPT is too crucial to be subjected to this type of diplomatic brinkmanship.

97   Finally, the NPT does not limit itself to nuclear disarmament. The Treaty's call for "general and complete disarmament" is an essential provision. The international community has a unique opportunity today to make progress in the regulation of armaments. The United Nations stands ready to help its Member States to fulfil this wish of their people everywhere.

BOUTROS BOUTROS-GHALI

Section Two
Chronology and Documents

I Chronology of events

25 March 1957
The Treaty formally establishing the European Atomic Energy Community (EURATOM) is signed at Rome.

29 July 1957
The Statute of the International Atomic Energy Agency (IAEA), opened for signature on 26 October 1956, comes into force. The Agency is established to facilitate the peaceful uses of nuclear energy, while ensuring that the assistance the Agency provides will not be used so as to further any military purposes.

20 November 1959
On the initiative of Ireland, the United Nations General Assembly adopts resolution 1380 (XIV), by which it suggests that the Ten-Nation Disarmament Committee consider the feasibility of an international agreement by which the nuclear-weapon Powers would not hand over control of those weapons to other Powers, and non-nuclear-weapon States would not manufacture such weapons.
See Document 1, page 45

1 December 1959
The Antarctic Treaty, stipulating that Antarctica shall be used for peaceful purposes only, is signed at Washington. The Treaty prohibits any measures of a military nature, including the testing of any type of weapons.

20 December 1960
On the initiative of Ireland, the General Assembly adopts resolution 1576 (XV), by which it calls upon both nuclear- and non-nuclear-weapon States, pending agreement on the prevention of wider dissemination of nuclear weapons, to refrain, as a temporary and voluntary measure, from acts that would lead to further proliferation.
See Document 2, page 45

1961
The IAEA establishes its first safeguards system.

4 December 1961
On the initiative of Sweden, the General Assembly adopts resolution 1664 (XVI), by which it requests the Secretary-General to inquire under what conditions States not possessing nuclear weapons would be willing to undertake not to acquire them.
See Document 3, page 46

On the initiative of Ireland, the General Assembly adopts, without a vote, resolution 1665 (XVI), by which it calls upon the nuclear-weapon States in particular to endeavour to conclude an international agreement on the non-dissemination of nuclear weapons and upon all States to cooperate for this purpose.
See Document 4, page 46

5 August 1963
The Treaty Banning Nuclear Weapon Tests in the Atmosphere, in Outer Space and under Water (the Partial Test-Ban Treaty) is signed by the Union of Soviet Socialist Republics (USSR), the United Kingdom of Great Britain and Northern Ireland and the United States of America. On 8 August, the Treaty is opened for signature by other States in Moscow, London and Washington.

17 August 1965
The United States submits to the Eighteen-Nation Committee on Disarmament a draft treaty to prevent the spread of nuclear weapons.

24 September 1965
The USSR submits to the General Assembly a draft treaty to prevent the spread of nuclear weapons.

19 November 1965
On the initiative of eight non-aligned States, the General Assembly adopts resolution 2028 (XX), which contains five principles on which negotiation of a non-proliferation treaty is to be based.
See Document 5, page 47

1965
The IAEA revises its safeguards system.

November 1966
The General Assembly adopts two resolutions on non-proliferation: resolution 2149 (XXI), by which it appeals to all States, pending the conclusion of a nuclear non-proliferation treaty, to renounce actions that might hamper agreement on such a treaty; and resolution 2153 A (XXI), in which it calls upon the Eighteen-Nation Committee on Disarmament to give priority to the question of non-proliferation and also to consider

the question of assurances to non-nuclear-weapon States.
See Document 7, page 49; and Document 8, page 49

27 January 1967
The Treaty on Principles Governing the Activities of States in the Exploration and Use of Outer Space, including the Moon and Other Celestial Bodies (the Outer Space Treaty) is opened for signature (A/RES/2222 (XXI), annex). The Treaty prohibits the placing of nuclear weapons or any other weapons of mass destruction in outer space, stipulating that that environment shall be used exclusively for peaceful purposes.

14 February 1967
The Treaty for the Prohibition of Nuclear Weapons in Latin America and the Caribbean (the Treaty of Tlatelolco) is opened for signature at Mexico City. The Treaty establishes the first nuclear-weapon-free zone in a densely populated region, and creates the Agency for the Prohibition of Nuclear Weapons in Latin America and the Caribbean to oversee its implementation.
See Document 9, page 50

August 1967
The Eighteen-Nation Committee on Disarmament considers two separate but identical draft texts of a non-proliferation treaty, submitted by the Soviet Union and the United States, as well as a number of amendments submitted by other members.

19 December 1967
The General Assembly adopts resolution 2346 A (XXII), in which it requests the Eighteen-Nation Committee on Disarmament to present it with a full report on the negotiations on a non-proliferation treaty on or before 15 March 1968.
See Document 10, page 59

1 January 1968
The Treaty establishing the European Atomic Energy Community (EURATOM) enters into force.

January - March 1968
The Eighteen-Nation Committee on Disarmament examines further revisions of the draft treaty texts submitted by the USSR and the United States, which incorporate some of the suggestions of the non-nuclear-weapon States, and submits another revision to the General Assembly at its resumed twenty-second session.

12 June 1968
After further revision — concerning mainly the preamble and articles IV and V — the General Assembly commends the draft text of the Treaty on the Non-Proliferation of Nuclear Weapons, which is annexed to Assembly resolution 2373 (XXII).
See Document 11, page 59

19 June 1968
The Security Council adopts resolution 255 (1968) on security assurances to non-nuclear-weapon States.
See Document 12, page 63

1 July 1968
The Treaty on the Non-Proliferation of Nuclear Weapons (also known as the "Non-Proliferation Treaty", or "NPT") is opened for signature at London, Moscow and Washington — the United Kingdom, the USSR and the United States having been designated the depositary Governments.
See Document 11, page 59

16 September 1968
The IAEA revises its safeguards system with further additional provisions for safeguarded nuclear material in conversion plants and fabrication plants.
See Document 13, page 64

5 March 1970
The Treaty on the Non-Proliferation of Nuclear Weapons enters into force. The IAEA establishes its safeguards system for NPT parties.
See Document 15, page 76

11 February 1971
The Treaty on the Prohibition of the Emplacement of Nuclear Weapons and Other Weapons of Mass Destruction on the Seabed and the Ocean Floor and in the Subsoil Thereof (the Seabed Treaty) is opened for signature (A/RES/2660 (XXV), annex).

26 May 1972
The United States and the Soviet Union sign two agreements to halt the growth in their strategic arms: the Treaty on the Limitation of Anti-Ballistic Missile Systems (the Anti-Ballistic Missile Treaty) and the Interim Agreement on Certain Measures with respect to the Limitation of Strategic Offensive Arms. These agreements are referred to as SALT I.

3 July 1974
The United States and the Soviet Union sign the Treaty on the Limitation of Underground Nuclear Weapon Tests (the Threshold Test-Ban Treaty).

5 - 30 May 1975

The First Review Conference of the Parties to the Treaty on the Non-Proliferation of Nuclear Weapons is held at Geneva. The Secretary-General of the United Nations and the Director General of the IAEA address the Conference. The Conference adopts a Final Declaration by consensus.
See Document 16, page 90; Document 17, page 92; and Document 18, page 93

28 May 1976

The United States and the Soviet Union sign the Treaty on Underground Nuclear Explosions for Peaceful Purposes.

21 September 1977

Fifteen nuclear supplier countries, known as the Nuclear Suppliers Group or the London Club, reach agreement in London on a set of principles and guidelines to govern the transfer of nuclear materials, equipment and technology. The suppliers' policies are based on a "trigger list" of nuclear and other materials for which certain conditions would have to be met before they would be exported.
See Document 19, page 116

23 May - 30 June 1978

The General Assembly holds its tenth special session — the first special session devoted to disarmament — in New York. The session ends with the adoption by consensus of a Final Document.
See Document 25, page 124

At the special session and later in the year, the five nuclear-weapon States make unilateral security assurances to non-nuclear-weapon States.
See Document 20, page 122; Document 21, page 123; Document 22, page 123; Document 23, page 123; Document 24, page 123; and Document 26, page 131

18 June 1979

The United States and the USSR sign the Treaty on the Limitation of Strategic Offensive Arms (referred to as SALT II).

3 March 1980

The Convention on the Physical Protection of Nuclear Material is opened for signature at Vienna and New York; the Convention applies to nuclear material used for peaceful purposes while in international nuclear transport (INFCIRC/274/Rev.1).

11 August - 7 September 1980

The Second Review Conference of the Parties to the Non-Proliferation Treaty is held at Geneva. The Secretary-General of the United Nations conveys a message to the Conference and the Director General of the IAEA addresses the Conference.
See Document 27, page 131; and Document 28, page 132

7 June - 10 July 1982

The General Assembly holds its second special session devoted to disarmament, in New York. At the special session, China, France and the Soviet Union make declarations regarding unilateral security assurances.
See Document 29, page 137; Document 30, page 137; and Document 31, page 137

6 August 1985

The South Pacific Nuclear Free Zone Treaty (the Treaty of Rarotonga) is opened for signature.
See Document 32, page 138

27 August - 21 September 1985

The Third NPT Review Conference is held at Geneva. The Secretary-General of the United Nations conveys a message to the Conference and the Director General of the IAEA addresses the Conference. The Conference adopts a Final Declaration by consensus.
See Document 33, page 145; Document 34, page 146; and Document 35, page 150

23 March - 10 April 1987

The United Nations Conference for the Promotion of International Cooperation in the Peaceful Uses of Nuclear Energy is held at Geneva, but is unable to reach agreement on principles for international cooperation that would promote the objectives of the full utilization of nuclear energy for peaceful purposes and the prevention of the proliferation of nuclear weapons.

16 April 1987

The Missile Technology Control Regime, established by seven industrialized nations, establishes guidelines for sensitive missile-relevant transfers.

30 November 1987

The General Assembly — by its resolution 42/38 C, and in conjunction with its resolution 41/59 N — establishes a system for an annual register of data on nuclear explosions to be submitted to it by the Secretary-General following notification of such tests by Member States.

8 December 1987

The United States and the Soviet Union sign the Treaty on the Elimination of Their Intermediate-Range and Shorter-Range Missiles (the INF Treaty).

20 August - 14 September 1990
The Fourth NPT Review Conference is held at Geneva. The Secretary-General of the United Nations conveys a message to the Conference and the Director General of the IAEA addresses the Conference.
See Document 36, page 162; and Document 37, page 163

7 - 18 January 1991
The Amendment Conference of the States Parties to the Treaty Banning Nuclear Weapon Tests in the Atmosphere, in Outer Space and under Water meets in New York.

10 July 1991
South Africa accedes to the Non-Proliferation Treaty as a non-nuclear-weapon State after terminating its nuclear weapons programme.

18 July 1991
Argentina and Brazil establish the Brazilian-Argentine Agency for Accounting and Control of Nuclear Materials.

31 July 1991
The United States and the Soviet Union sign the Treaty on the Reduction and Limitation of Strategic Offensive Arms (the START I Treaty), by which the two sides undertake to reduce their nuclear weapons from their current levels of between 10,000 and 11,000 weapons to between 8,000 and 9,000 weapons.

September - October 1991
The United States and the Soviet Union make unilateral announcements of further reductions and other measures for their respective nuclear arsenals.

31 January 1992
At a meeting of the Security Council held at the level of Heads of State and Government, the Council emphasizes the threat that the proliferation of weapons of mass destruction constitutes to international peace and security.
See Document 38, page 168

9 March 1992
China accedes to the Non-Proliferation Treaty.

3 April 1992
The Nuclear Suppliers Group, meeting at Warsaw, revises its "Guidelines for transfers of nuclear-related dual-use equipment, material and related technology".
See Document 39, page 169

23 May 1992
The Lisbon Protocol to the START I Treaty is signed by Belarus, Kazakhstan, the Russian Federation and

Ukraine, as successor States of the former USSR in connection with the Treaty, and by the United States. By the Protocol, Belarus, Kazakhstan and Ukraine undertake to adhere to the Non-Proliferation Treaty as non-nuclear-weapon States in the shortest possible time.

2 August 1992
France accedes to the Non-Proliferation Treaty.

27 October 1992
The Secretary-General submits to the First Committee of the General Assembly his report entitled "New dimensions of arms regulation and disarmament in the post-cold war era", in which he refers to the Non-Proliferation Treaty as providing an indispensable framework for global non-proliferation efforts.
See Document 40, page 170

3 January 1993
The United States and the Russian Federation sign the Treaty on Further Reduction and Limitation of Strategic Offensive Arms (the START II Treaty), by which they undertake further significant reductions in their nuclear arsenals.

9 February 1993
Belarus accedes to the Non-Proliferation Treaty as a non-nuclear-weapon State.

1 April 1993
The Nuclear Suppliers Group, meeting at Lucerne, Switzerland, revises the 1977 London Guidelines for Nuclear Transfers.
See Document 41, page 171

10 - 14 May 1993
The Preparatory Committee for the 1995 Conference of the Parties to the NPT holds its first session in New York.

10 August 1993
The Conference on Disarmament decides to give its Ad Hoc Committee on a Nuclear Test Ban a mandate to negotiate a comprehensive nuclear test-ban treaty. A special meeting (informal) of the Amendment Conference of the Partial Test-Ban Treaty is held in New York.

17 August 1993
The Russian Federation declares its policy regarding security assurances to non-nuclear-weapon States.
See Document 42, page 174

27 September 1993

The Secretary-General, in his message to the General Conference of the IAEA in Vienna, states that it is of vital importance that the Non-Proliferation Treaty be extended indefinitely and unconditionally when it comes up for review in 1995.
See Document 43, page 174

16 December 1993

The General Assembly adopts without a vote a resolution (48/70), sponsored by 157 States, on a comprehensive test-ban treaty, welcoming the decision of **10 August** by the Conference on Disarmament.

17 - 21 January 1994

The Preparatory Committee for the 1995 Conference of the Parties to the NPT holds its second session in New York.

February 1994

Negotiations on a comprehensive nuclear-test-ban treaty begin in the Conference on Disarmament. Consultations begin in the Conference on Disarmament regarding a mandate to negotiate a treaty on the prohibition of the production of fissile material for weapons purposes.

14 February 1994

Kazakhstan accedes to the NPT as a non-nuclear-weapon State.

March 1994

The drafting of a treaty establishing a nuclear-weapon-free zone in Africa enters its final stage.

12 - 16 September 1994

The Preparatory Committee for the 1995 Conference of the Parties to the NPT holds its third session at Geneva.

20 September 1994

The International Convention on Nuclear Safety is opened for signature in Vienna (INFCIRC/449 and Add.1).

5 December 1994

Ukraine accedes to the NPT as a non-nuclear-weapon State.

23-27 January 1995

The Preparatory Committee for the 1995 Conference of the Parties to the NPT holds its fourth session in New York.

17 April - 12 May 1995

The Review and Extension Conference of the States parties to the NPT is scheduled to convene in New York—25 years after the entry into force of the treaty—to decide whether the treaty shall continue in force indefinitely, or shall be extended for an additional fixed period or periods.

II   List of reproduced documents

*The documents reproduced in this book include relevant treaties,
resolutions of the General Assembly and the Security Council, reports
of the Secretary-General, the final declarations of the 1975 and 1985
Review Conferences of the Non-Proliferation Treaty (NPT), statements
by the Secretary-General, declarations by the nuclear-weapon States
and materials from the International Atomic Energy Agency (IAEA).*

Document 11
General Assembly resolution on the Treaty on the Non-Proliferation of Nuclear Weapons, with text of Treaty annexed.
A/RES/2373 (XXII), 12 June 1968
See page 59

Document 12
Security Council resolution on security assurances.
S/RES/255 (1968), 19 June 1968
See page 63

Document 13
The safeguards system of the IAEA, as approved in 1965 and provisionally extended in 1966 and 1968.
INFCIRC/66/Rev.2
See page 64

Document 14
Report of the Secretary-General on the work of the Organization, 1967-1968 (excerpt).
A/7201/Add.1, 24 September 1968
See page 75

Document 15
Structure and content of agreements between the IAEA and States parties, as required in connection with the NPT.
INFCIRC/153 (Corr), 1970
See page 76

Document 16
Statement by the Secretary-General of the United Nations at the First Review Conference of the Parties to the Treaty on the Non-Proliferation of Nuclear Weapons.
UN Press Release SG/SM/2181, 5 May 1975
See page 90

Document 17
Statement by the Director General of the IAEA at the 1975 Review Conference of the NPT.
Not issued as a United Nations document
See page 92

Document 18
Final declaration of the 1975 Review Conference of the NPT.
NPT/CONF/35/1, 30 May 1975
See page 93

Document 19
Guidelines for nuclear transfers, adopted by the 15-nation Nuclear Suppliers' Group, London, 21 September 1977.
INFCIRC/254, 1977
See page 116

Document 20
Declaration made by France on unilateral security assurances, 25 May 1978.
Official Records of the General Assembly (*GAOR*), tenth special session, plenary meetings, third meeting, paragraph 50
See page 122

Document 21
Declaration made by the Union of Soviet Socialist Republics (USSR) on unilateral security assurances, 26 May 1978.
GAOR, tenth special session, fifth meeting, paragraphs 84-85
See page 123

Document 22
Declaration made by China on unilateral security assurances, 7 June 1978.
A/S-10/AC.1/17
See page 123

Document 23
Declaration made by the United Kingdom of Great Britain and Northern Ireland on unilateral security assurances, 28 June 1978.
GAOR, tenth special session, twenty-sixth meeting, paragraph 12
See page 123

Document 24
Declaration made by France on unilateral security assurances, 30 June 1978.
GAOR, tenth special session, twenty-seventh meeting, paragraph 190
See page 123

Document 25
Final Document of the Tenth Special Session of the General Assembly, New York (excerpt).
General Assembly resolution S-10/2, 30 June 1978
See page 124

Document 26
Declaration made by the United States of America on unilateral security assurances, 17 November 1978.
A/C.1/33/7, annex, 17 November 1978
See page 131

Document 27
Message from the Secretary-General of the United Nations to the Second Review Conference of the Parties to the NPT.
NPT/CONF.II/SR.1, 11 August 1980
See page 131

Document 43
Message of the Secretary-General to the General Conference of the IAEA in Vienna.
UN Press Release SG/SM/5113, 27 September 1993
See page 174

Document 44
Statement of the Secretary-General before the Advisory Board on Disarmament Matters (excerpt), Geneva, 12 January 1994.
The Disarmament Agenda of the International Community in 1994 and Beyond: Statements of the Secretary-General. Published by the Centre for Disarmament Affairs, April 1994.
See page 176

Document 45
List of States parties to the NPT which had not concluded the required safeguards agreement with the IAEA.
NPT/CONF.1995/PC III/7, 1 July 1994
See page 177

Document 46
Situation with respect to the conclusion of safeguards agreements between the IAEA and non-nuclear-weapon States parties to the NPT.
NPT/CONF.1995/PC.III/7, 1 July 1994
See page 179

Document 47
Statement of the Secretary-General in the First Committee of the General Assembly (excerpts).
A/C.1/49/PV.3, New York, 17 October 1994
See page 184

Document 48
List of States parties to the NPT.
Not issued as a United Nations document
See page 185

Document 49
Nuclear fuel cycle.
Not issued as a United Nations document
See page 187

The following is a breakdown, by category, of the documents reproduced in this book.

Resolutions of the General Assembly
Documents 1, 2, 3, 4, 5, 7, 8, 10, 11

General Assembly: Tenth Special Session
Document 25

Resolution of the Security Council
Document 12

Statement by the President of the Security Council
Document 38

Reports of the Secretary-General
Documents 6, 14, 40

Statements and messages of the Secretary-General
Documents 16, 27, 33, 36, 43, 44, 47

Treaty on the Non-Proliferation of Nuclear Weapons
Documents 11, 18, 35, 45, 46, 48

Unilateral security assurances by nuclear-weapon States
Documents 20, 21, 22, 23, 24, 26, 29, 30, 31, 42

International Atomic Energy Agency (IAEA)
Documents 13, 15, 19, 39, 41

Statements by the Director General of the IAEA
Documents 17, 28, 34, 37

Other treaties
Documents 9, 32

Other
Document 49

III Other documents of interest

Readers seeking information about other significant events and developments related to the issue of nuclear non-proliferation might wish to consult the following documents, which are available in the Dag Hammarskjöld Library at United Nations Headquarters in New York City, at other libraries in the United Nations system or in libraries around the world which have been designated as depository libraries for United Nations documents and United Nations publications on disarmament.

Resolutions of the General Assembly

Resolution 41/59 N of 3 December 1986, by which the General Assembly calls upon the States concerned to provide the Secretary-General with data on their nuclear explosions and requests the Secretary-General to submit to it an annual register of such information.

Resolution 42/38 C of 30 November 1987, by which the General Assembly reiterates the provisions of resolution 41/59 N and invites all States to provide the Secretary-General with any data on nuclear explosions that they may have available.

Resolution 44/106 of 15 December 1989, by which the General Assembly makes recommendations concerning the convening of the Amendment Conference of the Parties to the Treaty Banning Nuclear Weapon Tests in the Atmosphere, in Outer Space and under Water.

Resolution 48/70 of 16 December 1993, by which the General Assembly urges the Conference on Disarmament to proceed intensively, as a priority task, in its negotiation of a universal and internationally and effectively verifiable comprehensive test-ban treaty.

Resolution 48/75 L of 16 December 1993, by which the General Assembly recommends the negotiation in the most appropriate international forum of a non-discriminatory, multilateral and internationally and effectively verifiable treaty banning the production of fissile material for weapons purposes.

General Assembly resolutions noting the establishment of Preparatory Committees for each Conference of Parties to the NPT

Resolution 3184 B (XXVIII) of 18 December 1973
Resolution 33/57 of 14 December 1978

Resolution 38/74 of 15 December 1983
Resolution 43/82 of 7 December 1988
Resolution 47/52 A of 9 December 1992

Resolutions of the Security Council

Resolution 687 (1991), by which the Security Council undertakes to make inspections and to supervise the destruction of proscribed weapons systems of mass destruction in Iraq.

Resolution 825 (1993), adopted following the announcement by the Democratic People's Republic of Korea that it would withdraw from the Non-Proliferation Treaty.

Treaties prohibiting nuclear testing and establishing demilitarized zones in certain environments*

1959 Antarctic Treaty. The Treaty ensures that Antarctica is preserved for peaceful purposes only. It prohibits all military activities other than the use of military personnel or equipment for scientific or for any other peaceful purpose.
United Nations, *Treaty Series*, vol. 402, No. I-5778

1963 Treaty Banning Nuclear Weapon Tests in the Atmosphere, in Outer Space and under Water (Partial Test Ban Treaty).
United Nations, *Treaty Series*, vol. 480, No. I-6964

1967 Treaty on Principles Governing the Activities of States in the Exploration and Use of Outer Space, including the Moon and Other Celestial Bodies.
General Assembly resolution 2222 (XXI), annex

*The texts of these treaties are reproduced in *Status of Multilateral Arms Regulation and Disarmament Agreements*, fourth edition: 1992 (United Nations publication, Sales No. E.93.IX.11 (vol. 1)).

1971 Treaty on the Prohibition of the Emplacement of Nuclear Weapons and Other Weapons of Mass Destruction on the Sea-Bed and the Ocean Floor and in the Subsoil Thereof.
General Assembly resolution 2660 (XXV), annex

1979 Agreement Governing the Activities of States on the Moon and Other Celestial Bodies.
General Assembly resolution 34/68, annex

Recent agreements between the United States and the Union of Soviet Socialist Republics and between the United States and the Russian Federation on reductions in their nuclear arsenals

Treaty between the United States of America and the Union of Soviet Socialist Republics (USSR) on the Elimination of Their Intermediate-Range and Shorter-Range Missiles (INF Treaty).
CD/798. The text of the Treaty is reproduced in *The United Nations Disarmament Yearbook*, vol. 12: 1987, appendix VII (United Nations publication, Sales No.E.88.IX.2).

Treaty between the United States and the USSR on the Reduction and Limitation of Strategic Offensive Arms (START I).
CD/1192. The text of the Treaty is reproduced in *The United Nations Disarmament Yearbook*, vol. 16: 1991, appendix II (United Nations publication, Sales No.E.92.IX.1).

Lisbon Protocol to START I.
CD/1193. The text of the Protocol is reproduced in *The United Nations Disarmament Yearbook*, vol. 17: 1992, appendix II (United Nations publication, Sales No.E.93.IX.1).

Treaty between the United States and the Russian Federation on Further Reduction and Limitation of Strategic Offensive Arms (START II).
CD/1194. The text of the Treaty is reproduced in *The*

United Nations Disarmament Yearbook, vol. 18: 1993, appendix II (United Nations publication, Sales No.E.94.IX.1).

Documents concerning nuclear-weapon-free zones

General Assembly resolution 3472 B (XXX) of 11 December 1975, by which the Assembly provides a definition of the concept of a nuclear-weapon-free zone and defines the principal obligations of the nuclear-weapon States towards such a zone.

Proposal by Egypt for the establishment of a zone free of weapons of mass destruction in the Middle East.
A/46/329 and CD/1098

Addis Ababa draft text of a treaty on an African nuclear-weapon-free zone.
A/49/436, appendix

Conference on Disarmament documents concerning negative security assurances

Draft agreement proposed by Nigeria on the prohibition of the use or threat of use of nuclear weapons against non-nuclear-weapon States parties to the NPT.
CD/967

Draft protocol on security assurances, to be attached to the NPT as its integral part, submitted to the Conference on Disarmament by members of the group of 21, States parties to the Treaty.
CD/1277

IAEA agreements

Convention on the Physical Protection of Nuclear Material of 1980.
INFCIRC/274/Rev.1

International Convention on Nuclear Safety of 1994.
INFCIRC/449 and Add.1

IV Texts of documents

The texts of the 49 documents listed on the preceding pages are reproduced below. The appearance of ellipses (. . .) in the text indicates that portions of the document have been omitted.
A subject index to the documents appears on page 193.

Document 1

General Assembly resolution drawing to the attention of the Ten-Nation Disarmament Committee the issue of an international agreement on the prevention of the wider dissemination of nuclear weapons

A/RES/1380 (XIV), 20 November 1959

The General Assembly,

Recognizing that the danger now exists that an increase in the number of States possessing nuclear weapons may occur, aggravating international tension and the difficulty of maintaining world peace, and thus rendering more difficult the attainment of general disarmament agreement,

Convinced therefore that consideration of this danger is appropriate within the framework of deliberations on disarmament,

Noting the resolution of the United Nations Disarmament Commission of 10 September 1959, 1/

Desiring to bring to the attention of the ten-nation disarmament committee its conviction that consideration should be given to this problem,

1.   *Suggests* that the ten-nation disarmament committee, in the course of its deliberations, should consider appropriate means whereby this danger may be averted, including the feasibility of an international agreement, subject to inspection and control, whereby the Powers producing nuclear weapons would refrain from handing over the control of such weapons to any nation not possessing them and whereby the Powers not possessing such weapons would refrain from manufacturing them;

2.   *Invites* the Committee to include the results of its deliberations on these matters in its report to the Disarmament Commission.

1/ *Official Records of the Disarmament Commission, Supplement for January to December 1959,* document DC/146.

Document 2

General Assembly resolution calling for efforts on the part of all Governments to achieve agreement on the prevention of the wider dissemination of nuclear weapons

A/RES/1576 (XV), 20 December 1960

The General Assembly,

Recalling its resolution 1380 (XIV) of 20 November 1959,

Recognizing the urgent danger that now exists that an increase in the number of States possessing nuclear weapons may occur, aggravating international tension and the difficulty of maintaining world peace, and thus

rendering more difficult the attainment of general disarmament agreement,

Noting with regret that the Ten-Nation Committee on Disarmament did not find it possible to consider this problem, which was referred to it by General Assembly resolution 1380 (XIV),

Believing in the necessity of an international agreement, subject to inspection and control, whereby the

Powers producing nuclear weapons would refrain from relinquishing control of such weapons to any nation not possessing them and whereby Powers not possessing such weapons would refrain from manufacturing them,

Believing further that, pending the conclusion of such an international agreement, it is desirable that temporary and voluntary measures be taken to avoid the aggravation of this danger,

1. *Calls upon* all Governments to make every effort to achieve permanent agreement on the prevention of the wider dissemination of nuclear weapons;

2. *Calls upon* Powers producing such weapons, as a temporary and voluntary measure pending the negotiation of such a permanent agreement, to refrain from relinquishing control of such weapons to any nation not possessing them and from transmitting to it the information necessary for their manufacture;

3. *Calls upon* Powers not possessing such weapons, on a similar temporary and voluntary basis, to refrain from manufacturing these weapons and from otherwise attempting to acquire them.

Document 3

General Assembly resolution requesting the Secretary-General to make an inquiry into the conditions under which non-nuclear-weapon States might be willing to undertake to refrain from manufacturing or acquiring nuclear weapons and to refuse to receive, in the future, such weapons in their territories on behalf of any other country

A/RES/1664 (XVI), 4 December 1961

The General Assembly,

Convinced that all measures should be taken that could halt further nuclear weapons tests and prevent the further spread of nuclear weapons,

Recognizing that the countries not possessing nuclear weapons have a grave interest, and an important part to fulfil, in the preparation and implementation of such measures,

Believing that action taken by those countries will facilitate agreement by the nuclear Powers to discontinue all nuclear tests and to prevent any increase in the number of nuclear Powers,

Taking note of the suggestion that an inquiry be made into the conditions under which countries not possessing nuclear weapons might be willing to enter into

specific undertakings to refrain from manufacturing or otherwise acquiring such weapons and to refuse to receive, in the future, nuclear weapons in their territories on behalf of any other country,

1. *Requests* the Secretary-General to make such an inquiry as soon as possible and to submit a report on its results to the Disarmament Commission not later than 1 April 1962;

2. *Requests* the Disarmament Commission to take such further measures as appear to be warranted in the light of that report;

3. *Calls upon* the nuclear Powers to extend their fullest cooperation and assistance with regard to the implementation of the present resolution.

Document 4

General Assembly resolution calling for efforts on the part of all States to reach agreement on the prevention of the wider dissemination of nuclear weapons

A/RES/1665 (XVI), 4 December 1961

The General Assembly,

Recalling its resolutions 1380 (XIV) of 20 November 1959 and 1576 (XV) of 20 December 1960,

Convinced that an increase in the number of States possessing nuclear weapons is growing more imminent and threatens to extend and intensify the arms race and to increase the difficulties of avoiding war and of establishing international peace and security based on the rule of law,

Believing in the necessity of an international agreement, subject to inspection and control, whereby the States producing nuclear weapons would refrain from relinquishing control of such weapons to any nation not possessing them and whereby States not possessing such weapons would refrain from manufacturing them,

1. *Calls upon* all States, and in particular upon the States at present possessing nuclear weapons, to use their best endeavours to secure the conclusion of an international agreement containing provisions under which the nuclear States would undertake to refrain from relinquishing control of nuclear weapons and from transmitting the information necessary for their manufacture to States not possessing such weapons, and provisions under which States not possessing nuclear weapons would undertake not to manufacture or otherwise acquire control of such weapons;

2. *Urges* all States to cooperate to those ends.

Document 5

General Assembly resolution calling upon the Conference of the Eighteen-Nation Committee on Disarmament to give urgent consideration to the negotiation of an international treaty to prevent the proliferation of nuclear weapons, based on five main principles

A/RES/2028 (XX), 19 November 1965

The General Assembly,

Conscious of its responsibility under the Charter of the United Nations for disarmament and the consolidation of peace,

Mindful of its responsibility in accordance with Article 11, paragraph 1, of the Charter, which stipulates that the General Assembly may consider the general principles of cooperation in the maintenance of international peace and security, including the principles governing disarmament and the regulation of armaments, and may make recommendations with regard to such principles to the Members or to the Security Council or to both,

Recalling its resolutions 1665 (XVI) of 4 December 1961 and 1908 (XVIII) of 27 November 1963,

Recognizing the urgency and great importance of the question of preventing the proliferation of nuclear weapons,

Noting with satisfaction the efforts of Brazil, Burma, Ethiopia, India, Mexico, Nigeria, Sweden and the United Arab Republic to achieve the solution of the problem of non-proliferation of nuclear weapons, as contained in their joint memorandum of 15 September 1965, 1/

Convinced that the proliferation of nuclear weapons would endanger the security of all States and make more difficult the achievement of general and complete disarmament under effective international control,

Noting the declaration adopted by the Assembly of Heads of State and Government of the Organization of African Unity at its first regular session, held at Cairo in July 1964, 2/ and the Declaration entitled "Programme for Peace and International Co-operation" 3/ adopted by the Second Conference of Heads of State or Government of Non-Aligned Countries, held at Cairo in October 1964,

Noting also the draft treaties to prevent the proliferation of nuclear weapons submitted by the United States of America 4/ and the Union of Soviet Socialist Republics, 5/ respectively,

Noting further that a draft unilateral non-acquisition declaration has been submitted by Italy, 6/

Convinced that General Assembly resolutions 1652 (XVI) of 24 November 1961 and 1911 (XVIII) of 27 November 1963 aim at preventing the proliferation of nuclear weapons,

Believing that it is imperative to exert further efforts to conclude a treaty to prevent the proliferation of nuclear weapons,

1. *Urges* all States to take all steps necessary for

1/ *Official Records of the Disarmament Commission, Supplement for January to December 1965,* document DC/227, annex l, sect. E.

2/ For the resolution entitled "Denuclearization of Africa" adopted by the Assembly of Heads of State and Government, see *Official Records of the General Assembly, Twentieth Session, Annexes,* agenda item 105, document A/5975.

3/ See A/5763.

4/ *Official Records of the Disarmament Commission, Supplement for January to December 1965,* document DC/227, annex 1, sect. A.

5/ *Official Records of the General Assembly, Twentieth Session, Annexes,* agenda item 106, document A/5976.

6/ *Official Records of the Disarmament Commission, Supplement for January to December 1965,* document DC/227, annex 1, sect. D.

the early conclusion of a treaty to prevent the proliferation of nuclear weapons;

2. *Calls upon* the Conference of the Eighteen-Nation Committee on Disarmament to give urgent consideration to the question of non-proliferation of nuclear weapons and, to that end, to reconvene as early as possible with a view to negotiating an international treaty to prevent the proliferation of nuclear weapons, based on the following main principles:

(a) The treaty should be void of any loop-holes which might permit nuclear or non-nuclear Powers to proliferate, directly or indirectly, nuclear weapons in any form;

(b) The treaty should embody an acceptable balance of mutual responsibilities and obligations of the nuclear and non-nuclear Powers;

(c) The treaty should be a step towards the achievement of general and complete disarmament and, more particularly, nuclear disarmament;

(d) There should be acceptable and workable provisions to ensure the effectiveness of the treaty;

(e) Nothing in the treaty should adversely affect the right of any group of States to conclude regional treaties in order to ensure the total absence of nuclear weapons in their respective territories;

3. *Transmits* the records of the First Committee relating to the discussion of the item entitled "Non-proliferation of nuclear weapons", together with all other relevant documents, to the Eighteen-Nation Committee for its consideration;

4. *Requests* the Eighteen-Nation Committee to submit to the General Assembly at an early date a report on the results of its work on a treaty to prevent the proliferation of nuclear weapons.

Document 6

Report of the Secretary-General on the work of the Organization, 1965-1966 (excerpt)

A/6301/Add.1, 15 September 1966

. . .

With regard to the question of preventing the spread of nuclear weapons, which was given the highest priority, the Eighteen-Nation Committee sought to agree on the text of a non-proliferation treaty based on the two draft treaties presented respectively by the Soviet Union and the United States, taking into account the principles laid down in General Assembly resolution 2028 (XX). While these efforts have not yet met with success, it can at least be said that the search for an agreed treaty is continuing. The positions of the parties have been clarified and all of them are aware of the compromises which have to be made if agreement is to be reached. I still hope, and I have continued to urge, that the Governments concerned will find it possible to make the necessary adjustments in their positions so that a treaty on non-proliferation can be agreed upon and put into force at the earliest possible date.

The dangers of nuclear proliferation are very real and very grave, more so than may be generally recognized. The use of nuclear reactors produces plutonium which, when processed in a separation plant, can be used to make nuclear weapons by techniques that are no longer secret. According to some estimates, by 1980 nuclear power reactors throughout the world will produce more than 100 kilogrammes of plutonium every day. It is always possible that cheaper and simpler methods of producing fissionable material may be discovered and that their availability for warlike purposes will increase astronomically. The risks that now exist of the further spread of nuclear weapons hold such peril for humanity that international safeguards should be established not only over nuclear power reactors but also over other nuclear plants which produce, use or process significant quantities of fissionable materials.

There may already be some countries which may, however misguidedly, hope—or in desperation persuade themselves—to try to improve their security by acquiring nuclear weapons as a deterrent against attack by a hostile neighbour. These countries may well be reluctant to forgo the option of acquiring such weapons unless other means of protection are found. Some countries may also be reluctant to give up the right to acquire such weapons unless the present nuclear Powers commit themselves—in the words of resolution 2028 (XX)—to "an acceptable balance of mutual responsibilities and obligations". These preoccupations of the non-nuclear countries raise serious and difficult problems and these problems must be faced. The responsibility for solving them must be shared by all States Members of the United Nations, and it rests as well with States not represented in the Organization.

. . .

Document 7

General Assembly resolution appealing to all States to take all necessary steps for the successful conclusion of a treaty on the non-proliferation of nuclear weapons

A/RES/2149 (XXI), 4 November 1966

The General Assembly,

Reaffirming its resolution 2028 (XX) of 19 November 1965,

Convinced that the proliferation of nuclear weapons would endanger the security of all States and hamper the achievement of general and complete disarmament,

Considering that international negotiations are now under way with a view to the preparation of a treaty on the non-proliferation of nuclear weapons, and wishing to create an atmosphere conducive to the successful conclusion of those negotiations,

Urgently appeals to all States, pending the conclusion of such a treaty:

(a) To take all the necessary steps to facilitate and achieve at the earliest possible time the conclusion of a treaty on the non-proliferation of nuclear weapons in accordance with the principles laid down in General Assembly resolution 2028 (XX);

(b) To refrain from any actions conducive to the proliferation of nuclear weapons or which might hamper the conclusion of an agreement on the non-proliferation of nuclear weapons.

Document 8

General Assembly resolution requesting the Conference of the Eighteen-Nation Committee on Disarmament to consider the issue of assurances to non-nuclear-weapon States and calling upon all States to adhere to the principles laid down in resolution 2028 (XX) for the negotiation of a treaty on the non-proliferation of nuclear weapons

A/RES/2153 A (XXI), 17 November 1966

The General Assembly,

Having discussed the report of the Conference of the Eighteen-Nation Committee on Disarmament on the non-proliferation of nuclear weapons, 1/

Noting that it has not yet been possible to reach agreement on an international treaty to prevent the proliferation of nuclear weapons,

Viewing with apprehension the possibility that such a situation may lead not only to an increase of nuclear arsenals and to a spread of nuclear weapons over the world but also to an increase in the number of nuclear-weapon Powers,

Believing that if such a situation persists it may lead to the aggravation of tensions between States and the risk of a nuclear war,

Believing further that the remaining differences between all concerned should be resolved quickly so as to prevent any further delay in the conclusion of an international treaty on the non-proliferation of nuclear weapons,

Convinced, therefore, that it is imperative to make further efforts to bring to a conclusion a treaty which reflects the mandate given by the General Assembly in its resolution 2028 (XX) of 19 November 1965 and which is acceptable to all concerned and satisfactory to the international community,

1. *Reaffirms* its resolution 2028 (XX);

2. *Urges* all States to take all the necessary steps conducive to the earliest conclusion of a treaty on the non-proliferation of nuclear weapons;

3. *Calls upon* all nuclear-weapon Powers to refrain from the use, or the threat of use, of nuclear weapons against States which may conclude treaties of the nature defined in paragraph 2 (e) of General Assembly resolution 2028 (XX);

4. *Requests* the Conference of the Eighteen-Nation Committee on Disarmament to consider urgently the

1/ *Official Records of the Disarmament Commission, Supplement for 1966,* document DC/228.

proposal that the nuclear-weapon Powers should give an assurance that they will not use, or threaten to use, nuclear weapons against non-nuclear-weapon States without nuclear weapons on their territories, and any other proposals that have been or may be made for the solution of this problem;

5. *Calls upon* all States to adhere strictly to the principles laid down in its resolution 2028 (XX) for the negotiation of the above-mentioned treaty;

6. *Calls upon* the Conference of the Eighteen-Nation Committee on Disarmament to give high priority to the question of the non-proliferation of nuclear weapons

in accordance with the mandate contained in General Assembly resolution 2028 (XX) ;

7. *Transmits* the records of the First Committee relating to the discussion of the item entitled "Non-proliferation of nuclear weapons", together with all other relevant documents, to the Conference of the Eighteen-Nation Committee on Disarmament;

8. *Requests* the Conference of the Eighteen-Nation Committee on Disarmament to submit to the General Assembly at an early date a report on the results of its work on the question of the non-proliferation of nuclear weapons.

Document 9

Treaty for the Prohibition of Nuclear Weapons in Latin America and the Caribbean (Treaty of Tlatelolco), 14 February 1967*

United Nations, *Treaty Series*, vol. 634, No. 9068

PREAMBLE

In the name of their peoples and faithfully interpreting their desires and aspirations, the Governments of the States which sign the Treaty for the Prohibition of Nuclear Weapons in Latin America,

Desiring to contribute, so far as lies in their power, towards ending the armaments race, especially in the field of nuclear weapons, and towards strengthening a world at peace, based on the sovereign equality of States, mutual respect and good neighbourliness,

Recalling that the United Nations General Assembly, in its resolution 808 (IX), adopted unanimously as one of the three points of a coordinated programme of disarmament "the total prohibition of the use and manufacture of nuclear weapons and weapons of mass destruction of every type",

Recalling that militarily denuclearized zones are not an end in themselves but rather a means for achieving general and complete disarmament at a later stage,

Recalling United Nations General Assembly resolution 1911 (XVIII), which established that the measures that should be agreed upon for the denuclearization of Latin America should be taken "in the light of the principles of the Charter of the United Nations and of regional agreements",

Recalling United Nations General Assembly resolution 2028 (XX), which established the principle of an acceptable balance of mutual responsibilities and duties for the nuclear and non-nuclear powers, and

Recalling that the Charter of the Organization of American States proclaims that it is an essential purpose

of the Organization to strengthen the peace and security of the hemisphere,

Convinced:

That the incalculable destructive power of nuclear weapons has made it imperative that the legal prohibition of war should be strictly observed in practice if the survival of civilization and of mankind itself is to be assured,

That nuclear weapons, whose terrible effects are suffered, indiscriminately and inexorably, by military forces and civilian population alike, constitute, through the persistence of the radioactivity they release, an attack on the integrity of the human species and ultimately may even render the whole earth uninhabitable,

That general and complete disarmament under effective international control is a vital matter which all the peoples of the world equally demand,

That the proliferation of nuclear weapons, which seems inevitable unless States, in the exercise of their sovereign rights, impose restrictions on themselves in order to prevent it, would make any agreement on disarmament enormously difficult and would increase the danger of the outbreak of a nuclear conflagration,

That the establishment of militarily denuclearized zones is closely linked with the maintenance of peace and security in the respective regions,

That the military denuclearization of vast geo-

* On 3 July 1990, the Agency for the Prohibition of Nuclear Weapons in Latin America decided, in its resolution 267 (E-V), to add to the legal title of the Treaty the terms "and the Caribbean", in conformity with article 7 of the Treaty.

graphical zones, adopted by the Sovereign decision of the States comprised therein, will exercise a beneficial influence on other regions where similar conditions exist,

That the privileged situation of the signatory States, whose territories are wholly free from nuclear weapons, imposes upon them the inescapable duty of preserving that situation both in their own interests and for the good of mankind,

That the existence of nuclear weapons in any country of Latin America would make it a target for possible nuclear attacks and would inevitably set off, throughout the region a ruinous race in nuclear weapons which would involve the unjustifiable diversion, for warlike purposes, of the limited resources required for economic and social development,

That the foregoing reasons, together with the traditional peace-loving outlook of Latin America, give rise to an inescapable necessity that nuclear energy should be used in that region exclusively for peaceful purposes, and that the Latin American countries should use their right to the greatest and most equitable possible access to this new source of energy in order to expedite the economic and social development of their peoples,

Convinced finally:

That the military denuclearization of Latin America—being understood to mean the undertaking entered into internationally in this Treaty to keep their territories forever free from nuclear weapons—will constitute a measure which will spare their peoples from the squandering of their limited resources on nuclear armaments and will protect them against possible nuclear attacks on their territories, and will also constitute a significant contribution towards preventing the proliferation of nuclear weapons and a powerful factor for general and complete disarmament, and

That Latin America, faithful to its tradition of universality, must not only endeavour to banish from its homelands the scourge of a nuclear war, but must also strive to promote the well-being and advancement of its peoples, at the same time cooperating in the fulfilment of the ideals of mankind, that is to say, in the consolidation of a permanent peace based on equal rights, economic fairness and social justice for all, in accordance with the principles and purposes set forth in the Charter of the United Nations and in the Charter of the Organization of American States,

Have agreed as follows:

OBLIGATIONS

Article 1

1. The Contracting Parties hereby undertake to use exclusively for peaceful purposes the nuclear mate-

rial and facilities which are under their jurisdiction, and to prohibit and prevent in their respective territories:

(a) The testing, use, manufacture, production or acquisition by any means whatsoever of any nuclear weapons, by the Parties themselves, directly or indirectly, on behalf of anyone else or in any other way, and

(b) The receipt, storage, installation, deployment and any form of possession of any nuclear weapons, directly or indirectly, by the Parties themselves, by anyone on their behalf or in any other way.

2. The Contracting Parties also undertake to refrain from engaging in, encouraging or authorizing, directly or indirectly, or in any way participating in the testing, use, manufacture, production, possession or control of any nuclear weapon.

DEFINITION OF THE CONTRACTING PARTIES

Article 2

For the purposes of this Treaty, the Contracting Parties are those for whom the Treaty is in force.

DEFINITION OF TERRITORY

Article 3

For the purposes of this Treaty, the term "territory" shall include the territorial sea, air space and any other space over which the State exercises sovereignty in accordance with its own legislation.

ZONE OF APPLICATION

Article 4

1. The zone of application of this Treaty is the whole of the territories for which the Treaty is in force.

2. Upon fulfilment of the requirements of article 28, paragraph 1, the zone of application of this Treaty shall also be that which is situated in the western hemisphere within the following limits (except the continental part of the territory of the United States of America and its territorial waters): starting at a point located at 35° north latitude, 75° west longitude; from this point directly southward to a point at 30° north latitude, 75° west longitude; from there, directly eastward to a point at 30° north latitude, 50° west longitude; from there, along a loxodromic line to a point at 5° north latitude, 20° west longitude; from there, directly southward to a point at 60° south latitude, 20° west longitude; from there, directly westward to a point at 60° south latitude, 115° west longitude; from there, directly northward to a point at 0 latitude, 115° west longitude; from there, along a loxodromic line to a point at 35° north latitude, 150° west

longitude; from there, directly eastward to a point at 35° north latitude, 75° west longitude.

DEFINITION OF NUCLEAR WEAPONS

Article 5

For the purposes of this Treaty, a nuclear weapon is any device which is capable of releasing nuclear energy In an uncontrolled manner and which has a group of characteristics that are appropriate for use for warlike purposes. An instrument that may be used for the transport or propulsion of the device is not included in this definition if it is separable from the device and not an indivisible part thereof.

MEETING OF SIGNATORIES

Article 6

At the request of any of the signatory States or if the Agency established by article 7 should so decide, a meeting of all the signatories may be convoked to consider in common questions which may affect the very essence of this instrument, including possible amendments to it. In either case, the meeting will be convoked by the General Secretary.

ORGANIZATION

Article 7

1. In order to ensure compliance with the obligations of this Treaty, the Contracting Parties hereby establish an international organization to be known as the Agency for the Prohibition of Nuclear Weapons in Latin America, hereinafter referred to as "the Agency". Only the Contracting Parties shall be affected by its decisions.

2. The Agency shall be responsible for the holding of periodic or extraordinary consultations among Member States on matters relating to the purposes, measures and procedures set forth in this Treaty and to the supervision of compliance with the obligations arising therefrom.

3. The Contracting Parties agree to extend to the Agency full and prompt cooperation in accordance with the provisions of this Treaty, of any agreements they may conclude with the Agency and of any agreements the Agency may conclude with any other international organization or body.

4. The headquarters of the Agency shall be in Mexico City.

ORGANS

Article 8

1. There are hereby established as principal organs of the Agency a General Conference, a Council and a Secretariat.

2. Such subsidiary organs as are considered necessary by the General Conference may be established within the purview of this Treaty.

THE GENERAL CONFERENCE

Article 9

1. The General Conference, the supreme organ of the Agency, shall be composed of all the Contracting Parties; it shall hold regular sessions every two years, and may also hold special sessions whenever this Treaty so provides or, in the opinion of the Council, the circumstances so require.

2. The General Conference:

(a) May consider and decide on any matters or questions covered by this Treaty, within the limits thereof, including those referring to powers and functions of any organ provided for in this Treaty;

(b) Shall establish procedures for the control system to ensure observance of this Treaty in accordance with its provisions;

(c) Shall elect the Members of the Council and the General Secretary;

(d) May remove the General Secretary from office if the proper functioning of the Agency so requires;

(e) Shall receive and consider the biennial and special reports submitted by the Council and the General Secretary;

(f) Shall initiate and consider studies designed to facilitate the optimum fulfilment of the aims of this Treaty, without prejudice to the power of the General Secretary independently to carry out similar studies for submission to and consideration by the Conference;

(g) Shall be the organ competent to authorize the conclusion of agreements with Governments and other international organizations and bodies.

3. The General Conference shall adopt the Agency's budget and fix the scale of financial contributions to be paid by Member States, taking into account the systems and criteria used for the same purpose by the United Nations.

4. The General Conference shall elect its officers for each session and may establish such subsidiary organs as it deems necessary for the performance of its functions.

5. Each Member of the Agency shall have one vote. The decisions of the General Conference shall be taken by a two-thirds majority of the Members present and voting in the case of matters relating to the control system and measures referred to in article 20, the admission of new Members, the election or removal of the General Secretary, adoption of the budget and matters related thereto. Decisions on other matters, as well as procedural questions and also determination of which questions

must be decided by a two-thirds majority, shall be taken by a simple majority of the Members present and voting.

6. The General Conference shall adopt its own rules of procedure.

THE COUNCIL

Article 10

1. The Council shall be composed of five Members of the Agency elected by the General Conference from among the Contracting Parties, due account being taken of equitable geographic distribution.

2. The Members of the Council shall be elected for a term of four years. However, in the first election three will be elected for two years. Outgoing Members may not be re-elected for the following period unless the limited number of States for which the Treaty is in force so requires.

3. Each Member of the Council shall have one representative.

4. The Council shall be so organized as to be able to function continuously.

5. In addition to the functions conferred upon it by this Treaty and to those which may be assigned to it by the General Conference, the Council shall, through the General Secretary, ensure the proper operation of the control system in accordance with the provisions of this Treaty and with the decisions adopted by the General Conference.

6. The Council shall submit an annual report on its work to the General Conference as well as such special reports as it deems necessary or which the General Conference requests of it.

7. The Council shall elect its officers for each session.

8. The decisions of the Council shall be taken by a simple majority of its Members present and voting.

9. The Council shall adopt its own rules of procedure.

THE SECRETARIAT

Article 11

1. The Secretariat shall consist of a General Secretary, who shall be the chief administrative officer of the Agency, and of such staff as the Agency may require. The term of office of the General Secretary shall be four years and he may be re-elected for a single additional term. The General Secretary may not be a national of the country in which the Agency has its headquarters. In case the office of General Secretary becomes vacant, a new election shall be held to fill the office for the remainder of the term.

2. The staff of the Secretariat shall be appointed by the General Secretary, in accordance with rules laid down by the General Conference.

3. In addition to the functions conferred upon him by this Treaty and to those which may be assigned to him by the General Conference, the General Secretary shall ensure, as provided by article 10, paragraph 5, the proper operation of the control system established by this Treaty, in accordance with the provisions of the Treaty and the decisions taken by the General Conference.

4. The General Secretary shall act in that capacity in all meetings of the General Conference and of the Council and shall make an annual report to both bodies on the work of the Agency and any special reports requested by the General Conference or the Council or which the General Secretary may deem desirable.

5. The General Secretary shall establish the procedures for distributing to all Contracting Parties information received by the Agency from governmental sources and such information from non-governmental sources as may be of interest to the Agency.

6. In the performance of their duties the General Secretary and the staff shall not seek or receive instructions from any Government or from any other authority external to the Agency and shall refrain from any action which might reflect on their position as international officials responsible only to the Agency; subject to their responsibility to the Agency, they shall not disclose any industrial secrets or other confidential information coming to their knowledge by reason of their official duties in the Agency.

7. Each of the Contracting Parties undertakes to respect the exclusively international character of the responsibilities of the General Secretary and the staff and not to seek to influence them in the discharge of their responsibilities.

CONTROL SYSTEM

Article 12

1. For the purpose of verifying compliance with the obligations entered into by the Contracting Parties in accordance with article 1, a control system shall be established which shall be put into effect in accordance with the provisions of articles 13-18 of this Treaty.

2. The control system shall be used in particular for the purpose of verifying:

(a) That devices, services and facilities intended for peaceful uses of nuclear energy are not used in the testing or manufacture of nuclear weapons;

(b) That none of the activities prohibited in article 1 of this Treaty are carried out in the territory of the

Contracting Parties with nuclear materials or weapons introduced from abroad; and

(c) That explosions for peaceful purposes are compatible with article 18 of this Treaty.

IAEA SAFEGUARDS

Article 13

Each Contracting Party shall negotiate multilateral or bilateral agreements with the International Atomic Energy Agency for the application of its safeguards to its nuclear activities. Each Contracting Party shall initiate negotiations within a period of 180 days after the date of the deposit of its instrument of ratification of this Treaty. These agreements shall enter into force, for each Party, not later than eighteen months after the date of the initiation of such negotiations except in case of unforeseen circumstances or force majeure.

REPORTS OF THE PARTIES

Article 14

1. The Contracting Parties shall submit to the Agency and to the International Atomic Energy Agency, for their information, semi-annual reports stating that no activity prohibited under this Treaty has occurred in their respective territories.

2. The Contracting Parties shall simultaneously transmit to the Agency a copy of any report they may submit to the International Atomic Energy Agency which relates to matters that are the subject of this Treaty and to the application of safeguards.

3. The Contracting Parties shall also transmit to the Organization of American States, for its information, any reports that may be of interest to it, in accordance with the obligations established by the Inter-American System.

SPECIAL REPORTS REQUESTED BY THE GENERAL SECRETARY

Article 15

1. With the authorization of the Council, the General Secretary may request any of the Contracting Parties to provide the Agency with complementary or supplementary information regarding any event or circumstance connected with compliance with this Treaty, explaining his reasons. The Contracting Parties undertake to cooperate promptly and fully with the General Secretary.

2. The General Secretary shall inform the Council and the Contracting Parties forthwith of such requests and of the respective replies.

SPECIAL INSPECTIONS

Article 16

1. The International Atomic Energy Agency and the Council established by this Treaty have the power of carrying out special inspections in the following cases:

(a) In the case of the International Atomic Energy Agency, in accordance with the agreements referred to in article 13 of this Treaty;

(b) In the case of the Council:

(i) When so requested, the reasons for the request being stated, by any Party which suspects that some activity prohibited by this Treaty has been carried out or is about to be carried out, either in the territory of any other Party or in any other place on such latter Party's behalf, the Council shall immediately arrange for such an inspection in accordance with article 10, paragraph 5;

(ii) When requested by any Party which has been suspected of or charged with having violated this shall immediately arrange for the special inspection requested in accordance with article 10, paragraph 5.

The above requests will be made to the Council through the General Secretary.

2. The costs and expenses of any special inspection carried out under paragraph 1, subparagraph (b), sections (i) and (ii) of this article shall be borne by the requesting Party or Parties, except where the Council concludes on the basis of the report on the special inspection that, in view of the circumstances existing in the case, such costs and expenses should be borne by the Agency.

3. The General Conference shall formulate the procedures for the organization and execution of the special inspections carried out in accordance with paragraph 1, subparagraph (b), sections (i) and (ii) of this article.

4. The Contracting Parties undertake to grant the inspectors carrying out such special inspections full and free access to all places and all information which may be necessary for the performance of their duties and which are directly and intimately connected with the suspicion of violation of this Treaty. If so requested by the authorities of the Contracting Party in whose territory the inspection is carried out, the inspectors designated by the General Conference shall be accompanied by representatives of said authorities, provided that this does not in any way delay or hinder the work of the inspectors.

5. The Council shall immediately transmit to all the Parties, through the General Secretary, a copy of any report resulting from special inspections.

6. Similarly, the Council shall send through the General Secretary to the Secretary-General of the United Nations, for transmission to the United Nations Security Council and General Assembly, and to the Council of the Organization of American States, for its information, a copy of any report resulting from any special inspection

carried out in accordance with paragraph 1, subparagraph (b), sections (i) and (ii) of this article.

7. The Council may decide, or any Contracting Party may request, the convening of a special session of the General Conference for the purpose of considering the reports resulting from any special inspection. In such a case, the General Secretary shall take immediate steps to convene the special session requested.

8. The General Conference, convened in special session under this article, may make recommendations to the Contracting Parties and submit reports to the Secretary-General of the United Nations to be transmitted to the United Nations Security Council and the General Assembly.

USE OF NUCLEAR ENERGY FOR PEACEFUL PURPOSES

Article 17

Nothing in the provisions of this Treaty shall prejudice the rights of the Contracting Parties, in conformity with this Treaty, to use nuclear energy for peaceful purposes, in particular for their economic development and social progress.

EXPLOSIONS FOR PEACEFUL PURPOSES

Article 18

1. The Contracting Parties may carry out explosions of nuclear devices for peaceful purposes—including explosions which involve devices similar to those used in nuclear weapons—or collaborate with third parties for the same purpose, provided that they do so in accordance with the provisions of this article and the other articles of the Treaty, particularly articles 1 and 5.

2. Contracting Parties intending to carry out, or to cooperate in carrying out, such an explosion shall notify the Agency and the International Atomic Energy Agency, as far in advance as the circumstances require, of the date of the explosion and shall at the same time provide the following information:

(a) The nature of the nuclear device and the source from which it was obtained;

(b) The place and purpose of the planned explosion;

(c) The procedures which will be followed in order to comply with paragraph 3 of this article;

(d) The expected force of the device; and

(e) The fullest possible information on any possible radioactive fall-out that may result from the explosion or explosions, and measures which will be taken to avoid danger to the population, flora, fauna and territories of any other Party or Parties.

3. The General Secretary and the technical personnel designated by the Council and the International Atomic Energy Agency may observe all the preparations, including the explosion of the device, and shall have unrestricted access to any area in the vicinity of the site of the explosion in order to ascertain whether the device and the procedures followed during the explosion are in conformity with the information supplied under paragraph 2 of this article and the other provisions of this Treaty.

4. The Contracting Parties may accept the collaboration of third parties for the purposes set forth in paragraph 1 of the present article, in accordance with paragraphs 2 and 3 thereof.

RELATIONS WITH OTHER INTERNATIONAL ORGANIZATIONS

Article 19

1. The Agency may conclude such agreements with the International Atomic Energy Agency as are authorized by the General Conference and as it considers likely to facilitate the efficient operation of the control system established by this Treaty.

2. The Agency may also enter into relations with any international Organization or body, especially any which may be established in the future to supervise disarmament or measures for the control of armaments in any part of the world.

3. The Contracting Parties may, if they see fit, request the advice of the Inter-American Nuclear Energy Commission on all technical matters connected with the application of this Treaty with which the Commission is competent to deal under its Statute.

MEASURES IN THE EVENT OF VIOLATION OF THE TREATY

Article 20

1. The General Conference shall take note of all cases in which, in its opinion, any Contracting Party is not complying fully with its obligations under this Treaty and shall draw the matter to the attention of the Party concerned, making such recommendations as it deems appropriate.

2. If, in its opinion, such non-compliance constitutes a violation of this Treaty which might endanger peace and security, the General Conference shall report thereon simultaneously to the United Nations Security Council and the General Assembly through the Secretary-General of the United Nations, and to the Council of the Organization of American States. The General Conference shall likewise report to the International Atomic Energy Agency for such purposes as are relevant in accordance with its Statute.

UNITED NATIONS AND ORGANIZATION OF AMERICAN STATES

Article 21

None of the provisions of this Treaty shall be construed as impairing the rights and obligations of the Parties under the Charter of the United Nations or, in the case of States Members of the Organization of American States, under existing regional treaties.

PRIVILEGES AND IMMUNITIES

Article 22

1. The Agency shall enjoy in the territory of each of the Contracting Parties such legal capacity and such privileges and immunities as may be necessary for the exercise of its functions and the fulfilment of its purposes.

2. Representatives of the Contracting Parties accredited to the Agency and officials of the Agency shall similarly enjoy such privileges and immunities as are necessary for the performance of their functions.

3. The Agency may conclude agreements with the Contracting Parties with a view to determining the details of the application of paragraphs 1 and 2 of this article.

NOTIFICATION OF OTHER AGREEMENTS

Article 23

Once this Treaty has entered into force, the Secretariat shall be notified immediately of any international agreement concluded by any of the Contracting Parties on matters with which this Treaty is concerned; the Secretariat shall register it and notify the other Contracting Parties.

SETTLEMENT OF DISPUTES

Article 24

Unless the Parties concerned agree on another mode of peaceful settlement, any question or dispute concerning the interpretation or application of this Treaty which is not settled shall be referred to the International Court of Justice with the prior consent of the Parties to the controversy.

SIGNATURE

Article 25

1. This Treaty shall be open indefinitely for signature by:

(a) All the Latin American Republics; and

(b) All other sovereign States situated in their entirety south of latitude 35° north in the western hemisphere; and, except as provided in paragraph 2 of this article, all such States which become sovereign, when they have been admitted by the General Conference.

2. The General Conference shall not take any decision regarding the admission of a political entity part or all of whose territory is the subject, prior to the date when this Treaty is opened for signature, of a dispute or claim between an extra-continental country and one or more Latin American States, so long as the dispute has not been settled by peaceful means.

RATIFICATION AND DEPOSIT

Article 26

1. This Treaty shall be subject to ratification by signatory States in accordance with their respective constitutional procedures.

2. This Treaty and the instruments of ratification shall be deposited with the Government of the Mexican United States, which is hereby designated the Depositary Government.

3. The Depositary Government shall send certified copies of this Treaty to the Governments of signatory States and shall notify them of the deposit of each instrument of ratification.

RESERVATIONS

Article 27

This Treaty shall not be subject to reservations.

ENTRY INTO FORCE

Article 28

1. Subject to the provisions of paragraph 2 of this article, this Treaty shall enter into force among the States that have ratified it as soon as the following requirements have been met:

(a) Deposit of the instruments of ratification of this Treaty with the Depositary Government by the Governments of the States mentioned in article 25 which are in existence on the date when this Treaty is opened for signature and which are not affected by the provisions of article 25, paragraph 2;

(b) Signature and ratification of Additional Protocol I annexed to this Treaty by all extra-continental or continental States having *de jure* or de facto international responsibility for territories situated in the zone of application of the Treaty;

(c) Signature and ratification of the Additional Protocol II annexed to this Treaty by all powers possessing nuclear weapons;

(d) Conclusion of bilateral or multilateral agreements on the application of the Safeguards System of the International Atomic Energy Agency in accordance with article 13 of this Treaty.

2. All signatory States shall have the imprescriptible right to waive, wholly or in part, the requirements laid

down in the preceding paragraph. They may do so by means of a declaration which shall be annexed to their respective instrument of ratification and which may be formulated at the time of deposit of the instrument or subsequently. For those States which exercise this right, this Treaty shall enter into force upon deposit of the declaration, or as soon as those requirements have been met which have not been expressly waived.

3. As soon as this Treaty has entered into force in accordance with the provisions of paragraph 2 for eleven States, the Depositary Government shall convene a preliminary meeting of those States in order that the Agency may be set up and commence its work.

4. After the entry into force of this Treaty for all the countries of the zone, the rise of a new power possessing nuclear weapons shall have the effect of suspending the execution of this Treaty for those countries which have ratified it without waiving requirements of paragraph 1, sub-paragraph (c) of this article, and which request such suspension; the Treaty shall remain suspended until the new power, on its own initiative or upon request by the General Conference, ratifies the annexed Additional Protocol II.

AMENDMENTS
Article 29

1. Any Contracting Party may propose amendments to this Treaty and shall submit its proposals to the Council through the General Secretary, who shall transmit them to all the other Contracting Parties and, in addition, to all other signatories in accordance with article 6. The Council, through the General Secretary, shall immediately following the meeting of signatories convene a special session of the General Conference to examine the proposals made, for the adoption of which a two-thirds majority of the Contracting Parties present and voting shall be required.

2. Amendments adopted shall enter into force as soon as the requirements set forth in article 28 of this Treaty have been complied with.

DURATION AND DENUNCIATION
Article 30

1. This Treaty shall be of a permanent nature and shall remain in force indefinitely, but any Party may denounce it by notifying the General Secretary of the Agency if, in the opinion of the denouncing State, there have arisen or may arise circumstances connected with the content of this Treaty or of the annexed Additional Protocols I and II which affect its supreme interests or the peace and security of one or more Contracting Parties.

2. The denunciation shall take effect three months after the delivery to the General Secretary of the Agency

of the notification by the Government of the signatory State concerned. The General Secretary shall immediately communicate such notification to the other Contracting Parties and to the Secretary-General of the United Nations for the information of the United Nations Security Council and the General Assembly. He shall also communicate it to the Secretary-General of the Organization of American States.

AUTHENTIC TEXTS AND REGISTRATION
Article 31

This Treaty, of which the Spanish, Chinese, English, French, Portuguese and Russian texts are equally authentic, shall be registered by the Depositary Government in accordance with article 102 of the United Nations Charter. The Depositary Government shall notify the Secretary-General of the United Nations of the signatures, ratifications and amendments relating to this Treaty and shall communicate them to the Secretary-General of the Organization of American States for its information.

Transitional Article

Denunciation of the declaration referred to in article 28, paragraph 2, shall be subject to the same procedures as the denunciation of this Treaty, except that it will take effect on the date of delivery of the respective notification.

IN WITNESS WHEREOF the undersigned Plenipotentiaries, having deposited their full powers, found in good and due form, sign this Treaty on behalf of their respective Governments.

Done at Mexico, Distrito Federal, on the Fourteenth day of February, one thousand nine hundred and sixty-seven.

Additional Protocol I

The undersigned Plenipotentiaries, furnished with full powers by their respective Governments,

Convinced that the Treaty for the Prohibition of Nuclear Weapons in Latin America, negotiated and signed in accordance with the recommendations of the General Assembly of the United Nations in Resolution 1911(XVIII) of 27 November 1963, represents an important step towards ensuring the non-proliferation of nuclear weapons,

Aware that the non-proliferation of nuclear weapons is not an end in itself but, rather, a means of achieving general and complete disarmament at a later stage, and

Desiring to contribute, so far as lies in their power, towards ending the armaments race, especially in the field of nuclear weapons, and towards strengthening a world peace, based on mutual respect and sovereign equality of States,

Have agreed as follows:

Article 1

To undertake to apply the statute of denuclearization in respect of warlike purposes as defined in articles 1, 3, 5 and 13 of the Treaty for the Prohibition of Nuclear Weapons in Latin America in territories for which, *de jure* or de facto, they are internationally responsible and which lie within the limits of the geographical zone established in that Treaty.

Article 2

The duration of this Protocol shall be the same as that of the Treaty for the Prohibition of Nuclear Weapons in Latin America of which this Protocol is an annex, and the provisions regarding ratification and denunciation contained in the Treaty shall be applicable to it.

Article 3

This Protocol shall enter into force, for the States which have ratified it, on the date of the deposit of their respective instruments of ratification.

IN WITNESS WHEREOF the undersigned Plenipotentiaries, having deposited their full powers, found in good and due form, sign this Protocol on behalf of their respective Governments.

Additional Protocol II

The undersigned Plenipotentiaries, furnished with full powers by their respective Governments,

Convinced that the Treaty for the Prohibition of Nuclear Weapons in Latin America, negotiated and signed in accordance with the recommendations of the General Assembly of the United Nations in Resolution 1911 (XVIII) of 27 November 1963, represents an important step towards ensuring the non-proliferation of nuclear weapons,

Aware that the non-proliferation of nuclear weapons is not an end in itself but, rather, a means of achieving general and complete disarmament at a later stage, and

Desiring to contribute, so far as lies in their power, towards ending the armaments race, especially in the field of nuclear weapons, and towards promoting and strengthening a world at peace, based on mutual respect and sovereign equality of States,

Have agreed as follows:

Article 1

The statute of denuclearization of Latin America in respect of warlike purposes, as defined, delimited and set forth in the Treaty for the Prohibition of Nuclear Weapons in Latin America of which this instrument is an annex, shall be fully respected by the Parties to this Protocol in all its express aims and provisions.

Article 2

The Governments represented by the undersigned Plenipotentiaries undertake, therefore, not to contribute in any way to the performance of acts involving a violation of the obligations of article 1 of the Treaty in the territories to which the Treaty applies in accordance with article 4 thereof.

Article 3

The Governments represented by the undersigned Plenipotentiaries also undertake not to use or threaten to use nuclear weapons against the Contracting Parties of the Treaty for the Prohibition of Nuclear Weapons in Latin America.

Article 4

The duration of this Protocol shall be the same as that of the Treaty for the Prohibition of Nuclear Weapons in Latin America of which this Protocol is an annex, and the definitions of territory and nuclear weapons set forth in articles 3 and 5 of the Treaty shall be applicable to this Protocol, as well as the provisions regarding ratification, reservations, denunciation, authentic texts and registration contained in articles 26, 27, 30 and 31 of the Treaty.

Article 5

This Protocol shall enter into force, for the States which have ratified it, on the date of the deposit of their respective instruments of ratification.

IN WITNESS WHEREOF, the undersigned Plenipotentiaries, having deposited their full powers, found to be in good and due form, hereby sign this Additional Protocol on behalf of their respective Governments.

Document 10

General Assembly resolution on the submission by the Eighteen-Nation Committee on Disarmament to the Assembly of a full report on the negotiations regarding a draft treaty on non-proliferation and recommending the early resumption of the Assembly's twenty-second session to consider the report

A/RES/2346 A (XXII), 19 December 1967

The General Assembly,

Having received the interim report of the Conference of the Eighteen-Nation Committee on Disarmament, 1/

Noting the progress that the Conference of the Eighteen-Nation Committee on Disarmament has made towards preparing a draft international treaty to prevent the proliferation of nuclear weapons,

Noting further that it has not been possible to complete the text of an international treaty to prevent the proliferation of nuclear weapons,

Reaffirming that it is imperative to make further efforts to conclude such a treaty at the earliest possible date,

Expressing the hope that the remaining differences between all the States concerned can be quickly resolved,

Taking into account the fact that the Conference of the Eighteen-Nation Committee on Disarmament is continuing its work with a view to negotiating a draft treaty on the non-proliferation of nuclear weapons and intends to submit a full report for the consideration of the General Assembly as soon as possible,

1. *Reaffirms* its resolutions 2028 (XX) of 19 November 1965, 2149 (XXI) of 4 November 1966 and 2153 A (XXI) of 17 November 1966;

2. *Calls upon* the Conference of the Eighteen-Nations Committee on Disarmament urgently to continue its work, giving all due consideration to all proposals submitted to the Committee and to the views expressed by Member States during the twenty-second session of the General Assembly;

3. *Requests* the Conference of the Eighteen-Nation Committee on Disarmament to submit to the General Assembly, on or before 15 March 1968, a full report on the negotiations regarding a draft treaty on the non-proliferation of nuclear weapons, together with the pertinent documents and records;

4. *Recommends* that upon the receipt of that report appropriate consultations should be initiated, in accordance with the rules of procedure of the General Assembly, on the setting of an early date after 15 March 1968 for the resumption of the twenty-second session of the General Assembly to consider agenda item 28 *(a)* entitled "Non-proliferation of nuclear weapons: report of the Conference of the Eighteen-Nation Committee on Disarmament".

1/ *Official Records of the General Assembly, Twenty-second Session, Annexes,* agenda item 28, document A/6951.

Document 11

General Assembly resolution on the Treaty on the Non-Proliferation of Nuclear Weapons, with text of Treaty annexed

A/RES/2373 (XXII), 12 June 1968

The General Assembly,

Recalling its resolutions 2346 A (XXII) of 19 December 1967, 2153 A (XXI) of 17 November 1966, 2149 (XXI) of 4 November 1966, 2028 (XX) of 19 November 1965 and 1665 (XVI) of 4 December 1961,

Convinced of the urgency and great importance of preventing the spread of nuclear weapons and of intensifying international cooperation in the development of peaceful applications of atomic energy,

Having considered the report of the Conference of the Eighteen-Nation Committee on Disarmament, dated 14 March 1968, 1/ and appreciative of the work of the Committee on the elaboration of the draft non-proliferation treaty, which is attached to that report, 2/

1/ *Official Records of the General Assembly, Twenty-second Session, Annexes,* agenda item 28, document A/7072-DC/230.
2/ *Ibid.,* annex I.

Convinced that, pursuant to the provisions of the treaty, all signatories have the right to engage in research, production and use of nuclear energy for peaceful purposes and will be able to acquire source and special fissionable materials, as well as equipment for the processing, use and production of nuclear material for peaceful purposes,

Convinced further that an agreement to prevent the further proliferation of nuclear weapons must be followed as soon as possible by effective measures on the cessation of the nuclear arms race and on nuclear disarmament, and that the non-proliferation treaty will contribute to this aim,

Affirming that in the interest of international peace and security both nuclear-weapon and non-nuclear-weapon States carry the responsibility of acting in accordance with the principles of the Charter of the United Nations that the sovereign equality of all States shall be respected, that the threat or use of force in international relations shall be refrained from and that international disputes shall be settled by peaceful means,

1. *Commends* the Treaty on the Non-Proliferation of Nuclear Weapons, the text of which is annexed to the present resolution;

2. *Requests* the Depositary Governments to open the Treaty for signature and ratification at the earliest possible date;

3. *Expresses the hope* for the widest possible adherence to the Treaty by both nuclear-weapon and non-nuclear-weapon States;

4. *Requests* the Conference of the Eighteen-Nation Committee on Disarmament and the nuclear-weapon States urgently to pursue negotiations on effective measures relating to the cessation of the nuclear arms race at an early date and to nuclear disarmament, and on a treaty on general and complete disarmament under strict and effective international control;

5. *Requests* the Conference of the Eighteen-Nation Committee on Disarmament to report on the progress of its work to the General Assembly at its twenty-third session.

ANNEX

Treaty on the Non-Proliferation of Nuclear Weapons

The States concluding this Treaty, hereinafter referred to as the "Parties to the Treaty",

Considering the devastation that would be visited upon all mankind by a nuclear war and the consequent need to make every effort to avert the danger of such a war and to take measures to safeguard the security of peoples,

Believing that the proliferation of nuclear weapons would seriously enhance the danger of nuclear war,

In conformity with resolutions of the United Nations General Assembly calling for the conclusion of an agreement on the prevention of wider dissemination of nuclear weapons,

Undertaking to cooperate in facilitating the application of International Atomic Energy Agency safeguards on peaceful nuclear activities,

Expressing their support for research, development and other efforts to further the application, within the framework of the International Atomic Energy Agency safeguards system, of the principle of safeguarding effectively the flow of source and special fissionable materials by use of instruments and other techniques at certain strategic points,

Affirming the principle that the benefits of peaceful applications of nuclear technology, including any technological by-products which may be derived by nuclear-weapon States from the development of nuclear explosive devices, should be available for peaceful purposes to all Parties to the Treaty, whether nuclear-weapon or non-nuclear-weapon States,

Convinced that, in furtherance of this principle, all Parties to the Treaty are entitled to participate in the fullest possible exchange of scientific information for, and to contribute alone or in cooperation with other States to, the further development of the applications of atomic energy for peaceful purposes,

Declaring their intention to achieve at the earliest possible date the cessation of the nuclear arms race and to undertake effective measures in the direction of nuclear disarmament,

Urging the cooperation of all States in the attainment of this objective,

Recalling the determination expressed by the Parties to the 1963 Treaty banning nuclear weapon tests in the atmosphere, in outer space and under water in its Preamble to seek to achieve the discontinuance of all test explosions of nuclear weapons for all time and to continue negotiations to this end,

Desiring to further the easing of international tension and the strengthening of trust between States in order to facilitate the cessation of the manufacture of nuclear weapons, the liquidation of all their existing stockpiles, and the elimination from national arsenals of nuclear weapons and the means of their delivery pursuant to a treaty on general and complete disarmament under strict and effective international control,

Recalling that, in accordance with the Charter of the United Nations, States must refrain in their international relations from the threat or use of force against the territorial integrity or political independence of any State, or in any other manner inconsistent with the purposes of the United Nations, and that the establishment and maintenance of international peace and security are to be promoted with the least diversion for armaments of the world's human and economic resources,

Have agreed as follows:

Article I

Each nuclear-weapon State Party to the Treaty undertakes not to transfer to any recipient whatsoever nuclear weapons or other nuclear explosive devices or control over such weapons or explosive devices directly, or indirectly; and not in any way to assist, encourage, or induce any non-nuclear-weapon State to manufacture or otherwise acquire nuclear weapons or other nuclear explosive devices, or control over such weapons or explosive devices.

Article II

Each non-nuclear-weapon State Party to the Treaty undertakes not to receive the transfer from any transferor whatsoever of nuclear weapons or other nuclear explosive devices or of control over such weapons or explosive devices directly, or indirectly; not to manufacture or otherwise acquire nuclear weapons or other nuclear explosive devices; and not to seek or receive any assistance in the manufacture of nuclear weapons or other nuclear explosive devices.

Article III

1. Each non-nuclear-weapon State Party to the Treaty undertakes to accept safeguards, as set forth in an agreement to be negotiated and concluded with the International Atomic Energy Agency in accordance with the Statute of the International Atomic Energy Agency and the Agency's safeguards system, for the exclusive purpose of verification of the fulfilment of its obligations assumed under this Treaty with a view to preventing diversion of nuclear energy from peaceful uses to nuclear weapons or other nuclear explosive devices. Procedures for the safeguards required by this article shall be followed with respect to source or special fissionable material whether it is being produced, processed or used in any principal nuclear facility or is outside any such facility. The safeguards required by this article shall be applied on all source or special fissionable material in all peaceful nuclear activities within the territory of such State, under its jurisdiction, or carried out under its control anywhere.

2. Each State Party to the Treaty undertakes not to provide: *(a)* source or special fissionable material, or *(b)* equipment or material especially designed or prepared for the processing, use or production of special fissionable material, to any non-nuclear-weapon State for peaceful purposes, unless the source or special fissionable material shall be subject to the safeguards required by this article.

3. The safeguards required by this article shall be implemented in a manner designed to comply with article IV of this Treaty, and to avoid hampering the economic or technological development of the Parties or international cooperation in the field of peaceful nuclear activities, including the international exchange of nuclear material and equipment for the processing, use or production of nuclear material for peaceful purposes in accordance with the provisions of this article and the principle of safeguarding set forth in the Preamble of the Treaty.

4. Non-nuclear-weapon States Party to the Treaty shall conclude agreements with the International Atomic Energy Agency to meet the requirements of this article either individually or together with other States in accordance with the Statute of the International Atomic Energy Agency. Negotiation of such agreements shall commence within 180 days from the original entry into force of this Treaty. For States depositing their instruments of ratification or accession after the 180-day period, negotiation of such agreements shall commence not later than the date of such deposit. Such agreements shall enter into force not later than eighteen months after the date of initiation of negotiations.

Article IV

1. Nothing in this Treaty shall be interpreted as affecting the inalienable right of all the Parties to the Treaty to develop research, production and use of nuclear energy for peaceful purposes without discrimination and in conformity with articles I and II of this Treaty.

2. All the Parties to the Treaty undertake to facilitate, and have the right to participate in, the fullest possible exchange of equipment, materials and scientific and technological information for the peaceful uses of nuclear energy. Parties to the Treaty in a position to do so shall also cooperate in contributing alone or together with other States or international organizations to the further development of the applications of nuclear energy for peaceful purposes, especially in the territories of non-nuclear-weapon States Party to the Treaty, with due consideration for the needs of the developing areas of the world.

Article V

Each Party to the Treaty undertakes to take appropriate measures to ensure that, in accordance with this Treaty, under appropriate international observation and through appropriate international procedures, potential benefits from any peaceful applications of nuclear explosions will be made available to non-nuclear-weapon States Party to the Treaty on a non-discriminatory basis and that the charge to such Parties for the explosive devices used will be as low as possible and exclude any charge for research and development. Non-nuclear-weapon States Party to the Treaty shall be able to obtain such benefits, pursuant to a special international agreement or agreements, through an appropriate international body with adequate representation of non-nuclear-weapon States. Negotiations on this subject shall commence as soon as possible after the Treaty enters into force. Non-nuclear-weapon States Party to the Treaty so desiring may also obtain such benefits pursuant to bilateral agreements.

Article VI

Each of the Parties to the Treaty undertakes to pursue negotiations in good faith on effective measures relating to cessation of the nuclear arms race at an early date and to nuclear disarmament, and on a treaty on general and complete disarmament under strict and effective international control.

Article VII

Nothing in this Treaty affects the right of any group of States to conclude regional treaties in order to assure the total absence of nuclear weapons in their respective territories.

Article VIII

1. Any Party to the Treaty may propose amendments to this Treaty. The text of any proposed amendment shall be submitted to the Depositary Governments which shall circulate it to all Parties to the Treaty. Thereupon, if requested to do so by one third or more of the Parties to the Treaty, the Depositary Governments shall convene a conference, to which they shall invite all the Parties to the Treaty, to consider such an amendment.

2. Any amendment to this Treaty must be approved by a majority of the votes of all the Parties to the Treaty, including the votes of all nuclear-weapon States Party to the Treaty and all other Parties which, on the date the amendment is circulated, are members of the Board of Governors of the International Atomic Energy Agency. The amendment shall enter into force for each Party that deposits its instrument of ratification of the amendment upon the deposit of such instruments of ratification by a majority of all the Parties, including the instruments of ratification of all nuclear-weapon States Party to the Treaty and all other Parties which, on the date the amendment is circulated, are members of the Board of Governors of the International Atomic Energy Agency, Thereafter, it shall enter into force for any other Party upon the deposit of its instrument of ratification of the amendment.

3. Five years after the entry into force of this Treaty, a conference of Parties to the Treaty shall be held in Geneva, Switzerland, in order to review the operation of this Treaty with a view to assuring that the purposes of the Preamble and the provisions of the Treaty are being realized. At intervals of five years thereafter, a majority of the Parties to the Treaty may obtain, by submitting a proposal to this effect to the Depositary Governments, the convening of further conferences with the same objective of reviewing the operation of the Treaty.

Article IX

1. This Treaty shall be open to all States for signature. Any State which does not sign the Treaty before its entry into force in accordance with paragraph 3 of this article may accede to it at any time.

2. This Treaty shall be subject to ratification by signatory States. Instruments of ratification and instruments of accession shall be deposited with the Governments of the Union of Soviet Socialist Republics, the United Kingdom of Great Britain and Northern Ireland and the United States of America, which are hereby designated the Depositary Governments.

3. This Treaty shall enter into force after its ratification by the States, the Governments of which are designated Depositaries of the Treaty, and forty other States signatory to this Treaty and the deposit of their instruments of ratification. For the purposes of this Treaty, a nuclear-weapon State is one which has manufactured and exploded a nuclear weapon or other nuclear explosive device prior to 1 January 1967.

4. For States whose instruments of ratification or accession are deposited subsequent to the entry into force of this Treaty, it shall enter into force on the date of the deposit of their instruments of ratification or accession.

5. The Depositary Governments shall promptly inform all signatory and acceding States of the date of each signature, the date of deposit of each instrument of ratification or of accession, the date of the entry into force of this Treaty, and the date of receipt of any requests for convening a conference or other notices.

6. This Treaty shall be registered by the Depositary Governments pursuant to article 102 of the Charter of the United Nations.

Article X

1. Each Party shall in exercising its national sovereignty have the right to withdraw from the Treaty if it decides that extraordinary events, related to the subject-matter of this Treaty, have jeopardized the supreme interests of its country. It shall give notice of such withdrawal to all other Parties to the Treaty and to the United Nations Security Council three months in advance. Such

notice shall include a statement of the extraordinary events it regards as having jeopardized its supreme interests.

2. Twenty-five years after the entry into force of the Treaty, a conference shall be convened to decide whether the Treaty shall continue in force indefinitely, or shall be extended for an additional fixed period or periods. This decision shall be taken by a majority of the Parties to the Treaty.

Article XI

This Treaty, the Chinese, English, French, Russian and Spanish texts of which are equally authentic, shall be deposited in the archives of the Depositary Governments. Duly certified copies of this Treaty shall be transmitted by the Depositary Governments to the Governments of the signatory and acceding States.

IN WITNESS WHEREOF the undersigned, duly authorized, have signed this Treaty.

DONE in . . . at . . . this . . . day of 3/

3/ The Treaty was signed at London, Moscow and Washington on 1 July 1968.

Document 12

Security Council resolution on security assurances

S/RES/255 (1968), 19 June 1968

The Security Council,

Noting with appreciation the desire of a large number of States to subscribe to the Treaty on the Non-Proliferation of Nuclear Weapons 1/ and thereby to undertake not to receive the transfer from any transferor whatsoever of nuclear weapons or other nuclear explosive devices or of control over such weapons or explosive devices directly or indirectly, not to manufacture or otherwise acquire nuclear weapons or other nuclear explosive devices, and not to seek or receive any assistance in the manufacture of nuclear weapons or other nuclear explosive devices,

Taking into consideration the concern of certain of these States that, in conjunction with their adherence to the Treaty on the Non-Proliferation of Nuclear Weapons, appropriate measures be undertaken to safeguard their security,

Bearing in mind that any aggression accompanied by the use of nuclear weapons would endanger the peace and security of all States,

1. *Recognizes* that aggression with nuclear weapons or the threat of such aggression against a non-nuclear-weapon State would create a situation in which the Security Council, and above all its nuclear-weapon State permanent members, would have to act immediately in accordance with their obligations under the United Nations Charter;

2. *Welcomes* the intention expressed by certain States that they will provide or support immediate assistance, in accordance with the Charter, to any non-nuclear-weapon State Party to the Treaty on the Non-Proliferation of Nuclear Weapons that is a victim of an act or an object of a threat of aggression in which nuclear weapons are used;

3. *Reaffirms* in particular the inherent right, recognized under Article 51 of the Charter, of individual and collective self-defence if an armed attack occurs against a Member of the United Nations, until the Security Council has taken measures necessary to maintain international peace and security.

1/ General Assembly resolution 2373 (XXII), annex.

Document 13

The safeguards system of the IAEA, as approved in 1965 and provisionally extended in 1966 and 1968

INFCIRC/66/Rev.2

1. The Agency's safeguards system, as approved by the Board of Governors in 1965, and provisionally extended in 1966 and 1968, is set forth in this document for the information of all Members.

2. The development of the system from 1961 onwards has been as follows:

	System	
Nature	*Name*	*Set forth in document*
The first system	The Agency's Safeguards System (1961)	INFCIRC/26
The 1961 system as extended to cover large reactor facilities	The Agency's Safeguards System (1961, as Extended in 1964)	INFCIRC/26 and Add.1
The revised system	The Agency's Safeguards System (1965)	INFCIRC/66
The revised system with additional provisions for reprocessing plants	The Agency's Safeguards System (1965, as Provisionally Extended in 1966)	INFCIRC/66/Rev.1
The revised system with further additional provisions for safeguarded nuclear material in conversion plants and fabrication plants	The Agency's Safeguards System (1965, as Provisionally Extended in 1966 and 1968)	INFCIRC/66/Rev.2

CONTENTS

THE AGENCY'S SAFEGUARDS SYSTEM (1965, AS PROVISIONALLY EXTENDED IN 1966 AND 1968)

I. GENERAL CONSIDERATIONS

A. THE PURPOSE OF THIS DOCUMENT

1. Pursuant to Article II of its Statute the Agency has the task of seeking "to accelerate and enlarge the contribution of atomic energy to peace, health and prosperity throughout the world". Inasmuch as the technology of nuclear energy for peaceful purposes is closely coupled with that for the production of materials for nuclear weapons, the same Article of the Statute provides that the Agency "shall ensure, so far as it is able, that assistance provided by it or at its request or under its supervision or control is not used in such a way as to further any military purpose".

2. The principal purpose of the present document is to establish a system of controls to enable the Agency to comply with this statutory obligation with respect to the activities of Member States in the field of the peaceful uses of nuclear energy, as provided in the Statute. The authority to establish such a system is provided by Article III.A.5. of the Statute, which authorizes the Agency to "establish and administer safeguards designed to ensure that special fissionable and other materials, services, equipment, facilities, and information made available by the Agency or at its request or under its supervision or control are not used in such a way as to further any military purpose". This Article further authorizes the Agency to "apply safeguards, at the request of the parties, to any bilateral or multilateral arrangement, or at the request of a State, to any of that State's activities in the field of atomic energy". Article XII.A sets forth the rights and responsibilities that the Agency is to have, to the extent relevant, with respect to any project or arrangement which it is to safeguard.

3. The principles set forth in this document and the procedures for which it provides are established for the information of Member States, to enable them to determine in advance the circumstances and manner in which the Agency would administer safeguards, and for the guidance of the organs of the Agency itself, to enable the Board and the Director General to determine readily what provisions should be included in agreements relating to safeguards and how to interpret such provisions.

4. Provisions of this document that are relevant to a particular project, arrangement or activity in the field of nuclear energy will only become legally binding upon the entry into force of a *safeguards agreement* 1/ and to the extent that they are incorporated therein. Such incorporation may be made by reference.

5. Appropriate provisions of this document may also be incorporated in bilateral or multilateral arrangements between Member States, including all those that provide for the transfer to the Agency of responsibility for administering safeguards. The Agency will not assume such responsibility unless the principles of the safeguards and the procedures to be used are essentially consistent with those set forth in this document.

1/ The use of italics indicates that a term has a specialized meaning in this document and is defined in Part IV.

6. Agreements incorporating provisions from the earlier version of the Agency's safeguards system 2/ will continue to be administered in accordance with such provisions, unless all States parties thereto request the Agency to substitute the provisions of the present document.

7. Provisions relating to types of *principal nuclear facilities*, other then *reactors*, which may produce, process or use safeguarded *nuclear material* will be developed as necessary.

8. The principles and procedures set forth in this document shall be subject to periodic review in the light of the further experience gained by the Agency as well as of technological developments.

B. GENERAL PRINCIPLES OF THE AGENCY'S SAFEGUARDS

The Agency's obligations

9. Bearing in mind Article II of the Statute, the Agency shall implement safeguards in a manner designed to avoid hampering a State's economic or technological development.

10. The safeguards procedures set forth in this document shall be implemented in a manner designed to be consistent with prudent management practices required for the economic and safe conduct of nuclear activities.

11. In no case shall the Agency request a State to stop the construction or operation of any *principal nuclear facility* to which the Agency's safeguards procedures extend, except by explicit decision of the Board.

12. The State or States concerned and the Director General shall hold consultations regarding the application of the provisions of the present document.

13. In implementing safeguards, the Agency shall take every precaution to protect commercial and industrial secrets. No member of the Agency's staff shall disclose, except to the Director General and to such other members of the staff as the Director General may authorize to have such information by reason of their official duties in connection with safeguards, any commercial or industrial secret or any other confidential information coming to his knowledge by reason of the implementation of safeguards by the Agency.

14. The Agency shall not publish or communicate to any State, organization or person any information obtained by it in connection with the implementation of safeguards, except that:

(a) Specific information relating to such implementation in a State may be given to the Board and to such Agency staff members as require such knowledge by reason of their official duties in connection with safeguards, but only to the extent necessary for the Agency to fulfil its safeguards responsibilities;

(b) Summarized lists of items being safeguarded by the Agency may be published upon decision of the Board; and

(c) Additional information may be published upon decision of the Board and if all States directly concerned agree.

Principles of implementation

15. The Agency shall implement safeguards in a State if:

(a) The Agency has concluded with the State a *project agreement* under which materials, services, equipment, facilities or information are supplied, and such agreement provides for the application of safeguards; or

(b) The State is a party to a bilateral or multilateral arrangement under which materials, services, equipment, facilities or information are supplied or otherwise transferred, and:

(i) All the parties to the arrangement have requested the Agency to administer safeguards; and

(ii) The Agency has concluded the necessary *safeguards agreement* with the State; or

(c) The Agency has been requested by the State to safeguard certain nuclear activities under the latter's jurisdiction, and the Agency has concluded the necessary *safeguards agreement* with the State.

16. In the light of Article XII.A.5 of the Statute, it is desirable that *safeguards agreements* should provide for the continuation of safeguards, subject to the provisions of this document, with respect to produced special fissionable material and to any materials substituted therefor.

17. The principal factors to be considered by the Board in determining the relevance of particular provisions of this document to various types of materials and facilities shall be the form, scope and amount of the assistance supplied, the character of each individual project and the degree to which such assistance could further any military purpose. The related *safeguards agreement* shall take account of all pertinent circumstances at the time of its conclusion.

18. In the event of any non-compliance by a State with a *safeguards agreement*, the Agency may take the measures set forth in Articles XII.A.7 and XII.C of the Statute.

2/ Set forth in documents INFCIRC/26 and Add.1.

II. CIRCUMSTANCES REQUIRING SAFEGUARDS

A. NUCLEAR MATERIALS SUBJECT TO SAFEGUARDS

19. Except as provided in paragraphs 21-28, *nuclear material* shall be subject to the Agency's safeguards if it is being or has been:

(a) Supplied under a *project agreement*; or

(b) Submitted to safeguards under a *safeguards agreement* by the parties to a bilateral or multilateral arrangement; or

(c) *Unilaterally submitted* to safeguards under a *safeguards agreement*; or

(d) Produced, processed or used in a *principal nuclear facility* which has been:

(i) Supplied wholly or substantially under a *project agreement*; or

(ii) Submitted to safeguards under a *safeguards agreement* by the parties to a bilateral or multilateral arrangement; or

(iii) Unilaterally submitted to safeguards under a *safeguards agreement*; or

(e) Produced in or by the use of safeguarded *nuclear material*; or

(f) Substituted, pursuant to paragraph 26(d), for safeguarded *nuclear material*.

20. A *principal nuclear facility* shall be considered as substantially supplied under a *project agreement* if the Board has so determined.

B. EXEMPTIONS FROM SAFEGUARDS

General exemptions

21. *Nuclear material* that would otherwise be subject to safeguards shall be exempted from safeguards at the request of the State concerned, provided that the material so exempted in that State may not at any time exceed:

(a) 1 kilogram in total of special fissionable material, which may consist of one or more of the following:

(i) Plutonium;

(ii) Uranium with an *enrichment* of 0.2 (20%) and above, taken account of by multiplying its weight by its *enrichment*;

(iii) Uranium with an *enrichment* below 0.2 (20%) and above that of natural uranium, taken account of by multiplying its weight by five times the square of its *enrichment*;

(b) 10 metric tons in total of natural uranium and depleted uranium with an *enrichment* above 0.005 (0.5%);

(c) 20 metric tons of depleted uranium with an *enrichment* of 0.005 (0.5%) or below; and

(d) 20 metric tons of thorium.

Exemptions related to reactors

22. Produced or used *nuclear material* that would otherwise be subject to safeguards pursuant to paragraph 19(d) or (e) shall be exempted from safeguards if:

(a) It is plutonium produced in the fuel of a *reactor* whose rate of production does not exceed 100 grams of plutonium per year; or

(b) It is produced in a *reactor* determined by the Agency to have a maximum calculated power for continuous operation of less than 3 thermal megawatts, or is used in such a *reactor* and would not be subject to safeguards except for such use, provided that the total power of the *reactors* with respect to which these exemptions apply in any State may not exceed 6 thermal megawatts.

23. Produced special fissionable material that would otherwise be subject to safeguards pursuant only to paragraph 19(e) shall in part be exempted from safeguards if it is produced in a *reactor* in which the ratio of fissionable isotopes within safeguarded *nuclear material* to all fissionable isotopes is less than 0.3 (calculated each time any change is made in the loading of the *reactor* and assumed to be maintained until the next such change). Such fraction of the produced material as corresponds to the calculated ratio shall be subject to safeguards.

C. SUSPENSION OF SAFEGUARDS

24. Safeguards with respect to *nuclear material* may be suspended while the material is transferred, under an arrangement or agreement approved by the Agency, for the purpose of processing, reprocessing, testing, research or development, within the State concerned or to any other Member State or to an international organization, provided that the quantities of *nuclear material* with respect to which safeguards are thus suspended in a State may not at any time exceed;

(a) 1 *effective kilogram* of special fissionable material;

(b) 10 metric tons in total of natural uranium and depleted uranium with an *enrichment* above 0.005 (0.5%);

(c) 20 metric tons of depleted uranium with an *enrichment* of 0.005 (0.5%) or below; and

(d) 20 metric tons of thorium.

25. Safeguards with respect to *nuclear material* in irradiated fuel which is transferred for the purpose of reprocessing may also be suspended if the State or States concerned have, with the agreement of the Agency, placed under safeguards substitute *nuclear material* in accordance with paragraph 26(d) for the period of suspension. In addition, safeguards with respect to plutonium contained in irradiated fuel which is transferred for the

purpose of reprocessing may be suspended for a period not to exceed six months if the State or States concerned have, with the agreement of the Agency, placed under safeguards a quantity of uranium whose *enrichment* in the isotope uranium-235 is not less than 0.9 (90%) and the uranium-235 content of which is equal in weight to such plutonium. Upon expiration of the said six months or the completion of reprocessing, whichever is earlier, safeguards shall, with the agreement of the Agency, be applied to such plutonium and shall cease to apply to the uranium substituted therefor.

D. TERMINATION OF SAFEGUARDS

26. *Nuclear material* shall no longer be subject to safeguards after:

(a) It has been returned to the State that originally supplied it (whether directly or through the Agency), if it was subject to safeguards only by reason of such supply and if:

(i) It was not *improved* while under safeguards; or

(ii) Any special fissionable material that was produced in it under safeguards has been separated out, or safeguards with respect to such produced material have been terminated; or

(b) The Agency has determined that:

(i) It was subject to safeguards only by reason of its use in a *principal nuclear facility* specified in paragraph 19(d);

(ii) It has been removed from such facility; and

(iii) Any special fissionable material that was produced in it under safeguards has been separated out, or safeguards with respect to such produced material have been terminated; or

(c) The Agency has determined that it has been consumed, or has been diluted in such a way that it is no longer usable for any nuclear activity relevant from the point of view of safeguards, or has become practicably irrecoverable; or

(d) The State or States concerned have, with the agreement of the Agency, placed under safeguards, as a substitute, such amount of the same element, not otherwise subject to safeguards, as the Agency has determined contains fissionable isotopes:

(i) Whose weight (with due allowance for processing losses) is equal to or greater than the weight of the fissionable isotopes of the material with respect to which safeguards are to terminate; and

(ii) Whose ratio by weight to the total substituted element is similar to or greater than the ratio by weight of the fissionable isotopes of the material with respect to which safeguards are to terminate to the total weight of such material;

provided that the Agency may agree to the substitution of plutonium for uranium-235 contained in uranium whose *enrichment* is not greater than 0.05 (5.0%); or

(e) It has been transferred out of the State under paragraph 28(d), provided that such material shall again be subject to safeguards if it is returned to the State in which the Agency had safeguarded it; or

(f) The conditions specified in the *safeguards agreement*, pursuant to which it was subject to Agency safeguards, no longer apply, by expiration of the agreement or otherwise.

27. If a State wishes to use safeguarded source material for non-nuclear purposes, such as the production of alloys or ceramics, it shall agree with the Agency on the circumstances under which the safeguards on such material may be terminated.

E. TRANSFER OF SAFEGUARDED NUCLEAR MATERIAL OUT OF THE STATE

28. No safeguarded *nuclear material* shall be transferred outside the jurisdiction of the State in which it is being safeguarded until the Agency has satisfied itself that one or more of the following conditions apply:

(a) The material is being returned, under the conditions specified in paragraph 26(a), to the State that originally supplied it; or

(b) The material is being transferred subject to the provisions of paragraph 24 or 25; or

(c) Arrangements have been made by the Agency to safeguard the material in accordance with this document in the State to which it is being transferred; or

(d) The material was not subject to safeguards pursuant to a *project agreement* and will be subject, in the State to which it is being transferred, to safeguards other than those of the Agency but generally consistent with such safeguards and accepted by the Agency.

III. SAFEGUARDS PROCEDURES

A. GENERAL PROCEDURES

Introduction

29. The safeguards procedures set forth below shall be followed, as far as relevant, with respect to safeguarded *nuclear materials*, whether they are being produced, processed or used in any *principal nuclear facility* or are outside any such facility. These procedures also extend to facilities containing or to contain such materials, including *principal nuclear facilities* to which the criteria in paragraph 19(d) apply.

Design review

30. The Agency shall review the design of *principal nuclear facilities*, for the sole purpose of satisfying itself that a facility will permit the effective application of safeguards.

31. The design review of a *principal nuclear facility* shall take place at as early a stage as possible. In particular, such review shall be carried out in the case of:

(a) An Agency project, before the project is approved;

(b) A bilateral or multilateral arrangement under which the responsibility for administering safeguards is to be transferred to the Agency, or an activity *unilaterally submitted* by a State, before the Agency assumes safeguards responsibilities with respect to the facility;

(c) A transfer of safeguarded *nuclear material* to a *principal nuclear facility* whose design has not previously been reviewed, before such transfer takes place; and

(d) A significant modification of a *principal nuclear facility* whose design has previously been reviewed, before such modification is undertaken.

32. To enable the Agency to perform the required design review, the State shall submit to it relevant design information sufficient for the purpose, including information on such basic characteristics of the *principal nuclear facility* as may bear on the Agency's safeguards procedures. The Agency shall require only the minimum amount of information and data consistent with carrying out its responsibility under this section. It shall complete the review promptly after the submission of this information by the State and shall notify the latter of its conclusions without delay.

Records

33. The State shall arrange for the keeping of records with respect to *principal nuclear facilities* and also with respect to all safeguarded *nuclear material* outside such facilities. For this purpose the State and the Agency shall agree on a system of records with respect to each facility and also with respect to such material, on the basis of proposals to be submitted by the State in sufficient time to allow the Agency to review them before the records need to be kept.

34. If the records are not kept in one of the working languages of the Board, the State shall make arrangements to facilitate their examination by inspectors.

35. The records shall consist, as appropriate, of:

(a) Accounting records of all safeguarded *nuclear material*; and

(b) Operating records for *principal nuclear facilities*.

36. All records shall be retained for at least two years.

Reports

GENERAL REQUIREMENTS

37. The State shall submit to the Agency reports with respect to the production, processing and use of safeguarded *nuclear material* in or outside *principal nuclear facilities*. For this purpose the State and the Agency shall agree on a system of reports with respect to each facility and also with respect to safeguarded *nuclear material* outside such facilities, on the basis of proposals to be submitted by the State in sufficient time to allow the Agency to review them before the reports need to be submitted. The reports need include only such information as is relevant for the purpose of safeguards.

38. Unless otherwise provided in the applicable *safeguards agreement*, reports shall be submitted in one of the working languages of the Board.

ROUTINE REPORTS

39. Routine reports shall be based on the records compiled in accordance with paragraphs 33-36 and shall consist, as appropriate, of:

(a) Accounting reports showing the receipt, transfer out, inventory and use of all safeguarded *nuclear material*. The inventory shall indicate the nuclear and chemical composition and physical form of all material and its location on the date of the report; and

(b) Operating reports showing the use that has been made of each *principal nuclear facility* since the last report and, as far as possible, the programme of future work in the period until the next routine report is expected to reach the Agency.

40. The first routine report shall be submitted as soon as:

(a) There is any safeguarded *nuclear material* to be accounted for; or

(b) The *principal nuclear facility* to which it relates is in a condition to operate.

PROGRESS IN CONSTRUCTION

41. The Agency may, if so provided in a *safeguards agreement*, request information as to when particular stages in the construction of a *principal nuclear facility* have been or are to be reached.

SPECIAL REPORTS

42. The State shall report to the Agency without delay:

(a) If any unusual incident occurs involving actual or potential loss or destruction of, or damage to, any safeguarded *nuclear material* or *principal nuclear facility*; or

(b) If there is good reason to believe that safeguarded *nuclear material* is lost or unaccounted for in quantities that exceed the normal operating and handling losses that have been accepted by the Agency as characteristic of the facility.

43. The State shall report to the Agency, as soon as possible, and in any case within two weeks, any transfer not requiring advance notification that will result in a significant change (to be defined by the Agency in agreement with the State) in the quantity of safeguarded *nuclear material* in a facility, or in a complex of facilities considered as a unit for this purpose by agreement with the Agency. Such report shall indicate the amount and nature of the material and its intended use.

AMPLIFICATION OF REPORTS

44. At the Agency's request the State shall submit amplifications or clarifications of any report, in so far as relevant for the purpose of safeguards.

Inspections
GENERAL PROCEDURES

45. The Agency may inspect safeguarded *nuclear material* and *principal nuclear facilities*.

46. The purpose of safeguards inspections shall be to verify compliance with *safeguards agreements* and to assist States in complying with such agreements and in resolving any questions arising out of the implementation of safeguards.

47. The number, duration and intensity of inspections actually carried out shall be kept to the minimum consistent with the effective implementation of safeguards, and if the Agency considers that the authorized inspections are not all required, fewer shall be carried out.

48. Inspectors shall neither operate any facility themselves nor direct the staff of a facility to carry out any particular operation.

ROUTINE INSPECTIONS

49. Routine inspections may include, as appropriate:

(a) Audit of records and reports;

(b) Verification of the amount of safeguarded *nuclear material* by physical inspection, measurement and sampling;

(c) Examination of *principal nuclear facilities*, including a check of their measuring instruments and operating characteristics; and

(d) Check of the operations carried out at *principal nuclear facilities* and at *research and development facilities* containing safeguarded *nuclear material*.

50. Whenever the Agency has the right of access to a *principal nuclear facility* at all times, 3/ it may perform inspections of which notice as required by paragraph 4 of the *Inspectors Document* need not be given, in so far

as this is necessary for the effective application of safeguards. The actual procedures to implement these provisions shall be agreed upon between the parties concerned in the *safeguards agreement*.

INITIAL INSPECTIONS OF PRINCIPAL NUCLEAR FACILITIES

51. To verify that the construction of a *principal nuclear facility* is in accordance with the design reviewed by the Agency, an initial inspection or inspections of the facility may be carried out, if so provided in a *safeguards agreement*:

(a) As soon as possible after the facility has come under Agency safeguards, in the case of a facility already in operation; or

(b) Before the facility starts to operate, in other cases.

52. The measuring instruments and operating characteristics of the facility shall be reviewed to the extent necessary for the purpose of implementing safeguards. Instruments that will be used to obtain data on the *nuclear materials* in the facility may be tested to determine their satisfactory functioning. Such testing may include the observation by inspectors of commissioning or routine tests by the staff of the facility, but shall not hamper or delay the construction, commissioning or normal operation of the facility.

SPECIAL INSPECTIONS

53. The Agency may carry out special inspections if:

(a) The study of a report indicates that such inspection is desirable; or

(b) Any unforeseen circumstance requires immediate action.

The Board shall subsequently be informed of the reasons for and the results of each such inspection.

54. The Agency may also carry out special inspections of substantial amounts of safeguarded *nuclear material* that are to be transferred outside the jurisdiction of the State in which it is being safeguarded, for which purpose the State shall give the Agency sufficient advance notice of any such proposed transfer.

B. SPECIAL PROCEDURES FOR REACTORS

Reports

55. The frequency of submission of routine reports shall be agreed between the Agency and the State, taking into account the frequency established for routine inspections. However, at least two such reports shall be submit-

---

3/ See para. 57.

ted each year and in no case shall more than 12 such reports be required in any year.

Inspections

56. One of the initial inspections of a *reactor* shall if possible be made just before the reactor first reaches criticality.

57. The maximum frequency of routine inspections of a *reactor* and of the safeguarded *nuclear material* in it shall be determined from the following table:

Whichever is the largest of: (a) Facility inventory (including loading): (b) Annual *throughput*; (c) Maximum potential annual production of special fissionable material *(Effective kilograms of nuclear material)*	Maximum number of routine inspections annually
Up to 1	0
More than 1 and up to 5	1
More than 5 and up to 10	2
More than 10 and up to 15	3
More than 15 and up to 20	4
More than 20 and up to 25	5
More than 25 and up to 30	6
More than 30 and up to 35	7
More than 35 and up to 40	8
More than 40 and up to 45	9
More than 45 and up to 50	10
More than 50 and up to 55	11
More than 55 and up to 60	12
More than 60	Right of access at all times

58. The actual frequency of inspection of a *reactor* shall take account of:

(a) Whether the State possesses irradiated-fuel reprocessing facilities;

(b) The nature of the *reactor*; and

(c) The nature and amount of the *nuclear material* produced or used in the *reactor*.

C. SPECIAL PROCEDURES RELATING TO SAFEGUARDED NUCLEAR MATERIAL OUTSIDE PRINCIPAL NUCLEAR FACILITIES

Nuclear material in research and development facilities

ROUTINE REPORTS

59. Only accounting reports need be submitted in respect of *nuclear material* in *research and development*

facilities. The frequency of submission of such routine reports shall be agreed between the Agency and the State, taking into account the frequency established for routine inspections; however, at least one such report shall be submitted each year and in no case shall more than 12 such reports be required in any year.

ROUTINE INSPECTIONS

60. The maximum frequency of routine inspections of safeguarded *nuclear material* in a *research and development facility* shall be that specified in the table in paragraph 57 for the total amount of material in the facility.

Source material in sealed storage

61. The following simplified procedures for safeguarding stockpiled source material shall be applied if a State undertakes to store such material in a sealed storage facility and not to remove it therefrom without previously informing the Agency.

DESIGN OF STORAGE FACILITIES

62. The State shall submit to the Agency information on the design of each sealed storage facility and agree with the Agency on the method and procedure for sealing it.

ROUTINE REPORTS

63. Two routine accounting reports in respect of source material in sealed storage shall be submitted each year.

ROUTINE INSPECTIONS

64. The Agency may perform one routine inspection of each sealed storage facility annually.

REMOVAL OF MATERIAL

65. The State may remove safeguarded source material from a sealed storage facility after informing the Agency of the amount, type and intended use of the material to be removed, and providing sufficient other data in time to enable the Agency to continue safeguarding the material after it has been removed.

Nuclear material in other locations

66. Except to the extent that safeguarded *nuclear material* outside of *principal nuclear facilities* is covered by any of the provisions set forth in paragraphs 59-65, the following procedures shall be applied with respect to such material (for example, source material stored elsewhere than in a sealed storage facility, or special fissionable material used in a sealed neutron source in the field).

ROUTINE REPORTS

67. Routine accounting reports in respect of all

safeguarded *nuclear material* in this category shall be submitted periodically. The frequency of submission of such reports shall be agreed between the Agency and the State, taking into account the frequency established for routine inspections; however, at least one such report shall be submitted each year and in no case shall more than 12 such reports be required in any year.

ROUTINE INSPECTIONS

68. The maximum frequency of routine inspections of safeguarded *nuclear material* in this category shall be one inspection annually if the total amount of such material does not exceed five *effective kilograms*, and shall be determined from the table in paragraph 57 if the amount is greater.

IV. DEFINITIONS

69. "Agency" means the International Atomic Energy Agency.

70. "Board" means the Board of Governors of the Agency.

71. "Director General" means the Director General of the Agency.

72. "Effective kilograms" means:

(a) In the case of plutonium, its weight in kilograms;

(b) In the case of uranium with an *enrichment* of 0.01 (1%) and above, its weight in kilograms multiplied by the square of its *enrichment*;

(c) In the case of uranium with an *enrichment* below 0.01 (1%) and above 0.005 (0.5%), its weight in kilograms multiplied by 0.0001; and

(d) In the case of depleted uranium with an *enrichment* of 0.005 (0.5 %) or below, and in the case of thorium, its weight in kilograms multiplied by 0.00005.

73. "Enrichment" means the ratio of the combined weight of the isotopes uranium-233 and uranium-235 to that of the total uranium in question.

74. "Improved" means, with respect to *nuclear material*, that either:

(a) The concentration of fissionable isotopes in it has been increased; or

(b) The amount of chemically separable fissionable isotopes in it has been increased; or

(c) Its chemical or physical form has been changed so as to facilitate further use or processing.

75. "Inspector" means an Agency official designated in accordance with the *Inspectors Document*.

76. "Inspectors Document" means the Annex to the Agency's document GC(V)/INF/39.

77. "Nuclear material" means any source or special fissionable material as defined in Article XX of the Statute.

78. "Principal nuclear facility" means a *reactor*, a plant for processing *nuclear material* irradiated in a *reactor*, a plant for separating the isotopes of a *nuclear material*, a plant for processing or fabricating *nuclear material* (excepting a mine or ore-processing plant) or a facility or plant of such other type as may be designated by the Board from time to time, including associated storage facilities.

79. "Project agreement" means a *safeguards agreement* relating to an Agency project and containing provisions as foreseen in Article XI.F.4(b) of the Statute.

80. "Reactor" means any device in which a controlled, self-sustaining fission chain-reaction can be maintained.

81. "Research and development facility" means a facility, other than a *principal nuclear facility*, used for research or development in the field of nuclear energy.

82. "Safeguards agreement" means an agreement between the Agency and one or more Member States which contains an undertaking by one or more of those States not to use certain items in such a way as to further any military purpose and which gives the Agency the right to observe compliance with such undertaking. Such an agreement may concern:

(a) An Agency project;

(b) A bilateral or multilateral arrangement in the field of nuclear energy under which the Agency may be asked to administer safeguards; or

(c) Any of a State's nuclear activities *unilaterally submitted* to Agency safeguards.

83. "Statute" means the Statute of the Agency.

84. "Throughput" means the rate at which *nuclear material* is introduced into a facility operating at full capacity.

85. "Unilaterally submitted" means submitted by a State Agency safeguards, pursuant to a *safeguards agreement*.

ANNEX I

Provisions for reprocessing plants

INTRODUCTION

1. The Agency's Safeguards System (1965) is so formulated as to permit application to *principal nuclear facilities* other than *reactors* as foreseen in paragraph 7. This Annex lays down the additional procedures which are applicable to the safeguarding of *reprocessing plants*. However, because of the possible need to revise these procedures in the light of experience, they shall be subject to review at any time and shall in any case be reviewed after two years' experience of their application has been gained.

SPECIAL PROCEDURES

Reports

2. The frequency of submission of routine reports shall be once each calendar month.

Inspections

3. A *reprocessing plant* having an annual *throughput* not exceeding 5 *effective kilograms* of *nuclear material* and the safeguarded nuclear material in it, may be routinely inspected twice a year. A *reprocessing plant* having an annual *throughput* exceeding 5 *effective kilograms* of *nuclear material*, and the safeguarded *nuclear material* in it, may be inspected at all times. The arrangements for inspections set forth in paragraph 50 shall apply to all inspections to be made under this paragraph. 1/

4. When a *reprocessing plant* is under Agency safeguards only because it contains safeguarded *nuclear material*, the inspection frequency shall be based on the rate of delivery of safeguarded *nuclear material*.

5. The State and the Agency shall cooperate in making all the necessary arrangements to facilitate the taking, shipping or analysis of samples, due account being taken of the limitations imposed by the characteristics of a plant already in operation when placed under Agency safeguards.

Mixtures of safeguarded and unsafeguarded nuclear material

6. By agreement between the State and the Agency, the following special arrangements may be made in the case of a *reprocessing plant* to which the criteria in paragraph 19(d) do not apply, and in which safeguarded and unsafeguarded *nuclear materials* are present:

(a) Subject to the provisions of sub-paragraph (b) below, the Agency shall restrict its safeguards procedures to the area in which irradiated fuel is stored, until such time as all or any part of such fuel is transferred out of the storage area into other parts of the plant. Safeguards procedures shall cease to apply to the storage area or plant when either contains no safeguarded *nuclear material*; and

(b) Where possible safeguarded *nuclear material* shall be measured and sampled separately from unsafeguarded material, and at as early a stage as possible. Where separate measurement, sampling or processing are not possible, the whole of the material being processed in that *campaign* shall be subject to the safeguards

procedures set out in this Annex. At the conclusion of the processing the *nuclear material* that is thereafter to be safeguarded shall be selected by agreement between the State and the Agency from the whole output of the plant resulting from that *campaign*, due account being taken of any processing losses accepted by the Agency.

DEFINITIONS

7. "Reprocessing plant" 2/ means a facility to separate irradiated *nuclear materials* and fission products, and includes the facility's head-end treatment section and its associated storage and analytical sections.

8. "Campaign" means the period during which the chemical processing equipment in a *reprocessing plant* is operated between two successive wash-outs of the *nuclear material* present in the equipment.

ANNEX II

Provisions for safeguarded nuclear material in conversion plants and fabrication plants

INTRODUCTION

1. The Agency's Safeguards System (1965, as Provisionally Extended in 1966) is so formulated as to permit application to *principal nuclear facilities* other than reactors as foreseen in paragraph 7. This Annex lays down the additional procedures which are applicable to safeguarded *nuclear material* in *conversion plants* and *fabrication plants*. 1/ However, because of the possible need to revise these procedures in the light of experience, they shall be subject to review at any time and shall in any case be reviewed after two years' experience of their application has been gained.

SPECIAL PROCEDURES

Reports

2. The frequency of submission of routine reports shall be once each calendar month.

Inspections

3. A *conversion plant* or *fabrication plant* to which the criteria in paragraph 19(d) apply and the *nuclear material* in it, may be inspected at all times if the plant inventory at any time, or the annual input, of *nuclear material* exceeds five *effective kilograms*. Where neither the inventory at any time, nor the annual input, exceeds five *effective kilograms* of *nuclear* material, the routine inspections shall not exceed two a year. The arrangements

---

1/ It is understood that for plants having an annual *throughput* of more than 60 *effective kilograms*, the right of access at all times would normally be implemented by means of continuous inspection.

2/ This term is synonymous with the term "a plant for processing nuclear material irradiated in a reactor" which is used in paragraph 78.

1/ This terminology is intended to be synonymous with the term "a plant for processing or fabricating *nuclear material* (excepting a mine or ore-processing plant")" which is used in paragraph 78.

for inspection set forth in paragraph 50 shall apply to all inspections to be made under this paragraph. 2/

4. When a *conversion plant* or *fabrication plant* to which the criteria in paragraph 19(d) do not apply contains safeguarded *nuclear material* the frequency of routine inspections shall be based on the inventory at any time and the annual input of safeguarded *nuclear material*. Where the inventory at any time, or the annual input, of safeguarded *nuclear material* exceeds five *effective kilograms* the plant may be inspected at all times. Where neither the inventory at any time, nor the annual input, exceeds five *effective kilograms* of safeguarded *nuclear material* the routine inspections shall not exceed two a year. The arrangements for inspection set forth in paragraph 50 shall apply to all inspections to be made under this paragraph. 2/

5. The intensity of inspection of safeguarded *nuclear material* at various steps in a *conversion plant* or *fabrication plant* shall take account of the nature, isotopic composition and amount of safeguarded *nuclear material* in the plant. Safeguards shall be applied in accordance with the general principles set forth in paragraphs 9-14. Emphasis shall be placed on inspection to control uranium of high enrichments and plutonium.

6. Where a plant may handle safeguarded and unsafeguarded *nuclear material*, the State shall notify the Agency in advance of the programme for handling safeguarded batches to enable the Agency to make inspections during these periods, due account being also taken of the arrangements under paragraph 10 below.

7. The State and the Agency shall cooperate in making all the necessary arrangements to facilitate the preparation of inventories of safeguarded *nuclear material* and the taking, shipping and/or analysis of samples, due account being taken of the limitations imposed by the characteristics of a plant already in operation when placed under Agency safeguards.

Residues, scrap and waste

8. The State shall ensure that safeguarded *nuclear material* contained in residues, scrap or waste created during conversion or fabrication is recovered, as far as is practicable, in its facilities and within a reasonable period of time. If such recovery is not considered practicable by the State, the State and the Agency shall cooperate in making arrangements to account for and dispose of the material.

Safeguarded and unsafeguarded nuclear material

9. By agreement between the State and the Agency, the following special arrangements may be made in the case of a *conversion plant* or a *fabrication plant* to which the criteria in paragraph 19(d) do not apply, and in which safeguarded and unsafeguarded *nuclear material* are both present:

(a) Subject to the provisions of sub-paragraph (b) below, the Agency shall restrict its safeguards procedures to the area in which safeguarded *nuclear material* is stored, until such time as all or any part of such *nuclear material* is transferred out of the storage area into other parts of the plant. Safeguards procedures shall cease to be applied to the storage area or plant when it contains no safeguarded *nuclear material*; and

(b) Where possible, safeguarded *nuclear material* shall be measured and sampled separately from unsafeguarded *nuclear material*, and at as early a stage as possible. Where separate measurement, sampling or processing is not possible, any *nuclear material* containing safeguarded *nuclear material* shall be subject to the safeguards procedures set out in this Annex. At the conclusion of processing, the *nuclear material* that is thereafter to be safeguarded shall be selected, in accordance with paragraph 11 below when applicable, by agreement between the State and the Agency, due account being taken of any processing losses accepted by the Agency.

Blending of nuclear material

10. When safeguarded *nuclear material* is to be blended with either safeguarded or unsafeguarded *nuclear material*, the State shall notify the Agency sufficiently in advance of the programme of blending to enable the Agency to exercise its right to obtain evidence, through inspection of the blending operation or otherwise, that the blending is performed according to the programme.

11. When safeguarded and unsafeguarded *nuclear material* are blended, if the ratio of fissionable isotopes in the safeguarded component going into the blend to all the fissionable isotopes in the blend is 0.3 or greater, and if the concentration of fissionable isotopes in the unsafeguarded *nuclear material* is increased by such blending, then the whole blend shall remain subject to safeguards. In other cases the following procedures shall apply:

(a) Plutonium/plutonium blending. The quantity of the blend that shall continue to be safeguarded shall be such that its weight, when multiplied by the square of the weight fraction of contained fissionable isotopes, is not less than the weight of originally safeguarded plutonium multiplied by the square of the weight fraction of fissionable isotopes therein, provided however that:

2/ It is understood that for plants having an inventory at any time, or an annual input, of more than 60 *effective kilograms* the right of access at all times would normally be implemented by means of continuous inspection. Where neither the inventory at any time nor the annual input exceeds one *effective kilogram* of *nuclear material* the plant would not normally be subject to routine inspection.

(i) In cases where the weight of the whole blend, when multiplied by the square of the weight fraction of contained fissionable isotopes, is less than the weight of originally safeguarded plutonium multiplied by the square of the weight fraction of fissionable isotopes therein, the whole of the blend shall be safeguarded; and

(ii) The number of fissionable atoms in the portion of the blend that shall continue to be under safeguards shall in no case be less than the number of fissionable atoms in the originally safeguarded plutonium;

(b) Uranium/uranium blending. The quantity of the blend that shall continue to be safeguarded shall be such that the number of *effective kilograms* is not less than the number of *effective kilograms* in the originally safeguarded uranium, provided however that:

(i) In cases where the number of *effective kilograms* in the whole blend is less than in the safeguarded uranium, the whole of the blend shall be safeguarded; and

(ii) The number of fissionable atoms in the portion of the blend that shall continue to be under safeguards shall in no case be less than the number of fissionable atoms in the originally safeguarded uranium;

(c) Uranium/plutonium blending. The whole of the resultant blend shall be safeguarded until the uranium and the plutonium constituents are separated. After separation of the uranium and plutonium, safeguards shall apply to the originally safeguarded component; and

(d) Due account shall be taken of any processing losses agreed upon between the State and the Agency.

DEFINITIONS

12. "Conversion plant" means a facility (excepting a mine or ore-processing plant) to *improve* unirradiated *nuclear material*, or irradiated *nuclear material* that has been separated from fission products, by changing its chemical or physical form so as to facilitate further use or processing. The term *conversion plant* includes the facility's storage and analytical sections. The term does not include a plant intended for separating the isotopes of a *nuclear material*.

13. "Fabrication plant" means a plant to manufacture fuel elements or other components containing *nuclear material* and includes the plant's storage and analytical sections.

Document 14

Report of the Secretary-General on the work of the Organization, 1967-1968 (excerpt)

A/7201/Add.1, 24 September 1968

...

The Treaty, which has been acclaimed as "the most important international agreement in the field of disarmament since the nuclear age began" and as "a major success for the cause of peace", is important on several accounts. First, the purpose of the Treaty is to prevent the further spread of nuclear weapons among countries which do not possess them and establishes a safeguards system for the purpose of verifying the fulfilment of the obligations assumed under the Treaty. If this international agreement is duly implemented, it will help to limit and contain the threat of nuclear war.

Secondly, the Treaty not only reaffirms the inalienable right of non-nuclear-weapon States to develop research and the production and use of nuclear energy for peaceful purposes without discrimination; it also provides that all parties to the Treaty are to facilitate, and have the right to participate in, the fullest possible exchange of equipment, materials and scientific and technological information for the peaceful uses of nuclear energy. In particular, the Treaty provides that, under appropriate international observation and through appropriate international procedures, potential benefits from any peaceful applications of nuclear explosions will be made available to non-nuclear-weapon States parties to the Treaty on a non-discriminatory basis, and that the charge to such parties for the explosive devices used will be as low as possible and will exclude any charge for research and development.

Thirdly, since the Treaty is not an end in itself but a step towards disarmament, each of the parties to the Treaty undertakes to pursue negotiations in good faith on effective measures relating to the cessation of the nuclear arms race at an early date and to nuclear disarmament, and also on a treaty on general and complete disarmament under strict and effective international control.

Agreement on these provisions, let us not forget, was reached only after several years of long and patient negotiations and even a longer period of preparatory work extending as far back as 1958, when the first draft resolution on preventing the spread of nuclear weapons was introduced in the General Assembly. Many adjustments and mutual concessions had to be made along the way by the parties concerned, both nuclear and non-nuclear. As a result, the final outcome necessarily represents a compromise solution. Yet, I am confident that, if this Treaty is accepted by the great majority of States and is faithfully implemented, it will play an essential role in the continuing pursuit of security, disarmament and peace.

Indeed, the question of the non-proliferation of nuclear weapons has provided additional evidence of how closely security and the regulation of armaments are linked together. It is enough to mention, in this connection, the debate in the Security Council, following the conclusion of the Treaty, which led, first, to declarations of intentions by the USSR, the United Kingdom and the United States that they would provide or support immediate assistance, in accordance with the Charter, to any non-nuclear-weapon State party to the Treaty that was a victim of an act or an object of a threat of aggression in which nuclear weapons were used, and secondly, to the adoption of Security Council resolution 255 (1968) on the question of the security of non-nuclear-weapon States.

. . .

Document 15

Structure and content of agreements between the IAEA and States parties, as required in connection with the NPT

INFCIRC/153 (Corr), 1970

The Board of Governors has requested the Director General to use the material reproduced in this booklet as the basis for negotiating safeguards agreements between the Agency and non-nuclear-weapon States party to the Treaty on the Non-Proliferation of Nuclear Weapons.

PART I

BASIC UNDERTAKING

1. The Agreement should contain, in accordance with Article III.1 of the Treaty on the Non-Proliferation of Nuclear Weapons, 1/ an undertaking by the State to accept safeguards, in accordance with the terms of the Agreement, on all source or special fissionable material in all peaceful nuclear activities within its territory, under its jurisdiction or carried out under its control anywhere, for the exclusive purpose of verifying that such material is not diverted to nuclear weapons or other nuclear explosive devices.

APPLICATION OF SAFEGUARDS

2. The Agreement should provide for the Agency's right and obligation to ensure that safeguards will be applied, in accordance with the terms of the Agreement, on all source or special fissionable material in all peaceful nuclear activities within the territory of the State, under its jurisdiction or carried out under its control anywhere, for the exclusive purpose of verifying that such material

is not diverted to nuclear weapons or other nuclear explosive devices.

COOPERATION BETWEEN THE AGENCY AND THE STATE

3. The Agreement should provide that the Agency and the State shall cooperate to facilitate the implementation of the safeguards provided for therein.

IMPLEMENTATION OF SAFEGUARDS

4. The Agreement should provide that safeguards shall be implemented in a manner designed:

(a) To avoid hampering the economic and technological development of the State or international cooperation in the field of peaceful nuclear activities, including international exchange of *nuclear material; 2/*

(b) To avoid undue interference in the State's peaceful nuclear activities, and in particular in the operation of *facilities;* and

(c) To be consistent with prudent management practices required for the economic and safe conduct of nuclear activities.

5. The Agreement should provide that the Agency shall take every precaution to protect commercial and industrial secrets and other confidential information

1/ Reproduced in document INFCIRC/140.

2/ Terms in italics have specialized meanings, which are defined in paragraphs 98-116 below.

coming to its knowledge in the implementation of the Agreement. The Agency shall not publish or communicate to any State, organization or person any information obtained by it in connection with the implementation of the Agreement, except that specific information relating to such implementation in the State may be given to the Board of Governors and to such Agency staff members as require such knowledge by reason of their official duties in connection with safeguards, but only to the extent necessary for the Agency to fulfil its responsibilities in implementing the Agreement. Summarized information on *nuclear material* being safeguarded by the Agency under the Agreement may be published upon decision of the Board if the States directly concerned agree.

6. The Agreement should provide that in implementing safeguards pursuant thereto the Agency shall take full account of technological developments in the field of safeguards, and shall make every effort to ensure optimum cost-effectiveness and the application of the principle of safeguarding effectively the flow of *nuclear material* subject to safeguards under the Agreement by use of instruments and other techniques at certain *strategic points* to the extent that present or future technology permits. In order to ensure optimum cost-effectiveness, use should be made, for example, of such means as:

(a) Containment as a means of defining *material balance areas* for accounting purposes;

(b) Statistical techniques and random sampling in evaluating the flow of *nuclear material*; and

(c) Concentration of verification procedures on those stages in the nuclear fuel cycle involving the production, processing, use or storage of *nuclear material* from which nuclear weapons or other nuclear explosive devices could readily be made, and minimization of verification procedures in respect of other *nuclear material*, on condition that this does not hamper the Agency in applying safeguards under the Agreement.

NATIONAL SYSTEM OF ACCOUNTING FOR AND CONTROL OF NUCLEAR MATERIAL

7. The Agreement should provide that the State shall establish and maintain a system of accounting for and control of all *nuclear material* subject to safeguards under the Agreement, and that such safeguards shall be applied in such a manner as to enable the Agency to verify, in ascertaining that there has been no diversion of *nuclear material* from peaceful uses to nuclear weapons or other nuclear explosive devices, findings of the State's system. The Agency's verification shall include, inter alia, independent measurements and observations conducted by the Agency in accordance with the procedures specified in Part II below. The Agency, in its verification, shall take due account of the technical effectiveness of the State's system.

PROVISION OF INFORMATION TO THE AGENCY

8. The Agreement should provide that to ensure the effective implementation of safeguards thereunder the Agency shall be provided, in accordance with the provisions set out in Part II below, with information concerning *nuclear material* subject to safeguards under the Agreement and the features of *facilities* relevant to safeguarding such material. The Agency shall require only the minimum amount of information and data consistent with carrying out its responsibilities under the Agreement. Information pertaining to *facilities* shall be the minimum necessary for safeguarding *nuclear material* subject to safeguards under the Agreement. In examining design information, the Agency shall, at the request of the State, be prepared to examine on premises of the State design information which the State regards as being of particular sensitivity. Such information would not have to be physically transmitted to the Agency provided that it remained available for ready further examination by the Agency on premises of the State.

AGENCY INSPECTORS

9. The Agreement should provide that the State shall take the necessary steps to ensure that Agency inspectors can effectively discharge their functions under the Agreement. The Agency shall secure the consent of the State to the designation of Agency inspectors to that State. If the State, either upon proposal of a designation or at any other time after a designation has been made, objects to the designation, the Agency shall propose to the State an alternative designation or designations. The repeated refusal of a State to accept the designation of Agency inspectors which would impede the inspections conducted under the Agreement would be considered by the Board upon referral by the Director General with a view to appropriate action. The visits and activities of Agency inspectors shall be so arranged as to reduce to a minimum the possible inconvenience and disturbance to the State and to the peaceful nuclear activities inspected, as well as to ensure protection of industrial secrets or any other confidential information coming to the inspectors' knowledge.

PRIVILEGES AND IMMUNITIES

10. The Agreement should specify the privileges and immunities which shall be granted to the Agency and its staff in respect of their functions under the Agreement. In the case of a State party to the Agreement on the Privileges and Immunities of the Agency, 3/ the provisions thereof, as in force for such State, shall apply. In the case of other States, the privileges and immunities granted should be such as to ensure that:

3/ Reproduced in document INFCIRC/9/Rev. 2.

(a) The Agency and its staff will be in a position to discharge their functions under the Agreement effectively; and

(b) No such State will be placed thereby in a more favourable position than States party to the Agreement on the Privileges and Immunities of the Agency.

TERMINATION OF SAFEGUARDS

Consumption or dilution of nuclear material

11. The Agreement should provide that safeguards shall terminate on *nuclear material* subject to safeguards thereunder upon determination by the Agency that it has been consumed, or has been diluted in such a way that it is no longer usable for any nuclear activity relevant from the point of view of safeguards, or has become practicably irrecoverable.

Transfer of nuclear material out of the State

12. The Agreement should provide, with respect to *nuclear material* subject to safeguards thereunder, for notification of transfers of such material out of the State, in accordance with the provisions set out in paragraphs 92-94 below. The Agency shall terminate safeguards under the Agreement on *nuclear material* when the recipient State has assumed responsibility therefor, as provided for in paragraph 91. The Agency shall maintain records indicating each transfer and, where applicable, the reapplication of safeguards to the transferred *nuclear material*.

Provisions relating to nuclear material to be used in non-nuclear activities

13. The Agreement should provide that if the State wishes to use *nuclear material* subject to safeguards thereunder in non-nuclear activities, such as the production of alloys or ceramics, it shall agree with the Agency on the circumstances under which the safeguards on such *nuclear material* may be terminated.

NON-APPLICATION OF SAFEGUARDS TO NUCLEAR MATERIAL TO BE USED IN NON-PEACEFUL ACTIVITIES

14. The Agreement should provide that if the State intends to exercise its discretion to use *nuclear material* which is required to be safeguarded thereunder in a nuclear activity which does not require the application of safeguards under the Agreement, the following procedures will apply:

(a) The State shall inform the Agency of the activity, making it clear:

(i) That the use of the *nuclear material* in a non-proscribed military activity will not be in conflict with an undertaking the State may have given and in respect of which Agency safeguards apply, that the *nuclear material* will be used only in a peaceful nuclear activity; and

(ii) That during the period of non-application of safeguards the *nuclear material* will not be used for the production of nuclear weapons or other nuclear explosive devices;

(b) The Agency and the State shall make an arrangement so that, only while the *nuclear material* is in such an activity, the safeguards provided for in the Agreement will not be applied. The arrangement shall identify, to the extent possible, the period or circumstances during which safeguards will not be applied. In any event, the safeguards provided for in the Agreement shall again apply as soon as the *nuclear material* is reintroduced into a peaceful nuclear activity. The Agency shall be kept informed of the total quantity and composition of such unsafeguarded *nuclear material* in the State and of any exports of such material; and

(c) Each arrangement shall be made in agreement with the Agency. The Agency's agreement shall be given as promptly as possible; it shall only relate to the temporal and procedural provisions, reporting arrangements, etc., but shall not involve any approval or classified knowledge of the military activity or relate to the use of the *nuclear material* therein.

FINANCE

15. The Agreement should contain one of the following sets of provisions:

(a) An agreement with a Member of the Agency should provide that each party thereto shall bear the expenses it incurs in implementing its responsibilities thereunder. However, if the State or persons under its jurisdiction incur extraordinary expenses as a result of a specific request by the Agency, the Agency shall reimburse such expenses provided that it has agreed in advance to do so. In any case the Agency shall bear the cost of any additional measuring or sampling which inspectors may request; or

(b) An agreement with a party not a Member of the Agency should in application of the provisions of Article XIV.C of the Statute, provide that the party shall reimburse fully to the Agency the safeguards expenses the Agency incurs thereunder. However, if the party or persons under its jurisdiction incur extraordinary expenses as a result of a specific request by the Agency, the Agency shall reimburse such expenses provided that it has agreed in advance to do so.

THIRD PARTY LIABILITY FOR NUCLEAR DAMAGE

16. The Agreement should provide that the State shall ensure that any protection against third party liability in respect of nuclear damage, including any insurance or other financial security, which may be available under its laws or regulations shall apply to the Agency and its

officials for the purpose of the implementation of the Agreement, in the same way as that protection applies to nationals of the State.

INTERNATIONAL RESPONSIBILITY

17. The Agreement should provide that any claim by one party thereto against the other in respect of any damage, other than damage arising out of a nuclear incident, resulting from the implementation of safeguards under the Agreement, shall be settled in accordance with international law.

MEASURES IN RELATION TO VERIFICATION OF NON-DIVERSION

18. The Agreement should provide that if the Board, upon report of the Director General, decides that an action by the State is essential and urgent in order to ensure verification that *nuclear material* subject to safeguards under the Agreement is not diverted to nuclear weapons or other nuclear explosive devices the Board shall be able to call upon the State to take the required action without delay, irrespective of whether procedures for the settlement of a dispute have been invoked.

19. The Agreement should provide that if the Board upon examination of relevant information reported to it by the Director General finds that the Agency is not able to verify that there has been no diversion of *nuclear material* required to be safeguarded under the Agreement to nuclear weapons or other nuclear explosive devices, it may make the reports provided for in paragraph C of Article XII of the Statute and may also take, where applicable, the other measures provided for in that paragraph. In taking such action the Board shall take account of the degree of assurance provided by the safeguards measures that have been applied and shall afford the State every reasonable opportunity to furnish the Board with any necessary reassurance.

INTERPRETATION AND APPLICATION OF THE AGREEMENT AND SETTLEMENT OF DISPUTES

20. The Agreement should provide that the parties thereto shall, at the request of either, consult about any question arising out of the interpretation or application thereof.

21. The Agreement should provide that the State shall have the right to request that any question arising out of the interpretation or application thereof be considered by the Board; and that the State shall be invited by the Board to participate in the discussion of any such question by the Board.

22. The Agreement should provide that any dispute arising out of the interpretation or application thereof except a dispute with regard to a finding by the Board under paragraph 19 above or an action taken by the Board pursuant to such a finding which is not settled by negotiation or another procedure agreed to by the parties should, on the request of either party, be submitted to an arbitral tribunal composed as follows: each party would designate one arbitrator, and the two arbitrators so designated would elect a third, who would be the Chairman. If, within 30 days of the request for arbitration, either party has not designated an arbitrator, either party to the dispute may request the President of the International Court of Justice to appoint an arbitrator. The same procedure would apply if, within 30 days of the designation or appointment of the second arbitrator, the third arbitrator had not been elected. A majority of the members of the arbitral tribunal would constitute a quorum, and all decisions would require the concurrence of two arbitrators. The arbitral procedure would be fixed by the tribunal. The decisions of the tribunal would be binding on both parties.

FINAL CLAUSES

Amendment of the Agreement

23. The Agreement should provide that the parties thereto shall, at the request of either of them, consult each other on amendment of the Agreement. All amendments shall require the agreement of both parties. It might additionally be provided, if convenient to the State, that the agreement of the parties on amendments to Part II of the Agreement could be achieved by recourse to a simplified procedure. The Director General shall promptly inform all Member States of any amendment to the Agreement.

Suspension of application of Agency safeguards under other agreements

24. Where applicable and where the State desires such a provision to appear, the Agreement should provide that the application of Agency safeguards in the State under other safeguards agreements with the Agency shall be suspended while the Agreement is in force. If the State has received assistance from the Agency for a project, the State's undertaking in the Project Agreement not to use items subject thereto in such a way as to further any military purpose shall continue to apply.

Entry into force and duration

25. The Agreement should provide that it shall enter into force on the date on which the Agency receives from the State written notification that the statutory and constitutional requirements for entry into force have been met. The Director General shall promptly inform all Member States of the entry into force.

26. The Agreement should provide for it to remain in force as long as the State is party to the Treaty on the Non-Proliferation of Nuclear Weapons . 1/

PART II

INTRODUCTION

27. The Agreement should provide that the purpose of Part II thereof is to specify the procedures to be applied for the implementation of the safeguards provisions of Part I.

OBJECTIVE OF SAFEGUARDS

28. The Agreement should provide that the objective of safeguards is the timely detection of diversion of significant quantities of *nuclear material* from peaceful nuclear activities to the manufacture of nuclear weapons or of other nuclear explosive devices or for purposes unknown, and deterrence of such diversion by the risk of early detection.

29. To this end the Agreement should provide for the use of material accountancy as a safeguards measure of fundamental importance, with containment and surveillance as important complementary measures.

30. The Agreement should provide that the technical conclusion of the Agency's verification activities shall be a statement, in respect of each *material balance area,* of the amount of *material unaccounted for* over a specific period, giving the limits of accuracy of the amounts stated.

NATIONAL SYSTEM OF ACCOUNTING FOR AND CONTROL OF NUCLEAR MATERIAL

31. The Agreement should provide that pursuant to paragraph 7 above the Agency, in carrying out its verification activities, shall make full use of the State's system of accounting for and control of all *nuclear material* subject to safeguards under the Agreement, and shall avoid unnecessary duplication of the State's accounting and control activities.

32. The Agreement should provide that the State's system of accounting for and control of all *nuclear material* subject to safeguards under the Agreement shall be based on a structure of material balance areas, and shall make provision as appropriate and specified in the Subsidiary Arrangements for the establishment of such measures as:

(a) A measurement system for the determination of the quantities of *nuclear material* received, produced, shipped, lost or otherwise removed from inventory, and the quantities on inventory;

(b) The evaluation of precision and accuracy of measurements and the estimation of measurement uncertainty;

(c) Procedures for identifying, reviewing and evaluating differences in shipper/receiver measurements;

(d) Procedures for taking a *physical inventory;*

(e) Procedures for the evaluation of accumulations of unmeasured inventory and unmeasured losses;

(f) A system of records and reports showing, for each *material balance area*, the inventory of *nuclear material* and the changes in that inventory including receipts into and transfers out of the *material balance area*;

(g) Provisions to ensure that the accounting procedures and arrangements are being operated correctly; and

(h) Procedures for the provisions of reports to the Agency in accordance with paragraphs 59-69 below.

STARTING POINT OF SAFEGUARDS

33. The Agreement should provide that safeguards shall not apply thereunder to material in mining or ore-processing activities.

34. The Agreement should provide that:

(a) When any material containing uranium or thorium which has not reached the stage of the nuclear fuel cycle described in sub-paragraph (c) below is directly or indirectly exported to a non-nuclear-weapon State, the State shall inform the Agency of its quantity, composition and destination, unless the material is exported for specifically non-nuclear purposes;

(b) When any material containing uranium or thorium which has not reached the stage of the nuclear fuel cycle described in sub-paragraph (c) below is imported, the State shall inform the Agency of its quantity and composition, unless the material is imported for specifically non-nuclear purposes; and

(c) When any *nuclear material* of a composition and purity suitable for fuel fabrication or for being isotopically enriched leaves the plant or the process stage in which it has been produced, or when such *nuclear material*, or any other *nuclear material* produced at a later stage in the nuclear fuel cycle, is imported into the State, the *nuclear material* shall become subject to the other safeguards procedures specified in the Agreement.

TERMINATION OF SAFEGUARDS

35. The Agreement should provide that safeguards shall terminate on *nuclear material* subject to safeguards thereunder under the conditions set forth in paragraph 11 above. Where the conditions of that paragraph are not met, but the State considers that the recovery of safeguarded *nuclear material* from residues is not for the time being practicable or desirable, the Agency and the State shall consult on the appropriate safeguards measures to be applied. It should further be provided that safeguards shall terminate on *nuclear material* subject to safeguards under the Agreement under the conditions set forth in paragraph 13 above, provided that the State and the

Agency agree that such *nuclear material* is practicably irrecoverable.

EXEMPTIONS FROM SAFEGUARDS

36. The Agreement should provide that the Agency shall, at the request of the State, exempt *nuclear material* from safeguards, as follows:

(a) Special fissionable material, when it is used in gram quantities or less as a sensing component in instruments;

(b) *Nuclear material*, when it is used in non-nuclear activities in accordance with paragraph 13 above, if such *nuclear material* is recoverable; and

(c) Plutonium with an isotopic concentration of plutonium-238 exceeding 80%.

37. The Agreement should provide that *nuclear material* that would otherwise be subject to safeguards shall be exempted from safeguards at the request of the State, provided that nuclear material so exempted in the State may not at any time exceed:

(a) One kilogram in total of special fissionable material, which may consist of one of more of the following:

(i) Plutonium;

(ii) Uranium with an *enrichment* of 0.2 (20%) and above, taken account of by multiplying its weight by its *enrichment*; and

(iii) Uranium with an *enrichment* below 0.2 (20%) and above that of natural uranium, taken account of by multiplying its weight by five times the square of its *enrichment*;

(b) Ten metric tons in total of natural uranium and depleted uranium with an *enrichment* above 0.005 (0.5%);

(c) Twenty metric tons of depleted uranium with an *enrichment* of 0.005 (0.5%) or below; and

(d) Twenty metric tons of thorium;

or such greater amounts as may be specified by the Board of Governors for uniform application.

38. The Agreement should provide that if exempted *nuclear material* is to be processed or stored together with safeguarded *nuclear material*, provision should be made for the reapplication of safeguards thereto.

SUBSIDIARY ARRANGEMENTS

39. The Agreement should provide that the Agency and the State shall make Subsidiary Arrangements which shall specify in detail, to the extent necessary to permit the Agency to fulfil its responsibilities under the Agreement in an effective and efficient manner, how the procedures laid down in the Agreement are to be applied. Provision should be made for the possibility of an exten-

sion or change of the Subsidiary Arrangements by agreement between the Agency and the State without amendment of the Agreement.

40. It should be provided that the Subsidiary Arrangements shall enter into force at the same time as, or as soon as possible after, the entry into force of the Agreement. The State and the Agency shall make every effort to achieve their entry into force within 90 days of the entry into force of the Agreement, a later date being acceptable only with the agreement of both parties. The State shall provide the Agency promptly with the information required for completing the Subsidiary Arrangements. The Agreement should also provide that, upon its entry into force, the Agency shall be entitled to apply the procedures laid down therein in respect of the *nuclear material* listed in the inventory provided for in paragraph 41 below.

INVENTORY

41. The Agreement should provide that, on the basis of the initial report referred to in paragraph 62 below, the Agency shall establish a unified inventory of all *nuclear material* in the State subject to safeguards under the Agreement, irrespective of its origin, and maintain this inventory on the basis of subsequent reports and of the results of its verification activities. Copies of the inventory shall be made available to the State at agreed intervals.

DESIGN INFORMATION

General

42. Pursuant to paragraph 8 above, the Agreement should stipulate that design information in respect of existing *facilities* shall be provided to the Agency during the discussion of the Subsidiary Arrangements, and that the time limits for the provision of such information in respect of new facilities shall be specified in the Subsidiary Arrangements. It should further be stipulated that such information shall be provided as early as possible before *nuclear material* is introduced into a new facility.

43. The Agreement should specify that the design information in respect of each *facility* to be made available to the Agency shall include, when applicable:

(a) The identification of the *facility*, stating its general character, purpose, nominal capacity and geographic location, and the name and address to be used for routine business purposes;

(b) A description of the general arrangement of the *facility* with reference, to the extent feasible, to the form, location and flow of *nuclear material* and to the general layout of important items of equipment which use, produce or process *nuclear material*;

(c) A description of features of the *facility* relating to material accountancy, containment and surveillance; and

(d) A description of the existing and proposed procedures at the *facility* for *nuclear material* accountancy and control, with special reference to *material balance areas* established by the operator, measurements of flow and procedures for *physical inventory* taking.

44. The Agreement should further provide that other information relevant to the application of safeguards shall be made available to the Agency in respect of each *facility*, in particular on organizational responsibility for material accountancy and control. It should also be provided that the State shall make available to the Agency supplementary information on the health and safety procedures which the Agency shall observe and with which the inspectors shall comply at *the facility*.

45. The Agreement should stipulate that design information in respect of a modification relevant for safeguards purposes shall be provided for examination sufficiently in advance for the safeguards procedures to be adjusted when necessary.

Purposes of examination of design information

46. The Agreement should provide that the design information made available to the Agency shall be used for the following purposes:

(a) To identify the features of *facilities* and *nuclear material* relevant to the application of safeguards to nuclear material in sufficient detail to facilitate verification;

(b) To determine *material balance areas* to be used for Agency accounting purposes and to select those *strategic points* which are *key measurement points* and which will be used to determine the *nuclear material* flows and inventories; in determining such *material balance areas* the Agency shall, inter alia, use the following criteria:

(i) The size of the *material balance area* should be related to the accuracy with which the material balance can be established;

(ii) In determining the *material balance area* advantage should be taken of any opportunity to use containment and surveillance to help ensure the completeness of flow measurements and thereby simplify the application of safeguards and concentrate measurement efforts at *key measurement points*;

(iii) A number of *material balance areas* in use at a *facility* or at distinct sites may be combined in one *material balance area* to be used for Agency accounting purposes when the Agency determines that this is consistent with its verification requirements; and

(iv) If the State so requests, a special material balance area around a process step involving commercially sensitive information may be established;

(c) To establish the nominal timing and procedures for taking of *physical inventory* for Agency accounting purposes;

(d) To establish the records and reports requirements and records evaluation procedures;

(e) To establish requirements and procedures for verification of the quantity and location of *nuclear material*; and

(f) To select appropriate combinations of containment and surveillance methods and techniques and the *strategic points* at which they are to be applied.

It should further be provided that the results of the examination of the design information shall be included in the Subsidiary Arrangements.

Re-examination of design information

47. The Agreement should provide that design information shall be re-examined in the light of changes in operating conditions, of developments in safeguards technology or of experience in the application of verification procedures, with a view to modifying the action the Agency has taken pursuant to paragraph 46 above.

Verification of design information

48. The Agreement should provide that the Agency, in cooperation with the State, may send inspectors to *facilities* to verify the design information provided to the Agency pursuant to paragraphs 42-45 above for the purposes stated in paragraph 46.

INFORMATION IN RESPECT OF NUCLEAR MATERIAL OUTSIDE FACILITIES

49. The Agreement should provide that the following information concerning *nuclear material customarily used outside* facilities shall be provided as applicable to the Agency:

(a) A general description of the use of the *nuclear material*, its geographic location, and the user's name and address for routine business purposes; and

(b) A general description of the existing and proposed procedures for *nuclear material* accountancy and control, including organizational responsibility for material accountancy and control.

The Agreement should further provide that the Agency shall be informed on a timely basis of any change in the information provided to it under this paragraph.

50. The Agreement should provide that the information made available to the Agency in respect of *nuclear material* customarily used outside *facilities* may be used, to the extent relevant, for the purposes set out in sub-paragraphs 46(b)-(f) above.

RECORDS SYSTEM
General

51. The Agreement should provide that in establishing a national system of accounting for and control of *nuclear material* as referred to in paragraph 7 above, the State shall arrange that records are kept in respect of each *material balance area*. Provision should also be made that the Subsidiary Arrangements shall describe the records to be kept in respect of each *material balance area*.

52. The Agreement should provide that the State shall make arrangements to facilitate the examination of records by inspectors, particularly if the records are not kept in English, French, Russian or Spanish.

53. The Agreement should provide that the records shall be retained for at least five years.

54. The Agreement should provide that the records shall consist, as appropriate, of:

(a) Accounting records of all *nuclear material* subject to safeguards under the Agreement; and

(b) Operating records for facilities containing such *nuclear material*.

55. The Agreement should provide that the system of measurements on which the records used for the preparation of reports are based shall either conform to the latest international standards or be equivalent in quality to such standards.

Accounting records

56. The Agreement should provide that the accounting records shall set forth the following in respect of each *material balance area*:

(a) All *inventory changes*, so as to permit a determination of the *book inventory* at any time;

(b) All measurement results that are used for determination of the *physical inventory*; and

(c) All *adjustments* and *corrections* that have been made in respect of *inventory changes*, *book inventories* and *physical inventories*.

57. The Agreement should provide that for all *inventory changes* and *physical inventories* the records shall show, in respect of each *batch* of *nuclear material*: material identification, *batch data* and *source data*. Provision should further be included that records shall account for uranium, thorium and plutonium separately in each *batch* of *nuclear material*. Furthermore, the date of the *inventory change* and, when appropriate, the originating *material balance area* and the receiving *material balance area* or the recipient, shall be indicated for each *inventory change*.

Operating records

58. The Agreement should provide that the operating records shall set forth as appropriate in respect of each *material balance area*:

(a) Those operating data which are used to establish changes in the quantities and composition of *nuclear material*;

(b) The data obtained from the calibration of tanks and instruments and from sampling and analyses, the procedures to control the quality of measurements and the derived estimates of random and systematic error;

(c) A description of the sequence of the actions taken in preparing for, and in taking, a *physical inventory*, in order to ensure that it is correct and complete; and

(d) A description of the actions taken in order to ascertain the cause and magnitude of any accidental or unmeasured loss that might occur.

REPORTS SYSTEM
General

59. The Agreement should specify that the State shall provide the Agency with reports as detailed in paragraphs 60-69 below in respect of *nuclear material* subject to safeguards thereunder.

60. The Agreement should provide that reports shall be made in English, French, Russian or Spanish, except as otherwise specified in the Subsidiary Arrangements.

61. The Agreement should provide that reports shall be based on the records kept in accordance with paragraphs 51-58 above and shall consist, as appropriate, of accounting reports and special reports.

Accounting reports

62. The Agreement should stipulate that the Agency shall be provided with an initial report on all *nuclear material* which is to be subject to safeguards thereunder. It should also be provided that the initial report shall be dispatched by the State to the Agency within 30 days of the last day of the calendar month in which the Agreement enters into force, and shall reflect the situation as of the last day of that month.

63. The Agreement should stipulate that for each *material balance area* the State shall provide the Agency with the following accounting reports:

(a) *Inventory change* reports showing changes in the inventory of *nuclear material*. The reports shall be dispatched as soon as possible and in any event within 30 days after the end of the month in which the *inventory changes* occurred or were established; and

(b) Material balance reports showing the material balance based on a *physical inventory* of *nuclear material* actually present in the *material balance area*. The reports shall be dispatched as soon as possible and in any event within 30 days after the *physical inventory* has been taken. The reports shall be based on data available as of the date of reporting and may be corrected at a later date as required.

64. The Agreement should provide that *inventory change* reports shall specify identification and *batch data* for each *batch* of *nuclear material*, the date of the *inventory change* and, as appropriate, the originating *material balance area* and the receiving *material balance area* or the recipient. These reports shall be accompanied by concise notes:

(a) Explaining the *inventory changes*, on the basis of the operating data contained in the operating records provided for under subparagraph 58(a) above; and

(b) Describing, as specified in the Subsidiary Arrangements, the anticipated operational programme, particularly the taking of a *physical inventory*.

65. The Agreement should provide that the State shall report each *inventory change*, *adjustment* and *correction* either periodically in a consolidated list or individually. The *inventory changes* shall be reported in terms of *batches*; small amounts, such as analytical samples, as specified in the Subsidiary Arrangements, may be combined and reported as one *inventory change*.

66. The Agreement should stipulate that the Agency shall provide the State with semi-annual statements of *book inventory* of *nuclear material* subject to safeguards, for each *material balance area*, as based on the *inventory change* reports for the period covered by each such statement.

67. The Agreement should specify that the material balance reports shall include the following entries, unless otherwise agreed by the Agency and the State:

(a) Beginning *physical inventory*;

(b) *Inventory changes* (first increases, then decreases);

(c) Ending *book inventory*;

(d) *Shipper/receiver differences*;

(e) Adjusted ending *book inventory*;

(f) Ending *physical inventory*; and

(g) *Material unaccounted for*.

A statement of the *physical inventory*, listing all *batches* separately and specifying material identification and *batch data* for each *batch*, shall be attached to each material balance report.

Special reports

68. The Agreement should provide that the State shall make special reports without delay:

(a) If any unusual incident or circumstances lead the State to believe that there is or may have been loss of *nuclear material* that exceeds the limits to be specified for this purpose in the Subsidiary Arrangements; or

(b) If the containment has unexpectedly changed from that specified in the Subsidiary Arrangements to the extent that unauthorized removal of *nuclear material* has become possible.

Amplification and clarification of reports

69. The Agreement should provide that at the Agency's request the State shall supply amplifications or clarifications of any report, in so far as relevant for the purpose of safeguards.

INSPECTIONS

General

70. The Agreement should stipulate that the Agency shall have the right to make inspections as provided for in paragraphs 71-82 below.

Purposes of inspections

71. The Agreement should provide that the Agency may make ad hoc inspections in order to:

(a) Verify the information contained in the initial report on the *nuclear material* subject to safeguards under the Agreement;

(b) Identify and verify changes in the situation which have occurred since the date of the initial report; and

(c) Identify, and if possible verify the quantity and composition of, *nuclear material* in accordance with paragraphs 93 and 96 below, before its transfer out of or upon its transfer into the State.

72. The Agreement should provide that the Agency may make routine inspections in order to:

(a) Verify that reports are consistent with records;

(b) Verify the location, identity, quantity and composition of all *nuclear material* subject to safeguards under the Agreement; and

(c) Verify information on the possible causes of *material unaccounted for*, *shipper/receiver differences* and uncertainties in the *book inventory*.

73. The Agreement should provide that the Agency may make special inspections subject to the procedures laid down in paragraph 77 below:

(a) In order to verify the information contained in special reports; or

(b) If the Agency considers that information made available by the State, including explanations from the

State and information obtained from routine inspections, is not adequate for the Agency to fulfil its responsibilities under the Agreement.

An inspection shall be deemed to be special when it is either additional to the routine inspection effort provided for in paragraphs 78-82 below, or involves access to information or locations in addition to the access specified in paragraph 76 for ad hoc and routine inspections, or both.

Scope of inspections

74. The Agreement should provide that for the purposes stated in paragraphs 71-73 above the Agency may:

(a) Examine the records kept pursuant to paragraphs 51-58;

(b) Make independent measurements of all *nuclear material* subject to safeguards under the Agreement;

(c) Verify the functioning and calibration of instruments and other measuring and control equipment;

(d) Apply and make use of surveillance and containment measures; and

(e) Use other objective methods which have been demonstrated to be technically feasible.

75. It should further be provided that within the scope of paragraph 74 above the Agency shall be enabled:

(a) To observe that samples at key *measurement points* for material balance accounting are taken in accordance with procedures which produce representative samples, to observe the treatment and analysis of the samples and to obtain duplicates of such samples;

(b) To observe that the measurements of *nuclear material* at *key measurement points* for material balance accounting are representative, and to observe the calibration of the instruments and equipment involved;

(c) To make arrangements with the State that, if necessary:

(i) Additional measurements are made and additional samples taken for the Agency's use;

(ii) The Agency's standard analytical samples are analysed;

(iii) Appropriate absolute standards are used in calibrating instruments and other equipment; and

(iv) Other calibrations are carried out;

(d) To arrange to use its own equipment for independent measurement and surveillance, and if so agreed and specified in the Subsidiary Arrangements, to arrange to install such equipment;

(e) To apply its seals and other identifying and tamper-indicating devices to containments, if so agreed and specified in the Subsidiary Arrangements; and

(f) To make arrangements with the State for the shipping of samples taken for the Agency's use.

Access for inspections

76. The Agreement should provide that:

(a) For the purposes specified in sub-paragraphs 71(a) and (b) above and until such time as the *strategic points* have been specified in the Subsidiary Arrangements, the Agency's inspectors shall have access to any location where the initial report or any inspections carried out in connection with it indicate that *nuclear material* is present;

(b) For the purposes specified in sub-paragraph 71(c) above the inspectors shall have access to any location of which the Agency has been notified in accordance with sub-paragraphs 92(c) or 95(c) below;

(c) For the purposes specified in paragraph 72 above the Agency's inspectors shall have access only to the *strategic points* specified in the Subsidiary Arrangements and to the records maintained pursuant to paragraphs 51-58; and

(d) In the event of the State concluding that any unusual circumstances require extended limitations on access by the Agency, the State and the Agency shall promptly make arrangements with a view to enabling the Agency to discharge its safeguards responsibilities in the light of these limitations. The Director General shall report each such arrangement to the Board.

77. The Agreement should provide that in circumstances which may lead to special inspections for the purposes specified in paragraph 73 above the State and the Agency shall consult forthwith. As a result of such consultations the Agency may make inspections in addition to the routine inspection effort provided for in paragraphs 78-82 below, and may obtain access in agreement with the State to information or locations in addition to the access specified in paragraph 76 above for ad hoc and routine inspections. Any disagreement concerning the need for additional access shall be resolved in accordance with paragraphs 21 and 22; in case action by the State is essential and urgent, paragraph 18 above shall apply.

Frequency and intensity of routine inspections

78. The Agreement should provide that the number, intensity, duration and timing of routine inspections shall be kept to the minimum consistent with the effective implementation of the safeguards procedures set forth therein, and that the Agency shall make the optimum and most economical use of available inspection resources.

79. The Agreement should provide that in the case of *facilities* and *material balance areas* outside *facilities* with a content or *annual throughput*, whichever is greater, of *nuclear material* not exceeding five *effective*

kilograms, routine inspections shall not exceed one per year. For other *facilities* the number, intensity, duration, timing and mode of inspections shall be determined on the basis that in the maximum or limiting case the inspection regime shall be no more intensive than is necessary and sufficient to maintain continuity of knowledge of the flow and inventory of *nuclear material*.

80. The Agreement should provide that the maximum routine inspection effort in respect of *facilities* with a content or *annual throughput* of *nuclear material* exceeding five *effective kilograms* shall be determined as follows:

(a) For reactors and sealed stores, the maximum total of routine inspection per year shall be determined by allowing one sixth of a *man-year of inspection* for each such *facility* in the State;

(b) For other *facilities* involving plutonium or uranium enriched to more than 5%, the maximum total of routine inspection per year shall be determined by allowing for each such *facility* $30 \times \sqrt{E}$ man-days of inspection per year, where E is the inventory or *annual throughput* of nuclear material, whichever is greater, expressed in *effective kilograms*. The maximum established for any such facility shall not, however, be less than 1.5 *man-years of inspection*; and

(c) For all other *facilities*, the maximum total of routine inspection per year shall be determined by allowing for each such *facility* one third of a *man-year of inspection* plus $0.4 \times E$ man-days of inspection per year, where E is the inventory or *annual throughput* of *nuclear material*, whichever is greater, expressed in *effective kilograms*.

The Agreement should further provide that the Agency and the State may agree to amend the maximum figures specified in this paragraph upon determination by the Board that such amendment is reasonable.

81. Subject to paragraphs 78-80 above the criteria to be used for determining the actual number, intensity, duration, timing and mode of routine inspections of any *facility* shall include:

(a) The form of *nuclear material*, in particular, whether the material is in bulk form or contained in a number of separate items; its chemical composition and, in the case of uranium, whether it is of low or high *enrichment*; and its accessibility;

(b) The effectiveness of the State's accounting and control system, including the extent to which the operators of *facilities* are functionally independent of the State's accounting and control system; the extent to which the measures specified in paragraph 32 above have been implemented by the State; the promptness of reports submitted to the Agency; their consistency with the Agency's independent verification; and the amount and accuracy of the *material unaccounted for*, as verified by the Agency;

(c) Characteristics of the State's nuclear fuel cycle, in particular, the number and types of *facilities* containing *nuclear material* subject to safeguards, the characteristics of such *facilities* relevant to safeguards, notably the degree of containment; the extent to which the design of such *facilities* facilitates verification of the flow and inventory of *nuclear material*; and the extent to which information from different *material balance areas* can be correlated;

(d) International interdependence, in particular, the extent to which *nuclear material* is received from or sent to other States for use or processing; any verification activity by the Agency in connection therewith; and the extent to which the State's nuclear activities are interrelated with those of other States; and

(e) Technical developments in the field of safeguards, including the use of statistical techniques and random sampling in evaluating the flow of *nuclear material*.

82. The Agreement should provide for consultation between the Agency and the State if the latter considers that the inspection effort is being deployed with undue concentration on particular *facilities*.

Notice of inspections

83. The Agreement should provide that the Agency shall give advance notice to the State before arrival of inspectors at *facilities* or *material balance areas* outside facilities, as follows:

(a) For ad hoc inspections pursuant to sub-paragraph 71(c) above, at least 24 hours, for those pursuant to sub-paragraphs 71(a) and (b), as well as the activities provided for in paragraph 48, at least one week;

(b) For special inspections pursuant to paragraph 73 above, as promptly as possible after the Agency and the State have consulted as provided for in paragraph 77, it being understood that notification of arrival normally will constitute part of the consultations; and

(c) For routine inspections pursuant to paragraph 72 above, at least 24 hours in respect of the *facilities* referred to in sub-paragraph 80(b) and sealed stores containing plutonium or uranium enriched to more than 5%, and one week in all other cases.

Such notice of inspections shall include the names of the inspectors and shall indicate the *facilities* and the *material balance areas* outside facilities to be visited and the periods during which they will be visited. If the inspectors are to arrive from outside the State the Agency shall also give advance notice of the place and time of their arrival in the State.

84. However, the Agreement should also provide that, as a supplementary measure, the Agency may carry out without advance notification a portion of the routine inspections pursuant to paragraph 80 above in accordance with the principle of random sampling. In performing any unannounced inspections, the Agency shall fully take into account any operational programme provided by the State pursuant to paragraph 64(b). Moreover, whenever practicable, and on the basis of the operational programme, it shall advise the State periodically of its general programme of announced and unannounced inspections, specifying the general periods when inspections are foreseen. In carrying out any unannounced inspections, the Agency shall make every effort to minimize any practical difficulties for *facility* operators and the State, bearing in mind the relevant provisions of paragraphs 44 above and 89 below. Similarly the State shall make every effort to facilitate the task of the inspectors.

Designation of inspectors

85. The Agreement should provide that:

(a) The Director General shall inform the State in writing of the name, qualifications, nationality, grade and such other particulars as may be relevant, of each Agency official he proposes for designation as an inspector for the State;

(b) The State shall inform the Director General within 30 days of the receipt of such a proposal whether it accepts the proposal;

(c) The Director General may designate each official who has been accepted by the State as one of the inspectors for the State, and shall inform the State of such designations; and

(d) The Director General, acting in response to a request by the State or on his own initiative, shall immediately inform the State of the withdrawal of the designation of any official as an inspector for the State.

The Agreement should also provide, however, that in respect of inspectors needed for the purposes stated in paragraph 48 above and to carry out ad hoc inspections pursuant to sub-paragraphs 71(a) and (b) the designation procedures shall be completed if possible within 30 days after the entry into force of the Agreement. If such designation appears impossible within this time limit, inspectors for such purposes shall be designated on a temporary basis.

86. The Agreement should provide that the State shall grant or renew as quickly as possible appropriate visas, where required, for each inspector designated for the State.

Conduct and visits of inspectors

87. The Agreement should provide that inspectors, in exercising their functions under paragraphs 48 and 71-75 above, shall carry out their activities in a manner designed to avoid hampering or delaying the construction, commissioning or operation of *facilities* or affecting their safety. In particular inspectors shall not operate any *facility* themselves or direct the staff of a *facility* to carry out any operation. If inspectors consider that in pursuance of paragraphs 74 and 75, particular operations in a *facility* should be carried out by the operator, they shall make a request therefor.

88. When inspectors require services available in the State, including the use of equipment, in connection with the performance of inspections, the State shall facilitate the procurement of such services and the use of such equipment by inspectors.

89. The Agreement should provide that the State shall have the right to have inspectors accompanied during their inspections by representatives of the State, provided that inspectors shall not thereby be delayed or otherwise impeded in the exercise of their functions.

STATEMENTS ON THE AGENCY'S VERIFICATION ACTIVITIES

90. The Agreement should provide that the Agency shall inform the State of:

(a) The results of inspections, at intervals to be specified in the Subsidiary Arrangements; and

(b) The conclusions it has drawn from its verification activities in the State, in particular by means of statements in respect of each *material balance area*, which shall be made as soon as possible after a *physical inventory* has been taken and verified by the Agency and a material balance has been struck.

INTERNATIONAL TRANSFERS

General

91. The Agreement should provide that *nuclear material* subject or required to be subject to safeguards thereunder which is transferred internationally shall, for purposes of the Agreement, be regarded as being the responsibility of the State:

(a) In the case of import, from the time that such responsibility ceases to lie with the exporting State, and no later than the time at which the *nuclear material* reaches its destination; and

(b) In the case of export, up to the time at which the recipient State assumes such responsibility, and no later than the time at which the *nuclear material* reaches its destination.

The Agreement should provide that the States concerned shall make suitable arrangements to determine the point at which the transfer of responsibility will take place. No State shall be deemed to have such responsibility for *nuclear material* merely by reason of the fact that the *nuclear material* is in transit on or over its territory or territorial waters, or that it is being transported under its flag or in its aircraft.

Transfers out of the State

92. The Agreement should provide that any intended transfer out of the State of safeguarded *nuclear material* in an amount exceeding one *effective kilogram*, or by successive shipments to the same State within a period of three months each of less than one *effective kilogram* but exceeding in total one *effective kilogram*, shall be notified to the Agency after the conclusion of the contractual arrangements leading to the transfer and normally at least two weeks before the *nuclear material* is to be prepared for shipping. The Agency and the State may agree on different procedures for advance notification. The notification shall specify:

(a) The identification and, if possible, the expected quantity and composition of the *nuclear material* to be transferred, and the *material balance area* from which it will come;

(b) The State for which the *nuclear material* is destined;

(c) The dates on and locations at which the *nuclear material* is to be prepared for shipping;

(d) The approximate dates of dispatch and arrival of the *nuclear material*; and

(e) At what point of the transfer the recipient State will assume responsibility for the *nuclear material*, and the probable date on which this point will be reached.

93. The Agreement should further provide that the purpose of this notification shall be to enable the Agency if necessary to identify, and if possible verify the quantity and composition of, *nuclear material* subject to safeguards under the Agreement before it is transferred out of the State and, if the Agency so wishes or the State so requests, to affix seals to the *nuclear material* when it has been prepared for shipping. However, the transfer of the *nuclear material* shall not be delayed in any way by any action taken or contemplated by the Agency pursuant to this notification.

94. The Agreement should provide that, if the *nuclear material* will not be subject to Agency safeguards in the recipient State, the exporting State shall make arrangements for the Agency to receive, within three months of the time when the recipient State accepts responsibility for the *nuclear material* from the exporting State, confirmation by the recipient State of the transfer.

Transfers into the State

95. The Agreement should provide that the expected transfer into the State of *nuclear material* required to be subject to safeguards in an amount greater than one *effective kilogram*, or by successive shipments from the same State within a period of three months each of less

than one *effective kilogram* but exceeding in total one *effective kilogram*, shall be notified to the Agency as much in advance as possible of the expected arrival of the *nuclear material*, and in any case not later than the date on which the recipient State assumes responsibility therefor. The Agency and the State may agree on different procedures for advance notification. The notification shall specify:

(a) The identification and, if possible, the expected quantity and composition of the *nuclear material*;

(b) At what point of the transfer responsibility for the *nuclear material* will be assumed by the State for the purposes of the Agreement, and the probable date on which this point will be reached; and

(c) The expected date of arrival, the location to which the *nuclear material* is to be delivered and the date on which it is intended that the *nuclear material* should be unpacked.

96. The Agreement should provide that the purpose of this notification shall be to enable the Agency if necessary to identify, and if possible verify the quantity and composition of, *nuclear material* subject to safeguards which has been transferred into the State, by means of inspection of the consignment at the time it is unpacked. However, unpacking shall not be delayed by any action taken or contemplated by the Agency pursuant to this notification.

Special reports

97. The Agreement should provide that in the case of international transfers a special report as envisaged in paragraph 68 above shall be made if any unusual incident or circumstances lead the State to believe that there is or may have been loss of *nuclear material*, including the occurrence of significant delay during the transfer.

DEFINITIONS

98. "Adjustment" means an entry into an accounting record or a report showing a *shipper/receiver difference* or *material unaccounted for*.

99. "Annual throughput" means, for the purposes of paragraphs 79 and 80 above, the amount of *nuclear material* transferred annually out of a *facility* working at nominal capacity.

100 "Batch" means a portion of *nuclear material* handled as a unit for accounting purposes at a *key measurement point* and for which the composition and quantity are defined by a single set of specifications or measurements. The *nuclear material* may be in bulk form or contained in a number of separate items.

101. "Batch data" means the total weight of each element of *nuclear material* and, in the case of plutonium

and uranium, the isotopic composition when appropriate. The units of account shall be as follows:

(a) Grams of contained plutonium;

(b) Grams of total uranium and grams of contained uranium-235 plus uranium-233 for uranium enriched in these isotopes; and

(c) Kilograms of contained thorium, natural uranium or depleted uranium.

For reporting purposes the weights of individual items in the batch shall be added together before rounding to the nearest unit.

102. "Book inventory" of a *material balance area* means the algebraic sum of the most recent *physical inventory* of that *material balance area* and of all *inventory changes* that have occurred since that *physical inventory* was taken.

103. "Correction" means an entry into an accounting record or a report to rectify an identified mistake or to reflect an improved measurement of a quantity previously entered into the record or report. Each correction must identify the entry to which it pertains.

104. "Effective kilogram" means a special unit used in safeguarding *nuclear material*. The quantity in "effective kilograms" is obtained by taking:

(a) For plutonium, its weight in kilograms;

(b) For uranium with an *enrichment* of 0.01 (1%) and above, its weight in kilograms multiplied by the square of its *enrichment*;

(c) For uranium with an *enrichment* below 0.01(1%) and above 0.005 (0.5%), its weight in kilograms multiplied by 0.0001; and

(d) For depleted uranium with an *enrichment* of 0.005 (0.5%) or below, and for thorium, its weight in kilograms multiplied by 0.00005.

105. "Enrichment" means the ratio of the combined weight of the isotopes uranium-233 and uranium-235 to that of the total uranium in question.

106. "Facility" means:

(a) A reactor, a critical facility, a conversion plant, a fabrication plant, a reprocessing plant, an isotope separation plant or a separate storage installation; or

(b) Any location where *nuclear material* in amounts greater than one *effective kilogram* is customarily used.

107. "Inventory change" means an increase or decrease, in terms of *batches*, of *nuclear material* in a *material balance area*; such a change shall involve one of the following:

(a) Increases:

(i) Import;

(ii) Domestic receipt: receipts from other *material balance areas*, receipts from a non-safeguarded

(non-peaceful) activity or receipts at the starting point of safeguards;

(iii) Nuclear production: production of special fissionable material in a reactor; and

(iv) De-exemption: reapplication of safeguards on *nuclear material* previously exempted therefrom on account of its use or quantity;

(b) Decreases:

(i) Export;

(ii) Domestic shipment: shipments to other *material balance areas* or shipments for a non-safeguarded (non-peaceful) activity;

(iii) Nuclear loss: loss of *nuclear material* due to its transformation into other element(s) or isotope(s) as a result of nuclear reactions;

(iv) Measured discard: *nuclear material* which has been measured, or estimated on the basis of measurements, and disposed of in such a way that it is not suitable for further nuclear use;

(v) Retained waste: *nuclear material* generated from processing or from an operational accident, which is deemed to be unrecoverable for the time being but which is stored;

(vi) Exemption: exemption of *nuclear material* from safeguards on account of its use or quantity; and

(vii) Other loss: for example, accidental loss (that is, irretrievable and inadvertent loss of *nuclear material* as the result of an operational accident) or theft.

108. "Key measurement point" means a location where *nuclear material* appears in such a form that it may be measured to determine material flow or inventory. "Key measurement points" thus include, but are not limited to, the inputs and outputs (including measured discards) and storages in *material balance areas*.

109. "Man-year of inspection" means, for the purposes of paragraph 80 above, 300 man-days of inspection, a man-day being a day during which a single inspector has access to a *facility* at any time for a total of not more than eight hours.

110. "Material balance area" means an area in or outside of a facility such that:

(a) The quantity of *nuclear material* in each transfer into or out of each "material balance area" can be determined; and

(b) The *physical inventory* of *nuclear material* in each "material balance area" can be determined when necessary, in accordance with specified procedures,

in order that the material balance for Agency safeguards purposes can be established.

111. "Material unaccounted for" means the difference between *book inventory* and *physical inventory*.

112. "Nuclear material" means any source or any special fissionable material as defined in Article XX of the Statute. The term source material shall not be interpreted as applying to ore or ore residue. Any determination by the Board under Article XX of the Statute after the entry into force of this Agreement which adds to the materials considered to be source material or special fissionable material shall have effect under this Agreement only upon acceptance by the State.

113. "Physical inventory" means the sum of all the measured or derived estimates of *batch* quantities of *nuclear material* on hand at a given time within a *material balance area*, obtained in accordance with specified procedures.

114. "Shipper/receiver difference" means the difference between the quantity of *nuclear material* in a *batch* as stated by the shipping *material balance area* and as measured at the receiving *material balance area*.

115. "Source data" means those data, recorded during measurement or calibration or used to derive empirical relationships, which identify *nuclear material* and provide *batch data*. "Source data" may include, for example, weight of compounds, conversion factors to determine weight of element, specific gravity, element concentration, isotopic ratios, relationship between volume and manometer readings and relationship between plutonium produced and power generated.

116. "Strategic point" means a location selected during examination of design information where, under normal conditions and when combined with the information from all "strategic points" taken together, the information necessary and sufficient for the implementation of safeguards measures is obtained and verified; a "strategic point" may include any location where key measurements related to material balance accountancy are made and where containment and surveillance measures are executed.

Document 16

Statement by the Secretary-General of the United Nations at the First Review Conference of the Parties to the Treaty on the Non-Proliferation of Nuclear Weapons

UN Press Release SG/SM/2181, 5 May 1975

Five years ago, the Treaty on the Non-Proliferation of Nuclear Weapons entered into force. This event was acclaimed as a major step towards the cessation of the nuclear arms race and an advance for the cause of peace. Since then, the Treaty has won wide international acceptance, and the General Assembly has repeatedly reaffirmed its support for the Treaty and for its full implementation.

Today, we are assembled here, in the Palais des Nations, where a very large part of the negotiations leading to the Non-Proliferation Treaty were conducted with such great competence and dedication by the Committee on Disarmament, following the pioneer efforts of the United Nations in the 1950s and early 1960s.

We are here to review the operation of this important international agreement and to make sure that its objectives and provisions are being fully realized. The presence in this hall of so many distinguished representatives is testimony to the importance that the world community attaches to that goal.

The basic goal of the Non-Proliferation Treaty is to avert the danger of a nuclear war. To achieve this end, the Treaty seeks to prevent the further spread of these weapons to an ever-increasing number of States and, on the other hand, it contains commitments to pursue negotiations on the cessation of the nuclear arms race at an early date and to nuclear disarmament. These two objectives are interrelated.

They have an even greater relevance today than they had during the process of negotiations leading to the conclusion of the Treaty. Recent events have demonstrated that the nuclear age leads inevitably towards a world where an increasing number of States manufacture nuclear explosives. Many will also have the raw materials and facilities needed in this context. The Conference should thus proceed in the clear and evident realization that the alternative to the implementation of the objectives of the Non-Proliferation Treaty is a world where nuclear weapons are ever more plentiful than they are today, and where they are owned by the many and not by the few. These are the sobering features of today's situation.

As the Review Conference begins its deliberations, more than 90 States are parties to the Treaty. This figure includes a number of recent, very significant ratifications. A constructive dialogue here at the Conference should improve even further the chances for broader acceptance of the Treaty, with a view to its ultimate acceptance by all.

This was the aim of the General Assembly of the United Nations when, in 1968, it commended the Treaty and called for the widest possible adherence to it. It will also be remembered that the General Assembly subsequently reiterated this call, in particular at its twenty-ninth session last year, when it urged all countries concerned "to ratify or accede to the Treaty on the Non-Proliferation of Nuclear Weapons or finalize their safeguards agreements with the International Atomic Energy Agency as soon as possible in accordance with the provisions of that Treaty, in view of the fact that the Review Conference of the Parties to the Treaty on the Non-Proliferation of Nuclear Weapons will take place in May 1975."

The Treaty embodies a balance of mutual responsibilities and obligations of the nuclear and non-nuclear-weapon States. The task of the Conference will be to review how these obligations have been implemented, with a view to strengthening the role of the Treaty in the promotion of non-proliferation, nuclear disarmament and international peace and security.

It has often been said that the Non-Proliferation Treaty is not an end in itself but a step towards arms limitations and disarmament. The Treaty certainly is very clear on this point and embodies an undertaking by each of the parties "to pursue negotiations in good faith on effective measures relating to cessation of the nuclear arms race at an early date and on nuclear disarmament, and on a treaty on general and complete disarmament under strict and effective international control". The way in which this undertaking is fulfilled cannot fail to have the most important consequences for the future.

My views on these matters are well known and need not be repeated here in any detail. They are summed up in a message to the 1975 opening session of the Conference of the Committee on Disarmament, where I stated: "The record reveals that although much has been achieved, a great deal still needs to be accomplished in the field of disarmament which is not only desirable but essential for our survival. It is sometimes said that it may be impossible to reconcile the desirable with the feasible in the affairs of States. I sincerely believe that in the field of disarmament we must keep trying to reconcile the positions of all parties concerned with perseverance, commitment and conviction. Although we have had many disappointments and only limited successes, we must not give up. The price of failure is too heavy, and too terrible, for mankind to bear."

Another element in the delicate balance of mutual responsibilities and obligations is a system of security guarantees to the non-nuclear-weapon States. The Security Council dealt with this question when it adopted resolution 255 (1968). This Conference will undoubtedly have the opportunity to further discuss this question.

One feature of the nuclear age, which we must necessarily take into account, is the interrelation between the peaceful and the military uses of nuclear energy. This dual aspect of nuclear energy is going to affect in an increasing degree the question of international security, as the peaceful uses of the atom continue to grow at a rapid pace.

The General Assembly had this situation clearly in mind when, at its last session in 1974, it expressed the hope that the Review Conference would give consideration to the role of peaceful nuclear explosions as provided for in the Non-Proliferation Treaty and would inform the Assembly at its thirtieth session of the results of its deliberations.

Similar calls were addressed by the Assembly to the International Atomic Energy Agency, the Conference of the Committee on Disarmament and the Secretary-General of the United Nations.

The Non-Proliferation Treaty, while encouraging the growth of the peaceful use of nuclear energy, at the same time provides for safeguards to prevent the transfer of fissile material from peaceful to military purposes. I had the privilege of taking part in the formulation of these safeguards as Chairman of the IAEA Safeguards Committee in the early 1970s. I can, therefore, highly appreciate the value of the work that the Agency, under the leadership of its distinguished Director General, Dr. Sigvard Eklund, devotes to the development and implementation of safeguards, as well as to the furthering of the peaceful uses of atomic energy.

The Review Conference will, undoubtedly, pay full attention to these aspects of the Non-Proliferation Treaty so as to further international cooperation in the territories of non-nuclear-weapon States parties to the Treaty, with due consideration for the needs of developing areas of the world.

Madame President, distinguished delegates, ladies and gentlemen, you have assembled here to meet a most challenging task, namely, to further enhance the security of all States by reviewing the operation and ensuring the widest possible acceptability of a Treaty which seeks to combine vital arms restraints with equally vital commitments to international cooperation in the peaceful nuclear field.

The United Nations, aware of its responsibilities under the Charter with regard to all matters pertaining to disarmament, and convinced of the urgency and great importance of preventing the spread of nuclear weapons and of intensifying international cooperation in the development of peaceful applications of atomic energy, has spared no effort to promote the cause of nuclear non-proliferation in the interest of all States. I therefore hope that all efforts will be made to bring about the full implementation of the Treaty and general acceptance of it by States as a contribution to the strengthening of international peace and security.

It is in this spirit that I extend to all of you my very best wishes for success in your difficult but most important task.

Document 17

Statement by the Director General of the IAEA at the 1975 Review Conference of the NPT

Not issued as a United Nations document

During the five years that the Non-Proliferation Treaty has been in force the International Atomic Energy Agency has gained considerable experience in the implementation of international safeguards under the Treaty. With the lesson learned since 1960 in operating the earlier safeguards system, this has enabled the Agency to make considerable improvements in safeguards operations. Our experience has been reported to the Review Conference in the documentation before you.

The development of nuclear energy during the last five years has been impressive and international collaboration in this field is described in reports to the Conference. In 1970 the installed nuclear power capacity outside the nuclear-weapon States amounted to about 5,000 MW in 11 countries of which nearly 50% was under IAEA safeguards. Today, with the ratification of the Treaty by the EURATOM countries this figure has grown to 24,000 MW in 15 countries of which almost 100% is under IAEA safeguards. It is expected that by 1980 a capacity of about 100,000 MW will be reached in 22 non-nuclear-weapon States.

However, two recent and conflicting trends may influence this development. On one hand public opposition to the use of nuclear power reactors has emerged and, in some cases, has gained such momentum as to hamper the realization of already approved projects. On the other hand, a marked change in the conventional energy situation has drawn renewed attention to the potentialities of nuclear power. The conflict of these two tendencies has led to a worldwide re-evaluation of the energy question, a re-evaluation of which the outcome is still open. One point is certain, however, and that is that electricity will take a steadily increasing share of total energy production and that the future demand for energy will exceed the conventional energy resources available. This gap will remain even if demand is reduced by conservation measures or by changes in the attitude of the industrial society towards the question of energy growth.

At present—and one can certainly include the next ten years—the gap can only be filled by nuclear energy, which is the only immediately available technical solution, even if all problems associated with it have not yet been entirely resolved. The development of nuclear energy will follow a different rhythm in various parts of the world; in some it will be slower than foreseen because of economic recession and public reluctance; in the developing countries new markets may emerge if adequate financial resources are available.

The figures I have just referred to give an indication of the increased requirements for the safeguarding activities of the Agency under the NPT during the next few years. As a result of the growth of nuclear power the spread of the capacity to make nuclear weapons is not, however, exclusively tied to this expansion.

I would here like to recall that a striking development since the NPT came into force has been the vast growth of both scientific and technical knowledge about nuclear energy and its wide dissemination throughout the world.

An illustration of this is that at present about 350 research reactors are in operation—one third of which are in some 50 non-nuclear-weapon States while the number of power reactors is only 180 in some 20 countries. Most of these research reactors are too small to be of significance with regard to production of fissile material but a few larger ones produce substantial amounts of plutonium.

Research reactors generally operate at low temperatures. This permits a vast simplification of their mode of operation compared with that of a power reactor. A country wishing to produce fissile material for explosives could do this so much more easily in a research reactor than in the complicated piece of equipment represented by a power reactor. All that a country would need is natural uranium and heavy water. The fabrication of the latter is a fairly well-known process.

Furthermore, the reprocessing of fuel from a research reactor to extract plutonium is far easier than handling highly irradiated fuel from a power reactor.

With regard to another road to nuclear explosive capacity, the impression from the recent conference in Paris on Nuclear Energy Maturity is that no new viable technology for isotope separation—outside the presently operating pilot, or full-scale installations—can be expected to emerge for at least a decade.

Let me sum up at this point. Mankind has not only entered the nuclear age, it has also entered a new phase where, whether we like it or not, we all share the common knowledge needed to exploit for peaceful or for military purposes one of the mightiest resources with which nature has endowed us. As nuclear knowledge cannot be safeguarded in the same way as installations or materials, the risk of proliferation of nuclear weapons is with us. The NPT offers a solution for dealing with this risk. Some countries may still feel that this is not an acceptable solution but given the critical situation we face, it is surely the path of wisdom to grasp even an imperfect solution rather than none at all. Moreover, I hope to see this conference devise the arrangements and the regimes which will permit those countries that have not yet found the NPT acceptable, to agree to measures which may offer equally effective safeguards for preventing further proliferation.

Let me close on an encouraging note. We must recognize that an important positive forward step has been taken. For the first time in the history of mankind an international inspection system has been established. A considerable amount of experience has been gained from the operation of this system which can certainly be further improved and which in the future may serve as a model for the other similar undertakings in the realm of disarmament.

Let me also say how much I share the conference's pleasure at the news of the action just taken by the non-nuclear-weapon States of the European Economic Community.

Document 18

Final declaration of the 1975 Review Conference of the NPT

NPT/CONF/35/1, 30 May 1975

PREAMBLE

The States Party to the Treaty on the Non-Proliferation of Nuclear Weapons which met in Geneva in May 1975, in accordance with the Treaty, to review the operation of the Treaty with a view to assuring that the purposes of the Preamble and the provisions of the Treaty are being realized,

Recognizing the continuing importance of the objectives of the Treaty,

Affirming the belief that universal adherence to the Treaty would greatly strengthen international peace and enhance the security of all States,

Firmly convinced that, in order to achieve this aim, it is essential to maintain, in the implementation of the Treaty, an acceptable balance of mutual responsibilities and obligations of all States Party to the Treaty, nuclear-weapon and non-nuclear-weapon States,

Recognizing that the danger of nuclear warfare remains a grave threat to the survival of mankind,

Convinced that the prevention of any further proliferation of nuclear weapons or other nuclear explosive devices remains a vital element in efforts to avert nuclear warfare, and that the promotion of this objective will be furthered by more rapid progress towards the cessation of the nuclear arms race and the limitation and reduction of existing nuclear weapons, with a view to the eventual elimination from national arsenals of nuclear weapons, pursuant to a Treaty on general and complete disarmament under strict and effective international control,

Recalling the determination expressed by the Parties to seek to achieve the discontinuance of all test explosions of nuclear weapons for all time,

Considering that the trend towards détente in relations between States provides a favourable climate within which more significant progress should be possible towards the cessation of the nuclear arms race,

Noting the important role which nuclear energy can, particularly in changing economic circumstances, play in power production and in contributing to the progressive elimination of the economic and technological gap between developing and developed States,

Recognizing that the accelerated spread and development of peaceful applications of nuclear energy will, in the absence of effective safeguards, contribute to further proliferation of nuclear explosive capability,

Recognizing the continuing necessity of full cooperation in the application and improvement of International Atomic Energy Agency (IAEA) safeguards on peaceful nuclear activities,

Recalling that all Parties to the Treaty are entitled to participate in the fullest possible exchange of scientific information for, and to contribute alone or in cooperation with other States to, the further development of the applications of atomic energy for peaceful purposes,

Reaffirming the principle that the benefits of peaceful applications of nuclear technology, including any technological by-products which may be derived by nuclear-weapon States from the development of nuclear explosive devices, should be available for peaceful purposes to all Parties to the Treaty, and

Recognizing that all States Parties have a duty to strive for the adoption of tangible and effective measures to attain the objectives of the Treaty,

Declares as follows:

PURPOSES

The States Party to the Treaty reaffirm their strong common interest in averting the further proliferation of nuclear weapons. They reaffirm their strong support for the Treaty their continued dedication to its principles and objectives, and their commitment to implement fully and more effectively its provisions.

They reaffirm the vital role of the Treaty in international efforts

—to avert further proliferation of nuclear weapons

—to achieve the cessation of the nuclear arms race and to undertake effective measures in the direction of nuclear disarmament, and

—to promote cooperation in the peaceful uses of nuclear energy under adequate safeguards.

REVIEW OF ARTICLES I AND II

The review undertaken by the Conference confirms that the obligations undertaken under Articles I and II of the Treaty have been faithfully observed by all Parties. The Conference is convinced that the continued strict observance of these Articles remains central to the shared objective of averting the further proliferation of nuclear weapons.

REVIEW OF ARTICLE III

The Conference notes that the verification activities of the IAEA under Article III of the Treaty respect the sovereign rights of States and do not hamper the economic, scientific or technological development of the Parties to the Treaty or international cooperation in peaceful nuclear activities. It urges that this situation be maintained. The Conference attaches considerable importance to the continued application of safeguards under Article III, 1, on a

non-discriminatory basis, for the equal benefit of all States Party to the Treaty.

The Conference notes the importance of systems of accounting for and control of nuclear material, from the standpoints both of the responsibilities of States Party to the Treaty and of cooperation with the IAEA in order to facilitate the implementation of the safeguards provided for in Article III, 1. The Conference expresses the hope that all States having peaceful nuclear activities will establish and maintain effective accounting and control systems and welcomes the readiness of the IAEA to assist States in so doing.

The Conference expresses its strong support for effective IAEA safeguards. In this context it recommends that intensified efforts be made towards the standardization and the universality of application of IAEA safeguards, while ensuring that safeguards agreements with non-nuclear-weapon States not Party to the Treaty are of adequate duration, preclude diversion to any nuclear explosive devices and contain appropriate provisions for the continuance of the application of safeguards upon re-export.

The Conference recommends that more attention and fuller support be given to the improvement of safeguards techniques, instrumentation, data-handling and implementation in order, among other things, to ensure optimum cost-effectiveness. It notes with satisfaction the establishment by the Director General of the IAEA of a standing advisory group on safeguards implementation.

The Conference emphasizes the necessity for the States Party to the Treaty that have not yet done so to conclude as soon as possible safeguards agreements with the IAEA.

With regard to the implementation of Article III, 2 of the Treaty, the Conference notes that a number of States suppliers of nuclear material or equipment have adopted certain minimum, standard requirements for IAEA safeguards in connection with their exports of certain such items to non-nuclear-weapon States not Party to the Treaty (IAEA document INFCIRC/209 and Addenda). The Conference attaches particular importance to the condition, established by those States, of an undertaking of non-diversion to nuclear weapons or other nuclear explosive devices, as included in the said requirements.

The Conference urges that:

(a) in all achievable ways, common export requirements relating to safeguards be strengthened, in particular by extending the application of safeguards to all peaceful nuclear activities in importing States not Party to the Treaty;

(b) such common requirements be accorded the

widest possible measure of acceptance among all suppliers and recipients;

(c) all Parties to the Treaty should actively pursue their efforts to these ends.

The Conference takes note of:

(a) The considered view of many Parties to the Treaty that the safeguards required under Article III, 2 should extend to all peaceful nuclear activities in importing States;

(b) (i) the suggestion that it is desirable to arrange for common safeguards requirements in respect of nuclear material processed, used or produced by the use of scientific and technological information transferred in tangible form to non-nuclear-weapon States not Party to the Treaty;

(ii) the hope that this aspect of safeguards could be further examined.

The Conference recommends that, during the review of the arrangements relating to the financing of safeguards in the IAEA which is to be undertaken by its Board of Governors at an appropriate time after 1975, the less favourable financial situation of the developing countries be fully taken into account. It recommends further that, on that occasion, the Parties to the Treaty concerned seek measures that would restrict within appropriate limits the respective shares of developing countries in safeguards costs.

The Conference attaches considerable importance, so far as safeguards inspectors are concerned, to adherence by the IAEA to Article VII.D of its Statute, prescribing, among other things, that "due regard shall be paid . . . to the importance of recruiting the staff on as wide a geographical basis as possible"; it also recommends that safeguards training be made available to personnel from all geographic regions.

The Conference, convinced that nuclear materials should be effectively protected at all times, urges that action be pursued to elaborate further, within the IAEA, concrete recommendations for the physical protection of nuclear material in use, storage and transit, including principles relating to the responsibility of States, with a view to ensuring a uniform, minimum level of effective protection for such material.

It calls upon all States engaging in peaceful nuclear activities (i) to enter into such international agreements and arrangements as may be necessary to ensure such protection; and (ii) in the framework of their respective physical protection systems, to give the earliest possible effective application, to the IAEA's recommendations.

REVIEW OF ARTICLE IV

The Conference reaffirms, in the framework of Article IV, 1, that nothing in the Treaty shall be interpreted as affecting, and notes with satisfaction that nothing in the Treaty has been identified as affecting, the inalienable right of all the Parties to the Treaty to develop research, production and use of nuclear energy for peaceful purposes without discrimination and in conformity with Articles I and II of the Treaty.

The Conference reaffirms, in the framework of Article IV, 2, the undertaking by all Parties to the Treaty to facilitate the fullest possible exchange of equipment, materials and scientific and technological information for the peaceful uses of nuclear energy and the right of all Parties to the Treaty to participate in such exchange and welcomes the efforts made towards that end. Noting that the Treaty constitutes a favourable framework for broadening international cooperation in the peaceful uses of nuclear energy, the Conference is convinced that on this basis, and in conformity with the Treaty, further efforts should be made to ensure that the benefits of peaceful applications of nuclear technology should be available to all Parties to the Treaty.

The Conference recognizes that there continues to be a need for the fullest possible exchange of nuclear materials, equipment and technology, including up-to-date developments, consistent with the objectives and safeguards requirements of the Treaty. The Conference reaffirms the undertaking of the Parties to the Treaty in a position to do so to cooperate in contributing, alone or together with other States or international organizations, to the further development of the applications of nuclear energy for peaceful purposes, especially in the territories of non-nuclear-weapon States Party to the Treaty, with due consideration for the needs of the developing areas of the world. Recognizing, in the context of Article IV, 2, those growing needs of developing States, the Conference considers it necessary to continue and increase assistance to them in this field bilaterally and through such multilateral channels as the IAEA and the United Nations Development Programme.

The Conference is of the view that, in order to implement as fully as possible Article IV of the Treaty, developed States Party to the Treaty should consider taking measures, making contributions and establishing programmes, as soon as possible, for the provision of special assistance in the peaceful uses of nuclear energy for developing States Party to the Treaty.

The Conference recommends that, in reaching decisions on the provision of equipment, materials, services and scientific and technological information for the peaceful uses of nuclear energy, on concessional and other appropriate financial arrangements and on the furnishing of technical assistance in the nuclear field, including cooperation related to the continuous operation of peaceful nuclear facilities, States Party to the Treaty should give weight to adherence to the Treaty by recipient States. The Conference recommends, in this connection, that any special measures of cooperation to meet the growing needs of developing States Party to the Treaty might include increased and supplemental voluntary aid provided bilaterally or through multilateral channels such as the IAEA's facilities for administering funds-in-trust and gifts-in-kind.

The Conference further recommends that States Party to the Treaty in a position to do so, meet, to the fullest extent possible, "technically sound" requests for technical assistance, submitted to the IAEA by developing States Party to the Treaty, which the IAEA is unable to finance from its own resources, as well as such "technically sound" requests as may be made by developing States Party to the Treaty which are not Members of the IAEA.

The Conference recognizes that regional or multinational nuclear fuel cycle centres may be an advantageous way to satisfy, safely and economically, the needs of many States in the course of initiating or expanding nuclear power programmes, while at the same time facilitating physical protection and the application of IAEA safeguards, and contributing to the goals of the Treaty.

The Conference welcomes the IAEA's studies in this area, and recommends that they be continued as expeditiously as possible. It considers that such studies should include, among other aspects, identification of the complex practical and organizational difficulties which will need to be dealt with in connection with such projects.

The Conference urges all Parties to the Treaty in a position to do so to cooperate in these studies, particularly by providing to the IAEA where possible economic data concerning construction and operation of facilities such as chemical reprocessing plants, plutonium fuel fabrication plants, waste management installations, and longer-term spent-fuel storage, and by assistance to the IAEA to enable it to undertake feasibility studies concerning the establishment of regional nuclear fuel cycle centres in specific geographic regions.

The Conference hopes that, if these studies lead to positive findings, and if the establishment of regional or multinational nuclear fuel cycle centres is undertaken, Parties to the Treaty in a position to do so, will cooperate in, and provide assistance for, the elaboration and realization of such projects.

REVIEW OF ARTICLE V

The Conference reaffirms the obligation of Parties to the Treaty to take appropriate measures to ensure that potential benefits from any peaceful applications of nuclear explosions are made available to non-nuclear-weapon States Party to the Treaty in full accordance with the provisions of Article V and other applicable international obligations. In this connection, the Conference also reaffirms that such services should be provided to non-nuclear-weapon States Party to the Treaty on a non-discriminatory basis and that the charge to such Parties for the explosive devices used should be as low as possible and exclude any charge for research and development.

The Conference notes that any potential benefits could be made available to non-nuclear-weapon States not Party to the Treaty by way of nuclear explosion services provided by nuclear-weapon States, as defined by the Treaty, and conducted under the appropriate international observation and international procedures called for in Article V and in accordance with other applicable international obligations. The Conference considers it imperative that access to potential benefits of nuclear explosions for peaceful purposes not lead to any proliferation of nuclear explosive capability.

The Conference considers the IAEA to be the appropriate international body, referred to in Article V of the Treaty, through which potential benefits from peaceful applications of nuclear explosions could be made available to any non-nuclear-weapon State. Accordingly, the Conference urges the IAEA to expedite work on identifying and examining the important legal issues involved in, and to commence consideration of, the structure and content of the special international agreement or agreements contemplated in Article V of the Treaty, taking into account the views of the Conference of the Committee on Disarmament (CCD) and the United Nations General Assembly and enabling States Party to the Treaty but not Members of the IAEA which would wish to do so to participate in such work.

The Conference notes that the technology of nuclear explosions for peaceful purposes is still at the stage of development and study and that there are a number of interrelated international legal and other aspects of such explosions which still need to be investigated.

The Conference commends the work in this field that has been carried out within the IAEA and looks forward to the continuance of such work pursuant to United Nations General Assembly resolution 3261 D (XXIX). It emphasizes that the IAEA should play the central role in matters relating to the provision of services for the application of nuclear explosions for peaceful purposes. It believes that the IAEA should broaden its consideration of this subject to encompass, within its area of competence, all aspects and implications of the practical applications of nuclear explosions for peaceful purposes. To this end it urges the IAEA to set up appropriate machinery within which intergovernmental discussion can take place and through which advice can be given on the Agency's work in this field.

The Conference attaches considerable importance to the consideration by the CCD, pursuant to United Nations General Assembly resolution 3261 D (XXIX) and taking due account of the views of the IAEA, of the arms control implications of nuclear explosions for peaceful purposes.

The Conference notes that the thirtieth session of the United Nations General Assembly will receive reports pursuant to United Nations General Assembly resolution 3261 D (XXIX) and will provide an opportunity for States to discuss questions related to the application of nuclear explosions for peaceful purposes. The Conference further notes that the results of discussion in the United Nations General Assembly at its thirtieth session will be available to be taken into account by the IAEA and the CCD for their further consideration.

REVIEW OF ARTICLE VI

The Conference recalls the provisions of Article VI of the Treaty under which all Parties undertook to pursue negotiations in good faith on effective measures relating

—to the cessation of the nuclear arms race at an early date and

—to nuclear disarmament and

—to a treaty on general and complete disarmament under strict and effective international control.

While welcoming the various agreements on arms limitation and disarmament elaborated and concluded over the last few years as steps contributing to the implementation of Article VI of the Treaty, the Conference expresses its serious concern that the arms race, in particular the nuclear arms race, is continuing unabated.

The Conference therefore urges constant and resolute efforts by each of the Parties to the Treaty, in particular by the nuclear-weapon States, to achieve an early and effective implementation of Article VI of the Treaty.

The Conference affirms the determination expressed in the preamble to the 1963 Partial Test Ban Treaty and reiterated in the preamble to the Non-Proliferation Treaty to achieve the discontinuance of all test explosions of nuclear weapons for all time. The Conference expresses the view that the conclusion of a treaty banning all nuclear weapons tests is one of the most important measures to halt the nuclear arms race. It expresses the hope that the nuclear-weapon States Party to the Treaty will take the lead in reaching an early solution of the technical and political difficulties on this issue. It appeals to these States to make every effort to reach agreement on the conclusion of an effective comprehensive test ban. To this end, the desire was expressed by a considerable number of delegations at the Conference that the nuclear-weapon States Party to the Treaty should as soon as possible enter into an agreement, open to all States and containing appropriate provisions to ensure its effectiveness, to halt all nuclear weapons tests of adhering States for a specified time, whereupon the terms of such an agreement would be reviewed in the light of the opportunity, at that time, to achieve a universal and permanent cessation of all nuclear weapons tests. The Conference calls upon the nuclear-weapon States signatories of the Treaty on the Limitation of Underground Nuclear Weapons tests, meanwhile, to limit the number of their underground nuclear weapons tests to a minimum. The Conference believes that such steps would constitute an incentive of particular value to negotiations for the conclusion of a treaty banning all nuclear weapons test explosions for all time.

The Conference appeals to the nuclear-weapon States Parties to the negotiations on the limitation of strategic arms to endeavour to conclude at the earliest possible date the new agreement that was outlined by their leaders in November 1974. The Conference looks forward to the commencement of follow-on negotiations on further limitations of, and significant reductions in, their nuclear weapons systems as soon as possible following the conclusion of such an agreement.

The Conference notes that, notwithstanding earlier progress, the CCD has recently been unable to reach agreement on new substantive measures to advance the objectives of Article VI of the Treaty. It urges, therefore, all members of the CCD Party to the Treaty, in particular the nuclear-weapon States Party, to increase their efforts to achieve effective disarmament agreements on all subjects on the agenda of the CCD.

The Conference expresses the hope that all States Party to the Treaty, through the United Nations and the CCD and other negotiations in which they participate, will work with determination towards the conclusion of arms limitation and disarmament agreements which will contribute to the goal of general and complete disarmament under strict and effective international control.

The Conference expresses the view that, disarmament being a matter of general concern, the provision of information to all governments and peoples on the situation in the field of the arms race and disarmament is of great importance for the attainment of the aims of Article VI. The Conference therefore invites the United Nations to consider ways and means of improving its existing facilities for collection, compilation and dissemination of information on disarmament issues, in order to keep all governments as well as world public opinion properly informed on progress achieved in the realization of the provisions of Article VI of the Treaty.

REVIEW OF ARTICLE VII AND THE SECURITY OF NON-NUCLEAR WEAPON STATES

Recognizing that all States have need to ensure their independence, territorial integrity and sovereignty, the Conference emphasizes the particular importance of assuring and strengthening the security of non-nuclear-weapon States Parties which have renounced the acquisition of nuclear weapons. It acknowledges that States Parties find themselves in different security situations and therefore that various appropriate means are necessary to meet the security concerns of States Parties.

The Conference underlines the importance of adherence to the Treaty by non-nuclear-weapon States as the best means of reassuring one another of their renunciation of nuclear weapons and as one of the effective means of strengthening their mutual security.

The Conference takes note of the continued determination of the Depositary States to honour their statements, which were welcomed by the United Nations Security Council in resolution 255 (1968), that, to ensure the security of the non-nuclear-weapon States Party to the Treaty, they will provide or support immediate assistance, in accordance with the Charter, to any non-nuclear-weapon State Party to the Treaty which is a victim of an act or an object of a threat of aggression in which nuclear weapons are used.

The Conference, bearing in mind Article VII of the Treaty, considers that the establishment of internationally recognized nuclear-weapon-free zones on the initiative and with the agreement of the directly concerned States of the zone, represents an effective means of curbing the spread of nuclear weapons, and could contribute significantly to the security of those States. It welcomes the steps which have been taken toward the establishment of such zones.

The Conference recognizes that for the maximum effectiveness of any Treaty arrangements for establishing a nuclear-weapon-free zone the cooperation of the nuclear-weapon States is necessary. At the Conference it was urged by a considerable number of delegations that nuclear-weapon States should provide, in an appropriate manner, binding security assurances to those States which become fully bound by the provisions of such regional arrangements.

At the Conference it was also urged that determined efforts must be made especially by the nuclear weapon States Party to the Treaty, to ensure the security of all non-nuclear-weapon States Parties. To this end the Conference urges all States, both nuclear-weapon States and non-nuclear-weapon States, to refrain, in accordance with the Charter of the United Nations, from the threat or the use of force in relations between States, involving either nuclear or non-nuclear weapons. Additionally, it stresses the responsibility of all Parties to the Treaty and especially the nuclear-weapon States, to take effective steps to strengthen the security of non-nuclear-weapon States and to promote in all appropriate fora the consideration of all practical means to this end, taking into account the views expressed at this Conference.

REVIEW OF ARTICLE VIII

The Conference invites States Party to the Treaty which are Members of the United Nations to request the Secretary-General of the United Nations to include the following item in the provisional agenda of the thirty-first session of the General Assembly: "Implementation of the conclusions of the first Review Conference of the Parties to the Treaty on the Non-Proliferation of Nuclear Weapons".

The States Party to the Treaty participating in the Conference propose to the Depositary Governments that a second Conference to review the operation of the Treaty be convened in 1980.

The Conference accordingly invites States Party to the Treaty which are Members of the United Nations to request the Secretary-General of the United Nations to include the following item in the provisional agenda of the thirty-third session of the General Assembly: "Implementation of the conclusions of the first Review Conference of the Parties to the Treaty on the Non-Proliferation of Nuclear Weapons and establishment of a preparatory committee for the second Conference."

REVIEW OF ARTICLE IX

The five years that have passed since the entry into force of the Treaty have demonstrated its wide international acceptance. The Conference welcomes the recent progress towards achieving wider adherence. At the same time, the Conference notes with concern that the Treaty has not as yet achieved universal adherence. Therefore, the Conference expresses the hope that States that have not already joined the Treaty should do so at the earliest possible date.

ANNEX II

Interpretative statements in connection with Final Declaration

MEXICO

The delegations of the States members of the Group of 77 Parties to the Treaty on the Non-Proliferation of Nuclear Weapons, taking part in the first Review Conference of the Parties to the Treaty, wish to place on record in the final document of the Conference that they have agreed not to oppose the consensus required in accordance with the rules of procedure for the adoption of the final declaration of the Conference, as a token of their great appreciation for the praiseworthy and unceasing endeavours of the President of the Conference, to whom we owe the preparation of the draft declaration (NPT/CONF/30/Rev.1), and on the condition *sine qua non* that the text of the present interpretative statement and the texts of the three draft resolutions NPT/CONF/L.2/Rev.1, NPT/CONF/L.3/Rev.1 and NPT/CONF/L.4/Rev.1, together with their annexed Working Papers NPT/CONF/17, NPT/CONF/18 and NPT/CONF/22 respectively, as well as documents NPT/CONF/C.I/L.1, NPT/CONF/C.I/L.2, NPT/CONF/C.I/L.3, NPT/CONF/C.II/L.1 and NPT/CONF/C.II/L.2, are reproduced in full in the final document, immediately following the text of the final declaration. The delegations I referred to earlier likewise wish to place on record that the relevant provisions of the declaration, particularly those relating to the implementation of the tenth preambular paragraph and to Article VI of the Treaty on the Non-Proliferation of Nuclear Weapons and to the need to safeguard the security of non-nuclear-weapon States Parties to the Treaty must, as regards the position of those delegations with respect to such provisions, be interpreted in the light of the content of the three Working Papers, NPT/CONF/17, NPT/CONF/18 and NPT/CONF/22 and of the other documents enumerated above.

BOLIVIA, ECUADOR, GHANA, HONDURAS, JAMAICA, LEBANON, LIBERIA, MEXICO, MOROCCO, NEPAL, NICARAGUA, NIGERIA, PERU, PHILIPPINES, ROMANIA, SENEGAL, SUDAN, SYRIAN ARAB REPUBLIC, YUGOSLAVIA AND ZAIRE

Draft resolution

(Document NPT/CONF/L.2/Rev.1)

The Review Conference of the Parties to the Treaty on the Non-Proliferation of Nuclear Weapons,

Noting the reiteration in the preamble of the Treaty on the Non-Proliferation of Nuclear Weapons of the determination proclaimed since 1963 in the Partial Test Ban Treaty to "achieve the discontinuance of all test explosions of nuclear weapons for all time",

Convinced that one of the most effective measures for strengthening the Treaty on the Non-Proliferation of Nuclear Weapons and promoting universal adherence to it would be to put into practice that determination,

Taking into account that the delegations of Bolivia, Ecuador, Ghana, Honduras, Jamaica, Lebanon, Liberia, Mexico, Morocco, Nepal, Nicaragua, Nigeria, Peru, Philippines, Romania, Sudan, Syria, Yugoslavia and Zaire have submitted to the Conference working paper NPT/CONF/17*, annexed to the present resolution, containing a draft additional protocol to the Treaty on the Non-Proliferation of Nuclear Weapons concerning nuclear weapon tests, with a view to establishing procedures

which, in the opinion of its co-sponsors, would facilitate the attainment of the permanent cessation of all test explosions of nuclear weapons,

Noting that it would be desirable that all States Party to the Treaty may examine this proposal and that over one third of them have been unable to send representatives to the Conference,

1. *Endorses* the aim of contributing to the attainment of the permanent cessation of all test explosions of nuclear weapons pursued by the draft additional protocol to the Treaty on the Non-Proliferation of Nuclear Weapons contained in working paper NPT/CONF/17* annexed to this resolution;

2. *Requests* the President of the Conference to transmit, through its Secretary-General, the present resolution with its annex to all States Party to the Treaty on the Non-Proliferation of Nuclear Weapons, in order that they may give it due consideration;

3. *Recommends* to those States to bear in mind the conclusions they may reach as a result of such consideration when they examine, at the thirty-first session of the General Assembly, the item: "Implementation of the decisions adopted by the first Review Conference of the Parties to the Treaty on the Non-Proliferation of Nuclear Weapons".

ANNEX

Working Paper Containing a Draft Additional Protocol to the Treaty on the Non-Proliferation of Nuclear Weapons Regarding Nuclear Weapon Tests

Introductory note

In its resolution 2373 (XXII) of 12 June 1968, the General Assembly of the United Nations expressed *inter alia* "the hope for the widest possible adherence to the Treaty" on the Non-Proliferation of Nuclear Weapons.

That hope was undoubtedly based on the conviction stated in unequivocal terms in the penultimate preambular paragraph of the same resolution in which the Assembly declared itself "convinced" that "an agreement to prevent the further proliferation of nuclear weapons must be followed as soon as possible by effective measures on the cessation of the nuclear arms race and on nuclear disarmament, and that the non-proliferation treaty will contribute to this aim".

To the foregoing one must add a whole series of facts which are equally pertinent in this regard, some of the most outstanding of which are recalled here:

That the Non-Proliferation Treaty itself has reiterated in its preamble the determination, proclaimed since 1963 in the Moscow Treaty, "to achieve the discontinuance of all test explosions of nuclear weapons for all time";

That in four of its very numerous resolutions on this

question, the Assembly has "condemned" with the utmost vigour all nuclear weapon tests, in whatever environment they may be conducted;

That the Assembly itself has repeatedly expressed the conviction that, "whatever may be the differences on the question of verification, there is no valid reason for delaying the conclusion of a comprehensive test ban";

That it is also the Assembly, the most representative body of the international community, which has affirmed, in its most recent resolution—3257 (XXIX) of 9 December 1974—on this subject, that "the continuance of nuclear weapon testing will intensify the arms race, thus increasing the danger of nuclear war";

That, as the Secretary-General of the United Nations emphatically stated more than three years ago, in his first address to the Conference of the Committee on Disarmament, on 20 February 1972: "All the technical and scientific aspects of the problem have been so fully explored that only a political decision is now necessary in order to achieve final agreement".

The inevitable conclusion which, in the opinion of the delegations co-sponsoring this working paper, is to be drawn from facts such as those just recalled is that one of the most effective measures for strengthening the Non-Proliferation Treaty and for promoting universal adherence to it would be that the three nuclear-weapon States, which are not only Parties to the Treaty but act as its depositaries as well, demonstrate their readiness to support with tangible deeds the provisions of the Treaty's preamble regarding the cessation of nuclear weapon tests.

For this reason the sponsoring delegations believe that they are making a positive contribution to the work of the Conference in submitting to it a draft "Additional Protocol I" on this subject. They are also convinced that the entry into force of the proposed instrument would in no way undermine the security of the depositary States, since the extent of the lead in nuclear war technology and the enormity of the nuclear arsenals of the USSR and the United States of America are such that, even if they were to suspend all nuclear weapon tests for half a century, it is absolutely certain that they would continue to maintain an indisputable superiority. As if this were not sufficient, the Treaty's provisions regarding withdrawal, which would apply as well to the Protocol, would give each of the Parties the right to withdraw from the Protocol, "in exercising its national sovereignty", should any of them reach the conclusion that, at a given moment, the supreme interests of its country require it. On the other hand, it is equally certain that a Protocol such as the one proposed would constitute an incentive of particular value in order to prompt the other nuclear-weapon States to commit themselves to put an end to all of their tests with such weapons.

The text of the draft Protocol which, basing themselves on the foregoing considerations, the sponsoring delegations submit to the Conference is the following:

Additional Protocol I to the Treaty on the Non-Proliferation of Nuclear Weapons

The Depositary Governments of the Treaty on the Non-Proliferation of Nuclear Weapons, referred to in this Protocol as "the Treaty",

Conscious that universal, or at least the widest possible, adherence to the Treaty will contribute to avoid an increase in the danger of nuclear war,

Convinced that one of the most effective procedures for attaining such adherence would be the implementation of the provisions of the Preamble of the Treaty reiterating the determination, proclaimed since 1963 in the Moscow Treaty, to achieve "the discontinuance of all test explosions of nuclear weapons for all time",

Have agreed as follows:

Article 1. They undertake to decree the suspension of all their underground nuclear weapon tests for a period of ten years, as soon as the number of Parties to the Treaty reaches one hundred.

Article 2. They undertake also to extend by three years the moratorium contemplated in the preceding article, each time that five additional States become Parties to the Treaty.

Article 3. They undertake to transform the moratorium into a permanent cessation of all nuclear weapon tests, through the conclusion of a multilateral treaty for that purpose, as soon as the other nuclear weapon States indicate their willingness to become parties to said treaty.

Article 4 This Protocol will be of the same duration as the Treaty. Nevertheless the provisions of the latter's Article X regarding withdrawal shall apply to it.

Article 5. This Protocol shall be subject to ratification by the three Depositary States of the Treaty to which it is open for signature and shall enter into force on the date that the instruments of ratification of two of them are received by the Secretary-General of the United Nations who shall be the depositary of the Protocol.

BOLIVIA, ECUADOR, GHANA, HONDURAS, JAMAICA, LEBANON, LIBERIA, MEXICO, MOROCCO, NEPAL, NICARAGUA, NIGERIA, PERU, ROMANIA, SENEGAL, SUDAN, SYRIAN ARAB REPUBLIC, YUGOSLAVIA AND ZAIRE

Draft resolution

(Document NPT/CONF/L.3/Rev.1)

The Review Conference of the Parties to the Treaty on the Non-Proliferation of Nuclear Weapons,

Recalling the provisions of article VI of the Treaty

on the Non-Proliferation of Nuclear Weapons whereby each of the Parties to the Treaty has undertaken *inter alia* "to pursue negotiations in good faith on effective measures relating to cessation of the nuclear arms race at an early date and to nuclear disarmament",

Convinced that one of the most effective measures for strengthening the Treaty and promoting universal adherence to it would be the achievement of tangible results in the field of nuclear disarmament,

Taking into account that the delegations of Bolivia, Ecuador, Ghana, Honduras, Jamaica, Lebanon, Liberia, Mexico, Morocco, Nepal, Nicaragua, Nigeria, Peru, Romania, Sudan, Syrian Arab Republic, Yugoslavia and Zaire have submitted to the Conference working paper NPT/CONF/18*, annexed to the present resolution, containing a draft additional protocol to the Treaty concerning nuclear disarmament, with a view to establishing procedures which, in the opinion of its co-sponsors, would facilitate the achievement at an early date of some important measures of nuclear disarmament,

Noting that it would be desirable that all States Party to the Treaty may examine this proposal and that over one third of them have been unable to send representatives to the Conference,

1. *Endorses* the aim of contributing to the attainment of effective measures towards the cessation of the nuclear arms race at an early date and to nuclear disarmament pursued by the draft additional protocol to the Treaty on the Non-Proliferation of Nuclear Weapons contained in working paper NPT/CONF/18* annexed to this resolution;

2. *Requests* the President of the Conference to transmit, through its Secretary-General, the present resolution with its annex to all States Party to the Treaty on the Non-Proliferation of Nuclear Weapons, in order that they may give it due consideration;

3. *Recommends* to those States to bear in mind the conclusions they may reach as a result of such consideration when they examine, at the thirty-first session of the General Assembly, the item: "Implementation of the decisions adopted by the first Review Conference of the Parties to the Treaty on the Non-Proliferation of Nuclear Weapons".

ANNEX

Working Paper containing a Draft Additional Protocol to the Treaty on the Non-Proliferation of Nuclear Weapons Regarding the Implementation of its Article VI

Introductory note

In its resolution 2373 (XXII) of 12 June 1968, the General Assembly of the United Nations expressed *inter alia* "the hope for the widest possible adherence to the Treaty" on the Non-Proliferation of Nuclear Weapons.

That hope was undoubtedly based on the conviction stated in unequivocal terms in the penultimate preambular paragraph of the same resolution in which the Assembly declared itself "convinced" that "an agreement to prevent the further proliferation of nuclear weapons must be followed as soon as possible by effective measures on the cessation of the nuclear arms race and on nuclear disarmament, and that the non-proliferation treaty will contribute to this aim".

It was no doubt for this same reason that the Treaty itself contains an article—article VI—aimed at reaffirming the Assembly's conviction referred to by providing that:

"Each of the Parties to the Treaty undertakes to pursue negotiations in good faith on effective measures relating to cessation of the nuclear arms race at an early date and to nuclear disarmament, and on a treaty on general and complete disarmament under strict and effective international control."

If, as set forth in the Treaty's article VIII, the basic objective of this Conference is to review how "the purposes of the Preamble and the provisions of the Treaty" have been, and are being, realized, the inevitable conclusions to be drawn from any objective analysis of reality are, with regard to the above-mentioned article, not only extremely disappointing but truly alarming. The nuclear arms race, far from ceasing as contemplated in the Treaty's article VI, has been stepped up in such a manner that it has given rise to the situation known as overkill. Implicit in such a situation is the constant threat of a nuclear holocaust, as shown by the two grave crises which in 1962 and 1973 gave rise to a general alert.

The imminence of this danger appears to have begun to find its way even in the highest political levels. Thus during the last session of the General Assembly, the Minister for Foreign Affairs of one of the two most powerful nuclear-weapon States stated emphatically:

"Stable and lasting peace is incompatible with the arms race. They are antipodes. One cannot seriously think of eliminating the threat of war, while at the same time increasing military budgets and endlessly building up armaments . . . The supreme interests not only of the peoples of the Soviet Union and the United States, but also of the peoples of the whole world require that the Soviet Union and the United States, possessing the colossal might of nuclear weapons, should make every effort to achieve appropriate understandings and agreements".

To date the only results which the Treaty's depositary States can point to regarding their commitment under article VI are the meagre ones obtained in the bilateral negotiations on the limitation of strategic nuclear-weapon systems (SALT) which have been going on for some years. If in the international sphere those negotiations have had some beneficial consequences of a political and psychological nature, their very modest scope as disarmament measures has in practice appeared to be of no account. This has prompted the Assembly to urge the Union of Soviet Socialist Republics and the United States repeatedly, as it did in its latest resolution in this regard—resolution 3261 C (XXIX) of 9 December 1974—to broaden the scope and accelerate the pace of their negotiations, stressing anew "the necessity and urgency of reaching agreement on important qualitative limitations and substantial reductions of their strategic nuclear-weapon systems as a positive step towards nuclear disarmament".

In the light of the foregoing, it is axiomatic that one of the most effective measures for strengthening the Non-Proliferation Treaty and for promoting universal adherence to it would be that the two States possessing by far the largest nuclear arsenals in existence demonstrate their readiness to support with tangible deeds the provisions of the Treaty's article VI relating to the cessation of the nuclear arms race and to nuclear disarmament.

For this reason the sponsoring delegations believe that they are making a positive contribution to the work of the Conference in submitting to it a draft "Additional Protocol II" on this subject. They are also convinced that the entry into force of the proposed instrument could not undermine the security of those two depositary States. On the one hand, the reductions suggested would in no way affect the system on which are based the proportions that they freely accepted in the Vladivostok accords. On the other hand, the extent of their lead in nuclear war technology and the enormity of their nuclear arsenals are such that, even after they had carried out the parity reductions called for in the Additional Protocol, the number of nuclear weapons and of delivery vehicles which each one would maintain would still be much superior to that which might be at the disposal of all of the other nuclear-weapon States taken together. As if this were not sufficient, the Treaty's provisions regarding withdrawal, which would apply as well to the Protocol, would give each of the Parties the right to withdraw from the Protocol, "in exercising its national sovereignty", should either of them reach the conclusion that, at a given moment, the supreme interests of its country require it. Moreover, it should be borne in mind that a Protocol such as the one proposed would constitute an incentive of particular value in order to prompt the other nuclear-weapon States to adopt measures for reductions similar to those set forth in it.

The text of the draft Protocol which, basing themselves on the foregoing considerations, the sponsoring delegations submit to the Conference is the following:

Additional Protocol II to the Treaty on the Non-Proliferation of Nuclear Weapons

The Depositary Governments of the Treaty on the Non-Proliferation of Nuclear Weapons referred to in this Protocol as "the Treaty"—which participate in the bilateral negotiations on the limitation of strategic nuclear-weapon systems (SALT),

Conscious that universal, or at least the widest possible, adherence to the Treaty will contribute to avoid an increase in the danger of nuclear war,

Convinced that one of the most effective procedures for attaining such adherence would be the parallel achievement of tangible results relating to nuclear disarmament,

Bearing in mind that in the accords reached at Vladivostok in November of 1974 both Governments agreed that each side would be entitled to have an aggregate maximum of 2,400 intercontinental ballistic missiles, submarine-launched ballistic missiles and heavy bombers, and that only 1,320 of the ballistic missiles may be equipped with multiple independently targetable warheads (MIRVs),

Have agreed as follows:

Article 1. They solemnly reaffirm the obligations undertaken in article VI of the Treaty to pursue "negotiations in good faith on effective measures relating to cessation of the nuclear arms race at an early date and to nuclear disarmament".

Article 2. They undertake, as soon as the number of Parties to the Treaty has reached one hundred:

(a) To reduce by fifty per cent the ceiling of 2,400 nuclear strategic delivery vehicles contemplated for each side under the Vladivostok accords;

(b) To reduce likewise by fifty per cent the ceiling of 1,320 strategic ballistic missiles which, under those accords, each side may equip with multiple independently targetable warheads (MIRVs).

Article 3. They also undertake, once such reductions have been carried out, to reduce by ten per cent the ceilings of 1,200 strategic nuclear delivery vehicles and of 660 strategic ballistic missiles that may be equipped with multiple independently targetable warheads (MIRVs), each time that ten additional States become Parties to the Treaty.

Article 4. This Protocol will be of the same duration as the Treaty. Nevertheless the provisions of the latter's article X regarding withdrawal shall apply to it.

Article 5. This Protocol shall be subject to ratification by the two States to which it is open for signature and shall enter into force on the date both instruments of ratification have been received by the Secretary-General of the United Nations who shall be the depositary of the Protocol.

BOLIVIA, ECUADOR, GHANA, MEXICO, NIGERIA, PERU, ROMANIA, SENEGAL, SUDAN, YUGO-SLAVIA AND ZAIRE

Draft resolution

(Document NPT/CONF/L.4/Rev.1)

The Review Conference of the Parties to the Treaty on the Non-Proliferation of Nuclear Weapons,

Reiterating the provisions of the first preambular paragraph of the Treaty on the non-proliferation of nuclear weapons to the effect that every effort should be made in order to take measures to safeguard the security of peoples,

Taking into account resolution 3261 G (XXIX) adopted unanimously by the United Nations General Assembly which considered that it is imperative for the international community to devise effective measures in order to ensure the security of non-nuclear-weapon States and recommend *inter alia* to Member States to consider in all appropriate forums, without loss of time, the question of strengthening the security of non-nuclear-weapon States,

Convinced that one of the most effective measures for strengthening the Treaty on Non-Proliferation of Nuclear Weapons and promoting universal adherence to it would be to establish a system of security assurances within the framework of the Treaty,

Taking into account that the delegations of Bolivia, Ecuador, Ghana, Mexico, Nigeria, Peru, Romania, Sudan, Yugoslavia and Zaire have submitted to the Conference Working Paper NPT/CONF/22, annexed to the present resolution, containing a draft additional protocol to the Treaty on the Non-Proliferation of Nuclear Weapons which in the opinion of its co-sponsors would facilitate the establishment of a system of security assurances within the framework of the Treaty,

Noting that it would be desirable that all States Party to the Treaty may examine this proposal and that over a third of them have been unable to send representatives to the Conference,

1. *Endorses* the aim of contributing to the ensuring and strengthening of the security of non-nuclear-weapon States Parties to the Treaty on the Non-Proliferation of Nuclear Weapons which have renounced the acquisition of nuclear weapons pursued by the draft additional protocol to the Treaty on the Non-Proliferation of Nuclear Weapons contained in Working Paper NPT/CONF/22* annexed to this resolution;

2. *Requests* the President of the Conference to transmit, through its Secretary-General, the present resolution with its annex to all States Party to the Treaty on the Non-Proliferation of Nuclear Weapons, in order that they may give it due consideration;

3. *Recommends* to those States to bear in mind the conclusions they may reach as a result of such consideration when they examine, at the thirty-first session of the General Assembly, the item: "Implementation of the decisions adopted by the first Review Conference of the Parties to the Treaty on the Non-Proliferation of Nuclear Weapons".

ANNEX

Working Paper containing a Draft Additional Protocol to the Treaty on the Non-Proliferation of Nuclear Weapons Regarding the Establishment of a System of Security Assurances within the Framework of the Treaty

Introductory note

It is generally accepted that the non-nuclear-weapon States, by renouncing to acquire such weapons in accordance with Articles II and III of the Treaty, have the right to have their independence, territorial integrity and sovereignty guaranteed against the use or threat of use of nuclear weapons.

On the other hand, the acceleration of the arms race and the accumulation of a great amount of arms during the period since the entry into force of the Treaty have led to the increase of the degree of insecurity in the world.

Resolution 255 (1968) of the Security Council relates to the possible action to be taken by the Security Council only when a nuclear attack has occurred. It does not offer, therefore, appropriate assurances for the prevention of the use or of the threat of use of nuclear weapons.

Finally, it should be borne in mind, in connection with this matter, that the United Nations General Assembly in its Declaration of 24 November 1961 solemnly proclaimed that the use of nuclear and thermo-nuclear weapons is contrary to the rules of international law and to the laws of humanity.

For the above reasons the sponsoring delegations believe that they are making a positive contribution to the work of the Conference in submitting to it the following draft:

Additional Protocol III to the Treaty on the Non-Proliferation of Nuclear Weapons

The Depositary Governments of the Treaty on the Non-Proliferation of Nuclear Weapons, referred to in this Protocol as "The Treaty",

Recalling that, according to the Charter of the United Nations, the States have the obligation to refrain in their international relations from the threat or use of force against the territorial integrity or political independence of any State, or in any other manner inconsistent with the purposes of the United Nations,

Taking into account resolution 3261 G (XXIX) which considered *inter alia* that it is imperative for the international community to devise effective measures in order to ensure the security of non-nuclear-weapon States,

Recognizing that the effectiveness of the Treaty, its viability and universality depend, to a great extent, on its balanced character and on the existence of appropriate assurances for the States which have consented, by virtue of the Treaty, to renounce acquiring or manufacturing nuclear weapons,

Have agreed as follows:

Article 1.   They solemnly undertake

(a) never and under no circumstances to use or threaten to use nuclear weapons against non-nuclear-weapon States Parties to the Treaty whose territories are completely free from nuclear weapons, and

(b) to refrain from first use of nuclear weapons against any other non-nuclear-weapon States Parties to the Treaty.

Article 2.   They undertake to encourage negotiations initiated by any group of States Parties to the Treaty or others to establish nuclear-weapon-free zones in their respective territories or regions, and to respect the statute of nuclear-weapon-free zones established.

Article 3.   In the event a non-nuclear-weapon State Party to the Treaty becomes a victim of an attack with nuclear weapons or of a threat with the use of such weapons, the States Parties to this Protocol, at the request of the victim of such threat or attack, undertake to provide to it immediate assistance without prejudice to their obligations under the United Nations Charter.

Article 4.   This Protocol will be of the same duration as the Treaty. Nevertheless, the provisions of the latter's Article X regarding withdrawal shall apply to it.

Article 5.   This Protocol shall be subject to ratification by the three Depositary States of the Treaty to which it is open for signature and shall enter into force on the date that the instruments of ratification of two of them are received by the Secretary-General of the United Nations who shall be the depositary of the Protocol.

GHANA, NEPAL, NIGERIA, ROMANIA, YUGOSLAVIA

Draft resolution

(Document NPT/CONF/C.I/L.1)

The Review Conference of the Parties to the Treaty on the Non-Proliferation of Nuclear Weapons,

Recalling General Assembly resolution 2661 A (XXV) of 1970 by which it urged the Governments of nuclear-weapon Powers to bring about an immediate halt in the nuclear arms race and to cease all testing as well as deployment of offensive and defensive nuclear-weapon systems,

Taking into account that peace and security in the world cannot be maintained unless an immediate stop is put to the nuclear arms race followed by nuclear disarmament,

Convinced that only the nuclear-weapon States can stop vertical proliferation of nuclear weapons which would substantially contribute towards preventing their horizontal proliferation as well,

Noting with satisfaction that the non-nuclear-weapon States Party to the Treaty have been faithfully abiding by the spirit and letter of Articles II and III of the Treaty on the Non-Proliferation of Nuclear Weapons,

Deeply convinced that the halting of the nuclear arms race and the undertaking of further measures of nuclear disarmament would significantly enhance the creation of essential conditions for the establishment of nuclear-weapon-free zones,

1. *Invites* the nuclear-weapon States Party to the Treaty to initiate, as soon as possible but not later than the end of 1976, negotiations on the conclusion of a treaty on the withdrawal from the territories of the non-nuclear-weapon States Party to the Treaty of all nuclear-weapon delivery systems, especially tactical nuclear weapons;

2. *Requests* the nuclear-weapon States Party to the Treaty to immediately discontinue further deployment of all types of tactical and other nuclear-weapon-delivery systems within the territories of the non-nuclear-weapon States Party to the Treaty and to simultaneously commence with their gradual withdrawal pending the entry into force of the aforementioned treaty;

3. *Invites* also the non-nuclear-weapon States Party to the Treaty on whose territories, waterways or air space the nuclear-weapon delivery systems are deployed not to allow the use or threat of use of nuclear weapons against other non-nuclear-weapon States Party to the Treaty.

IRAN

Draft resolution on Article VII of the Treaty on the Non-Proliferation of Nuclear Weapons

(Document NPT/CONF/C.I/L.2)

The Review Conference of the Parties to the Treaty on the Non-Proliferation of Nuclear Weapons,

Considering that article VII of the Treaty on the Non-Proliferation of Nuclear Weapons stresses the right of any group of States to conclude regional treaties to assure the total absence of nuclear weapons in their respective territories;

Recognizing that the establishment of internationally recognized nuclear weapon-free zones in appropriate regions of the world on the initiative of States directly concerned represent a most effective means to curb the spread of nuclear weapons;

Recognizing in this connection the particular value of the Treaty on the Prohibition of Nuclear Weapons in Latin America (Treaty of Tlatelolco) and its Additional Protocols;

Recalling the Declaration on Denuclearization of Africa by the Assembly of Heads of State and Government of the Organization of African Unity in July 1964 and resolutions 1652 (XVI) of 24 November 1961, 2033 (XX) of 3 December 1965 and 3261 E (XXIX) of 9 December 1974 of the United Nations General Assembly on the same subject;

Recalling resolution 3263 (XXIX) of 9 December 1974 of the United Nations General Assembly on the Establishment of a Nuclear Weapon-Free Zone in the region of the Middle East;

Recalling resolution 3265 (XXIX) of 9 December 1974 of the United Nations on the Declaration and Establishment of a Nuclear-Free Zone in South Asia;

Recalling further the United Nations General Assembly resolution 3261 F (XXIX) of 9 December 1974 in which the Assembly decided to undertake a comprehensive study of the question of nuclear weapon-free zones in all its aspects;

Noting that in implementation of this decision a group of governmental experts has been set up to carry out this study under the auspices of the Conference of the Committee on Disarmament,

1. *Invites* the Parties to the Treaty and in particular the nuclear weapon States to cooperate with the States in appropriate regions of the world which decide to establish nuclear weapon-free zones, under effective conditions and an adequate system of safeguards, in order to assure the total absence of such weapons in their respective territories,

2. *Urges* the nuclear-weapon States to undertake a solemn obligation never to use or threaten to use nuclear weapons against countries which have become Parties to and are fully bound by the provisions of such regional arrangements.

ROMANIA

Draft resolution on Article VI

(Document NPT/CONF/C.I/L.3)

The Review Conference of the Parties to the Treaty on the Non-Proliferation of Nuclear Weapons,

Recalling the obligations assumed by each of the Parties to the Treaty under its Article VI, to pursue negotiations in good faith on effective measures relating to cessation of the nuclear arms race at an early date and to nuclear disarmament and on a Treaty on general and complete disarmament under strict and effective international control,

Recalling further General Assembly resolution 2373 (XXII) of 12 June 1968 by which it expressed, *inter alia*, the conviction "that an agreement to prevent the further proliferation of nuclear weapons must be followed as soon as possible by effective measures on the cessation of the nuclear arms race and on nuclear disarmament" and it requested the then existing Conference of the Eighteen-Nation Committee on Disarmament and the Nuclear-Weapon States urgently to pursue negotiations to that end,

Deeply concerned that during the period since the entry into force of the Treaty the nuclear arms race has, nevertheless, continued at an accelerated pace, resulting in accumulation of a great amount of nuclear weapons in the world,

Reaffirming the role of the Conference of the Committee on Disarmament in the negotiation of those effective measures relating to the cessation of the nuclear arms race at an early date and to nuclear disarmament and of a Treaty on general and complete disarmament under strict and effective international control, which have been referred to in Article VI of the Treaty,

Mindful of the importance of the cooperation of governments and all media in the attainment of the objectives of the Treaty,

1. *Requests* all Governments Party to the Treaty on the Non-Proliferation of Nuclear Weapons which are members of the Conference of the Committee on Disarmament, particularly the Depositary Governments, to bring their decisive contribution, in conformity with the obligations assumed by them under Article VI of the Treaty, to developing within the Conference the necessary conditions which would enable it to effectively deal with the measures provided in Article VI of the Treaty as follows:

(a) to offer the disarmament negotiations the required perspective in achieving the aims of Article VI of the Treaty most urgently, by a comprehensive approach to the matters relating to cessation of the nuclear arms race and nuclear disarmament and to a Treaty on general and complete disarmament under strict and effective international control,

(b) to continuously review the operation and the methods of work of the Conference to assure that the negotiations are conducted in the most efficient manner, fully compatible with the principles of equality and the security and the interests of all States;

2. *Considers it necessary* that a system of retrieval and distribution as well as of assessment and analysis of information on armaments and disarmament issues be established within the United Nations in order to keep properly informed all governments, as well as international public opinion, of the progress achieved in the realization of the provisions of Article VI of the Treaty.

GHANA, MEXICO, NIGERIA, PERU, PHILIPPINES, ROMANIA SYRIAN ARAB REPUBLIC AND YUGOSLAVIA

Draft resolution

(Document NPT/CONF/C.II/L.1)

The Review Conference of the Parties to the Treaty on the Non-Proliferation of Nuclear Weapons,

Reaffirming the provisions of article V of the Treaty on the Non-Proliferation of Nuclear Weapons, according to which non-nuclear-weapon States Party to the Treaty shall be able to obtain the "potential benefits from any peaceful applications of nuclear explosions" under the favourable conditions described therein,

Recalling that the same article provides for the obtainment of such benefits "pursuant to a special international agreement or agreements" and that "negotiations on this subject shall commence as soon as possible after the Treaty enters into force",

Taking into account the authoritative interpretation which, at the 1577th meeting of the First Committee of the United Nations General Assembly, held on 31 May 1968, the representatives of the Union of Soviet Socialist Republics and the United States of America gave to the above-mentioned provisions, as evidenced in Conference document NPT/CONF/14 of 24 February 1975,

Noting that, although five years have elapsed since the Treaty entered into force, the pertinent negotiations have yet to begin,

Urges the Depositary Governments of the Treaty on the Non-Proliferation of Nuclear Weapons to initiate immediate consultations with all of the other States Party to the Treaty in order to reach agreement on the most appropriate place and date for holding a meeting of the Parties in order to conclude the basic special international agreement contemplated in article V of that Treaty.

MEXICO, NIGERIA, REPUBLIC OF KOREA AND THE PHILIPPINES

Draft resolution

(Document NPT/CONF/C.II/L.2)

The Review Conference of the Parties to the Treaty on the Non-Proliferation of Nuclear Weapons,

Convinced of the common responsibilities of Parties to the Treaty for the effective implementation of the principle that the benefits of peaceful applications of nuclear energy, including any technological by-products which may be derived from the development of nuclear explosive devices, shall be made available for peaceful purposes to all Parties to the Treaty,

Convinced further that, in furtherance of the effective implementation of this principle, all Parties to the Treaty should participate in the fullest possible exchange of materials, equipment and scientific and technological information, and to contribute through international cooperation to the further development of the application of atomic energy for peaceful purposes,

Conscious of the need in particular of developing countries to obtain technology of all types, including nuclear technology, at low costs and on fair terms of transfer, in order to promote their economic and social development, thus strengthening international peace and security,

Taking note of the activity so far undertaken by the International Atomic Energy Agency with a view to facilitating the international cooperation in the field of the peaceful uses of nuclear energy, provided in Article IV of the Treaty,

Hoping that the nuclear-weapon States Parties to the Treaty would make available, through the International Atomic Energy Agency, part of the fissionable material resulting from the measures of nuclear disarmament to the non-nuclear-weapon States Parties to the Treaty.

1. *Decides,*

(a) that preferential treatment and concessional terms shall be provided by the Parties to the Treaty to developing non-nuclear-weapon States Parties to the Treaty in the supply of equipment, material and scientific and technological information for the peaceful uses of nuclear energy which would include, *inter alia*, fissionable material and the related service in the nuclear fuel cycle;

(b) that a Special Fund be established for the provision of technical assistance in the peaceful uses of nuclear energy to developing non-nuclear-weapon States Parties to the Treaty. This Fund, which shall also be utilized for the provision of nuclear research facilities including research reactors and fuel needed for the continuing operation of research reactors in developing non-nuclear-weapon States Parties to the Treaty, shall be maintained at an adequate level to meet the required needs. The Depositary States shall contribute 60 per cent of the Fund and the developed non-nuclear-weapon States Parties to the Treaty shall provide the balance. The schedule for the division of costs for the present Review Conference, appropriately pro-rated, shall serve as the basis for determining the contribution to this Fund of each respective State Party to the Treaty. The International Atomic Energy Agency shall be entrusted with the administration and management of the Fund which shall not form part of the regular or operational budgets of the Agency;

(c) that a Special Nuclear Fund be established to provide financing under concessional terms for the nuclear projects in the territories of developing non-nuclear-weapon States Parties to the Treaty. The Fund shall be kept at a reasonable minimum annual level and contributions to this Fund shall be assessed in the same manner as the Special Fund referred to under paragraph 1(b) above. These amounts shall be administered on an ad hoc basis by an international organization or an existing regional financing institution located in Africa, Asia or Latin America, to be designated by the donor country with the agreement of the recipient country;

2. *Decides further* that preferential treatment shall be provided by the Parties to the Treaty to developed non-nuclear weapon States Parties to the Treaty in the supply of equipment, materials and scientific and technological information for the peaceful uses of nuclear energy, which would include, *inter alia*, the supply of uranium and enrichment and re-processing services.

GERMAN DEMOCRATIC REPUBLIC

On behalf of the delegations of the People's Republic of Bulgaria, the Hungarian People's Republic, the Mongolian People's Republic, the People's Republic of Poland, the Czechoslovakian Socialist Republic and on behalf of my own delegation, I would like to declare that these delegations fully support the statement made by the Delegation of the Union of Soviet Socialist Republics, in particular as to the contents of the Final Declaration.

We came to this Conference with the determination to strengthen the non-proliferation regime and thus to contribute to the cause of disarmament and arms limitation.

The aim of the Conference was to strengthen the Treaty and to make it still more effective. In this constructive spirit we participated in this Conference and worked together with other delegations. We believe that the Declaration which was adopted by the Conference will promote this aim. In the course of the Conference, evident proof of the fact has been furnished that the Treaty has become an irreversible and extraordinary positive reality of international life. The Treaty has not only proved to be advantageous for the Parties to it, but also corresponds to the interests of all peoples and States.

The fact that immediately before as well as during the Conference some ten other States have acceded to the Treaty, thus demonstrating their agreement with the

Treaty, is also evidence of its continued attractiveness. We express the hope that countries still outside the Treaty will join us in order to strengthen peace and international security.

I ask you, Madame President, to include this statement in the Final Document

FEDERAL REPUBLIC OF GERMANY

The Delegation of the Federal Republic of Germany welcomes that consensus could be reached on the general declaration. At the conclusion of the Conference, we want to put the following statement on the record of this Conference to be included in the appropriate Annex of the final document:

—We support the recommendations of the final declaration and will, within the framework of our possibilities, work for their implementation;

—The Federal Republic of Germany considers the Treaty to be a necessary and important instrument for the maintenance of peace;

—It is, therefore, the strong belief of my Government that security and world peace would best be served if all States became members to the NPT;

—We repeat the hope expressed in our opening statement that all States members to the NPT submit their peaceful nuclear activities to IAEA safeguards;

—The text of the final declaration can be regarded as encouraging in this respect;

—My delegation is satisfied that the Conference has endorsed the standard export requirements introduced by the vast majority of the supplier countries of nuclear material or equipment, and wishes to reiterate its firm resolve to strengthen and to broaden common export safeguards requirements in the future, by a gradual process and with the objective of non-proliferation firmly in mind;

—The paragraphs in the declaration relating to Article IV also meet with our approval, although some delegations, including mine, had to make certain concessions in negotiating these texts. I want to take this opportunity to emphasize that, in our view, Article IV is too often misconstrued as merely a device for establishing new development assistance funds. In reality it is the charter of the universal exchange of knowledge in the nuclear realm.

IRAN

Our aim in this Conference has been to reach consensus. We had sought to achieve two objectives:

(i) To review the NPT after five years: come to an agreement on its implementation, discuss its strengths and weaknesses in the light of technological and political transformations and

(ii) To reaffirm our commitment to the NPT as an extremely important means of controlling proliferation.

Now, in affirming our support of the NPT we have sought to show its success and demonstrate our solidarity to those States which, for their own reasons, have chosen not to adhere to the Treaty as yet. Now the *type* of consensus, that is the *content* of the consensus that we have sought to achieve here in the past four weeks, has been extremely important.

In seeking to achieve a realistic consensus by emphasizing the content of the consensus as much as the achievement of *any* consensus—we have sought to demonstrate the vitality of the NPT regime to those States presently outside it. As we are all aware, several of the States outside the NPT have an overdeveloped sense of realism. It has been our belief that nothing could be calculated to appeal to these States *less* than the achievement of a false, weak, evasive, or generally equivocal text emanating from this Review Conference.

To our mind, the heart of the NPT is a balance of obligations and rights between those States possessing nuclear weapons and those renouncing the option so to do.

We therefore place a particular emphasis on Articles VI, VII of the Treaty and the question of Security Assurances. And here I will deal with two specific points I mentioned before:

1. We cannot accept the view that at *this* Conference the conventional arms race is as important as the nuclear arms race, that non-nuclear-weapon States have the same responsibilities as nuclear-weapon States in implementing Article VI, or that the major focus of Article VI is an equivalent emphasis on general and complete disarmament as well as on the cessation of the nuclear arms race. Both are referred to in Article VI, but clearly the cessation of the nuclear arms race is the major focus of that Article.

Unfortunately, in the formulation of the final Declaration regarding Article VI on pages 7-8 of the English text, we find a quite different interpretation of that article. The wording here appears to reflect a quite different focus. It is a subtle shifting of the primary emphasis on Article VI from the nuclear arms race and the consequent responsibilities of the nuclear-weapon States in its implementation. This interpretation of Article VI, in our opinion, seriously imbalances the Treaty, and my delegation would like to register its reservation with respect to this particular part of the Declaration.

2. On Article VII, it is our conviction that the creation of nuclear-weapon-free zones undertaken on the initiative of the States of the region, recognized internationally, and under adequate safeguards would enhance the prospects of containing nuclear proliferation. We sought to have the Conference acknowledge the responsibility of nuclear-weapon States to these zones. A corollary of this, we believe, is an undertaking by the nuclear States to respect the provisions of such zones and to pledge not to use or threaten to use nuclear weapons against them.

Although the final Declaration deals with this, in paragraph 5 of page 9, the formulation of this passage is not satisfactory to my delegation.

In spite of these remarks, we would like to once again stress our general support of the final declaration as an affirmation of our commitment to the success of the Treaty.

ITALY

Madame President,

I feel it is my duty to join other speakers and put on record the position of my Government on some of the items of the draft declaration you have submitted to us.

On paragraph 5 of the Preamble, I want to underline that that paragraph is interpreted by us as falling within the scope of Articles I and II of the Treaty. I recall, in this connection, the statement made by the Italian Government with the approval of the Italian Parliament at the time of ratification, as well as at the time of signature of the NPT, concerning nuclear explosive devices for peaceful purposes. This reading of the Treaty also covers the last sentence of the second paragraph of the Section "Review of Article V". We agree of course on the need to avert any risk of further proliferation of nuclear weapons. However, in our view the language adopted can in no way alter and does not alter the scope of Article V.

As to the part of the Document concerning the "Purposes", an agreement had been reached, in the working group in which I had the honour to participate, on a compromise formula. This agreement concerned the last item in the list of purposes as contained in document NPT/CONF/C.1/3. The formula read as follows: "To bring about an expanded and more effective cooperation in the peaceful uses of nuclear energy under adequate safeguards".

I am therefore surprised that in a subsequent meeting of another group, at which I was not present, the addition which had then been suggested by another delegation:—"under adequate safeguards"—has been inserted in the text, while the other component of the compromise formula, on which a clear consensus had been achieved, was ignored.

As to the Section "Review of Article III", it is important for me to stress that any initiative in the field of safeguards must be taken with due regard to the provisions of article III, 3 of the Treaty.

Furthermore, on "Review of Article III", I should like to spend one moment on physical protection of nuclear materials. I have no reservation on this text, which we approve. However, we think that it should have been placed elsewhere as it is not related to the obligations envisaged in Article III, which strictly concerns safeguards. I mention this in order to stress that physical protection should involve—as indicated by the language used in the document—the whole international community, all the members of which should share an interest in physical protection.

With regard to the Section "Review of Article IV", I must express the opinion that the text falls short of our expectations. Naturally, we are confronted with a compromise to which we have ourselves contributed. Yet we want to emphasize again the importance that the Italian Government attach to the fulfilment of the provision of Article IV. Speaking two days ago in Paris at the meeting of the International Energy Agency, the Italian Foreign Minister, Mr. Rumor, in indicating the limiting factors to the success of the vast nuclear power programme which we are undertaking, recalled again the vital importance of the problems connected with access to nuclear technology and to the nuclear fuel market, under equal and stable conditions.

The implementation of the Treaty obligations concerning such matters—and I refer in particular to equity and stability of prices and continuity of fuel supply—is not clearly reviewed in the document before us. Moreover, preferential treatment for the Parties to the Treaty—in the very interest of universal adherence—could have been more clearly spelled out. We trust that the discussions which have taken place in this hall, and the views expressed by a number of Delegations on these same matters, will have a real impact on the future policies of all concerned.

On the review regarding the same Article IV, we have taken note that the problem of regional fuel cycle centres will be the object of study. We trust that this exercise will not weaken the impact of Article IV. We reserve, however, our position with regard to the assessment of this part of the text until we will be able to evaluate the results of the projected study.

Concerning the Section "Review of Article VII" and in particular the security of non-nuclear States, we have repeatedly stressed the different objective situations in which States find themselves in this respect. Consequently, in our view, a specific reference would be necessary to the arrangements which many States—in the exercise of the right of individual and collective self-defence—have freely entered.

Similarly, while recognizing the importance of the establishment of nuclear-free zones in appropriate regions of the world as a means of curbing nuclear proliferation, as well as the importance of guaranteeing the security of the States concerned, we interpret the relevant provisions of the Document in the sense that the creation of such nuclear-free zones must not detract from existing security arrangements.

In conclusion, I should like to say that my remarks should be understood as in no way diminishing our interest in, and appreciation for this first NPT review. We are happy to see that a second Review Conference will follow: an objective that, as you know, was much in the mind of the Italian Delegation.

In our view, full compliance with the Treaty is the best way through which we can hope to achieve wider participation. This is an essential element for the same attainment of the vital purposes of the Treaty. It is in this spirit that our remarks were made.

PERU

The delegation of Peru states for the record that the review of the operation of the Treaty has made clear the responsibility of the Depositary States for the failure to implement Articles VI and VII of the Treaty attributed to them by the non-nuclear States Parties; that said responsibility is clearly set forth in the draft resolutions submitted by the non-nuclear States and reproduced in this final document; and that, therefore, the consensus on which the adoption of the draft Final Declaration of the Conference prepared by the President is based is subject to the interpretation contained in those draft resolutions

ROMANIA

In his statement of 7 May, before this Assembly, the head of the Romanian delegation stressed the importance that my country attaches to this Conference as a collective means of verification, with the participation of all States, of the way in which the provisions of the Treaty on the Non-Proliferation of Nuclear Weapons are being realized.

After the Treaty's first five years of operation, our basic conclusion was, and it remains the same today, that while the non-nuclear-weapon States had scrupulously fulfilled their undertakings not to acquire or manufacture nuclear weapons, the vertical proliferation of nuclear weapons and the nuclear arms race have continued and even accelerated. As a result of the increasing destructive capacity of the new generation of nuclear weapons and of the massive stockpiling of armaments, nuclear weapons in particular, the whole world is in a grave state of insecurity. At the same time, despite the IAEA's efforts, the non-nuclear-weapon States and especially the developing countries are far from having received the assistance they have counted on, so that nuclear energy should become the instrument expected to help their economic development.

My delegation came therefore to this Conference with the expectation that, in view of the above, practical measures would be considered and adopted, aimed: (1) at giving a new impetus to nuclear disarmament negotiations; (2) at contributing to the ensuring and strengthening of the security of non-nuclear-weapon States Party to the Treaty, which under the Treaty have renounced the acquisition of nuclear weapons; (3) at promoting true international cooperation and assistance in the field of the use of nuclear energy for peaceful purposes.

During the last four weeks, intensive work, following that performed by the Preparatory Committee, has been carried out. In this process each delegation has had the occasion to present, in a responsible manner, the views and the positions of its respective Government.

Regretfully, this valuable process of negotiations has not reached the expected practical results. It has only underlined the unsatisfactory state of affairs within the membership of the Treaty, the shortcomings of this important international document and, in fact, even a certain degree of lack of communication between the nuclear and the non-nuclear-weapon States.

Nevertheless, the Conference has offered a good occasion for all Parties to express their views and has pointed to the main fields of vital interests for each of them, towards the solution of which we all have to continue to work, collectively, in the future.

Today we have before us, due to your most appreciative efforts, Madame President, a text which constituted an attempt at achieving a compromise in the difficult situation in which the Conference found itself, but which falls short of our expectations.

The tacit acceptance by all of us, including my own delegation, of the proposed General Declaration should be interpreted only as an expression of the attachment of the States Parties to the noble goals and aspirations pursued by the Treaty. At the same time we want to state that as a whole the present text is exceedingly unbalanced. The vital issues on which the viability of the Treaty and its universality depend are not reflected in an appropriate manner. The Declaration does not contain any concrete measures directed to giving the necessary impetus to disarmament negotiations, to ensuring the security of the non-nuclear-weapon States, to broadening international cooperation for peaceful uses of nuclear energy as expected by all of mankind. We are expressing our deep regret and dissatisfaction that there was no possibility to

agree on generally acceptable measures on such outstanding issues of global concern.

The document confines itself to evaluating the past in an over-optimistic manner, while the measures designed to assure the realization of the purposes of the Preamble and of the provisions of the Treaty, which was the basic objective of the Conference, are practically non-existent.

In addition, attempts have been made to extend the interpretation of the purposes of the Treaty in some respects, to deepen even more the imbalance existing in the field of peaceful utilization of nuclear energy.

As regards the review of Article III, paragraphs 7 and 8 of the Declaration, the Romanian delegation wishes to reserve its position by interpreting them solely in accordance with the letter of Article III, point 2 of the Treaty.

At the same time we want to state that in our interpretation all the measures of safeguards included in the Declaration should strictly respect the sovereign rights of all States.

They should be implemented in such a manner as to avoid any obstacle to the economic or technological development of the Parties or of international cooperation in the field of peaceful nuclear activities, including the international exchange of nuclear material and equipment for the processing, use or production of nuclear material for peaceful purposes, as provided by the Treaty itself.

We are firmly convinced that it is only on this basis that all the Parties to the Treaty will equally benefit from peaceful applications of nuclear technology.

The Romanian delegation asks, therefore, that these reservations be duly recorded.

As I have already pointed out, from the very moment of becoming a Party to this Treaty, which was an act of full responsibility on the part of my Government, in considering the general interests of all the international community, Romania has resolutely acted for the achievement of the main objectives of the Non-Proliferation Treaty, including the strengthening of the security of non-nuclear-weapon States, an issue which had been left pending at the conclusion of the Treaty.

It is in this spirit that we have also given particular attention at this Conference to the question of security guarantees for the non-nuclear-weapon States Party to the Treaty.

The solution of this issue consists in the legal obligation by the nuclear-weapon States Party to the Treaty never and under no circumstances to use or threaten to use nuclear weapons against non-nuclear-weapon States Party to the Treaty. This is the interpretation which the

Romanian delegation gives to the chapter of the Declaration on this issue, and we ask that it be recorded.

The draft Additional Protocol (document NPT/CONF/22) initiated by Romania was intended to respond to this shortcoming of the Treaty.

Fully aware of the vital interest of all countries in their security, but first of all of the non-nuclear-weapon States, which in their majority are small and medium-sized countries, the draft Additional Protocol represented a concrete measure to be taken by the Conference, aimed at ensuring and strengthening the security of the States which undertook to renounce the nuclear option.

We realize the complexity of the problem and our draft sought only to advance an idea to be negotiated with good will.

Unfortunately, a dialogue could not be started on this issue either. Naturally an international conference cannot progress when it does not treat on an equal basis all the views and opinions put forward by all sovereign and independent States participating in it. Nevertheless the discussion proved that the issue of security guarantees is of vital interest to most of the States. It has been consolidated as a basic issue of general interest for our future work in strengthening the Treaty.

We hope that the transmission of the draft Protocol for study by States Parties to the Treaty, and subsequently its consideration by the United Nations General Assembly, may stimulate concrete negotiations.

The stand of my delegation at this Conference reflected the general line of the policy of Romania, firmly committed to the strengthening of international peace and security.

On the basis of the mandate received from its Government, the Romanian delegation has done its best to contribute to the attainment of the common goals of humanity: peace, disarmament and cooperation with all States. We have constructively cooperated with all those who shared the same objective.

We leave this Conference with the sentiment that such endeavours should be stronger in the future, if we want to succeed in our common goals.

SWEDEN

The Swedish Delegation supports the part of the general declaration which deals with article VII and the security of NNWS. With respect to the paragraph dealing with Security Council Resolution 255 (1968), my Delegation wishes to put on record its view that should assistance to a country be contemplated under these provisions, that country shall have the right to decide if and under what conditions assistance might be granted.

SYRIAN ARAB REPUBLIC

Madame President,

In your statement of 6 May 1975, you emphatically stated that the Conference was embarking on a momentous task, the result of which might well extend far into the future. You also reminded us of the repercussions of a possible failure to reach agreement on basic problems facing the Review Conference; this was when you said "over the world people of goodwill and common sense and knowledge are looking to the Conference for positive results".

These remarks have remained vivid in our mind throughout the long hours spent in discussions, negotiations and debates.

At the darkest hours, when it became clear that the future of non-proliferation was at stake, you launched what you rightly called "a new initiative" contained now in the declaration before us. We welcomed it because, like you, we believe that the Review Conference must produce "something" or the entire structure of non-proliferation would probably collapse. A collapse would surely have played into the hands of the aggressor, the blackmailer, the racist and the expansionist. It would have shaken the foundation of universal adherence—a goal that we all are firmly committed to.

The document just adopted has got that "something", which we had to produce willingly or unwillingly, but its content, and I am sure you agree with us, does not solve the basic problems that were identified in your 12 May statement.

But we have chosen to accept a quarter of a loaf instead of half a loaf because we wanted to preserve the achievements already realized under the NPT regime and hope for a better future.

Nonetheless, we must put on record some reservations or interpretations relating to the following parts:

1. *Review of Article VII and problems of security guarantees*

   This part as it is formulated now constitutes a set-back to a strong momentum which has been gathering strength from 1968 onward, to obtain security guarantees that would protect non-nuclear NPT Parties against nuclear aggression and nuclear blackmail. This part of the Declaration does not, and regrettably so, contain any formulation, not even an indication, relating to obligations of Depositary States to extend both positive and negative security guarantees to NPT Parties. Instead, there is an attempt to shift the urgency of extending guarantees from Parties directly concerned to non-nuclear-weapon Parties through the creation of nuclear-free zones, an effort that we would have lauded if it had been accompanied by an equal attempt at supporting security guarantees. This lacuna has, in cur opinion, weakened to a certain extent the credibility of the assurances under Security Council resolution 255 and the tripartite declaration.

2. *On the Review of Article III*

It is our firm belief that irrespective of the field of competence of the IAEA, the Declaration should have extended safeguards measures to all nuclear activities of non-NPT countries receiving any nuclear material or equipment. Therefore, whenever the following or a similar sentence reading "application of safeguards to all peaceful nuclear activities" appears in the text, we should read the word "activities" as meaning activities of all kinds, peaceful or non-peaceful, declared to be such or not declared as such.

3. *Review of Article IV*

We reserve our position on those parts relating to Article IV which do not fulfil the following conditions:

—Preferential treatment to developing NPT Parties without harming the interests of any developing non-party;

—Concessional and preferential arrangements to developing nations, whether Parties or non-parties to the NPT;

— The establishment of a "Special Fund" as well as a "Special Nuclear Fund", as provided for in operative paragraph 1 of the draft resolution proposed by Mexico, Nigeria and the Philippines, (NPT/CONF/C.II/L.2) in order to institutionalize and stabilize the flow of assistance to developing nations in accordance with Article IV of the NPT.

Now, allow me to raise two issues closely related to our work, namely, the issue of participation and that of attendance. We cannot hush the fact that only 55 out of 94 Parties to the NPT participated in our work. Absenteeism is a phenomenon that should be carefully studied. It betrays, in our opinion, either a lack of interest in improving the NPT regime or a loss of faith in the utility of a dialogue between nuclear and non-weapon Parties to the NPT. Whatever may be the case, the results of the Conference have immensely suffered from the absence of so many NPT Parties. This was mostly felt in the ranks of developing nations.

Our second remark relates to the admission of Israel and South Africa to attend as observers. The Conference did show a positive attitude towards their request. But these two countries did not show any positive interest in the work of the Conference. We are at the end, yet we have seen no contribution on their part. Their presence was only felt when it came to sabotaging certain constructive proposals or exerting pressures directly or indirectly. We did not object to their presence because we knew beforehand that they had come for diversionary and for propaganda purposes. But the Conference was not deceived, because it must have realized that their contribution to the cause of the NPT was nil. The Conference must have regretted its decision.

We can be critical of the progress achieved at this Conference, but our criticism should be construed as a constructive one. We wish to the NPT all success; and despite the limited objectives we achieved, we shall increase our efforts to strengthen the NPT regime in all its aspects. We hope that the nuclear-weapon Powers Parties to the NPT will take our legitimate demands and concern into serious consideration.

I should like to signify the wish of my Delegation to see this statement annexed to the final document of the Conference.

UNION OF SOVIET SOCIALIST REPUBLICS

For almost a month—the duration of this Conference—its participants have carefully and thoroughly reviewed the operation of the Treaty on the Non-Proliferation of Nuclear Weapons, expressed opinions on the practical application of the Treaty and made numerous proposals concerning the implementation of its provisions.

Taken as a whole, the results of the Conference permit the conclusion that it has convincingly demonstrated the obvious fact that the five years of the Treaty's existence have confirmed its vitality, its effectiveness and its continued importance in today's world.

As regards the significance of the Conference, one is justified in laying special emphasis on the constructive role it has played in increasing the universality of the Treaty and in making the non-proliferation regime even more effective. It is already clear that the Conference has promoted the adherence of a whole series of States to the Treaty. Just before and during the Conference, the number of Parties was expanded by the addition of an important group of States, including some with a highly developed atomic industry, and this has been a significant step towards the future strengthening of the Treaty. We hope that the outcome of the Conference will encourage accession by additional States as well as completion of the process of ratification by the countries which have signed the Treaty.

A significant fact recognized in the statements of all delegations is that the key Articles and essential part of the Treaty—Articles I and II—are being strictly observed by all Parties.

We regard the unanimous confirmation of the effective implementation of those Articles and of the Article on international control as the most important result of the Conference, and we note with satisfaction that this result has been reflected in the final declaration.

In that connection, it is worth noting that the Conference has also discussed a series of proposals aimed at achieving maximum effectiveness for the Treaty. There has been unanimous support for proposals relating to Article III, paragraph 2 of the Treaty, the physical protection of nuclear material, the establishment of regional nuclear fuel-cycle centres, and other matters.

As to the situation with regard to the implementation of Article IV, we are pleased to note that the Non-Proliferation Treaty has made a very significant contribution to the development of international cooperation in the utilization of nuclear energy.

Great significance must also be attached to the recommendations adopted by the Conference concerning the implementation of Article V of the Treaty which provide that any non-nuclear-weapon State deciding to use, on the basis of the Treaty's provisions, the energy of a nuclear explosion for purposes of its economic development, would be able to obtain effective assistance both from the Depositary States and from the International Atomic Energy Agency.

All of these constructive recommendations for the further strengthening of the non-proliferation regime have been duly reflected in the final declaration of the Conference.

It cannot be overlooked that proposals were also made at the Conference which were not in harmony with the objective of strengthening the Non-Proliferation Treaty and which really sought to revise it. And that is how we assessed them in our statements during the Conference. Naturally it was not such proposals, which were not approved by the Conference, that determined the direction of the Conference's work or its results. They only represented the opinions of particular delegations.

The Soviet delegation is gratified that the Conference has succeeded in arriving at a draft final document whose provisions, on the whole, are of a constructive nature.

Nevertheless, the Soviet delegation would like to state that it has certain reservations with regard to some of the declaration's provisions relating to the implementation of Articles VI and VII of the Treaty.

It is the position of the Soviet Union, which is an advocate of nuclear disarmament, that measures in that field must not be prejudicial to the security of the parties concerned. The Soviet Union also considers that the basic problems of disarmament—and especially of nuclear disarmament—can only be solved with the participation of all the nuclear Powers.

As regards the cessation of nuclear weapon tests, we deem it necessary to emphasize that the Soviet Union is in favour of the cessation of all testing, including underground testing, by all States. That is the position of principle of the Soviet Union.

As to the provisions of the draft declaration dealing with the Soviet-American Strategic Arms Limitation Talks, the delegation of the USSR wishes to state that the Soviet Union attaches great significance to the talks and considers agreements and understandings reached in those talks to be of exceptional importance for the cause of peace and international security. The position of the Soviet Union on that question is set forth in the Soviet-American declaration adopted at the Vladivostok meeting in November 1974.

On the question of security guarantees for non-nuclear States Parties to the Treaty, the Soviet delegation would like to observe that Security Council resolution 255 (1968) and the declarations made by the Soviet Union, the United States of America and the United Kingdom in relation thereto constitute an effective instruments for guaranteeing the security of Parties to the Treaty not possessing nuclear weapons.

The strengthening of the security of States is the object of the resolution of the twenty-seventh session of the United Nations General Assembly on the non-use of force in international relations and simultaneous permanent prohibition of the use of nuclear weapons. Adoption by the Security Council of a decision approving that resolution would give it binding force and constitute an important step for strengthening the security of the non-nuclear States.

That purpose would also be served by the creation of nuclear-free zones. We favour the creation of such zones in various regions of the world on condition that measures are carried out which genuinely transform the territories of the States concerned into zones completely free of nuclear weapons and which exclude any loopholes for violating the non-nuclear status of the zones. As regards the Treaty on the nuclear-free zone in Latin America, our position is well known and there is no need to redefine it.

The USSR delegation does not support the proposal mentioned in the final declaration of the Conference concerning United Nations facilities for the collection, compilation and dissemination of information on disarmament issues because the existing organs of the United Nations suffice to ensure that all States and world opinion are informed on such issues.

With reference to the recommendation in the draft declaration on the convening of the next Conference to review the operation of the Non-Proliferation Treaty, the USSR delegation wishes to state that the procedure for reviewing the operation of the Treaty is clearly laid down in the text of the Treaty itself—in Article VIII, paragraph 3.

In conclusion, the Soviet delegation would like to express its conviction that the Conference, now about to conclude its work, will endow the Treaty on the Non-Proliferation of Nuclear Weapons with even greater effectiveness and thereby contribute to intensifying and expanding the process of international détente.

The Soviet delegation requests that its statement be included in the final document of the Conference.

UNITED STATES OF AMERICA

My delegation is pleased to have joined in the adoption of the Final Declaration of this, the first NPT Review Conference. We believe that, by reaching agreement on the Conference Declaration—which is the culmination of our efforts over the last four weeks—we have taken an important step forward.

The Declaration is a realistic document, containing recommendations for improving the effectiveness of the Treaty's operation and most important of the non-proliferation regime generally. Some ideas, including those relating to international cooperation on physical security, to improvements of safeguards on exports, and to regional solutions to fuel-cycle needs, are innovative, and are receiving broad international endorsement for the first time. In addition, the Conference Declaration strongly underlines the need for determined and timely efforts to achieve widely shared objectives. Taken as a whole, the Final Declaration establishes a practical and comprehensive course of action for strengthening the non-proliferation regime. It shows clearly that we all have a shared and overriding interest in the success of efforts to curb nuclear proliferation, which is a continuing and complicated process. We recognize that no delegation can give unqualified support to each of the conclusions and recommendations contained in the Declaration. Some may have reservations about particular ideas expressed in the document; others may regret that some of their suggestions were not included, or were given less emphasis than they would have preferred. This is as true of our delegation as it is of others.

I would like to take this opportunity to briefly state for the record our views on some of the issues covered in the Final Declaration. First, I would like to reiterate that we look forward, as soon as possible after the conclusion of the agreement outlined at Vladivostok, to the commencement of follow-on negotiations on further limitations and reductions in the level of strategic arms.

Second, with respect to the question of restraints on nuclear testing, my government joins in affirming the determination of participants of this Conference to achieve the discontinuance of all explosions of nuclear weapons for all time. The Final Declaration notes that a number of Delegations at the Conference expressed the desire that the nuclear-weapon States Parties enter as soon as possible into an agreement to halt all nuclear-weapon tests for a specified period of time. Our view is that any treaty or agreement on nuclear-weapons testing must contain provisions for adequate verification and must solve the problem of peaceful nuclear explosions. It would not be realistic to assume that an agreement banning all nuclear-weapons testing, whether by nuclear-weapon States Party to the NPT or by all testing Powers, could be concluded before solutions to these problems are found.

With reference to nuclear-free zones, we believe that the creation of such zones could effectively complement the NPT as a means of preventing the spread of nuclear explosive capabilities. We have emphasized that, to be effective, regional arrangements should meet the following criteria:

The initiative should be taken by the States in the region concerned. The zone should preferably include all States in the area whose participation is deemed important. The creation of the zone should not disturb necessary security arrangements; and provision must be made for adequate verification. Finally, we do not believe that the objective of non-proliferation would be served if a nuclear-free zone arrangement permitted the indigenous development of nuclear explosives for any purpose. No effort to achieve non-proliferation could succeed if it permitted such indigenous development of nuclear explosives by non-nuclear-weapon States, or failed to safeguard against diversion of nuclear materials to such use.

A number of Delegations at the Conference urged that nuclear-weapon States provide, in an appropriate manner, binding security assurances to those States which became fully bound by the provisions of a regional arrangement. My government adhered to Protocol II of the Latin American Nuclear-Weapon-Free-Zone Treaty, which contains such a binding security assurance, after determining that that treaty met the criteria noted above. However, we believe that each nuclear-free zone proposal must be judged on its own merits to determine whether the provision of specific security assurances would be likely to have a favourable effect. Moreover, we do not believe it would be realistic to expect nuclear-weapon States to make implied commitments to provide such assurances before the scope and content of any nuclear-free zone arrangement are worked out.

I ask that this written statement be incorporated in Annex II of the final document.

YUGOSLAVIA

Madame President,

You have in your opening address quite correctly posed a number of questions to which this Conference should provide answers. Let us now see what has actually been accomplished.

The Yugoslav delegation to the Review Conference of the Parties to the Treaty considers that:

—The nuclear-weapons States have not fulfilled their basic obligation assumed under the Treaty:

1. They have not discontinued the nuclear arms race;

2. They have not stopped the nuclear weapon tests;

3. Vertical proliferation of nuclear weapons has continued;

4. No substantial assistance has been given to the non-nuclear weapon States, that is, the developing countries, in the application of nuclear energy for peaceful purposes;

—The non-nuclear-weapon States have fulfilled, in every respect, their obligations ensuing from the Treaty.

The Conference has revealed contradictions both in the comprehension of the substance and the meaning of the Treaty, as well as regarding the fundamental issues on the agenda of the Conference:

1. The nuclear-weapon States and the States sharing their views have made an effort to preserve the NPT as an instrument by which they will retain all the advantages which the Treaty offers them;

2. The non-nuclear-weapon States, and in particular the developing countries, demand a programme of measures strengthening and consolidating the Treaty, measures that would enhance the equality in the rights and duties between the nuclear and non-nuclear States.

The Conference has failed to reach a consensus both in the informal working groups and in the Committees on any substantive issue. This reflects profound divergences on fundamental issues.

The responsibility for such a situation at the Conference, in our opinion, rests primarily with the nuclear-weapon States—the Depositaries.

The submitted draft final declaration, contained in document NPT/CONF/30, does not faithfully reflect the deliberations and positions stated at the Conference, nor does it contain all pertinent elements of the proposed documents.

The Yugoslav delegations would like to state that, had the vote been taken on the Declaration, my delegation would not have taken part in the voting. However, since voting did not take place, it will not stand in the way of consensus, provided that this statement is fully recorded.

In conclusion, I would like to state that my Government, bearing in mind the above-mentioned points, finds itself in a position to re-examine its attitude towards the Treaty and to draw corresponding conclusions.

Draft resolutions NPT/CONF/L.2/Rev.1, NPT/CONF/L.3/Rev.1 and NPT/CONF/L.4/Rev.1

See Annex II for the text of the three resolutions above.

Draft resolutions NPT/CONF/L.1; NPT/CONF/C.I/ L.1-3; NPT/CONF/29; NPT/CONF/C.II/L.1-2

1. Draft resolutions NPT/CONF/L.1 and NPT/CONF/29 are attached.

2. See Annex II for the text of draft resolutions NPT/CONF/C.1/L.1-3 and NPT/CONF/C.II/L.1-2.

BOLIVIA, ECUADOR, GHANA, HONDURAS, JAMAICA, LEBANON, LIBERIA, MEXICO, MOROCCO, NICARAGUA, NIGERIA, PERU, PHILIPPINES, ROMANIA, SENEGAL, SUDAN, SYRIAN ARAB REPUBLIC, THAILAND, YUGO-SLAVIA AND ZAIRE

Draft resolution

(Document NPT/CONF/L.1)

The Review Conference of the Parties to the Treaty on the Non-Proliferation of Nuclear Weapons,

Having reviewed the operation of the Treaty in accordance with the provisions of its article VIII,

Noting that such a review has demonstrated the necessity that effective measures be taken in order to promote the realization of the purposes of the Preamble and the provisions of the Treaty,

Convinced of the desirability that a second Conference with the same purposes as the first be convened in five years,

Convinced further that it is necessary that the General Assembly of the United Nations have the opportunity to review every two years the implementation of the resolutions and other instruments adopted by the first Conference,

1. *Requests* the Secretary-General of the United Nations to include the following item in the provisional agenda of the thirty-first session of the General Assembly: "Implementation of the resolutions and other instruments adopted by the first Review Conference of the Parties to the Treaty on the Non-Proliferation of Nuclear Weapons";

2. *Requests* also the Secretary-General of the United Nations to include the following item in the provisional agenda of the thirty-third session of the General Assembly: "Implementation of the resolutions and other instruments adopted by the first Review Conference of the Parties to the Treaty on the Non-Proliferation of Nuclear Weapons and establishment of a preparatory committee for the second Conference to be held in 1980 for the same purposes as the first".

Proposal on the follow-up of the Conference

(Document NPT/CONF/29)

The Review Conference of the Parties to the Treaty on the Non-Proliferation of Nuclear Weapons,

Considering that paragraph 3 of Article VIII of the Treaty on the Non-Proliferation of Nuclear Weapons provides that "at intervals of five years" after the first review conference contemplated in that paragraph, "a majority of the Parties to the Treaty may obtain, by submitting a proposal to this effect to the Depositary Governments, the convening of further conferences with the ... objective of reviewing the operation of the Treaty",

Considering that review conferences are an important instrument in the endeavour to assure "that the purposes of the Preamble and the provisions of the Treaty are being realized" in that they ensure a continuity in the evaluation of the actions severally and jointly undertaken or pursued by the Parties in order fully to comply with the obligations incumbent upon them under the Treaty,

Considering that the results of the Conference demonstrate that a second review conference should be held, within the framework of paragraph 3 of article VIII, at the earliest possible time in view of the necessity that a further assessment of the implementation of the Treaty be made at an early date,

Considering that delegations to the Conference have expressed a firm belief in the necessity of such a second review conference,

Urges all the Parties to the Treaty to submit to the Depositary Governments at the earliest possible time a proposal for a new review conference to be held in Geneva, Switzerland, in the year 1980, in accordance with Article VIII, paragraph 3 of the Treaty and for the purposes indicated therein.

Document 19

Guidelines for nuclear transfers adopted by the 15-nation Nuclear Suppliers' Group, London, 21 September 1977

INFCIRC/254, 1977

1. The following fundamental principles for safeguards and export controls should apply to nuclear transfers to any non-nuclear-weapon State for peaceful purposes. In this connection, suppliers have defined an export trigger list and agreed on common criteria for technology transfers.

Prohibition on nuclear explosives

2. Suppliers should authorize transfer of items identified in the trigger list only upon formal governmental assurances from recipients explicitly excluding uses which would result in any nuclear explosive device.

Physical protection

3. (a) All nuclear materials and facilities identified by the agreed trigger list should be placed under effective physical protection to prevent unauthorized use and handling. The levels of physical protection to be ensured in relation to the type of materials, equipment and facilities, have been agreed by suppliers, taking account of international recommendations.

(b) The implementation of measures of physical protection in the recipient country is the responsibility of the Government of that country. However, in order to implement the terms agreed upon amongst suppliers, the levels of physical protection on which these measures have to be based should be the subject of an agreement between supplier and recipient.

(c) In each case special arrangements should be made for a clear definition of responsibilities for the transport of trigger list items.

Safeguards

4. Suppliers should transfer trigger list items only when covered by IAEA safeguards, with duration and coverage provisions in conformance with the GOV/1621 guidelines. Exceptions should be made only after consultation with the parties to this understanding.

5. Suppliers will jointly reconsider their common safeguards requirements, whenever appropriate.

Safeguards triggered by the transfer of certain technology

6. (a) The requirements of paragraphs 2, 3 and 4 above should also apply to facilities for reprocessing, enrichment, or heavy-water production, utilizing technology directly transferred by the supplier or derived from transferred facilities, or major critical components thereof.

(b) The transfer of such facilities, or major critical components thereof, or related technology, should require an undertaking (1) that IAEA safeguards apply to any facilities of the same type (i.e. if the design, construction or operating processes are based on the same or similar physical or chemical processes, as defined in the trigger list) constructed during an agreed period in the recipient country and (2) that there should at all times be in effect a safeguards agreement permitting the IAEA to apply Agency safeguards with respect to such facilities identified by the recipient, or by the supplier in consultation with the recipient, as using transferred technology.

Special controls on sensitive exports

7. Suppliers should exercise restraint in the transfer of sensitive facilities, technology and weapons-usable materials. If enrichment or reprocessing facilities, equipment or technology are to be transferred, suppliers should encourage recipients to accept, as an alternative to national plants, supplier involvement and/or other appropriate multinational participation in resulting facilities. Suppliers should also promote international (including IAEA) activities concerned with multinational regional fuel cycle centres.

Special controls on export of enrichment facilities, equipment and technology

8. For a transfer of an enrichment facility, or technology therefor, the recipient nation should agree that neither the transferred facility, nor any facility based on such technology, will be designed or operated for the production of greater than 20% enriched uranium without the consent of the supplier nation, of which the IAEA should be advised.

Controls on supplied or derived weapons-usable material

9. Suppliers recognize the importance, in order to advance the objectives of these guidelines and to provide opportunities further to reduce the risks of proliferation, of including in agreements on supply of nuclear materials or of facilities which produce weapons-usable material, provisions calling for mutual agreement between the supplier and the recipient on arrangements for reprocessing, storage, alteration, use, transfer or retransfer of any weapons-usable material involved. Suppliers should endeavour to include such provisions whenever appropriate and practicable.

Controls on retransfer

10. (a) Suppliers should transfer trigger list items, including technology defined under paragraph 6, only upon the recipient's assurance that in the case of:

(1) retransfer of such items, or

(2) transfer of trigger list items derived from facilities originally transferred by the supplier, or with the help of equipment or technology originally transferred by the supplier;

the recipient of the retransfer or transfer will have provided the same assurances as those required by the supplier for the original transfer.

(b) In addition the supplier's consent should be required for: (1) any retransfer of the facilities, major critical components, or technology described in paragraph 6; (2) any transfer of facilities or major critical components derived from those items; (3) any retransfer of heavy water or weapons-usable material.

SUPPORTING ACTIVITIES

Physical security

11. Suppliers should promote international co-operation on the exchange of physical security information, protection of nuclear materials in transit, and recovery of stolen nuclear materials and equipment.

Support for effective IAEA safeguards

12. Suppliers should make special efforts in support of effective implementation of IAEA safeguards. Suppliers should also support the Agency's efforts to assist Member States in the improvement of their national systems of accounting and control of nuclear material and to increase the technical effectiveness of safeguards.

Similarly, they should make every effort to support the IAEA in increasing further the adequacy of safeguards in the light of technical developments and the rapidly growing number of nuclear facilities, and to support appropriate initiatives aimed at improving the effectiveness of IAEA safeguards.

Sensitive plant design features

13. Suppliers should encourage the designers and makers of sensitive equipment to construct it in such a way as to facilitate the application of safeguards.

Consultations

14. (a) Suppliers should maintain contact and consult through regular channels on matters connected with the implementation of these guidelines.

(b) Suppliers should consult, as each deems appropriate, with other Governments concerned on specific sensitive cases, to ensure that any transfer does not contribute to risks of conflict or instability.

(c) In the event that one or more suppliers believe that there has been a violation of supplier/recipient understandings resulting from these guidelines, particularly in the case of an explosion of a nuclear device, or illegal termination or violation of IAEA safeguards by a recipient, suppliers should consult promptly through diplomatic channels in order to determine and assess the reality and extent of the alleged violation.

Pending the early outcome of such consultations, suppliers will not act in a manner that could prejudice any measure that may be adopted by other suppliers concerning their current contacts with that recipient.

Upon the findings of such consultations, the suppliers, bearing in mind Article XII of the IAEA Statute, should agree on an appropriate response and possible action which could include the termination of nuclear transfers to that recipient.

15. In considering transfers, each supplier should exercise prudence having regard to all the circumstances of each case, including any risk that technology transfers not covered by paragraph 6, or subsequent retransfers, might result in unsafeguarded nuclear materials.

16. Unanimous consent is required for any changes in these guidelines, including any which might result from the reconsideration mentioned in paragraph 5.

ANNEX A

Trigger List referred to in guidelines

PART A. Material and equipment

1. Source or special fissionable material as defined in Article XX of the Statute of the International Atomic Energy Agency; provided that items specified in sub-paragraph (a) below, and exports of source or special fissionable material to a given recipient country, within a period of 12 months, below the limits specified in sub-paragraph (b) below, shall not be included:

(a) Plutonium with an isotopic concentration of plutonium-238 exceeding 80%.

Special fissionable material when used in gram quantities or less as a sensing component in instruments; and

Source material which the Government is satisfied is to be used only in non-nuclear activities, such as the production of alloys or ceramics;

(b) Special fissionable material 50 effective grams;
Natural uranium   500 kilograms;
Depleted uranium   1000 kilograms; and
Thorium   1000 kilograms.

2.1. *Reactors and equipment therefor*:

2.1.1. Nuclear reactors capable of operation so as to maintain a controlled self-sustaining fission chain reaction, excluding zero energy reactors, the latter being defined as reactors with a designed maximum rate of production of plutonium not exceeding 100 grams per year.

2.1.2. Reactor pressure vessels:

Metal vessels, as complete units or as major shop-fabricated parts therefor, which are especially designed or prepared to contain the core of a nuclear reactor as defined in paragraph 2.1.1 above and are capable of withstanding the operating pressure of the primary coolant.

2.1.3. Reactor fuel charging and discharging machines:

Manipulative equipment especially designed or pre-pared for inserting or removing fuel in a nuclear reactor as defined in paragraph 2.1.1 above, capable of on-load operation or employing technically sophisticated positioning or alignment features to allow complex off-load fuelling operations such as those in which direct viewing of or access to the fuel is not normally available.

2.1.4. Reactor control rods:

Rods especially designed or prepared for the control of the reaction rate in a nuclear reactor as defined in paragraph 2.1.1 above.

2.1.5. Reactor pressure tubes:

Tubes which are especially designed or prepared to contain fuel elements and the primary coolant in a reactor as defined in paragraph 2.1.1 above at an operating pressure in excess of 50 atmospheres.

2.1.6. Zirconium tubes:

Zirconium metal and alloys in the form of tubes or assemblies of tubes, and in quantities exceeding 500 kg per year, especially designed or prepared for use in a reactor as defined in paragraph 2.1.1 above, and in which the relationship of hafnium to zirconium is less than 1:500 parts by weight.

2.1.7. Primary coolant pumps:

Pumps especially designed or prepared for circulating liquid metal as primary coolant for nuclear reactors as defined in paragraph 2.1.1 above.

2.2. *Non-nuclear materials for reactors*:

2.2.1. Deuterium and heavy water:

Deuterium and any deuterium compound in which the ratio of deuterium to hydrogen exceeds 1:5000 for use in a nuclear reactor as defined in paragraph 2.1.1 above in quantities exceeding 200 kg of deuterium atoms for any one recipient country in any period of 12 months.

2.2.2. Nuclear grade graphite:

Graphite having a purity level better than 5 parts per million boron equivalent and with a density greater than 1.50 grams per cubic centimetre in quantities exceeding 30 metric tons for any one recipient country in any period of 12 months.

2.3.1. Plants for the reprocessing of irradiated fuel elements, and equipment especially designed or prepared therefor.

2.4.1. Plants for the fabrication of fuel elements.

2.5.1. Equipment, other than analytical instruments, especially designed or prepared for the separation of isotopes of uranium.

2.6.1. Plants for the production of heavy water, deuterium and deuterium compounds and equipment especially designed or prepared therefor.

Clarifications of certain of the items on the above list are annexed.

PART B. *Common criteria for technology transfers under paragraph 6 of the Guidelines*

(1) "Technology" means technical data in physical form designated by the supplying country as important to the design, construction, operation, or maintenance of enrichment, reprocessing, or heavy water production facilities or major critical components thereof, but excluding data available to the public, for example, in published books and periodicals, or that which has been made available internationally without restrictions upon its further dissemination.

(2) "Major critical components" are:

(a) in the case of an isotope separation plant of the gaseous diffusion type: *diffusion barrier;*

(b) in the case of an isotope separation plant of the gas centrifuge type: *gas centrifuge assemblies, corrosion-resistant to UF*$_6$;

(c) in the case of an isotope separation plant of the jet nozzle type: the *nozzle units;*

(d) in the case of an isotope separation plant of the vortex type: the *vortex units.*

(3) For facilities covered by paragraph 6 of the Guidelines for which no major critical component is described in paragraph 2 above, if a supplier nation should transfer in the aggregate a significant fraction of the items essential to the operation of such a facility, together with the knowhow for construction and operation of that facility, that transfer should be deemed to be a transfer of "facilities or major critical components thereof".

(4) The definitions in the preceding paragraphs are solely for the purposes of paragraph 6 of the Guidelines and this Part B, which differ from those applicable to Part A of this Trigger List, which should not be interpreted as limited by such definition.

(5) For the purposes of implementing paragraph 6 of the Guidelines, the following facilities should be deemed to be "of the same type (i.e. if their design, construction or operating processes are based on the same or similar physical or chemical processes)":

Where the technology transferred is such as to make possible the construction in the recipient State of a facility of the following type, or major facilities critical components thereof:	The following will be deemed to be facilities of the same type:
(a) an isotope separation plant of the gaseous diffusion type	any other isotope separation plant using the gaseous diffusion process.
(b) an isotope separation plant of the gas centrifuge type	any other isotope separation plant using the gas centrifuge process.
(c) an isotope separation plant of the jet nozzle type	any other isotope separation plant using the jet nozzle process.
(d) an isotope separation plant of the vortex type	any other isotope separation plant using the vortex process.
(e) a fuel reprocessing plant using the solvent extraction process	any other fuel reprocessing plant using the solvent extraction process.
(f) a heavy water plant using the exchange process	any other heavy water plant using the exchange process.
(g) a heavy water plant using the electrolytic process	any other heavy water plant using the electrolytic process.
(h) a heavy water plant using the hydrogen distillation process	any other heavy water plant using the hydrogen distillation process.

Note: In the case of reprocessing, enrichment, and heavy water facilities whose design, construction, or operation processes are based on physical or chemical processes other than those enumerated above, a similar approach would be applied to define facilities "of the same type", and a need to define major critical components of such facilities might arise.

(6) The reference in paragraph 6(b) of the Guidelines to "any facilities of the same type constructed during an agreed period in the recipient's country" is understood to refer to such facilities (or major critical components thereof), the first operation of which commences within a period of at least 20 years from the date of the first operation of (1) a facility which has been transferred or incorporates transferred major critical components or of (2) a facility of the same type built after the transfer of technology. It is understood that during that period there would be a conclusive presumption that any facility of the same type utilized transferred technology. But the agreed period is not intended to limit the duration of the safeguards imposed or the duration of the right to identify facilities as being constructed or operated on the basis of or by the use of transferred technology in accordance with paragraph 6(b)(2) of the Guidelines.

ANNEX

Clarifications of items on the Trigger List

A. *Complete nuclear reactors*
(Item 2.1.1 of the Trigger List)

1. A "nuclear reactor" basically includes the items within or attached directly to the reactor vessel, the equipment which controls the level of power in the core,

and the components which normally contain or come in direct contact with or control the primary coolant of the reactor core.

2. The export of the whole set of major items within this boundary will take place only in accordance with the procedures of the Guidelines. Those individual items within this functionally defined boundary which will be exported only in accordance with the procedures of the Guidelines are listed in paragraphs 2.1.1 to 2.1.5.

The Government reserves to itself the right to apply the procedures of the Guidelines to other items within the functionally defined boundary.

3. It is not intended to exclude reactors which could reasonably be capable of modification to produce significantly more than 100 grams of plutonium per year. Reactors designed for sustained operation at significant power levels, regardless of their capacity for plutonium production, are not considered as "zero energy reactors".

B. *Pressure vessels*
(Item 2.1.2 of the Trigger List)

4. A top plate for a reactor pressure vessel is covered by item 2.1.1 as a major shop-fabricated part of a pressure vessel.

5. Reactor internals (e.g. support columns and plates for the core and other vessel internals, control rod guide tubes, thermal shields, baffles, core grid plates, diffuser plates, etc.) are normally supplied by the reactor supplier. In some cases, certain internal support components are included in the fabrication of the pressure vessel. These items are sufficiently critical to the safety and reliability of the operation of the reactor (and, therefore, to the guarantees and liability of the reactor supplier), so that their supply, outside the basic supply arrangement for the reactor itself, would not be common practice. Therefore, although the separate supply of these unique, especially designed and prepared, critical, large and expensive items would not necessarily be considered as falling outside the area of concern, such a mode of supply is considered unlikely.

C. *Reactor control rods*
(Item 2.1.4 of the Trigger List)

6. This item includes, in addition to the neutron absorbing part, the support or suspension structures therefor if supplied separately.

D. *Fuel reprocessing plants*
(Item 2.3.1 of the Trigger List)

7. A "plant for the reprocessing of irradiated fuel elements" includes the equipment and components which normally come in direct contact with and directly control the irradiated fuel and the major nuclear material and fission product processing streams. The export of the whole set of major items within this boundary will take place only in accordance with the procedures of the Guidelines. In the present state of technology, the following items of equipment are considered to fall within the meaning of the phrase "and equipment especially designed or prepared therefor":

(a) Irradiated fuel element chopping machines: remotely operated equipment especially designed or prepared for use in a reprocessing plant as identified above and intended to cut, chop or shear irradiated nuclear fuel assemblies, bundles or rods; and

(b) Critically safe tanks (e.g. small diameter, annular or slab tanks) especially designed or prepared for use in a reprocessing plant as identified above, intended for dissolution of irradiated nuclear fuel and which are capable of withstanding hot, highly corrosive liquid, and which can be remotely loaded and maintained.

8. The Government reserves to itself the right to apply the procedures of the Guidelines to other items within the functionally defined boundary.

E. *Fuel fabrication plants*
(Item 2.4.1 of the Trigger List)

9. A "plant for the fabrication of fuel elements" includes the equipment:

(a) Which normally comes in direct contact with, or directly processes, or controls, the production flow of nuclear material, or

(b) Which seals the nuclear material within the cladding.

10. The export of the whole set of items for the foregoing operations will take place only in accordance with the procedures of the Guidelines. The Government will also give consideration to application of the procedures of the Guidelines to individual items intended for any of the foregoing operations, as well as for other fuel fabrication operations such as checking the integrity of the cladding or the seal, and the finish treatment to the sealed fuel.

F. *Isotope separation plant equipment*
(Item 2.5.1 of the Trigger List)

11. "Equipment, other than analytical instruments, especially designed or prepared for the separation of isotopes of uranium" includes each of the major items of equipment especially designed or prepared for the separation process. Such items include:

—gaseous diffusion barriers,

—gaseous diffuser housings,

—gas centrifuge assemblies, corrosion-resistant to UF_6,

—jet nozzle separation units,

—vortex separation units,

—large UF_6 corrosion-resistant axial or centrifugal compressors,

—special compressor seals for such compressors.

ANNEX B

Criteria for levels of physical protection

1. The purpose of physical protection of nuclear materials is to prevent unauthorized use and handling of these materials. Paragraph 3(a) of the Guidelines document calls for agreement among suppliers on the levels of protection to be ensured in relation to the type of materials, and equipment and facilities containing these materials, taking account of international recommendations.

2. Paragraph 3(b) of the Guidelines document states that implementation of measures of physical protection in the recipient country is the responsibility of the Government of that country. However, the levels of physical protection on which these measures have to be based should be the subject of an agreement between supplier and recipient. In this context these requirements should apply to all States.

3. The document INFCIRC/225 of the International Atomic Energy Agency entitled "The Physical Protection of Nuclear Material" and similar documents which from time to time are prepared by international groups of experts and updated as appropriate to account for changes in the state of the art and state of knowledge with regard to physical protection of nuclear material are a useful basis for guiding recipient States in designing a system of physical protection measures and procedures.

4. The categorization of nuclear material presented in the attached table or as it may be updated from time to time by mutual agreement of suppliers shall serve as the agreed basis for designating specific levels of physical protection in relation to the type of materials, and equipment and facilities containing these materials, pursuant to paragraph 3(a) and 3(b) of the Guidelines document.

5. The agreed levels of physical protection to be ensured by the competent national authorities in the use, storage and transportation of the materials listed in the attached table shall as a minimum include protection characteristics as follows:

CATEGORY III

Use and Storage within an area to which access is controlled.

Transportation under special precautions including prior arrangements among sender, recipient and carrier, and prior agreement between entities subject to the jurisdiction and regulation of supplier and recipient States, respectively, in case of international transport specifying time, place and procedures for transferring transport responsibility.

CATEGORY II

Use and Storage within a protected area to which access is controlled, i.e. an area under constant surveillance by guards or electronic devices, surrounded by a physical barrier with a limited number of points of entry under appropriate control, or any area with an equivalent level of physical protection.

Transportation under special precautions including prior arrangements among sender, recipient and carrier, and prior agreement between entities subject to the jurisdiction and regulation of supplier and recipient States, respectively, in case of international transport, specifying time, place and procedures for transferring transport responsibility.

CATEGORY I

Materials in this Category shall be protected with highly reliable systems against unauthorized use as follows:

Use and Storage within a highly protected area, i.e. a protected area as defined for Category II above, to which, in addition, access is restricted to persons whose trustworthiness has been determined, and which is under surveillance by guards who are in close communication with appropriate response forces. Specific measures taken in this context should have as their objective the detection and prevention of any assault, unauthorized access or unauthorized removal of material.

Transportation under special precautions as identified above for transportation of Category II and III materials and, in addition, under constant surveillance by escorts and under conditions which assure close communication with appropriate response forces.

6. Suppliers should request identification by recipients of those agencies or authorities having responsibility for ensuring that levels of protection are adequately met and having responsibility for internally coordinating response/recovery operations in the event of unauthorized use or handling of protected materials. Suppliers and recipients should also designate points of contact within their national authorities to cooperate on matters of out-of-country transportation and other matters of mutual concern.

TABLE: CATEGORIZATION OF NUCLEAR MATERIAL

Material	Form	Category		
		I	II	III
1. Plutonium [a]	Unirradiated [b]	2 kg or more	Less than 2 kg but more than 500 g	500 g or less [c]
2. Uranium-235	Unirradiated [b]			
	—uranium enriched to 20% ^{235}U or more	5 kg or more	Less than 5 kg but more than 1 kg	1 kg or less [c]
	—uranium enriched to 10% ^{235}U but less than 20%		10 kg or more	Less than 10 kg [c]
	—uranium enriched above natural, but less than 10% ^{235}U [d]			10 kg or more
3. Uranium-233	Unirradiated [b]	2 kg or more	Less than 2 kg but more than 500 g	500 g or less [c]
4. Irradiated fuel			Depleted or natural uranium, thorium or low-enriched fuel (less than 10% fissile content) [e, f]	

a/ As identified in the Trigger List.

b/ Material not irradiated in a reactor or material but with a radiation level equal to or less than 100 rads/hour at one metre unshielded.

c/ Less than a radiologically significant quantity should be exempted.

d/ Natural uranium, depleted uranium and thorium and quantities of uranium enriched to less than 10% not falling in Category III should be protected in accordance with prudent management practice.

e/ Although this level of protection is recommended, it would be open to States, upon evaluation of the specific circumstances, to assign a different category of physical protection.

f/ Other fuel which by virtue of its original fissile material content is classified as Category I or II before irradiation may be reduced one category level while the radiation level from the fuel exceeds 100 rads/hour at one metre unshielded.

Document 20

Declaration made by France on unilateral security assurances, 25 May 1978

Official Records of the General Assembly (GAOR), tenth special session, plenary meetings, third meeting, paragraph 5

In terms of their security, the decision by the States of a region to preserve a nuclear-free status should entail an obligation for the nuclear-weapon States to refrain from seeking a military advantage from the situation. Nuclear-weapon States should in particular preclude, according to a formula to be defined, any use or threat of the use of nuclear weapons against States that are part of a nuclear-free zone.

Document 21

Declaration made by the Union of Soviet Socialist Republics (USSR) on unilateral security assurances, 26 May 1978

GAOR, tenth special session, fifth meeting, paragraphs 84-85

From the rostrum of the special session our country declares that the Soviet Union will never use nuclear weapons against those States which renounce the production and acquisition of such weapons and do not have them on their territories.

We are aware of the responsibility which would thus fall on us as a result of such a commitment. But we are convinced that such a step to meet the wishes of non-nuclear States to have stronger security guarantees is in the interests of peace in the broadest sense of the word. We expect that the goodwill evinced by our country in this manner will lead to more active participation by a large number of States in strengthening the non-proliferation regime.

Document 22

Declaration made by China on unilateral security assurances, 7 June 1978

A/S-10/AC.1/17

For the present, all the nuclear countries, particularly the super-Powers, which possess nuclear weapons in large quantities, should immediately undertake not to resort to the threat or use of nuclear weapons against the non-nuclear countries and nuclear-free zones. China is not only ready to undertake this commitment but wishes to reiterate that at no time and in no circumstances will it be the first to use nuclear weapons.

Document 23

Declaration made by the United Kingdom of Great Britain and Northern Ireland on unilateral security assurances, 28 June 1978

GAOR, tenth special session, twenty-sixth meeting, paragraph 12

The United Kingdom is now ready formally to give such an assurance. I accordingly give the following assurance, on behalf of my Government, to non-nuclear-weapon States which are parties to the Treaty on the Non-Proliferation of Nuclear Weapons [resolution 2373 (XXII), annex] and to other internationally binding commitments not to manufacture or acquire nuclear explosive devices: Britain undertakes not to use nuclear weapons against such States except in the case of an attack on the United Kingdom, its dependent territories, its armed forces or its allies by such a State in association or alliance with a nuclear-weapon State.

Document 24

Declaration made by France on unilateral security assurances, 30 June 1978

GAOR, tenth special session, twenty-seventh meeting, paragraph 190

Furthermore, as regards paragraph 59 concerning assurances of the non-use of nuclear weapons against non-nuclear States, the delegation of France would recall that France is prepared to give such assurances, in accordance with arrangements to be negotiated, to States which constitute non-nuclear zones.

Document 25

Final Document of the Tenth Special Session of the General Assembly, New York (excerpt)

General Assembly resolution S-10/2, 30 June 1978

II. Declaration

11. Mankind today is confronted with an unprecedented threat of self-extinction arising from the massive and competitive accumulation of the most destructive weapons ever produced. Existing arsenals of nuclear weapons alone are more than sufficient to destroy all life on earth. Failure of efforts to halt and reverse the arms race, in particular the nuclear arms race, increases the danger of the proliferation of nuclear weapons. Yet the arms race continues. Military budgets are constantly growing, with enormous consumption of human and material resources. The increase in weapons, especially nuclear weapons, far from helping to strengthen international security, on the contrary weakens it. The vast stockpiles and tremendous build-up of arms and armed forces and the competition for qualitative refinement of weapons of all kinds, to which scientific resources and technological advances are diverted, pose incalculable threats to peace. This situation both reflects and aggravates international tensions, sharpens conflicts in various regions of the world, hinders the process of detente, exacerbates the differences between opposing military alliances, jeopardizes the security of all States, heightens the sense of insecurity among all States, including the non-nuclear-weapon States, and increases the threat of nuclear war.

12. The arms race, particularly in its nuclear aspect, runs counter to efforts to achieve futher relaxation of international tension, to establish international relations based on peaceful coexistence and trust between all States, and to develop broad international cooperation and understanding. The arms race impedes the realization of the purposes, and is incompatible with the principles, of the Charter of the United Nations, especially respect for sovereignty, refraining from the threat or use of force against the territorial integrity or political independence of any State, the peaceful settlement of disputes and non-intervention and non-interference in the internal affairs of States. It also adversely affects the right of peoples freely to determine their systems of social and economic development, and hinders the struggle for self-determination and the elimination of colonial rule, racial or foreign domination or occupation. Indeed, the massive accumulation of armaments and the acquisition of armaments technology by racist regimes, as well as their possible acquisition of nuclear weapons, present a challenging and

increasingly dangerous obstacle to a world community faced with the urgent need to disarm. It is, therefore, essential for purposes of disarmament to prevent any further acquisition of arms or arms technology by such regimes, especially through strict adherence by all States to relevant decisions of the Security Council.

13. Enduring international peace and security cannot be built on the accumulation of weaponry by military alliances nor be sustained by a precarious balance of deterrence or doctrines of strategic superiority. Genuine and lasting peace can only be created through the effective implementation of the security system provided for in the Charter of the United Nations and the speedy and substantial reduction of arms and armed forces, by international agreement and mutual example, leading ultimately to general and complete disarmament under effective international control. At the same time, the causes of the arms race and threats to peace must be reduced and to this end effective action should be taken to eliminate tensions and settle disputes by peaceful means.

14. Since the process of disarmament affects the vital security interests of all States, they must all be actively concerned with and contribute to the measures of disarmament and arms limitation, which have an essential part to play in maintaining and strengthening international security. Therefore the role and responsibility of the United Nations in the sphere of disarmament, in accordance with its Charter, must be strengthened.

15. It is essential that not only Governments but also the peoples of the world recognize and understand the dangers in the present situation. In order that an international conscience may develop and that world public opinion may exercise a positive influence, the United Nations should increase the dissemination of information on the armaments race and disarmament with the full cooperation of Member States.

16. In a world of finite resources there is a close relationship between expenditure on armaments and economic and social development. Military expenditures are reaching ever higher levels, the highest percentage of which can be attributed to the nuclear-weapon States and most of their allies, with prospects of further expansion and the danger of further increases in the expenditures of other countries. The hundreds of billions of dollars spent annually on the manufacture or improvement of weapons are in sombre and dramatic contrast to the want and

poverty in which two thirds of the world's population live. This colossal waste of resources is even more serious in that it diverts to military purposes not only material but also technical and human resources which are urgently needed for development in all countries, particularly in the developing countries. Thus, the economic and social consequences of the arms race are so detrimental that its continuation is obviously incompatible with the implementation of the new international economic order based on justice, equity and cooperation. Consequently, resources released as a result of the implementation of disarmament measures should be used in a manner which will help to promote the well-being of all peoples and to improve the economic conditions of the developing countries.

17.   Disarmament has thus become an imperative and most urgent task facing the international community. No real progress has been made so far in the crucial field of reduction of armaments. However, certain positive changes in international relations in some areas of the world provide some encouragement. Agreements have been reached that have been important in limiting certain weapons or eliminating them altogether, as in the case of the Convention on the Prohibition of the Development, Production and Stockpiling of Bacteriological (Biological) and Toxin Weapons and on Their Destruction 1/ and excluding particular areas from the arms race. The fact remains that these agreements relate only to measures of limited restraint while the arms race continues. These partial measures have done little to bring the world closer to the goal of general and complete disarmament. For more than a decade there have been no negotiations leading to a treaty on general and complete disarmament. The pressing need now is to translate into practical terms the provisions of this Final Document and to proceed along the road of binding and effective international agreements in the field of disarmament.

18.   Removing the threat of a world war—a nuclear war—is the most acute and urgent task of the present day. Mankind is confronted with a choice: we must halt the arms race and proceed to disarmament or face annihilation.

19.   The ultimate objective of the efforts of States in the disarmament process is general and complete disarmament under effective international control. The principal goals of disarmament are to ensure the survival of mankind and to eliminate the danger of war, in particular nuclear war, to ensure that war is no longer an instrument for settling international disputes and that the use and the threat of force are eliminated from international life, as provided for in the Charter of the United Nations. Progress towards this objective requires the conclusion and implementation of agreements on the cessation of the arms race and on genuine measures of disarmament, taking into account the need of States to protect their security.

20.   Among such measures, effective measures of nuclear disarmament and the prevention of nuclear war have the highest priority. To this end, it is imperative to remove the threat of nuclear weapons, to halt and reverse the nuclear arms race until the total elimination of nuclear weapons and their delivery systems has been achieved, and to prevent the proliferation of nuclear weapons. At the same time, other measures designed to prevent the outbreak of nuclear war and to lessen the danger of the threat or use of nuclear weapons should be taken.

21.   Along with these measures, agreements or other effective measures should be adopted to prohibit or prevent the development, production or use of other weapons of mass destruction. In this context, an agreement on elimination of all chemical weapons should be concluded as a matter of high priority.

22.   Together with negotiations on nuclear disarmament measures, negotiations should be carried out on the balanced reduction of armed forces and of conventional armaments, based on the principle of undiminished security of the parties with a view to promoting or enhancing stability at a lower military level, taking into account the need of all States to protect their security. These negotiations should be conducted with particular emphasis on armed forces and conventional weapons of nuclear-weapon States and other militarily significant countries. There should also be negotiations on the limitation of international transfer of conventional weapons, based in particular on the same principle, and taking into account the inalienable right to self-determination and independence of peoples under colonial or foreign domination and the obligations of States to respect that right, in accordance with the Charter of the United Nations and the Declaration on Principles of International Law concerning Friendly Relations and Cooperation among States, 2/ as well as the need of recipient States to protect their security.

23.   Further international action should be taken to prohibit or restrict for humanitarian reasons the use of specific conventional weapons, including those which may be excessively injurious, cause unnecessary suffering or have indiscriminate effects.

24.   Collateral measures in both the nuclear and conventional fields, together with other measures specifically designed to build confidence, should be undertaken in order to contribute to the creation of favourable con-

1/ Resolution 2826 (XXVI), annex.
2/ Resolution 2625 (XXV), annex.

ditions for the adoption of additional disarmament measures and to further the relaxation of international tension.

25. Negotiations and measures in the field of disarmament shall be guided by the fundamental principles set forth below.

26. All States Members of the United Nations reaffirm their full commitment to the purposes of the Charter of the United Nations and their obligation strictly to observe its principles as well as other relevant and generally accepted principles of international law relating to the maintenance of international peace and security. They stress the special importance of refraining from the threat or use of force against the sovereignty, territorial integrity or political independence of any State, or against peoples under colonial or foreign domination seeking to exercise their right to self-determination and to achieve independence; non-intervention and non-interference in the internal affairs of other States; the inviolability of international frontiers; and the peaceful settlement of disputes, having regard to the inherent right of States to individual and collective self-defence in accordance with the Charter.

27. In accordance with the Charter, the United Nations has a central role and primary responsibility in the sphere of disarmament. In order effectively to discharge this role and facilitate and encourage all measures in this field, the United Nations should be kept appropriately informed of all steps in this field, whether unilateral, bilateral, regional or multilateral, without prejudice to the progress of negotiations.

28. All the peoples of the world have a vital interest in the success of disarmament negotiations. Consequently, all States have the duty to contribute to efforts in the field of disarmament. All States have the right to participate in disarmament negotiations. They have the right to participate on an equal footing in those multilateral disarmament negotiations which have a direct bearing on their national security. While disarmament is the responsibility of all States, the nuclear-weapon States have the primary responsibility for nuclear disarmament and, together with other militarily significant States, for halting and reversing the arms race. It is therefore important to secure their active participation.

29. The adoption of disarmament measures should take place in such an equitable and balanced manner as to ensure the right of each State to security and to ensure that no individual State or group of States may obtain advantages over others at any stage. At each stage the objective should be undiminished security at the lowest possible level of armaments and military forces.

30. An acceptable balance of mutual responsibilities and obligations for nuclear and non-nuclear-weapon States should be strictly observed.

31. Disarmament and arms limitation agreements should provide for adequate measures of verification satisfactory to all parties concerned in order to create the necessary confidence and ensure that they are being observed by all parties. The form and modalities of the verification to be provided for in any specific agreement depend upon and should be determined by the purposes, scope and nature of the agreement. Agreements should provide for the participation of parties directly or through the United Nations system in the verification process. Where appropriate, a combination of several methods of verification as well as other compliance procedures should be employed.

32. All States, in particular nuclear-weapon States, should consider various proposals designed to secure the avoidance of the use of nuclear weapons, and the prevention of nuclear war. In this context, while noting the declarations made by nuclear-weapon States, effective arrangements, as appropriate, to assure non-nuclear-weapon States against the use or the threat of use of nuclear weapons could strengthen the security of those States and international peace and security.

33. The establishment of nuclear-weapon-free zones on the basis of agreements or arrangements freely arrived at among the States of the zone concerned and the full compliance with those agreements or arrangements, thus ensuring that the zones are genuinely free from nuclear weapons, and respect for such zones by nuclear-weapon States constitute an important disarmament measure.

34. Disarmament, relaxation of international tension, respect for the right to self-determination and national independence, the peaceful settlement of disputes in accordance with the Charter of the United Nations and the strengthening of international peace and security are directly related to each other. Progress in any of these spheres has a beneficial effect on all of them; in turn, failure in one sphere has negative effects on others.

35. There is also a close relationship between disarmament and development. Progress in the former would help greatly in the realization of the latter. Therefore resources released as a result of the implementation of disarmament measures should be devoted to the economic and social development of all nations and contribute to the bridging of the economic gap between developed and developing countries.

36. Non-proliferation of nuclear weapons is a matter of universal concern. Measures of disarmament must be consistent with the inalienable right of all States, without discrimination, to develop, acquire and use nuclear technology, equipment and materials for the peaceful use of nuclear energy and to determine their peaceful nuclear programmes in accordance with their national

priorities, needs and interests, bearing in mind the need to prevent the proliferation of nuclear weapons. International cooperation in the peaceful uses of nuclear energy should be conducted under agreed and appropriate international safeguards applied on a non-discriminatory basis.

37. Significant progress in disarmament, including nuclear disarmament, would be facilitated by parallel measures to strengthen the security of States and to improve the international situation in general.

38. Negotiations on partial measures of disarmament should be conducted concurrently with negotiations on more comprehensive measures and should be followed by negotiations leading to a treaty on general and complete disarmament under effective international control.

39. Qualitative and quantitative disarmament measures are both important for halting the arms race. Efforts to that end must include negotiations on the limitation and cessation of the qualitative improvement of armaments, especially weapons of mass destruction and the development of new means of warfare so that ultimately scientific and technological achievements may be used solely for peaceful purposes.

40. Universality of disarmament agreements helps create confidence among States. When multilateral agreements in the field of disarmament are negotiated, every effort should be made to ensure that they are universally acceptable. The full compliance of all parties with the provisions contained in such agreements would also contribute to the attainment of that goal.

41. In order to create favourable conditions for success in the disarmament process, all States should strictly abide by the provisions of the Charter of the United Nations, refrain from actions which might adversely affect efforts in the field of disarmament, and display a constructive approach to negotiations and the political will to reach agreements. There are certain negotiations on disarmament under way at different levels, the early and successful completion of which could contribute to limiting the arms race. Unilateral measures of arms limitation or reduction could also contribute to the attainment of that goal.

42. Since prompt measures should be taken in order to halt and reverse the arms race, Member States hereby declare that they will respect the objectives and principles stated above and make every effort faithfully to carry out the Programme of Action set forth in section III below.

III. Programme of Action

43. Progress towards the goal of general and complete disarmament can be achieved through the implementation of a programme of action on disarmament, in accordance with the goals and principles established in the Declaration on disarmament. The present Programme of Action contains priorities and measures in the field of disarmament that States should undertake as a matter of urgency with a view to halting and reversing the arms race and to giving the necessary impetus to efforts designed to achieve genuine disarmament leading to general and complete disarmament under effective international control.

44. The present Programme of Action enumerates the specific measures of disarmament which should be implemented over the next few years, as well as other measures and studies to prepare the way for future negotiations and for progress towards general and complete disarmament.

45. Priorities in disarmament negotiations shall be: nuclear weapons; other weapons of mass destruction, including chemical weapons; conventional weapons, including any which may be deemed to be excessively injurious or to have indiscriminate effects; and reduction of armed forces.

46. Nothing should preclude States from conducting negotiations on all priority items concurrently.

47. Nuclear weapons pose the greatest danger to mankind and to the survival of civilization. It is essential to halt and reverse the nuclear arms race in all its aspects in order to avert the danger of war involving nuclear weapons. The ultimate goal in this context is the complete elimination of nuclear weapons.

48. In the task of achieving the goals of nuclear disarmament, all the nuclear-weapon States, in particular those among them which possess the most important nuclear arsenals, bear a special responsibility.

49. The process of nuclear disarmament should be carried out in such a way, and requires measures to ensure, that the security of all States is guaranteed at progressively lower levels of nuclear armaments, taking into account the relative qualitative and quantitative importance of the existing arsenals of the nuclear-weapon States and other States concerned.

50. The achievement of nuclear disarmament will require urgent negotiation of agreements at appropriate stages and with adequate measures of verification satisfactory to the States concerned for:

(a) Cessation of the qualitative improvement and development of nuclear-weapon systems;

(b) Cessation of the production of all types of nuclear weapons and their means of delivery, and of the production of fissionable material for weapons purposes;

(c) A comprehensive, phased programme with agreed time-frames, whenever feasible, for progressive and balanced reduction of stockpiles of nuclear weapons and their means of delivery, leading to their ultimate and complete elimination at the earliest possible time.

Consideration can be given in the course of the negotiations to mutual and agreed limitation or prohibition, without prejudice to the security of any State, of any types of nuclear armaments.

51. The cessation of nuclear-weapon testing by all States within the framework of an effective nuclear disarmament process would be in the interest of mankind. It would make a significant contribution to the above aim of ending the qualitative improvement of nuclear weapons and the development of new types of such weapons and of preventing the proliferation of nuclear weapons. In this context the negotiations now in progress "on a treaty prohibiting nuclear-weapon tests, and a protocol covering nuclear explosions for peaceful purposes, which would be an integral part of the treaty," should be concluded urgently and the result submitted for full consideration by the multilateral negotiating body with a view to the submission of a draft treaty to the General Assembly at the earliest possible date. All efforts should be made by the negotiating parties to achieve an agreement which, following endorsement by the General Assembly, could attract the widest possible adherence. In this context, various views were expressed by non-nuclear-weapon States that, pending the conclusion of this treaty, the world community would be encouraged if all the nuclear-weapon States refrained from testing nuclear weapons. In this connection, some nuclear-weapon States expressed different views.

52. The Union of Soviet Socialist Republics and the United States of America should conclude at the earliest possible date the agreement they have been pursuing for several years in the second series of the strategic arms limitation talks. They are invited to transmit in good time the text of the agreement to the General Assembly. It should be followed promptly by further strategic arms limitation negotiations between the two parties, leading to agreed significant reductions of, and qualitative limitations on, strategic arms. It should constitute an important step in the direction of nuclear disarmament and, ultimately, of establishment of a world free of such weapons.

53. The process of nuclear disarmament described in the paragraph on this subject should be expedited by the urgent and vigorous pursuit to a successful conclusion of ongoing negotiations and the urgent initiation of further negotiations among the nuclear-weapon States.

54. Significant progress in nuclear disarmament would be facilitated both by parallel political or international legal measures to strengthen the security of States and by progress in the limitation and reduction of armed forces and conventional armaments of the nuclear-weapon States and other States in the regions concerned.

55. Real progress in the field of nuclear disarmament could create an atmosphere conducive to progress in conventional disarmament on a worldwide basis.

56. The most effective guarantee against the danger of nuclear war and the use of nuclear weapons is nuclear disarmament and the complete elimination of nuclear weapons.

57. Pending the achievement of this goal, for which negotiations should be vigorously pursued, and bearing in mind the devastating results which nuclear war would have on belligerents and non-belligerents alike, the nuclear-weapon States have special responsibilities to undertake measures aimed at preventing the outbreak of nuclear war, and of the use of force in international relations, subject to the provisions of the Charter of the United Nations, including the use of nuclear weapons.

58. In this context all States, in particular nuclear-weapon States, should consider as soon as possible various proposals designed to secure the avoidance of the use of nuclear weapons, the prevention of nuclear war and related objectives, where possible through international agreement, and thereby ensure that the survival of mankind is not endangered. All States should actively participate in efforts to bring about conditions in international relations among States in which a code of peaceful conduct of nations in international affairs could be agreed and which would preclude the use or threat of use of nuclear weapons.

59. In the same context, the nuclear-weapon States are called upon to take steps to assure the non-nuclear-weapon States against the use or threat of use of nuclear-weapons. The General Assembly notes the declarations made by the nuclear-weapon States and urges them to pursue efforts to conclude, as appropriate, effective arrangements to assure non-nuclear-weapon States against the use or threat of use of nuclear weapons.

60. The establishment of nuclear-weapon-free zones on the basis of arrangements freely arrived at among the States of the region concerned constitutes an important disarmament measure.

61. The process of establishing such zones in different parts of the world should be encouraged with the ultimate objective of achieving a world entirely free of nuclear weapons. In the process of establishing such zones, the characteristics of each region should be taken into account. The States participating in such zones should undertake to comply fully with all the objectives, purposes and principles of the agreements or arrangements establishing the zones, thus ensuring that they are genuinely free from nuclear weapons.

62. With respect to such zones, the nuclear-weapon

States in turn are called upon to give undertakings, the modalities of which are to be negotiated with the competent authority of each zone, in particular:

(a) To respect strictly the status of the nuclear-weapon-free zone;

(b) To refrain from the use or threat of use of nuclear weapons against the States of the zone.

63. In the light of existing conditions, and without prejudice to other measures which may be considered in other regions, the following measures are especially desirable:

(a) Adoption by the States concerned of all relevant measures to ensure the full application of the Treaty for the Prohibition of Nuclear Weapons in Latin America (Treaty of Tlatelolco), 3/ taking into account the views expressed at the tenth special session on the adherence to it;

(b) Signature and ratification of the Additional Protocols of the Treaty for the Prohibition of Nuclear Weapons in Latin America (Treaty of Tlatelolco) by the States entitled to become parties to those instruments which have not yet done so;

(c) In Africa, where the Organization of African Unity has affirmed a decision for the denuclearization of the region, the Security Council of the United Nations shall take appropriate effective steps whenever necessary to prevent the frustration of this objective;

(d) The serious consideration of the practical and urgent steps, as described in paragraphs above, required for the implementation of the proposal to establish a nuclear-weapon-free zone in the Middle East, in accordance with the relevant General Assembly resolutions, where all parties directly concerned have expressed their support for the concept and where the danger of nuclear-weapon proliferation exists. The establishment of a nuclear-weapon-free zone in the Middle East would greatly enhance international peace and security. Pending the establishment of such a zone in the region, States of the region should solemnly declare that they will refrain on a reciprocal basis from producing, acquiring or in any other way possessing nuclear weapons and nuclear explosive devices and from permitting the stationing of nuclear weapons on their territory by any third party, and agree to place all their nuclear activities under International Atomic Energy Agency safeguards. Consideration should be given to a Security Council role in advancing the establishment of a nuclear-weapon-free zone in the Middle East;

(e) All States in the region of South Asia have expressed their determination to keep their countries free of nuclear weapons. No action should be taken by them which might deviate from that objective. In this context, the question of establishing a nuclear-weapon-free zone in South Asia has been dealt with in several resolutions of the General Assembly, which is keeping the subject under consideration.

64. The establishment of zones of peace in various regions of the world under appropriate conditions, to be clearly defined and determined freely by the States concerned in the zone, taking into account the characteristics of the zone and the principles of the Charter of the United Nations, and in conformity with international law, can contribute to strengthening the security of States within such zones and to international peace and security as a whole. in this regard, the General Assembly notes the proposals for the establishment of zones of peace, *inter alia*, in:

(a) South-East Asia where States in the region have expressed interest in the establishment of such a zone, in conformity with their views;

(b) The Indian Ocean, taking into account the deliberations of the General Assembly and its relevant resolutions and the need to ensure the maintenance of peace and security in the region.

65. It is imperative, as an integral part of the effort to halt and reverse the arms race, to prevent the proliferation of nuclear weapons. The goal of nuclear non-proliferation is on the one hand to prevent the emergence of any additional nuclear-weapon States besides the existing five nuclear-weapon States, and on the other progressively to reduce and eventually eliminate nuclear weapons altogether. This involves obligations and responsibilities on the part of both nuclear-weapon States and non-nuclear-weapon States, the former undertaking to stop the nuclear arms race and to achieve nuclear disarmament by urgent application of the measures outlined in the relevant paragraphs of this Final Document, and all States undertaking to prevent the spread of nuclear weapons.

66. Effective measures can and should be taken at the national level and through international agreements to minimize the danger of the proliferation of nuclear weapons without jeopardizing energy supplies or the development of nuclear energy for peaceful purposes. Therefore, the nuclear-weapon States and the non-nuclear-weapon States should jointly take further steps to develop an international consensus of ways and means, on a universal and non-discriminatory basis, to prevent the proliferation of nuclear weapons.

67. Full implementation of all the provisions of existing instruments on non-proliferation, such as the Treaty on the Non-Proliferation of Nuclear Weapons 4/ and/or the Treaty for the Prohibition of Nuclear Weapons in Latin America (Treaty of Tlatelolco) by States parties

3/ United Nations, *Treaty Series*, vol. 634, No. 9068.
4/ Resolution 2373 (XXII), annex.

to those instruments will be an important contribution to this end. Adherence to such instruments has increased in recent years and the hope has been expressed by the parties that this trend might continue.

68. Non-proliferation measures should not jeopardize the full exercise of the inalienable rights of all States to apply and develop their programmes for the peaceful uses of nuclear energy for economic and social development in conformity with their priorities, interests and needs. All States should also have access to and be free to acquire technology, equipment and materials for peaceful uses of nuclear energy, taking into account the particular needs of the developing countries. International cooperation in this field should be under agreed and appropriate international safeguards applied through the international Atomic Energy Agency on a non-discriminatory basis in order to prevent effectively the proliferation of nuclear weapons.

69. Each country's choices and decisions in the field of the peaceful uses of nuclear energy should be respected without jeopardizing their respective fuel cycle policies or international cooperation, agreements and contracts for the peaceful uses of nuclear energy, provided that the agreed safeguard measures mentioned above are applied.

70. In accordance with the principles and provisions of General Assembly resolution 32/50 of 8 December 1977, international cooperation for the promotion of the transfer and utilization of nuclear technology for economic and social development, especially in the developing countries, should be strengthened.

71. Efforts should be made to conclude the work of the International Nuclear Fuel Cycle Evaluation strictly in accordance with the objectives set out in the final communique of its Organizing Conference. 5/

72. All States should adhere to the Protocol for the Prohibition of the Use in War of Asphyxiating, Poisonous or Other Gases, and of Bacteriological Methods of Warfare, signed at Geneva on 17 June 1925. 6/

73. All States which have not yet done so should consider adhering to the Convention on the Prohibition of the Development, Production and Stockpiling of Bacteriological (Biological) and Toxin Weapons and on Their Destruction.

74. States should also consider the possibility of adhering to multilateral agreements concluded so far in the disarmament field which are mentioned below in this section.

75. The complete and effective prohibition of the development, production and stockpiling of all chemical weapons and their destruction represent one of the most urgent measures of disarmament. Consequently, the conclusion of a convention to this end, on which negotiations have been going on for several years, is one of the most urgent tasks of multilateral negotiations. After its conclusion, all States should contribute to ensuring the broadest possible application of the convention through its early signature and ratification.

76. A convention should be concluded prohibiting the development, production, stockpiling and use of radiological weapons.

77. In order to help prevent a qualitative arms race and so that scientific and technological achievements may ultimately be used solely for peaceful purposes, effective measures should be taken to avoid the danger and prevent the emergence of new types of weapons of mass destruction based on new scientific principles and achievements. Efforts should be appropriately pursued aiming at the prohibition of such new types and new systems of weapons of mass destruction. Specific agreements could be concluded on particular types of new weapons of mass destruction which may be identified. This question should be kept under continuing review.

78. The Committee on Disarmament should keep under review the need for a further prohibition of military or any other hostile use of environmental modification techniques in order to eliminate the dangers to mankind from such use.

79. In order to promote the peaceful use of and to avoid an arms race on the sea-bed and the ocean floor and the subsoil thereof, the Committee on Disarmament is requested—in consultation with the States parties to the Treaty on the Prohibition of the Emplacement of Nuclear Weapons and Other Weapons of Mass Destruction on the Sea-Bed and the Ocean Floor and in the Subsoil Thereof, 7/ and taking into account the proposals made during the 1977 Review Conference of the parties to that Treaty and any relevant technological developments—to proceed promptly with the consideration of further measures in the field of disarmament for the prevention of an arms race in that environment.

80. In order to prevent an arms race in outer space, further measures should be taken and appropriate international negotiations held in accordance with the spirit of the Treaty on Principles Governing the Activities of States in the Exploration and Use of Outer Space, including the Moon and Other Celestial Bodies. 8/

5/ See A/C.1/32/7.
6/ League of Nations, *Treaty Series*, vol. XCIV (1929), No. 2138.
7/ Resolution 2660 (XXV), annex.
8/ Resolution 2222 (XXI), annex.

Document 26

Declaration made by the United States of America on unilateral security assurances, 17 November 1978

A/C.1/33/7, annex, 17 November 1978

The United States will not use nuclear weapons against any non-nuclear-weapons State party to the NPT (Non-Proliferation Treaty) or any comparable internationally binding commitment not to acquire nuclear explosive devices, except in the case of an attack on the United States, its territories or armed forces, or its allies, by such a State allied to a nuclear-weapons state or associated with a nuclear-weapons State in carrying out or sustaining the attack.

Document 27

Message from the Secretary-General of the United Nations to the Second Review Conference of the Parties to the NPT

NPT/CONF.II/SR.1, 11 August 1980

I wish to extend my greetings to the participants in the second Review Conference of the Parties to the Treaty on the Non-Proliferation of Nuclear Weapons. This Conference is very timely in view of the apparently increasing danger of the spread of nuclear weapons in recent years. Consequently, there is now greater urgency than before to achieve universal acceptance of the Treaty. The task of the Conference is to examine how this objective can be attained.

The goal of non-proliferation, as the Final Document of the tenth special session of the General Assembly made clear, is twofold: to prevent the emergence of nuclear-weapon States in addition to the existing five and progressively to reduce nuclear weapons with a view to their eventual elimination. This involved obligations and responsibilities on the part of nuclear and non-nuclear-weapon States. Nuclear disarmament remains an overriding priority and it is evident that initiatives towards it have to come from States which possess the largest nuclear arsenals. A significant reduction of strategic arms is a matter of crucial importance in this regard as it would greatly help in building the atmosphere of international confidence essential for giving an impetus to the process of nuclear disarmament. Recent achievements towards this end need to be consolidated and followed by negotiations for further meaningful limitations of strategic arms.

I also wish to stress once again the vital importance of the measures to halt and reverse the nuclear arms race, in particular of a general and complete ban on the testing of nuclear weapons which is an indispensable first step in this endeavour.

Another aspect of the balance of mutual responsibilities and obligations is the strengthening of the security of non-nuclear-weapon States. I note with satisfaction that in recent years there have been new initiatives in this area and that negotiations are under way in the framework of the Committee on Disarmament with a view to reaching agreement on effective international arrangements to assure non-nuclear-weapon States against the threat or use of nuclear weapons.

Finally, there is the question of minimizing the danger of the proliferation of nuclear weapons without jeopardizing the supply or the development of nuclear energy for peaceful purposes. The principle of sovereign equality connotes that all States should be able to have access to, and benefit from, nuclear technology for peaceful purposes. At the same time, humanity's survival requires that this access or utilization must be subject to international safeguards so that it does not serve as an avenue for the proliferation of nuclear weapons. The International Atomic Energy Agency, under the distinguished leadership of Dr. Sigvard Eklund, has performed invaluable work in the development and implementation of such safeguards. The International Nuclear Fuel Cycle Evaluation, which was made this year with the participation of both developed and developing States, has provided a comprehensive technical analysis that will no doubt facilitate the search for widely acceptable solutions in the years ahead.

This Review Conference is faced with a range of difficult and delicate issues that have a direct bearing on such fundamental matters as international peace and security, assured energy supplies, scientific and technological self-reliance and economic development. Different States approach those issues from different perspectives. I am sure, however, that all delegations here have the common desire to ensure the widest possible acceptability of a treaty which remains the pillar of international efforts to prevent the spread of nuclear weapons. I am, therefore, confident that your deliberations will be animated by a spirit of mutual understanding and cooperation towards ensuring the full implementation of the Treaty in the near future.

I extend to you my best wishes for success in this most important endeavour.

Document 28

Statement by the Director General of the IAEA at the Second Review Conference of the NPT

Not issued as a United Nations document

The Treaty on the Non-Proliferation of Nuclear Weapons makes provision for a periodical review of the operation of the Treaty.

Since the first Review Conference in 1975, there have been a number of significant developments which are noteworthy. Briefly, these can be summarized as follows:

(i) A number of additional States have joined the NPT—among them are several countries with extensive nuclear facilities and programmes;

(ii) A considerable number of additional safeguards agreements have been concluded with the non-nuclear weapon States;

(iii) There has been substantial progress in the implementation of safeguards agreements, in particular in the agreement with EURATOM non-nuclear-weapon States, and in organizing the first safeguard field offices.

(iv) There have been significant improvements in safeguards techniques, implementation and instrumentation, and safeguards procedures. The possibility of introducing a system of international plutonium storage to give practical effect to the safeguards measures foreseen in the Agency's Statute has also been under study since December 1978. Another study is presently engaged in examining the potential for international management of spent fuel and problems created by growing accumulations of spent fuel;

(v) An international Convention on the Physical Protection of Nuclear Material has been successfully negotiated and already signed by 26 Member States;

(vi) Considerable advance has been made towards the realization of the full potential of the Treaty for the Prohibition or Nuclear Weapons in Latin America, known as the Treaty of Tlatelolco. With the ratification of the additional protocol II to that Treaty by the Soviet Union, all five nuclear-weapon States now adhere to that protocol;

(vii) The International Nuclear Fuel Cycle Evaluation, a technical study completed in February this year, has examined a range of options on how nuclear power could be made widely available while minimizing the risk of nuclear weapons proliferation. By identifying some useful concepts for strengthening international cooperation, this study may lead to better mutual understanding amongst the supplier and the consumer countries of their respective concerns in regard both to proliferation and assurance of supply.

The five years that have elapsed since the first NPT Review Conference are thus marked by a number of achievements and it is of fundamental importance that the NPT continues to serve as the essential framework for international non-proliferation efforts. However, one must not forget that the Treaty not only prohibits the acquisition of nuclear weapons by non-nuclear-weapon Parties but also places an obligation on the Parties to the Treaty to facilitate and promote peaceful nuclear activities and to work towards reducing nuclear arsenals. This two-fold objective represents an indivisible goal of the Treaty to which all Parties, both nuclear and non-nuclear-weapon States, are pledged and stand equally committed. It is my considered opinion that upon the success or failure to realize this goal may ultimately depend the very fate of the Treaty and its consequential effect on the fabric of international security and human survival.

I should now like to refer to the role of the IAEA in the operation of the NPT. Our principal concern is related to the implementation of Articles III, IV and V and, in response to the request made by the Preparatory Committee of this Conference for background papers on the Agency's activities related to the Treaty, we have submitted analytical and technical reports which are before you.

Article III

Our obligations are most clearcut and specific under Article III which, in effect, calls upon the IAEA to apply safeguards to all nuclear material in all peaceful activities of the non-nuclear-weapon States that are Party to the Treaty. Furthermore, nuclear items may not be exported unless the relevant nuclear material will be subject to safeguards in the importing non-nuclear-weapon State.

Of the 113 Parties to the Treaty, 110 are non-nuclear-weapon States. Of these, 69 have concluded the required safeguards agreements with the Agency. I take the opportunity of calling upon the other 41 Governments that have not yet concluded their relevant safeguards agreements to do so without further delay.

Let me turn now to the scope and dimensions of the safeguards operation itself. The Agency's budget for safeguards has increased from approximately one million dollars in 1970, when the Treaty entered into force, to approximately five million dollars at the time of the First Review Conference and to 22 million this year. I should like, however, to stress that these costs represent only a completely insignificant fraction of the cost per nuclear kwh produced. While part of this growth in expenditure has reflected the impact of inflation and the declining value of the dollar, there has also been a very substantial expansion in the safeguards programme. Thus, for instance, the professional staff of the Department of Safeguards has increased from 54 in 1970 to 101 in 1975, to 206 in 1980 of whom 138 are full-time inspectors. The number of power reactors under safeguards has risen from 10 in 1970 to 117 at the beginning of 1980. The amount of plutonium has increased from 770 kg in 1970 to 17 tons in 1975 and 68 tons at the beginning of this year.

In fact, today over 95% of the nuclear plants in all non-nuclear-weapon States of the world, whether Parties to the NPT or not, are under IAEA safeguards. Less than a dozen significant facilities in all non-nuclear-weapon States are unsafeguarded. However, some of these unsafeguarded plants are very significant. I shall return to this point later.

The IAEA has also begun applying safeguards under the voluntary offer by the United Kingdom to place its civilian nuclear material under IAEA safeguards where their breeder reactor will be of special interest. The safeguards agreement under the US offer has been approved by the Board and recently also by the United States Senate. A somewhat similar agreement with France has been approved by the Board and signed and is awaiting ratification from the French Parliament.

Instead of trying to describe technical improvements of the safeguards system, I recommend that you visit the two exhibits adjacent to this Hall, where some equipment used is being exposed as well as some explanatory maps and diagrams.

For the past four years, the Secretariat has provided the Board with a detailed statistical analysis and evaluation of the effectiveness of the safeguards operation during the preceding year, the so-called SIR report. In no case has the Agency detected any discrepancy which would indicate the diversion of a significant amount of safeguarded nuclear material, and it has concluded that all such material remained in peaceful nuclear activities or was otherwise adequately accounted for.

The system has now evolved to the stage where safeguards can be or are being applied to every category of plant from small research reactors to reprocessing plants, and other highly sensitive facilities, including gas centrifuge enrichment facilities with respect to nuclear material in the storage area of such facilities.

Experience underlines the need for designing nuclear plants of all kinds in such a way as to permit the easy, effective and inexpensive application of safeguards.

The safeguards procedures for enrichment plants still have to be fully developed. The same holds true for large commercial reprocessing plants in which a thousand or more tons of spent fuel will be handled each year. At this time, only a couple of such plants exist. It is only in the 1990s that they are likely to come into operation in non-nuclear-weapon States. Meanwhile, the development of safeguards procedures for this type of plant is under way and this would of course be facilitated if the plants were regionally or internationally managed as already concluded by the First Review Conference.

Summing up, although there are a number of problem areas, the Agency has not encountered any insurmountable technical difficulties in the effective application of safeguards and does not foresee any in the immediate future. On the contrary, we believe that we shall be able to continue to increase the technical effectiveness of the safeguards system as it becomes a routine industrial operation. The cost effectiveness will be improved by this as well as—and I underline this—*by a proper selection of the objects to be safeguarded.*

The application of safeguards is not, however, only a technical matter. The safeguards system is only as good as Member States want it to be. Its efficacy depends crucially on the willingness of Governments to cooperate with the Agency. On several occasions I have reported to the Board of Governors that we are running into serious difficulties in the designation and acceptance of inspectors. It is, of course, the right of every State to reject the proposed designation of an individual who is personally unacceptable. The practice however of rejecting whole categories of inspectors on political, linguistic or nationality grounds is, unfortunately, growing and inevitably leads to retaliatory discrimination and distortion of the recruitment pattern and effective deployment of inspectors in the field. I once more appeal through your Conference, to all concerned, for consideration of this problem.

Article IV

I should now like to turn to the implementation of this Article.

When the last Conference opened on 5 May 1975, I reported that the world's installed nuclear power capacity then stood at 20,000 MW and that by 1980 it would reach 100,000 MW. In fact, by the end of last year, 122,000 MW of plant were in operation. By 1985, this figure is likely to reach between 290,000 and 350,000 MW (more than a two-fold increase). The annual amount of power produced from nuclear energy will then be the equivalent of what would be generated by using the complete oil production last year of Saudi Arabia and will represent about 15% of the world's electricity production.

In a world which is sliding into a deepening energy supply crisis, such a growth in nuclear power production is no more than one would expect. It is almost a truism that, for the rest of the century at least, and probably well into the next, the only way that the world can hope to compensate for dwindling oil supplies is by conservation and a far greater use of nuclear energy and coal.

Generally speaking, the energy course followed in the Socialist countries and a number of Western industrial countries is forward-looking and pragmatic. In France, for example, nuclear energy will account for 50% of electricity production in 1985. Perhaps, because of domestic reactions, a number of industrial countries seem unable to cope effectively with the energy supply crisis. There is no starker illustration of this than the fact that, during last year, the total amount of nuclear power plant on order throughout the world decreased by 8,000 MW. Eight new orders were placed, but no less than fourteen earlier orders were cancelled.

It is instructive but depressing to contrast the powerful affirmation of the need for nuclear energy which was pronounced recently at the Venice Summit Conference with the bleak realities of domestic nuclear politics. The statesmen meeting at Venice said: "We underline the vital contribution of nuclear power to a more secure energy supply. The role of nuclear energy has to be increased if world energy needs are to be met. We shall, therefore, have to expand our nuclear generating capacity."

Speaking now of the situation in the developing world, in 1975, nuclear energy plants were being built or operated in eight developing countries of Asia, Africa and Latin America. Today, with the discontinuance of the Iranian programme, this figure has dropped to seven. It will rise to nine when the Philippine and Cuban projects are completed, but at present, there seems no definite prospect of a significant further spread, of nuclear power in developing countries during this decade though it seems likely that existing nuclear power programmes in certain developing countries might expand quite rapidly.

It is obvious that there is still much to do in order to realize the potential of Article IV of the Treaty under which all Parties are "to facilitate and . . . to participate in the fullest possible exchange of equipment, materials and scientific and technological information on the peaceful uses of nuclear energy" and in the "further development of the applications of nuclear energy for peaceful purposes . . . with due consideration for the needs of the developing areas of the world".

Progress towards these objectives (which were the counterpart of the obligation assumed under Article III of the Treaty) was certainly not favoured by the wave of restrictions which rose in the late 1970s. Billion-dollar investments in nuclear power plants are hardly encouraged when contractual commitments for nuclear supplies may be called into question. Fortunately, I believe we are beginning to emerge from these difficulties. The International Nuclear Fuel Cycle Evaluation, which completed its work in February, provided a pause for a return to the procedures of multilateral consultation.

This has now been followed up by the decision of the IAEA Board of Governors, two months ago, to establish a Committee open to all Member States to consider and advise the Agency's Board of Governors on ways and means in which supplies of nuclear material, equipment and technology and fuel cycle services can be assured on a more predictable and long-term basis in accordance with mutually acceptable considerations of non-proliferation and on the Agency's role and responsibilities thereto. This Committee could serve as an important instrument for rebuilding, on the basis of Article IV of the NPT, confidence in the long-term security of nuclear supplies which is essential for the worldwide promotion of the peaceful uses of nuclear energy.

The Secretary-General of the United Nations, Dr. Kurt Waldheim, in his message to this Conference, has, as we have just heard, succinctly summed up the problem in the following words and I quote him:

"There is the question of minimizing the danger of the proliferation of nuclear weapons without jeopardizing the supply or the development of nuclear energy for peaceful purposes. The principle of sovereign equality connotes that all States should be able to have access to, and benefit from, nuclear technology for peaceful purposes. At the same time, humanity's survival requires that this access or utilization must be subject to international safeguards so that it does not serve as an avenue for the proliferation of nuclear weapons."

Article V
Turning now to Article V of the Treaty, most of us would agree that it has been overtaken by events, and that the peaceful uses of nuclear explosives may entail greater risks than the benefits they would bring. There seems to be a general understanding that the technology involved is not an ordinary technology. Perhaps, therefore, it may be the course of wisdom to leave Article V where it is, for the time being at least.

Geographical Coverage of NPT
Despite the problems I have referred to, the Non-Proliferation Treaty itself has continued to demonstrate its viability. Since the First Review Conference, 28 non-nuclear-weapon States have joined the Treaty bringing the total membership to 113. Amongst these countries is Japan, which is now the world's second largest producer of nuclear electricity. Today, all but three countries in Europe, all of North America, most of the countries bordering the Western Pacific, most Latin American countries and half the countries of Africa are Parties to the Treaty.

However, we cannot afford to be complacent. At present there are eleven non-nuclear-weapon States which operate nuclear facilities and which still remain outside the Treaty. Amongst these, there are five countries which are operating unsafeguarded nuclear facilities. There are disquieting reports that the day may not be far when, besides those which are known to already have the capability of producing nuclear explosive material, one or more additional non-nuclear-weapon State has also acquired this capability. Whatever the situation, such reports reflect the fears of further proliferation which are fed by the operation of unsafeguarded facilities.

All the sensitive unsafeguarded nuclear plants are, moreover, in regions of acute political tension. We cannot ignore the risk that localized but perilous nuclear arms races may break out in these volatile areas which are also uncomfortably near the world's main oil resources or the routes by which this oil is carried.

It seems self-evident, therefore, that one of the highest priorities of international diplomacy should be to render inert the nuclear fuse which could add a new dimension to the political tensions in these regions.

Three of the States operating nuclear facilities which have not joined the NPT are in another region of the world, Latin America, and this group includes two countries with major nuclear power programmes. In these cases, however, as far as the Agency is aware, all nuclear plants and material are at present under IAEA safeguards. Moreover, there has been encouraging progress in the ratification and full application of the Tlatelolco Treaty. Latin America is thus the only major region in the world which has foresworn the manufacture of nuclear weapons and in which all nuclear plants are under IAEA safeguards. It does seem to me that this situation offers an opportunity to establish a nuclear-free zone by the full-scale application of the Tlatelolco Treaty in all countries of the region, banning nuclear explosives in every form and setting an example for the world to follow.

Comprehensive Test Ban
The Agency is not directly involved in the implementation of Article VI except in the sense that the lack of progress in implementing this Article may in time detract from the viability of Articles III and IV which are crucial to us, and from the credibility of the Treaty as a whole.

I can only repeat what I said here five years ago in reference to a major commitment expressed in Article VI and in the Preamble to the Treaty, namely, the declared determination of the Parties to achieve the discontinuance of all test explosions of nuclear weapons for all time and to continue negotiations to this end. I said then that an effective Treaty banning every kind of nuclear weapons test would be the most important single action that could be taken to strengthen and universalize the beneficial regime of non-proliferation of nuclear weapons. Events since 1975 have only served to strengthen this conviction. Nuclear weapons testing has continued at a steady rate. In 1979 alone, 53 nuclear tests have been performed bringing a total of 420 of those tests performed by the five nuclear-weapon States during the last ten years and one test by another State. In the long term, the non-proliferation regime can only survive on the tripod of the Non-Proliferation Treaty, effective international safeguards and a comprehensive nuclear test ban treaty.

As Dr. Waldheim has rightly stressed in his message, a general and complete ban on the testing of nuclear weapons is an indispensable first step if we are to realize the goal of halting and reversing the nuclear arms race.

Disarmament
The nuclear arsenals in the world have continued to grow both in numbers and in their destructive capacity. It is unfortunately true that in many cases technology dictates national policy and that new weapon systems often emerge not so much from national security requirements but from the sheer momentum of the technological process. This trend carries with it an intrinsic element of

danger. It is therefore imperative that political leaders of the world accept their responsibility and control these forces rather than be controlled by them. If they do not, the arms race will get out of control.

In the Final Document, adopted by consensus, at the first special session of the General Assembly devoted to Disarmament in 1978, it is stated categorically that "enduring international peace and security cannot be built on the accumulation of weaponry by military alliances nor sustained by a precarious balance of deterrence or doctrine of strategic superiority". The idea that permanent establishment of a world system of nuclear-weapon States and non-nuclear-weapon States could serve as a solution is no doubt fallacious and there are strong moral and political arguments against a continued reliance on such a situation. Besides, this very system carries within it the seed of nuclear weapons proliferation.

As mentioned already in my statement, the possible increase in the number of nuclear-weapon States that may take place overtly or covertly is of a growing concern. This problem requires urgent attention of the world community because it represents a development in a direction opposite to that of non-proliferation and of nuclear disarmament. Looking ahead, in the absence of the nuclear powers' ability to halt and reverse the prevailing competitive nuclear arms race, this will inevitably face the world with a problem of the most serious nature.

The important question is: what can be done to create the necessary political will to bear on this situation? My answer would be that the mobilization of a forceful public opinion could create this climate and lead to the elimination of all nuclear weapons.

In concluding, I should like to leave with you, if I may, some of my personal thoughts bearing on the tasks before this Conference.

In the continuing discussion about the Treaty's usefulness and importance, it must be kept in mind that up to now only six countries have developed and tested nuclear explosives. This is a most remarkable proof of the wisdom of statesmen, especially of the non-nuclear-weapon States who have recognized that the world would not be a safer place if a large number of countries possessed nuclear explosives and could use them for military purposes.

The NPT has provided a frame within which it should be possible to develop, under mutual assistance, nuclear power for peaceful purposes with the non-nuclear-weapon States Party to the Treaty voluntarily abstaining from production of nuclear explosives, and with the IAEA safeguards regime applied on all their nuclear activities.

The main question to be raised at this Second Review Conference of the NPT is undoubtedly that of the stability of the system. Will the Treaty with its shortcomings which will certainly be discussed intensively during the Conference—I am especially thinking of Articles IV and VI—survive another five or ten or 15-year period?

What is the alternative? Let me here recall to your minds that it was 35 years ago that the world witnessed the first use of the atomic bomb in Hiroshima and we are all painfully aware of its massive devastation at that time. But, by today's standards, the Hiroshima bomb would not even rank as a minimum nuclear destructive capability. Today, there may exist some 50,000 nuclear weapons, the combined explosive power of which is believed to be equal to that of more than one million Hiroshima bombs, or, to put it differently, representing not less than 3 tons of TNT for every individual in the world. In spite of this global overkill capacity, the nuclear weapon powers are continually increasing their nuclear arsenals and improving their lethality and effectiveness. It is indeed one of the more ominous paradoxes of history that, instead of a sense of universal revulsion arising from the tragedy of Hiroshima and Nagasaki, the world today should be seeing an ever-increasing number and sophistication of the weapon that had demonstrated this horrendous capability for destruction and has now become an abiding menace to human society.

How I wish that in a way consistent with the limited test-ban Treaty the nuclear weapon powers would now arrange a demonstration explosion of a weapon, not necessarily the most sophisticated one from their point of view, to give the news media the world over an idea of the destructive power of the new nuclear weapons. This would create massive public reaction against nuclear weapons both in the nuclear-weapon States and the non-nuclear-weapon States.

The NPT is the result of substantive efforts to find a common ground on which proliferation could be prevented. To maintain stability in the system it is, in my opinion, necessary to start work on eliminating some of the discriminatory features of the manner in which the Treaty is being implemented and, at the same time, remove the obstacles which seem to prevent about a dozen countries with nuclear weapon potential from joining the Treaty. They, more than the NNWS Parties to the Treaty, raise the most interesting issues for your attention.

All serious studies of the energy situation in the world come to the conclusion that nuclear energy is indispensable for maintaining the present standard of living in the industrialized countries and improving the situation in the developing countries. This implies that nuclear power technology should be still more widely spread; in fact, this is the implicit assumption and basis of NPT. I repeat what I have said on many occasions that there is no direct link between nuclear power for peaceful purposes and nuclear weapons. The elimination of nuclear power for peaceful purposes will not lead to elimination of nuclear weapons. Of course, the same situation prevails here as in other technologies—a country able to construct merchant ships can probably more easily produce a submarine than a country without a shipyard; similarly, a country engaged in nuclear power technology can probably more easily reach the nuclear weapon potential than a country without any nuclear experience. That is why the NPT is so fundamentally important.

You, Parties to the Treaty, have certainly goals which you want to reach at this Conference. In wishing you every success, may I take the liberty of stressing a threefold wish of my own, namely:

(i) Within the shortest possible time, an effective and enduring ban on all nuclear tests;

(ii) Fulfillment of the spirit of Article IV of the Treaty; and

(iii) Adherence to the Treaty by those nuclear threshold States who up to now have preferred to remain outside the Treaty.

Document 29

Declaration made by China on unilateral security assurances, 28 April 1982

A/S-12/11, 28 April 1982

Pending the realization of complete prohibition and thorough destruction of nuclear weapons, all nuclear countries must undertake unconditionally not to use or threaten to use such weapons against non-nuclear countries and nuclear-free zones.

As is known to all, the Chinese Government has long declared on its own initiative and unilaterally that at no time and under no circumstances will China be the first to use nuclear weapons, and that it undertakes unconditionally not to use or threaten to use nuclear weapons against non-nuclear countries and nuclear-free zones.

Document 30

Declaration made by France on unilateral security assurances, 11 June 1982

GAOR, twelfth special session, ninth meeting, paragraph 175

For its part, it [France] states that it will not use nuclear arms against a State that does not have them and that has pledged not to seek them, except if an act of aggression is carried out in association or alliance with a nuclear-weapon State against France or against a State with which France has a security commitment.

Document 31

Declaration made by the USSR on unilateral security assurances, 12 June 1982

GAOR, twelfth special session, twelfth meeting, paragraph 73

Guided by the desire to do all in its power to deliver the world's peoples from the threat of nuclear devastation and ultimately to exclude its very possibility from the life of mankind, the Soviet State solemnly declares: the Union of Soviet Socialist Republics assumes an obligation not to be the first to use nuclear weapons. This obligation shall become effective immediately, from the moment when it is announced from the rostrum of the General Assembly.

Document 32

South Pacific Nuclear Free Zone Treaty (Treaty of Rarotonga),
6 August 1985

CD/633 and Corr.1

PREAMBLE

The Parties to this Treaty,

United in their commitment to a world at peace;

Gravely concerned that the continuing nuclear arms race presents the risk of nuclear war which would have devastating consequences for all people;

Convinced that all countries have an obligation to make every effort to achieve the goal of eliminating nuclear weapons, the terror which they hold for humankind and the threat which they pose to life on earth;

Believing that regional arms control measures can contribute to global efforts to reverse the nuclear arms race and promote the national security of each country in the region and the common security of all;

Determined to ensure, so far as lies within their power, that the bounty and beauty of the land and sea in their region shall remain the heritage of their peoples and their descendants in perpetuity to be enjoyed by all in peace;

Reaffirming the importance of the Treaty on the Non-Proliferation of Nuclear Weapons (NPT) in preventing the proliferation of nuclear weapons and in contributing to world security;

Noting, in particular, that Article VII of the NPT recognizes the right of any group of States to conclude regional treaties in order to assure the total absence of nuclear weapons in their respective territories;

Noting that the prohibitions of emplantation and emplacement of nuclear weapons on the seabed and the ocean floor and in the subsoil thereof contained in the Treaty on the Prohibition of Emplacement of Nuclear Weapons and Other Weapons of Mass Destruction on the Seabed and the Ocean Floor and in the Subsoil Thereof apply in the South Pacific;

Noting also that the prohibition of testing of nuclear weapons in the atmosphere or under water, including territorial waters or high seas, contained in the Treaty Banning Nuclear Weapon Tests in the Atmosphere, in Outer Space and Under Water applies in the South Pacific;

Determined to keep the region free of environmental pollution by radioactive wastes and other radioactive matter;

Guided by the decision of the Fifteenth South Pacific Forum at Tuvalu that a nuclear free zone should be established in the region at the earliest possible opportunity in accordance with the principles set out in the communique of that meeting;

Have agreed as follows:

Article 1

USAGE OF TERMS

For the purposes of this Treaty and its Protocols:

(a) "South Pacific Nuclear Free Zone" means the areas described in Annex 1 as illustrated by the map attached to that Annex;

(b) "territory" means internal waters, territorial sea and archipelagic waters, the seabed and subsoil beneath, the land territory and the airspace above them;

(c) "nuclear explosive device" means any nuclear weapon or other explosive device capable of releasing nuclear energy, irrespective of the purpose for which it could be used. The term includes such a weapon or device in unassembled and partly assembled forms, but does not include the means of transport or delivery of such a weapon or device if separable from and not an indivisible part of it;

(d) "stationing" means emplantation, emplacement, transportation on land or inland waters, stockpiling, storage, installation and deployment.

Article 2

APPLICATION OF THE TREATY

1. Except where otherwise specified, this Treaty and its Protocols shall apply to territory within the South Pacific Nuclear Free Zone.

2. Nothing in this Treaty shall prejudice or in any way affect the rights, or the exercise of the rights, of any State under international law with regard to freedom of the seas.

Article 3

RENUNCIATION OF NUCLEAR EXPLOSIVE DEVICES

Each Party undertakes:

(a) not to manufacture or otherwise acquire, possess or have control over any nuclear explosive device by any means anywhere inside or outside the South Pacific Nuclear Free zone;

(b) not to seek or receive any assistance in the manufacture or acquisition of any nuclear explosive device;

(c) not to take any action to assist or encourage the manufacture or acquisition of any nuclear explosive device by any State.

Article 4

PEACEFUL NUCLEAR ACTIVITIES

Each Party undertakes:

(a) not to provide source or special fissionable material, or equipment or material especially designed or prepared for the processing, use or production of special fissionable material for peaceful purposes to:

(i) any non-nuclear-weapon State unless subject to the safeguards required by Article III.1 of the NPT, or

(ii) any nuclear-weapon State unless subject to applicable safeguards agreements with the International Atomic Energy Agency (IAEA).

Any such provisions shall be in accordance with strict non-proliferation measures to provide assurance of exclusively peaceful non-explosive use;

(b) to support the continued effectiveness of the international non-proliferation system based on the NPT and the IAEA safeguards system.

Article 5

PREVENTION OF STATIONING OF NUCLEAR EXPLOSIVE DEVICES

1. Each Party undertakes to prevent in its territory the stationing of any nuclear explosive device.

2. Each Party in the exercise of its sovereign rights remains free to decide for itself whether to allow visits by foreign ships and aircraft to its ports and airfields, transit of its airspace by foreign aircraft, and navigation by foreign ships in its territorial sea or archipelagic waters in a manner not covered by the rights of innocent passage, archipelagic sea lane passage or transit passage of straits.

Article 6

PREVENTION OF TESTING OF NUCLEAR EXPLOSIVE DEVICES

Each Party undertakes:

(a) to prevent in its territory the testing of any nuclear explosive device;

(b) not to take any action to assist or encourage the testing of any nuclear explosive device by any State.

Article 7

PREVENTION OF DUMPING

1. Each Party undertakes:

(a) not to dump radioactive wastes and other radioactive matter at sea anywhere within the South Pacific Nuclear Free Zone;

(b) to prevent the dumping of radioactive wastes and other radioactive matter by anyone in its territorial sea;

(c) not to take any action to assist or encourage the dumping by anyone of radioactive wastes and other radioactive matter at sea anywhere within the South Pacific Nuclear Free Zone;

(d) to support the conclusion as soon as possible of the proposed Convention relating to the protection of the natural resources and environment of the South Pacific region and its Protocol for the prevention of pollution of the South Pacific region by dumping, with the aim of precluding dumping at sea of radioactive wastes and other radioactive matter by anyone anywhere in the region.

2. Paragraphs 1(a) and 1(b) of this Article shall not apply to areas of the South Pacific Nuclear Free Zone in respect of which such a Convention and Protocol have entered into force.

Article 8

CONTROL SYSTEM

1. The Parties hereby establish a control system for the purpose of verifying compliance with their obligations under this Treaty.

2. The control system shall comprise:

(a) reports and exchange of information as provided for in Article 9;

(b) consultations as provided for in Article 10 and Annex 4 (1);

(c) the application to peaceful nuclear activities of safeguards by the IAEA as provided for in Annex 2;

(d) a complaints procedure as provided for in Annex 4.

Article 9

REPORTS AND EXCHANGES OF INFORMATION

1. Each Party shall report to the Director of the South Pacific Bureau for Economic Co-operation (the Director) as soon as possible any significant event within its jurisdiction affecting the implementation of this Treaty. The Director shall circulate such reports promptly to all Parties.

2. The Parties shall endeavour to keep each other informed on matters arising under or in relation to this Treaty. They may exchange information by communicating it to the Director, who shall circulate it to all Parties.

3. The Director shall report annually to the South Pacific Forum on the status of this Treaty and matters arising under or in relation to it, incorporating reports and communications made under paragraphs 1 and 2 of this Article and matters arising under Articles 8(2)(d) and 10 and Annex 2(4).

Article 10

CONSULTATIONS AND REVIEW

Without prejudice to the conduct of consultations among Parties by other means, the Director, at the request of any Party, shall convene a meeting of the Consultative Committee established by Annex 3 for consultation and cooperation on any matter arising in relation to this Treaty or for reviewing its operation.

Article 11

AMENDMENT

The Consultative Committee shall consider proposals for amendment of the provisions of this Treaty proposed by any Party and circulated by the Director to all Parties not less than three months prior to the convening of the Consultative Committee for this purpose. Any proposal agreed upon by consensus by the Consultative Committee shall be communicated to the Director who shall circulate it for acceptance to all Parties. An amendment shall enter into force thirty days after receipt by the depositary of acceptances from all Parties.

Article 12

SIGNATURE AND RATIFICATION

1. This Treaty shall be open for signature by any member of the South Pacific Forum.

2. This Treaty shall be subject to ratification. Instruments of ratification shall be deposited with the Director who is hereby designated depositary of this Treaty and its Protocols.

3. If a member of the South Pacific Forum whose territory is outside the South Pacific Nuclear Free Zone becomes a party to this Treaty, Annex 1 shall be deemed to be amended so far as is required to enclose at least the territory of that Party within the boundaries of the South Pacific Nuclear Free Zone. The delineation of any area added pursuant to this paragraph shall be approved by the South Pacific Forum.

Article 13

WITHDRAWAL

1. This Treaty is of a permanent nature and shall remain in force indefinitely, provided that in the event of a violation by any party of a provision of this Treaty essential to the achievement of the objectives of the Treaty or of the spirit of the Treaty, every other Party shall have the right to withdraw from the Treaty.

2. Withdrawal shall be effected by giving notice twelve months in advance to the Director who shall circulate such notice to all other Parties.

Article 14

RESERVATIONS

This Treaty shall not be subject to reservations.

Article 15

ENTRY INTO FORCE

1. This Treaty shall enter into force on the date of deposit of the eighth instrument of ratification.

2. For a signatory which ratifies this Treaty after the date of deposit of the eighth instrument of ratification, the Treaty shall enter into force on the date of deposit of its instrument of ratification.

Article 16

DEPOSITARY FUNCTIONS

The depositary shall register this Treaty and its Protocols pursuant to Article 102 of the Charter of the United Nations and shall transmit certified copies of the Treaty and its Protocols to all Members of the South Pacific Forum and all States eligible to become Party to the Protocols to the Treaty and shall notify them of signatures and ratifications of the Treaty and its Protocols.

IN WITNESS WHEREOF the undersigned, being duly authorized by their Governments, have signed this Treaty.

DONE at Rarotonga, this sixth day of August, One thousand nine hundred and eighty-five, in a single original in the English language.

ANNEX 1

South Pacific Nuclear Free Zone

A. The area bounded by a line:

(1) commencing at the point of intersection of the Equator by the maritime boundary between Indonesia and Papua New Guinea;

(2) running thence northerly along that maritime boundary to its intersection by the outer limit of the exclusive economic zone of Papua New Guinea;

(3) thence generally north-easterly, easterly and south-easterly along that outer limit to its intersection by the Equator;

(4) thence east along the Equator to its intersection by the meridian of Longitude 163 degrees East;

(5) thence north along that meridian to its intersection by the parallel of Latitude 3 degrees North;

(6) thence east along that parallel to its intersection by the meridian of Longitude 171 degrees East;

(7) thence north along that meridian to its intersection by the parallel of Latitude 4 degrees North;

(8) thence east along that parallel to its intersection by the meridian of Longitude 180 degrees East;

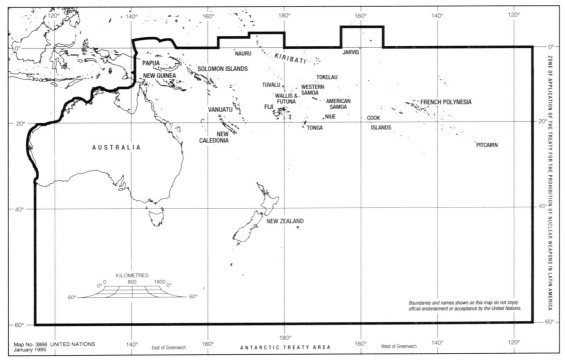

(9) thence south along that meridian to its intersection by the Equator;

(10) thence east along the Equator to its intersection by the meridian of Longitude 165 degrees West;

(11) thence north along that meridian to its intersection by the parallel of Latitude 5 degrees 30 minutes North;

(12) thence east along that parallel to its intersection by the meridian of Longitude 154 degrees West;

(13) thence south along that meridian to its intersection by the Equator;

(14) thence east along the Equator to its intersection by the meridian of Longitude 115 degrees West;

(15) thence south along that meridian to its intersection by the parallel of Latitude 60 degrees South;

(16) thence west along that parallel to its intersection by the meridian of Longitude 115 degrees East;

(17) thence north along that meridian to its southern-most intersection by the outer limit of the territorial sea of Australia;

(18) thence generally northerly and easterly along the outer limit of the territorial sea of Australia to its intersection by the meridian of Longitude 136 degrees 45 minutes East;

(19) thence north-easterly along the geodesic to the point of Latitude 10 degrees 50 minutes South, Longitude 139 degrees 12 minutes East;

(20) thence north-easterly along the maritime boundary between Indonesia and Papua New Guinea to where it joins the land border between those two countries;

(21) thence generally northerly along that land border to where it joins the maritime boundary between Indonesia and Papua New Guinea, on the northern coastline of Papua New Guinea; and

(22) thence generally northerly along that boundary to the point of commencement.

B. The areas within the outer limits of the territorial seas of all Australian islands lying westward of the area described in paragraph A and north of Latitude 60 degrees South, provided that any such areas shall cease to be part of the South Pacific Nuclear Free Zone upon receipt by the depositary of written notice from the

Government of Australia stating that the areas have become subject to another treaty having an object and purpose substantially the same as that of this Treaty.

ANNEX 2

IAEA safeguards

1. The safeguards referred to in Article 8 shall in respect of each Party be applied by the IAEA as set forth in an agreement negotiated and concluded with the IAEA on all source or special fissionable mater in all peaceful nuclear activities within the territory of the Party, under its jurisdiction or carried out under its control anywhere.

2. The agreement referred to in paragraph 1 shall be, or shall be equivalent in its scope and effect to, an agreement required in connection with the NPT on the basis of the material reproduced in document INFCIRC/153 (Corrected) of the IAEA. Each Party shall take all appropriate steps to ensure that such an agreement is in force for it not later than 18 months after the date of entry into force for that party of this Treaty.

3. For the purposes of this Treaty, the safeguards referred to in paragraph 1 shall have as their purpose the verification of the non-diversion of nuclear material from peaceful nuclear activities to nuclear explosive devices.

4. Each Party agrees upon the request of any other Party to transmit to that party and to the Director for the information of all Parties a copy of the overall conclusions of the most recent report by the IAEA on its inspection activities in the territory of the Party concerned, and to advise the Director promptly of any subsequent findings of the Board of Governors of the IAEA in relation to those conclusions for the information of all Parties.

ANNEX 3

Consultative Committee

1. There is hereby established a Consultative Committee which shall be convened by the Director from time to time pursuant to Articles 10 and 11 and Annex 4(2). The Consultative Committee shall be constituted of representatives of the Parties, each Party being entitled to appoint one representative who may be accompanied by advisers. Unless otherwise agreed, the Consultative Committee shall be chaired at any given meeting by the representative of the Party which last hosted the meeting of Heads of Government of Members of the South Pacific Forum. A quorum shall be constituted by representatives of half the Parties. Subject to the provisions of Article 11, decisions of the Consultative Committee shall be taken by consensus or, failing consensus, by a two-thirds majority of those present and voting. The Consultative Committee shall adopt such other rules of procedure as it sees fit.

2. The costs of the Consultative Committee, in-

cluding the costs of special inspections pursuant to Annex 4, shall be borne by the South Pacific Bureau for Economic Co-operation. It may seek special funding should this be required.

ANNEX 4

Complaints procedure

1. A Party which considers that there are grounds for a complaint that another Party is in breach of its obligations under this Treaty shall, before bringing such a complaint to the Director, bring the subject matter of the complaint to the attention of the Party complained of and shall allow the latter reasonable opportunity to provide it with an explanation and to resolve the matter.

2. If the matter is not so resolved, the complainant Party may bring the complaint to the Director with a request that the Consultative Committee be convened to consider it. Complaints shall be supported by an account of evidence of breach of obligations known to the complainant Party. Upon receipt of a complaint the Director shall convene the Consultative Committee as quickly as possible to consider it.

3. The Consultative Committee, taking account of efforts made under paragraph 1, shall afford the Party complained of a reasonable opportunity to provide it with an explanation of the matter.

4. If, after considering any explanation given to it by the representatives of the Party complained of, the Consultative Committee decides that there is sufficient substance in the complaint to warrant a special inspection in the territory of that Party or elsewhere, the Consultative Committee shall direct that such special inspection be made as quickly as possible by a special inspection team of three suitably qualified special inspectors appointed by the Consultative Committee in consultation with the complained of and complainant Parties, provided that no national of either Party shall serve on the special inspection team. If so requested by the Party complained of, the special inspection team shall be accompanied by a representative of that Party. Neither the right of consultation on the appointment of special inspectors, nor the right to accompany special inspectors, shall delay the work of the special inspection team.

5. In making a special inspection, special inspectors shall be subject to the direction only of the Consultative Committee and shall comply with such directives concerning tasks, objectives, confidentiality and procedures as may be decided upon by it. Directives shall take account of the legitimate interests of the Party complained of in complying with its other international obligations and commitments and shall not duplicate safeguards procedures to be undertaken by the IAEA pursuant to agreements referred to in Annex 2 (1). The special inspec-

tors shall discharge their duties with due respect for the laws of the Party complained of.

6. Each Party shall give to special inspectors full and free access to all information and places within its territory which may be relevant to enable the special inspectors to implement the directives given to them by the Consultative Committee.

7. The Party complained of shall take all appropriate steps to facilitate the special inspection, and shall grant to special inspectors privileges and immunities necessary for the performance of their functions, including inviolability for all papers and documents and immunity from arrest, detention and legal process for acts done and words spoken and written, for the purpose of the special inspection.

8. The special inspectors shall report in writing as quickly as possible to the Consultative Committee, outlining their activities, setting out relevant facts and information ascertained by them, with supporting evidence and documentation as appropriate, and stating their conclusions. The Consultative Committee shall report fully to all Members of the South Pacific Forum, giving its decision as to whether the Party complained of is in breach of its obligations under this Treaty.

9. If the Consultative Committee has decided that the Party complained of is in breach of its obligations under this Treaty, or that the above provisions have not been complied with, or at any time at the request of either the complainant or complained of Party, the Parties shall meet promptly at a meeting of the South Pacific Forum.

Protocol 1

The Parties to this Protocol

Noting the South Pacific Nuclear Free Zone Treaty (the Treaty)

Have agreed as follows:

Article I1

Each Party undertakes to apply, in respect of the territories for which it is internationally responsible situated within the South Pacific Nuclear Free Zone, the prohibitions contained in Articles 3, 5 and 6, in so far as they relate to the manufacture, stationing and testing of any nuclear explosive device within those territories, and the safeguards specified in Article 8(2)(c) and Annex 2 of the Treaty.

Article 2

Each Party may, by written notification to the depositary, indicate its acceptance from the date of such notification of any alteration to its obligation under this Protocol brought about by the entry into force of an amendment to the Treaty pursuant to Article 11 of the Treaty.

Article 3

This Protocol shall be open for signature by the French Republic, the United Kingdom of Great Britain and Northern Ireland and the United States of America.

Article 4

This Protocol shall be subject to ratification.

Article 5

This Protocol is of a permanent nature and shall remain in force indefinitely, provided that each Party shall, in exercising its national sovereignty, have the right to withdraw from this Protocol if it decides that extraordinary events, related to the subject matter of this Protocol, have jeopardized its supreme interest. It shall give notice of such withdrawal to the depositary three months in advance. Such notice shall include a statement of the extraordinary events it regards as having jeopardized its supreme interests.

Article 6

This Protocol shall enter into force for each State on the date of its deposit with the depositary of its instrument of ratification.

IN WITNESS WHEREOF the undersigned, being duly authorized by their Governments, have signed this Protocol.

DONE at Suva, this Eighth day of August, One thousand nine hundred and eighty-six, in a single original in the English language.

Protocol 2

The Parties to this Protocol

Noting the South Pacific Nuclear Free Zone Treaty (the Treaty)

Have agreed as follows:

Article 1

Each Party undertakes not to use or threaten to use any nuclear explosive device against:

(a) Parties to the Treaty; or

(b) any territory within the South Pacific Nuclear Free Zone for which a State that has become a Party to Protocol 1 is internationally responsible.

Article 2

Each Party undertakes not to contribute to any act of a Party to the Treaty which constitutes a violation of the Treaty, or to any act of another Party to a Protocol which constitutes a violation of a Protocol.

Article 3

Each Party may, by written notification to the

depositary, indicate its acceptance from the date of such notification of any alteration to its obligation under this Protocol brought about by the entry into force of an amendment to the Treaty pursuant to Article II of the Treaty or by the extension of the South Pacific Nuclear Free Zone pursuant to Article 12(3) of the Treaty.

Article 4

This Protocol shall be open for signature by the French Republic, the People's Republic of China, the Union of Soviet Socialist Republics, the United Kingdom of Great Britain and Northern Ireland and the United States of America.

Article 5

This Protocol shall be subject to ratification.

Article 6

This Protocol is of a permanent nature and shall remain in force indefinitely, provided that each Party shall, in exercising its national sovereignty, have the right to withdraw from this Protocol if it decides that extraordinary events, related to the subject matter of this Protocol, have jeopardized its supreme interests. It shall give notice of such withdrawal to the depositary three months in advance. Such notice shall include a statement of the extraordinary events it regards as having jeopardized its supreme interests.

Article 7

This Protocol shall enter into force for each State on the date of its deposit with the depositary of its instrument of ratification.

IN WITNESS WHEREOF the undersigned, being duly authorized by their Governments, have signed this Protocol.

DONE at Suva, this eighth day of August, One thousand nine hundred and eighty-six, in a single original in the English language.

Protocol 3

The Parties to this Protocol

Noting the South Pacific Nuclear Free Zone Treaty (the Treaty)

Have agreed as follows:

Article 1

Each Party undertakes not to test any nuclear explosive device anywhere within the South Pacific Nuclear Free Zone.

Article 2

Each Party may, by written notification to the depositary, indicate its acceptance from the date of such notification of any alteration to its obligation under this Protocol brought about by the entry into force of an amendment to the Treaty pursuant to Article 11 of the Treaty or by the extension of the South Pacific Nuclear Free Zone pursuant to Article 12(3) of the Treaty.

Article 3

This Protocol shall be open for signature by the French Republic, the People's Republic of China, the Union of Soviet Socialist Republics, the United Kingdom of Great Britain and Northern Ireland and the United States of America.

Article 4

This Protocol shall be subject to ratification.

Article 5

This Protocol is of a permanent nature and shall remain in force indefinitely, provided that each Party shall, in exercising its national sovereignty, have the right to withdraw from this Protocol if it decides that extraordinary events, related to the subject matter of this Protocol, have jeopardized its supreme interests. It shall give notice of such withdrawal to the depositary three months in advance. Such notice shall include a statement of the extraordinary events it regards as having jeopardized its supreme interests.

Article 6

This Protocol shall enter into force for each State on the date of its deposit with the depositary of its instrument of ratification.

IN WITNESS WHEREOF the undersigned, being duly authorized by their Governments, have signed this Protocol.

DONE at Suva, this eighth day of August, One thousand nine hundred and eighty-six, in a single original in the English language.

Document 33

Message from the Secretary-General of the United Nations to the Third NPT Review Conference

NPT/CONF.III/SR.1, 27 August 1985

Forty years ago Hiroshima and Nagasaki were in ruins. Smoke hung over the desolate wastelands. The survivors were exposed to the incurable afflictions of atomic radiation. Still today, thousands touched by that frightful phenomenon are burdened with an agonizing existence and demonstrate the horror caused by the use of what now must be seen as two small, primitive and inefficient atomic bombs.

As the Third Review Conference of the Treaty on the Non-Proliferation of Nuclear Weapons opens in Geneva, preparations are under way in New York for the fortieth session of the General Assembly of the World Organization that was created "to save succeeding generations from the scourge of war". In the 40 years of its existence, it has been a major objective of the United Nations to prevent the further use of nuclear weapons. This challenge must now be faced in the alarming circumstances of even more sophisticated arms systems, and of the awareness that even a limited nuclear exchange could well jeopardize human survival.

Thus, for those vested with responsibility for the well-being of their countries, avoidance of a nuclear war is surely the most critical obligation. Political differences must not be allowed to impede that task. I particularly wish to stress again on this occasion, that unless the nuclear arms race between the major Powers is halted and the further spread of military nuclear capability deterred, the terrible possibility of wholesale destruction will increase yet further and the fear of a final catastrophe will shadow our daily existence.

The Treaty on the Non-Proliferation of Nuclear Weapons was agreed upon as an important means of reducing the likelihood of this eventuality. It has already been a central element in efforts to restrain the horizontal spread of nuclear weapons. Many States now have the technical capability to undertake military nuclear programmes of their own, but consciously adopt a policy of restraint in this regard. The existence of the Non-Proliferation Treaty permits them to do so the more readily because of the confidence engendered by the safeguards applied under the Treaty.

But the Treaty is not a one-way street. In signing it, the nuclear-weapons States Parties agreed to pursue in good faith negotiations on effective measures relating to cessation of the nuclear arms race at an early date and to nuclear disarmament. In this respect, the implementation of the Treaty has been largely one-sided, to the understandable concern and profound dissatisfaction of its non-nuclear-weapons parties. There must be recognition of the fact that restraint on one side can not reasonably be demanded in the face of unlimited expansion on the other. No doubt, as in the past, this issue will figure prominently in the present Review Conference and in discussions on the future of the Treaty.

The Treaty parties—nuclear and non-nuclear-weapons States alike—have a fundamental interest in its effectiveness and viability. This can be furthered by full compliance with the Treaty's provisions by all the parties and by progress towards nuclear disarmament, each of which can encourage the universal adherence to the Treaty that is also critical to its long-term effectiveness. It is highly welcome in this regard that the two most powerful nuclear States are again engaged in disarmament talks, although there has been no visible progress so far. Agreement between them that would lead to real progress in nuclear disarmament would accord with the expectations arising from the Non-Proliferation Treaty and with the most basic interests of the entire international community.

This Review Conference will be dealing with subjects that can profoundly influence the present world and the prospects for future generations. I send you my most sincere wishes for productive deliberations and a positive outcome.

Document 34

Statement by the Director General of the IAEA to the Third NPT Review Conference

NPT/CONF.III/SR.1, 27 August 1985

. . .

10. Mr. Blix (Director General of the International Atomic Energy Agency) said that although the Agency was not a mechanism for disarmament, one of its objectives was that nuclear energy should be used for exclusively peaceful purposes, and it had acquired practical experience in that field, particularly in the implementation of the safeguards system, which might throw some light on obstacles to disarmament and the means of overcoming them.

11. While disarmament and non-proliferation of nuclear weapons were crucial issues which deserved to be resolved whatever the world political climate, the importance of the state of international relations for their solution should not be overlooked. It was therefore essential to create a climate in which Governments would feel less likely to resort to the nuclear deterrent in order to defend themselves. States could not be expected to give up their legitimate interests and ambitions for influence, but it was essential that they should adopt a code of conduct to limit competition between countries and social systems. Such a code of conduct would be based in particular on the principles of non-use of force, non-intervention and peaceful settlement of disputes. States should reach an understanding on the significance of those principles and respect them, thereby helping to create a climate of international confidence.

12. In addition, States should more consistently make use of the opportunities provided by the intergovernmental organizations which they themselves had created to serve as instruments of cooperation. Of course, those organizations did not have the power simply to make conflicts of interest disappear, but they had the advantage of helping States little by little to build up the habit of institutionalized cooperation, which was perhaps even more important.

13. The verification of the implementation of treaties relating to arms control and disarmament was a *sine qua non* for creating and maintaining international confidence. It was most certainly at the level of safeguards that the experience of the Agency had most to offer.

14. First, if States had deemed it necessary to establish an elaborate verification system simply to guarantee the observance of the principle of non-acquisition of nuclear weapons, any agreement relating to actual nuclear disarmament would presumably require reliable verification measures. But it could not be expected that such a system would become an international police force which would intervene in cases of non-application of the Treaty nor that the whole of the territory of a State would be open to inspection.

15. Secondly, implementation of the safeguards system by the Agency showed that the more sensitive the installation, the more intensive the verification, plants for reprocessing or enriching or manufacturing nuclear fuel were inspected more closely than, for example, light-water reactors.

16. Thirdly, there were those who would no doubt consider on-site inspections as an encroachment on the sovereignty of States. The fact should not be overlooked that, as was the case for the Agency, safeguards inspections only took place at the invitation of a sovereign State and on the basis of an agreement with it. It would be more appropriate to view the verification system as a service to a State wishing to acquire credibility it could not obtain by itself.

17. Fourthly, by agreeing to such inspection, a State naturally expected that other parties would be reassured about the peaceful use of the safeguarded installations and would act accordingly. It was for that reason that the Israeli attack in June 1981 on the IAEA-safeguarded nuclear research centre in Iraq had given cause for serious concern. Clearly a legal instrument should be adopted which explicitly prohibited any armed attack against nuclear installations devoted to peaceful purposes. It should perhaps be emphasized that anyone with doubts about the peaceful nature of a safeguarded installation should refer back to the international machinery responsible for safeguards.

18. Turning to matters dealt with in background papers submitted by the Agency and bearing on articles III, IV and V of the Treaty, he observed that whereas some aspects of the Treaty were very controversial, the international community was practically unanimous in its support of the broad objectives of the non-proliferation regime.

19. First, it was encouraging to note that almost all Governments agreed that the spread of nuclear weapons

was to be avoided at all costs. That attitude ought to find expression in further formal adherence to the Treaty, the Treaty for the prohibition of Nuclear Weapons in Latin America (Treaty of Tlatelolco), of 14 February 1967, 1/ or other arrangements or full-scope safeguards agreements.

20 Secondly, Governments were practically all in agreement that the safeguards system maintained by the Agency was useful and even essential for maintaining nuclear trade, facilitating the transfer of nuclear technology and creating a climate of international confidence.

21. Thirdly, there was universal support for the idea of continuous transfer of knowledge and technology concerning the peaceful use of nuclear energy. Some criticized the restraints imposed on transfer but did not contest the principle.

22. The most important application of nuclear energy was certainly nuclear power, and the Agency was devoting an important part of its activities to that. Expert meetings organized by the Agency and its many publications constituted an important way in which States parties to the Treaty and other States might participate in the exchange of scientific and technological information on the peaceful uses of nuclear energy. Although the expansion of nuclear power worldwide had lagged behind anticipated growth for a number of reasons (low increase in electricity demand during the recession, high interest rates, public opposition etc.), he was confident that the economic viability, reliability and safety of nuclear plants, particularly from the environmental point of view, would in due course lead to a renewed upswing in demand for plants. One of the prime tasks of the Agency was to facilitate that evolution and solve some of the problems which it posed. Nuclear power for the production of electricity was very unevenly spread among countries. One of the reasons was the size of current types of power reactors, which were often too large for the small grids of many developing countries. Inadequate skilled manpower, weak organizational and industrial infrastructures as well as the financial burden were also obstacles in the way of the adoption of nuclear power. The Agency was seeking to assist Member States to solve those problems and had undertaken a study on the viability of small and medium-sized power reactors.

23. Countries which might decide to install nuclear power plants would naturally wish to have the assurance that they would be able to continue to import fuel, spare parts and relevant technologies without any problem. Suppliers on the other hand would demand that importers should continue to show by their acts that they were respecting the commitment to use imported equipment or

material for purely peaceful purposes. The Committee on Assurances of Supply had been dealing with that question within the Agency for five years. Its activities, as well as the evolution of the situation, had contributed towards attenuating the problem somewhat. While the number of suppliers of nuclear plant and uranium had increased, thereby giving a wider choice to importers and helping to ensure supply, the market trend in the field of enrichment, reduced interest in reprocessing, and the fact that suppliers were beginning to be aware that they must maintain or restore a record of reliability, had reduced the incentive to importing countries to acquire an expensive independence in their fuel cycle through technologies which might be used for military purposes. Lastly, the Committee itself had reached positive conclusions in its consideration of several practical measures to facilitate international cooperation, including measures for alleviating technical and administrative problems with international shipments, emergency and back-up mechanisms and mechanisms for the revision of intergovernmental nuclear co-operation agreements.

24. In his view it would be possible to take a number of other practical measures which could facilitate the use of nuclear power and increase international confidence. The existence of multinational facilities, for example, would give their owners a stronger feeling of participation, assurance and influence. Cooperation in the establishment of a system of international spent fuel storage might be a solution to a problem which would become urgent in a few years.

25. It would certainly be interesting to link fuel cycle services with high-level nuclear waste storage and disposal services. With the rapid progress being made in technology for the storage and disposal of such waste it should not be an insurmountable problem. Importing countries with limited nuclear programmes would probably be more inclined to turn to existing suppliers for reprocessing. Once they wished to ensure that their supplies were not contributing to the proliferation of nuclear weapons, ought suppliers not to feel an obligation to facilitate the storage and disposal of the high-level waste which their technology generated?

26. There were many applications of nuclear technology, particularly in industry and medicine and above all in agriculture. They were making their way rapidly in industrialized and developing countries alike. Nuclear techniques to improve crops and preserve food—radiation-induced mutation in plants, the use of radioisotopes to measure the uptake of fertilizers or to trace groundwater and the use of irradiation as a means of decontami-

1/ United Nations, *Treaty Series*, vol. 634, No. 9068, page 326.

nating food—were assuming particular importance for many developing countries. In all those fields the Agency was assisting Governments to build up local scientific capacity through the supply of equipment, materials and scientific and technological information. It was also assisting them in the field of radiation protection and had been instrumental in the worldwide emergence of secondary standard dosimetry laboratories.

27. Generally speaking, nuclear techniques had come out of the laboratory to be put to practical use and that trend was reflected in the Agency's technical assistance and cooperation programme. Requests for training assistance were today focused less on pure science and more on applied topics. A training element was being increasingly integrated into projects and combined with provision of equipment and expert advice.

28. Resources available for technical assistance and cooperation through the Agency had increased by about 20 per cent per year through the 1980-1984 period. Targets for the Technical Assistance and Co-operation Fund, which were established each year on the basis of IPFs, had doubled from $13 million for 1981 to $26 million for 1985 and would increase to $30 million for 1986. The institution of IPFs was an important step towards making the financing of technical assistance predictable and assured. The Fund was supplemented by extra-budgetary resources, which, at the request of the donor, were often used preferentially or exclusively for non-nuclear-weapon States parties to the Treaty. While it was obvious that the Agency could not fund large-scale projects such as power reactors, the fact remained that if given more resources it could do much more to assist developing countries in the early stages of introducing nuclear power and in an advisory capacity during siting, construction and operation.

29. Turning to the safeguards system, he observed that its establishment, development and functioning had certainly not been without problems, but many features of it were encouraging.

30. First, the fact that 125 States had explicitly accepted safeguards by accepting the Treaty, in addition to those States which were parties to other agreements and conventions, was in itself remarkable, even though the idea of full-scope safeguards remained unacceptable to some States.

31. Secondly, some 98 per cent of all nuclear installations in non-nuclear-weapon States were under safeguards. Throughout its existence the system had not once experienced any diversion of fissionable materials under safeguard or other misuse of safeguarded material or installation. In one case the installations of a State had

been deemed inadequate from the point of view of safeguards, and that had been reported. The matter had subsequently been remedied with the cooperation of the State concerned. What was more serious, although it did not reflect on the manner in which the safeguards system operated, was that since 1979 the number of non-nuclear-weapon States constructing or operating unsafeguarded facilities and having the capacity to produce material that could be used for weapons had increased from three to five.

32. Thirdly, 18 additional States had concluded safeguards agreements within the framework of the Treaty since the Second Review Conference. Some 40 States still had to conclude agreements, but since hardly any of them had significant nuclear activities, the problem was more a legal than a practical one.

33. Fourthly, there was nothing to suggest that the safeguards system had ever hampered production or use of nuclear energy or obstructed research in that field.

34. Fifthly, while the number and complexity of installations subjected to safeguards had continuously posed new challenges to the system, the Agency and the Governments had helped to keep the system viable through their programmes to support safeguards. Thus the problems raised by the safeguarding of on-load reactors, long-term storage facilities for spent fuel elements and enrichment plants using ultracentrifuge technology had been successfully tackled. However, it should not be forgotten that there must be adequate resources to maintain and improve the system so that it created the desired confidence while keeping the cost of verification as low as possible. The construction of facilities handling large quantities of enriched uranium or plutonium, or new technologies such as lasers, raised new problems which should really be addressed already at the stage when such technologies and facilities were being devised.

35. It was true that the safeguards system was still grappling with a number of problems. All Governments would naturally like to spend as few resources as possible on it, and most countries felt that it was more urgent to tackle development. The secretariat, which was responsible for the credibility of the system, was doing all it could to increase efficiency, but would like to see a steady increase in the resources made available. In view of what the safeguards system represented the $30 million spent on it annually would seem to be a very modest sum, and the 180 inspectors, backed up by 75 headquarters staff, would seem a very modest force to cover almost 900 nuclear facilities. On the whole, the secretariat enjoyed excellent cooperation with the Governments which invited the Agency to inspect their facilities. That

was hardly surprising, since the issuing of safeguards reports was really a service to the safeguarded State, providing an assurance of the peaceful nature of its activities.

36.   In his opinion, the formulation used to define the objective of safeguards, namely to deter from diversion by risk of detection, was misleading. Countries did not invite safeguards to avoid succumbing to temptation but to prove that they were continuing in good faith to pursue exclusively non-military aims with their safeguarded nuclear activities as pledged. However, it was true that in order to be credible, safeguards operations must be sufficiently thorough and frequent to make the risk of detection a deterrent against any idea of diversion.

37.   In principle, safeguarded States and the Agency had an interest in allowing safeguards activities to proceed in the smoothest and most economical manner possible. In practice, however, problems might arise. For example, safeguards equipment might not be considered acceptable or the inspectors designated might not be accepted in sufficient numbers to permit the Agency to operate with maximum efficiency. All those problems could, however, be solved given good will. Governments had undoubtedly already gained very great benefits from the existence of the safeguards system in that it gave them increased confidence so that their nuclear trade was not obstructed by non-proliferation concerns. In addition, they were also provided with an opportunity to check on the effectiveness of their own national safeguards systems, particularly for the physical protection of nuclear material within their jurisdiction, for example against seizure of nuclear material by terrorists. In that context it should be mentioned that the Convention on Physical Protection of Nuclear Material had been ratified by 14

States. Seven more ratifications were necessary for its entry into force.

38.   Given the slower pace of nuclear development foreseen for the years ahead, it could be expected that there would be a consolidation of the safeguards system, which had rapidly evolved to become a professional, experienced verification system serving the Treaty and relied on by the Treaty. Four of the nuclear-weapon States had concluded agreements with the Agency on safeguards in their peaceful nuclear sectors, and the fifth, China, had negotiated nuclear cooperation agreements with other States requiring safeguards on nuclear trade between the parties. It might thus be concluded that all nuclear-weapon States were ready to accept safeguard verification. Inspections had already taken place in the United States of America, the United Kingdom and France, and the first such inspection had recently taken place in the Soviet Union.

39.   The importance of the safeguards system in the nuclear-weapon States was not so much what it implied in the field of non-proliferation as the fact that it constituted a precedent for verification of nuclear activities in those States and a first experience of such activities in that field which, it was to be hoped, would prove useful in discussions on the question of verification within the framework of agreements on nuclear disarmament. The world had been successful so far in preventing the spread of nuclear weapons to other countries. To sustain that success, an expanded transfer of technology in the peaceful nuclear field, a strengthening of the safeguards system and, above all, tangible results in nuclear disarmament negotiations were necessary. Only then could the Treaty be said to have lived up to the expectations placed on it in 1968.

Document 35

Final declaration of the Third NPT Review Conference

NPT/CONF.III/64/I, 21 September 1985

The States Party to the Treaty on the Non-Proliferation of Nuclear Weapons which met in Geneva from 27 August to 21 September 1985 to review the operation of the Treaty solemnly declare:

—their conviction that the Treaty is essential to international peace and security,

—their continued support for the objectives of the Treaty which are:

—the prevention of proliferation of nuclear weapons or other nuclear explosive devices;

—the cessation of the nuclear arms race, nuclear disarmament and a Treaty on general and complete disarmament;

—the promotion of cooperation between States Parties in the field of the peaceful uses of nuclear energy,

—the reaffirmation of their firm commitment to the purposes of the Preamble and the provisions of the Treaty,

—their determination to enhance the implementation of the Treaty and to further strengthen its authority.

Review of the Operation of the Treaty and Recommendations

Articles I and II and preambular paragraphs 1-3

The Conference noted the concerns and convictions expressed in preambular paragraphs 1 to 3 and agreed that they remain valid. The States Party to the Treaty remain resolved in their belief in the need to avoid the devastation that a nuclear war would bring. The Conference remains convinced that any proliferation of nuclear weapons would seriously increase the danger of a nuclear war.

The Conference agreed that the strict observance of the terms of Articles I and II remains central to achieving the shared objectives of preventing under any circumstances the further proliferation of nuclear weapons and preserving the Treaty's vital contribution to peace and security, including to the peace and security of non-Parties.

The Conference acknowledged the declarations by nuclear-weapons States Party to the Treaty that they had fulfilled their obligations under Article I. The Conference further acknowledged the declarations that non-nuclear-weapons States Party to the Treaty had fulfilled their obligations under Article II. The Conference was of the view therefore that one of the primary objectives of the Treaty had been achieved in the period under review.

The Conference also expressed deep concern that the national nuclear programmes of some States non-Party to the Treaty may lead them to obtain a nuclear weapon capability. States Party to the Treaty stated that any further detonation of a nuclear explosive device by any non-nuclear-weapon State would constitute a most serious breach of the non-proliferation objective.

The Conference noted the great and serious concerns expressed about the nuclear capability of South Africa and Israel. The Conference further noted the calls on all States for the total and complete prohibition of the transfer of all nuclear facilities, resources or devices to South Africa and Israel and to stop all exploitation of Namibian uranium, natural or enriched, until the attainment of Namibian independence.

Article III and preambular paragraphs 4 and 5

1. The Conference affirms its determination to strengthen further the barriers against the proliferation of nuclear weapons and other nuclear explosive devices to additional States. The spread of nuclear explosive capabilities would add immeasurably to regional and international tensions and suspicions. It would increase the risk of nuclear war and lessen the security of all States. The Parties remain convinced that universal adherence to the Non-Proliferation Treaty is the best way to strengthen the barriers against proliferation and they urge all States not party to the Treaty to accede to it. The Treaty and the regime of non-proliferation it supports play a central role in promoting regional and international peace and security, *inter alia*, by helping to prevent the spread of nuclear explosives. The non-proliferation and safeguards commitments in the Treaty are essential also for peaceful nuclear commerce and cooperation.

2. The Conference expresses the conviction that IAEA safeguards provide assurance that States are complying with their undertakings and assist States in demonstrating this compliance. They thereby promote further confidence among States and, being a fundamental element of the Treaty, help to strengthen their collective security. IAEA safeguards play a key role in preventing the proliferation of nuclear weapons and other nuclear explosive devices. Unsafeguarded nuclear activities in non-nuclear-weapon States pose serious proliferation dangers.

3. The Conference declares that the commitment to non-proliferation by nuclear-weapon States Party to the Treaty pursuant to Article I, by non-nuclear-weapon States Party to the Treaty pursuant to Article II, and by the acceptance of IAEA safeguards on all peaceful nuclear activities within non-nuclear-weapon States Party to the Treaty pursuant to Article III is a major contribution by those States to regional and international security. The Conference notes with satisfaction that the commitments in Articles I-III have been met and have greatly helped prevent the spread of nuclear explosives.

4. The Conference therefore specifically urges all non-nuclear-weapon States not party to the Treaty to make an international legally-binding commitment not to acquire nuclear weapons or other nuclear explosive devices and to accept IAEA safeguards on all their peaceful nuclear activities, both current and future, to verify that commitment. The Conference further urges all States in their international nuclear cooperation and in their nuclear export policies and, specifically as a necessary basis for the transfer of relevant nuclear supplies to non-nuclear-weapon States, to take effective steps towards achieving such a commitment to non-proliferation and acceptance of such safeguards by those States. The Conference expresses its view that accession to the Non-Proliferation Treaty is the best way to achieve that objective.

5. The Conference expresses its satisfaction that four of the five nuclear-weapon States have voluntarily concluded safeguards agreements with the IAEA, covering all or part of their peaceful nuclear activities. The Conference regards those agreements as further strengthening the non-proliferation regime and increasing the authority of IAEA and the effectiveness of its safeguards system. The Conference calls on the nuclear-weapon States to continue to cooperate fully with the IAEA in the implementation of these agreements and calls on IAEA to take full advantage of this cooperation. The Conference urges the People's Republic of China similarly to conclude a safeguards agreement with IAEA. The Conference recommends the continued pursuit of the principle of universal application of IAEA safeguards to all peaceful nuclear activities in all States. To this end, the Conference recognizes the value of voluntary offers and recommends further evaluation of the economic and practical possibility of extending application of safeguards to additional civil facilities in the nuclear-weapon States as and when IAEA resources permit and consideration of separation of the civil and military facilities in the nuclear-weapon States. Such an extending of safeguards will enable the further development and application of an effective regime in both nuclear-weapon States and non-nuclear-weapon States.

6. The Conference also affirms the great value to the non-proliferation regime of commitments by the nuclear-weapon States that nuclear supplies provided for peaceful use will not be used for nuclear weapons or other nuclear explosive purposes. Safeguards in nuclear-weapon States pursuant to their safeguards agreements with IAEA can verify observance of those commitments.

7. The Conference notes with satisfaction the adherence of further Parties to the Treaty and the conclusion of further safeguards agreements in compliance with the undertaking of the Treaty and recommends that:

(a) The non-nuclear-weapon States Party to the Treaty that have not concluded the agreements required under Article III (4) conclude such agreements with IAEA as soon as possible;

(b) The Director-General of IAEA intensify his initiative of submitting to States concerned draft agreements to facilitate the conclusion of corresponding safeguards agreements, and that Parties to the Treaty, in particular Depositary Parties, should actively support these initiatives;

(c) All States Party to the Treaty make strenuous individual and collective efforts to make the Treaty truly universal.

8. The Conference notes with satisfaction that IAEA in carrying out its safeguards activities has not detected any diversion of a significant amount of safeguarded material to the production of nuclear weapons, other nuclear explosive devices or to purposes unknown.

9. The Conference notes that IAEA safeguards activities have not hampered the economic, scientific or technological development of the Parties to the Treaty, or international cooperation in peaceful nuclear activities, and it urges that this situation be maintained.

10. The Conference commends IAEA on its implementation of safeguards pursuant to this Treaty and urges it to continue to ensure the maximum technical and cost effectiveness and efficiency of its operations, while maintaining consistency with the economic and safe conduct of nuclear activities.

11. The Conference notes with satisfaction the improvement of IAEA safeguards which has enabled it to continue to apply safeguards effectively during a period of rapid growth in the number of safeguarded facilities. It also notes that IAEA safeguards approaches are capable of adequately dealing with facilities under safeguards. In this regard, the recent conclusion of the project to design a safeguards regime for centrifuge enrichment plants and its implementation is welcomed. This project allows the application of an effective regime to all plants of this type in the territories both of nuclear-weapon States and non-nuclear-weapon States Parties to the Treaty.

12. The Conference emphasizes the importance of continued improvements in the effectiveness and efficiency of IAEA safeguards, for example, but not limited to:

(a) Uniform and non-discriminatory implementation of safeguards;

(b) The expeditious implementation of new instruments and techniques;

(c) The further development of methods for evaluation of safeguards effectiveness in combination with safeguards information;

(d) Continued increases in the efficiency of the use of human and financial resources and of equipment.

13. The Conference believes that further improvement of the list of materials and equipment which, in accordance with Article III (2) of the Treaty, calls for the application of IAEA safeguards should take account of advances in technology.

14. The Conference recommends that IAEA establish an internationally agreed effective system of international plutonium storage in accordance with Article XII(A)5 of its statute.

15. The Conference welcomes the significant contributions made by States Parties in facilitating the application of IAEA safeguards and in supporting research, development and other supports to further the application of effective and efficient safeguards. The Conference urges that such cooperation and support be continued and that other States Parties provide similar support.

16. The Conference calls upon all States to take IAEA safeguards requirements fully into account while planning, designing and constructing new nuclear fuel-cycle facilities and while modifying existing nuclear fuel-cycle facilities.

17. The Conference also calls on States Parties to the Treaty to assist IAEA in applying its safeguards, *inter alia*, through the efficient operation of State systems of accounting for and control of nuclear material, and including compliance with all notification requirements in accordance with safeguards agreements.

18. The Conference welcomes the Agency's endeavours to recruit and train staff of the highest professional standards for safeguards implementation with due regard to the widest possible geographical distribution, in accordance with Article VII D of the IAEA Statute. It calls upon States to exercise their right regarding proposals of designation of IAEA inspectors in such a way as to facilitate the most effective use of safeguards manpower.

19. The Conference also commends to all States Parties the merits of establishment of international fuel-cycle facilities, including multination participation, as a positive contribution to reassurance of the peaceful use and non-diversion of nuclear materials. While primarily a national responsibility, the Conference sees advantages in international cooperation concerning spent fuel storage and nuclear waste storage.

20. The Conference calls upon States Parties to continue their political, technical and financial support of the IAEA safeguards system.

21. The Conference underlines the need for IAEA to be provided with the necessary financial and human resources to ensure that the Agency is able to continue to meet effectively its safeguards responsibilities.

22. The Conference urges all States that have not done so to adhere to the Convention on the physical protection of nuclear material at the earliest possible date.

Article IV and preambular paragraphs 6 and 7

1. The Conference affirms that the NPT fosters the worldwide peaceful use of nuclear energy and reaffirms that nothing in the Treaty shall be interpreted as affecting the inalienable right of any Party to the Treaty to develop research, production and use of nuclear energy for peaceful purposes without discrimination and in conformity with Articles I and II.

2. The Conference reaffirms the undertaking by all Parties to the Treaty, in accordance with Article IV and preambular paragraphs 6 and 7, to facilitate the fullest possible exchange of equipment, materials and scientific and technological information for the peaceful uses of nuclear energy and the right of all Parties to the Treaty to participate in such exchange. In this context, the Conference recognizes the importance of services. This can contribute to progress in general and to the elimination of technological and economic gaps between the developed and developing countries.

3. The Conference reaffirms the undertaking of the Parties to the Treaty in a position to do so to cooperate in contributing, alone or together with other States or international organizations, to the further development of the applications of nuclear energy for peaceful purposes, especially in the territories of the non-nuclear-weapon States Party to the Treaty, with due consideration for the needs of the developing areas of the world. In this context the Conference recognizes the particular needs of the least developed countries.

4. The Conference requests that States Parties consider possible bilateral cooperation measures to further improve the implementation of Article IV. To this end, States Parties are requested to give in written form their experiences in this area in the form of national contributions to be presented in a report to the next Review Conference.

5. The Conference recognizes the need for more

predictable long-term supply assurances with effective assurances of non-proliferation.

6. The Conference commends the recent progress which the IAEA's Committee on Assurances of Supply (CAS) has made towards agreeing a set of principles related to this matter, and expresses the hope that the Committee will complete this work soon. The Conference further notes with satisfaction the measures which CAS has recommended to the IAEA Board of Governors for alleviating technical and administrative problems in international shipments of nuclear items, emergency and back-up mechanisms, and mechanisms for the revision of international nuclear cooperation agreements and calls for the early completion of the work of CAS and the implementation of its recommendations.

7. The Conference reaffirms that in accordance with international law and applicable treaty obligations, States should fulfil their obligations under agreements in the nuclear field, and any modification of such agreements, if required, should be made only by mutual consent of the parties concerned.

8. The Conference confirms that each country's choices and decisions in the field of peaceful uses of nuclear energy should be respected without jeopardizing their respective fuel-cycle policies. International cooperation in this area, including international transfer and subsequent operations, should be governed by effective assurances of non-proliferation and predictable long-term supply assurances. The issuance of related licences and authorization involved should take place in a timely fashion.

9. While recognizing that the operation and management of the back-end of the fuel cycle including nuclear waste storage are primarily a national responsibility, the Conference acknowledges the importance for the peaceful uses of nuclear energy of international and multilateral collaboration for arrangements in this area.

10. The Conference expresses its profound concern about the Israeli military attack on Iraq's safeguarded nuclear reactor on 7 June 1981. The Conference recalls Security Council Resolution 487 of 1981, strongly condemning the military attack by Israel, which was unanimously adopted by the Council and which considered that the said attack constituted a serious threat to the entire IAEA safeguards regime which is the foundation of the Non-Proliferation Treaty. The Conference also takes note of the decisions and resolutions adopted by the United Nations General Assembly and the International Atomic Energy Agency on this attack, including Resolution 425 of 1984 adopted by the General Conference of the IAEA.

11. The Conference recognizes that an armed attack on a safeguarded nuclear facility, or threat of attack, would create a situation in which the Security Council would have to act immediately in accordance with provisions of the United Nations Charter. The Conference further emphasizes the responsibilities of the Depositaries of the NPT in their capacity as permanent members of the Security Council to endeavour, in consultation with the other members of the Security Council, to give full consideration to all appropriate measures to be undertaken by the Security Council to deal with the situation, including measures under Chapter VII of the United Nations Charter.

12. The Conference encourages Parties to be ready to provide immediate peaceful assistance in accordance with international law to any Party to the NPT, if it so requests, whose safeguarded nuclear facilities have been subject to an armed attack, and calls upon all States to abide by any decisions taken by the Security Council in accordance with the United Nations Charter in relation to the attacking State.

13. The Conference considers that such attacks could involve grave dangers due to the release of radioactivity and that such attacks or threats of attack jeopardize the development of the peaceful uses of nuclear energy. The Conference also acknowledges that the matter is under consideration by the Conference on Disarmament and urges cooperation of all States for its speedy conclusion.

14. The Conference acknowledges the importance of the work of the International Atomic Energy Agency (IAEA) as the principal agent for technology transfer amongst the international organizations referred to in Article IV (2) and welcomes the successful operation of the Agency's technical assistance and cooperation programmes. The Conference records with appreciation that projects supported from these programmes covered a wide spectrum of applications, related both to power and non-power uses of nuclear energy, notably in agriculture, medicine, industry and hydrology. The Conference notes that the Agency's assistance to the developing States Party to the Treaty has been chiefly in the non-power uses of nuclear energy.

15. The Conference welcomes the establishment by the IAEA, following a recommendation of the First Review Conference of the Parties to the Treaty, of a mechanism to permit the channelling of extra-budgetary funds to projects additional to those financed from the IAEA Technical Assistance and Cooperation Fund. The Conference notes that this channel has been used to make additional resources available for a wide variety of projects in developing States Party to the Treaty.

16. In this context, the Conference proposes the following measures for consideration by the IAEA:

(i) IAEA assistance to developing countries in siting, construction, operation and safety of nuclear power projects and the associated trained manpower provision to be strengthened.

(ii) To provide, upon request, assistance in securing financing from outside sources for nuclear power projects in developing countries, and in particular the least developed countries.

(iii) IAEA assistance in nuclear planning systems for developing countries to be strengthened in order to help such countries draw up their own nuclear development plans.

(iv) IAEA assistance on country-specific nuclear development strategies to be further developed, with a view to identifying the application of nuclear technology that can be expected to contribute most to the development both of individual sectors and developing economies as a whole.

(v) Greater support for regional cooperative agreements, promoting regional projects based on regionally agreed priorities and using inputs from regional countries.

(vi) Exploration of the scope for multi-year, multi-donor projects financed from the extra-budgetary resources of the IAEA.

(vii) The IAEA's technical cooperation evaluation activity to be further developed, so as to enhance the Agency's effectiveness providing technical assistance.

17. The Conference underlines the need for the provision to the IAEA of the necessary financial and human resources to ensure that the Agency is able to continue to meet effectively its responsibilities.

18. The Conference notes the appreciable level of bilateral cooperation in the peaceful uses of nuclear energy, and urges that States in a position to do so should continue and where possible increase the level of their cooperation in these fields.

19. The Conference urges that preferential treatment should be given to the non-nuclear-weapon States Party to the Treaty in access to or transfer of equipment, materials, services and scientific and technological information for the peaceful uses of nuclear energy, taking particularly into account needs of developing countries.

20. Great and serious concerns were expressed at the Conference about the nuclear capability of South Africa and Israel and that the development of such a capability by South Africa and Israel would undermine the credibility and stability of the non-proliferation Treaty regime. The Conference noted the demands made on all States to suspend any cooperation which would contribute to the nuclear programme of South Africa and Israel. The Conference further noted the demands made on South Africa and Israel to accede to the NPT, to accept IAEA safeguards on all their nuclear facilities and to pledge themselves not to manufacture or acquire nuclear weapons or other nuclear explosive devices.

21. The Conference recognizes the growing nuclear energy needs of the developing countries as well as the difficulties which the developing countries face in this regard, particularly with respect to financing their nuclear power programmes. The Conference calls upon States Party to the Treaty to promote the establishment of favourable conditions in national, regional and international financial institutions for financing of nuclear energy projects including nuclear power programmes in developing countries. Furthermore, the Conference calls upon the IAEA to initiate and the Parties to the Treaty to support the work of an expert group study on mechanisms to assist developing countries in the promotion of their nuclear power programmes, including the establishment of a Financial Assistance Fund.

22. The Conference recognizes that further IAEA assistance in the preparation of feasibility studies and infrastructure development might enhance the prospects for developing countries for obtaining finance, and recommends such countries as are members of the Agency to apply for such help under the Agency's technical assistance and cooperation programmes. The Conference also acknowledges that further support for the IAEA's Small and Medium Power Reactor (SMPR) Study could help the development of nuclear reactors more suited to the needs of some of the developing countries.

23. The Conference expresses its satisfaction at the progress in the preparations for the United Nations Conference for the Promotion of International Cooperation in the Peaceful Uses of Nuclear Energy (UNCPICPUNE) and its conviction that UNCPICPUNE will fully realize its goals in accordance with the objectives of resolution 32/50 and relevant subsequent resolutions of the General Assembly for the development of national programmes of peaceful uses of nuclear energy for economic and social development, especially in the developing countries.

24. The Conference considers that all proposals related to the promotion and strengthening of international cooperation in the peaceful uses of nuclear energy which have been produced by the Third Review Conference of the NPT, be transmitted to the Preparatory Committee of the UNCPICPUNE.

Article V

1. The Conference reaffirms the obligation of Parties to the Treaty to take appropriate measures to ensure that potential benefits from any peaceful applications of nuclear explosions are made available to non-nuclear-

weapon States Party to the Treaty in full accordance with the provisions of article V and other applicable international obligations, that such services should be provided to non-nuclear-weapon States Party to the Treaty on a non-discriminatory basis and that the charge to such Parties for the explosive devices used should be as low as possible and exclude any charge for research and development.

2. The Conference confirms that the IAEA would be the appropriate international body through which any potential benefits of the peaceful applications of nuclear explosions could be made available to non-nuclear-weapon States under the terms of article V of the Treaty.

3. The Conference notes that the potential benefits of the peaceful applications of nuclear explosions have not been demonstrated and that no requests for services related to the peaceful applications of nuclear explosions have been received by the IAEA since the Second NPT Review Conference.

Article VI and preambular paragraphs 8-12

A.

1. The Conference recalled that under the provisions of article VI all parties have undertaken to pursue negotiations in good faith:

—on effective measures relating to cessation of the nuclear arms race at an early date;

—on effective measures relating to nuclear disarmament;

—on a Treaty on general and complete disarmament under strict and effective international control.

2. The Conference undertook an evaluation of the achievements in respect of each aspect of the article in the period under review, and paragraphs 8 to 12 of the preamble, and in particular with regard to the goals set out in preambular paragraph 10 which recalls the determination expressed by the parties to the Partial Test Ban Treaty to:

—continue negotiations to achieve the discontinuance of all test explosions of nuclear weapons for all time.

3. The Conference recalled the declared intention of the parties to the Treaty to achieve at the earliest possible date the cessation of the nuclear arms race and to undertake effective measures in the direction of nuclear disarmament and their urging made to all States Parties to cooperate in the attainment of this objective. The Conference also recalled the determination expressed by the parties to the 1963 Treaty Banning Nuclear Weapons Tests in the Atmosphere, in Outer Space and under Water in its preamble to seek to achieve the discontinuance of all test explosions of nuclear weapons for all time and the desire to further the easing of international tension and the strengthening of trust between States in order to facilitate the cessation of the manufacture of nuclear weapons, the liquidation of all existing stockpiles, and the elimination from national arsenals of nuclear weapons and the means of their delivery.

4. The Conference notes that the tenth special session of the General Assembly of the United Nations concluded, in paragraph 50 of its Final Document, that the achievement of nuclear disarmament will require urgent negotiations of agreements at appropriate stages and with adequate measures of verification satisfactory to the States concerned for:

(a) Cessation of the qualitative improvement and development of nuclear-weapon systems;

(b) Cessation of the production of all types of nuclear weapons and their means of delivery, and of the production of fissionable material for weapons purposes;

(c) A comprehensive, phased programme with agreed timetables whenever feasible, for progressive and balanced reduction of stockpiles of nuclear weapons and their means of delivery, leading to their ultimate and complete elimination at the earliest possible time.

5. The Conference also recalled that in the Final Declaration of the First Review Conference, the parties expressed the view that the conclusion of a treaty banning all nuclear-weapon tests was one of the most important measures to halt the nuclear arms race and expressed the hope that the nuclear-weapon States party to the Treaty would take the lead in reaching an early solution of the technical and political difficulties of this issue. .

6. The Conference examined developments relating to the cessation of the nuclear arms race in the period under review and noted in particular that the destructive potentials of the nuclear arsenals of nuclear-weapon States Parties were undergoing continuing development, including a growing research and development component in military spending, continued nuclear testing, development of new delivery systems and their deployment.

7. The Conference noted the concerns expressed regarding developments with far-reaching implications and the potential of a new environment, space, being drawn into the arms race. In that regard the Conference also noted the fact that the United States of America and the Union of Soviet Socialist Republics are pursuing bilateral negotiations on a broad complex of questions concerning space and nuclear arms, with a view to achieving effective agreements aimed at preventing an arms race in space and terminating it on Earth.

8. The Conference noted with regret that the development and deployment of nuclear weapon systems had continued during the period of review.

9. The Conference also took note of numerous proposals and actions, multilateral and unilateral, ad-

vanced during the period under review by many States with the aim of making progress towards the cessation of the nuclear arms race and nuclear disarmament.

10. The Conference examined the existing situation in the light of the undertaking assumed by the parties in Article VI to pursue negotiations in good faith on effective measures relating to cessation of the nuclear arms race at an early date and to nuclear disarmament. The Conference recalled that a stage of negotiations on the Strategic Arms Limitations Talks (SALT II) had been concluded in 1979, by the signing of the Treaty, which had remained unratified. The Conference noted that both the Union of Soviet Socialist Republics and the United States of America have declared that they are abiding by the provisions of SALT II.

11. The Conference recalled that the bilateral negotiations between the Union of Soviet Socialist Republics and the United States of America which were held between 1981 and 1983 were discontinued without any concrete results.

12. The Conference noted that bilateral negotiations between the Union of Soviet Socialist Republics and the United States of America had been held in 1985 to consider questions concerning space and nuclear arms, both strategic and intermediate-range, with all the questions considered and resolved in their interrelationship. No agreement has emerged so far. These negotiations are continuing.

13. The Conference evaluated the progress made in multilateral nuclear disarmament negotiations in the period of the Review.

14. The Conference recalled that the trilateral negotiations on a comprehensive test ban treaty, begun in 1977 between the Union of Soviet Socialist Republics, the United Kingdom of Great Britain and Northern Ireland and the United States of America, had not continued after 1980, that the Committee on Disarmament and later the Conference on Disarmament had been called upon by the General Assembly of the United Nations in successive years to begin negotiations on such a Treaty, and noted that such negotiations had not been initiated, despite the submission of draft treaties and different proposals to the Conference on Disarmament in this regard.

15. The Conference noted the lack of progress on relevant items of the agenda of the Conference on Disarmament, in particular those relating to the cessation of the nuclear arms race and nuclear disarmament, the prevention of nuclear war including all related matters and effective international arrangements to assure non-nuclear-weapon States against the use or threat of use of nuclear weapons.

16. The Conference noted that two Review Conferences had taken place since 1980, one on the Sea-bed

Treaty and one on the Environmental Modification Treaty and three General Conferences of the Agency for the Prohibition of Nuclear Weapons in Latin America. In 1982, a Special United Nations General Assembly Session on Disarmament took place without any results in matters directly linked to nuclear disarmament.

17. The Conference also noted the last five years had thus not given any results concerning negotiations on effective measures relating to cessation of the nuclear arms race and to nuclear disarmament.

B.

1. The Conference concluded that, since no agreements had been reached in the period under review on effective measures relating to the cessation of an arms race at an early date, on nuclear disarmament and on a Treaty on general and complete disarmament under strict and effective international control, the aspirations contained in preambular paragraphs 8 to 12 had still not been met, and the objectives under Article VI had not yet been achieved.

2. The Conference reiterated that the implementation of Article VI is essential to the maintenance and strengthening of the Treaty, reaffirmed the commitment of all States Parties to the implementation of this Article and called upon the States Parties to intensify their efforts to achieve fully the objectives of the Article. The Conference addressed a call to the nuclear-weapon States Parties in particular to demonstrate this commitment.

3. The Conference welcomes the fact that the United States of America and the Union of Soviet Socialist Republics are conducting bilateral negotiations on a complex of questions concerning space and nuclear arms—both strategic and intermediate-range—with all these questions considered and resolved in their interrelationship. It hopes that these negotiations will lead to early and effective agreements aimed at preventing an arms race in space and terminating it on Earth, at limiting and reducing nuclear arms, and at strengthening strategic stability. Such agreements will complement and ensure the positive outcome of multilateral negotiations on disarmament, and would lead to the reduction of international tensions and the promotion of international peace and security. The Conference recalls that the two sides believe that ultimately the bilateral negotiations, just as efforts in general to limit and reduce arms, should lead to the complete elimination of nuclear arms everywhere.

4. The Conference urges the Conference on Disarmament, as appropriate, to proceed to early multilateral negotiations on nuclear disarmament in pursuance of paragraph 50 of the Final Document of the First Special Session of the General Assembly of the United Nations devoted to disarmament.

5. The Conference reaffirms the determination expressed in the preamble of the 1963 Partial Test Ban Treaty, confirmed in Article I (b) of the said Treaty and reiterated in preambular paragraph 10 of the Non-Proliferation Treaty, to achieve the discontinuance of all test explosions of nuclear weapons for all time.

6. The Conference also recalls that in the Final Document of the First Review Conference, the Parties expressed the view that the conclusion of a Treaty banning all nuclear weapons tests was one of the most important measures to halt the nuclear arms race. The Conference stresses the important contribution that such a treaty would make toward strengthening and extending the international barriers against the proliferation of nuclear weapons; it further stresses that adherence to such a treaty by all States would contribute substantially to the full achievement of the non-proliferation objective.

7. The Conference also took note of the appeals contained in five successive United Nations General Assembly resolutions since 1981 for a moratorium on nuclear weapons testing pending the conclusion of a comprehensive test ban Treaty, and of similar calls made at this Conference. It also took note of the measure announced by the Union of Soviet Socialist Republics for a unilateral moratorium on all nuclear explosions from 6 August 1985 until 1 January 1986, which would continue beyond that date if the United States of America, for its part, refrained from carrying out nuclear explosions. The Union of Soviet Socialist Republics suggested that this would provide an example for other nuclear-weapon States and would create favourable conditions for the conclusion of a Comprehensive Test Ban Treaty and the promotion of the fuller implementation of the Non-Proliferation Treaty.

8. The Conference took note of the unconditional invitation extended by the United States of America to the Union of Soviet Socialist Republics to send observers, who may bring any equipment they deem necessary, to measure a United States of America nuclear test in order to begin a process which in the view of the United States of America would help to ensure effective verification of limitations on underground nuclear testing.

9. The Conference also took note of the appeals contained in five United Nations General Assembly resolutions since 1982 for a freeze on all nuclear weapons in quantitative and qualitative terms, which should be taken by all nuclear-weapon States or, in the first instance and simultaneously, by the Union of Soviet Socialist Republics and the United States of America on the understanding that the other nuclear-weapon States would follow their example, and of similar calls made at this Conference.

10. The Conference took note of proposals by the Union of Soviet Socialist Republics and the United States of America for the reduction of nuclear weapons.

11. The Conference took note of proposals submitted by States Parties on a number of related issues relevant to achieving the purposes of Article VI and set out in Annex I to this document and in the statements made in the General Debate of the Conference.

12. The Conference reiterated its conviction that the objectives of Article VI remained unfulfilled and concluded that the nuclear-weapon States should make greater efforts to ensure effective measures for the cessation of the nuclear arms race at an early date, for nuclear disarmament and for a Treaty on general and complete disarmament under strict and effective international control.

The Conference expressed the hope for rapid progress in the United States-USSR bilateral negotiations.

The Conference except for certain States whose views are reflected in the following subparagraph deeply regretted that a comprehensive multilateral Nuclear Test Ban Treaty banning all nuclear tests by all States in all environments for all time had not been concluded so far and, therefore, called on the nuclear-weapon States Party to the Treaty to resume trilateral negotiations in 1985 and called on all the nuclear-weapon States to participate in the urgent negotiation and conclusion of such a Treaty as a matter of the highest priority in the Conference on Disarmament.

At the same time, the Conference noted that certain States Party to the Treaty, while committed to the goal of an effectively verifiable comprehensive Nuclear Test Ban Treaty, considered deep and verifiable reductions in existing arsenals of nuclear weapons as the highest priority in the process of pursuing the objectives of Article VI.

The Conference also noted the statement of the USSR, as one of the nuclear-weapon States Party to the Treaty, recalling its repeatedly expressed readiness to proceed forthwith to negotiations trilateral and multilateral, with the aim of concluding a comprehensive Nuclear Test Ban Treaty and the submission by it of a draft Treaty proposal to this end.

Article VII and the Security of Non-Nuclear-Weapon States

1. The Conference observes the growing interest in utilizing the provisions of Article VII of the Non-Proliferation Treaty, which recognizes the right of any group of States to conclude regional treaties in order to assure the absence of nuclear weapons in their respective territories.

2. The Conference considers that the establishment of nuclear-weapon-free zones on the basis of arrangements freely arrived at among the States of the region

concerned constitutes an important disarmament measure and therefore the process of establishing such zones in different parts of the world should be encouraged with the ultimate objective of achieving a world entirely free of nuclear weapons. In the process of establishing such zones, the characteristics of each region should be taken into account.

3. The Conference emphasizes the importance of concluding nuclear-weapon-free zone arrangements in harmony with internationally recognized principles, as stated in the Final Document of the First Special Session of the United Nations devoted to disarmament.

4. The Conference holds the view that, under appropriate conditions, progress towards the establishment of nuclear-weapon-free zones will create conditions more conducive to the establishment of zones of peace in certain regions of the world.

5. The Conference expresses its belief that concrete measures of nuclear disarmament would significantly contribute to creating favourable conditions for the establishment of nuclear-weapon-free zones.

6. The Conference expresses its satisfaction at the continued successful operation of the Treaty for the Prohibition of Nuclear Weapons in Latin America (Treaty of Tlatelolco). It reaffirms the repeated exhortations of the General Assembly to France, which is already a signatory of Additional Protocol I, to ratify it, and calls upon the Latin American States that are eligible to become parties to the treaty to do so. The Conference welcomes the signature and ratification of Additional Protocol II to this Treaty by all nuclear-weapon States.

7. The Conference also notes the continued existence of the Antarctic Treaty.

8. The Conference notes the endorsement of the South Pacific Nuclear Free Zone Treaty by the South Pacific Forum on 6 August 1985 at Rarotonga and welcomes this achievement as consistent with Article VII of the Non-Proliferation Treaty. The Conference also takes note of the draft Protocols to the South Pacific Nuclear Free Zone Treaty and further notes the agreement at the South Pacific Forum that consultations on the Protocols should be held between members of the Forum and the nuclear-weapon States eligible to sign them.

9. The Conference takes note of the existing proposals and the ongoing regional efforts to achieve nuclear-weapon-free zones in different areas of the world.

10. The Conference recognizes that for the maximum effectiveness of any treaty arrangements for establishing a nuclear-weapon-free zone the cooperation of the nuclear-weapon States is necessary. In this connection, the nuclear-weapon States are invited to assist the efforts of States to create nuclear-weapon-free zones, and to enter into binding undertakings to respect strictly the

status of such a zone and to refrain from the use or threat of use of nuclear weapons against the States of the zone.

11. The Conference welcomes the consensus reached by the United Nations General Assembly at its thirty-fifth session that the establishment of a nuclear-weapon-free zone in the region of the Middle East would greatly enhance international peace and security, and urges all parties directly concerned to consider seriously taking the practical and urgent steps required for the implementation of the proposal to establish a nuclear-weapon-free zone in the region of the Middle East.

12. The Conference also invites the nuclear-weapon States and all other States to render their assistance in the establishment of the zone and at the same time to refrain from any action that runs counter to the letter and spirit of United Nations General Assembly resolution 39/54.

13. The Conference considers that acceding to the Non-Proliferation Treaty and acceptance of IAEA safeguards by all States in the region of the Middle East will greatly facilitate the creation of a nuclear-weapon-free zone in the region and will enhance the credibility of the Treaty.

14. The Conference considers that the development of a nuclear weapon capability by South Africa at any time frustrates the implementation of the Declaration on the Denuclearization of Africa and that collaboration with South Africa in this area would undermine the credibility and the stability of the Non-Proliferation Treaty regime. South Africa is called upon to submit all its nuclear installations and facilities to IAEA safeguards and to accede to the Non-Proliferation Treaty. All States Parties directly concerned are urged to consider seriously taking the practical and urgent steps required for the implementation of the proposal to establish a nuclear-weapon-free zone in Africa. The nuclear weapon States are invited to assist the efforts of States to create a nuclear-weapon-free zone in Africa, and to enter into binding undertakings to respect strictly the status of such a zone and to refrain from the use or threat of use of nuclear weapons against the States of the zone.

15. The Conference considers that the most effective guarantee against the possible use of nuclear weapons and the danger of nuclear war is nuclear disarmament and the complete elimination of nuclear weapons. Pending the achievement of this goal on a universal basis and recognizing the need for all States to ensure their independence, territorial integrity and sovereignty, the Conference reaffirms the particular importance of assuring and strengthening the security of non-nuclear-weapon States Parties which have renounced the acquisition of nuclear weapons. The Conference recognizes that different approaches

may be required to strengthen the security of non-nuclear-weapon States Parties to the Treaty.

16. The Conference underlines again the importance of adherence to the Treaty by non-nuclear-weapon States as the best means of reassuring one another of their renunciation of nuclear weapons and as one of the effective means of strengthening their mutual security.

17. The Conference takes note of the continued determination of the Depositary States to honour their statements, which were welcomed by the United Nations Security Council in resolution 255 (1968), that, to ensure the security of the non-nuclear-weapon States Parties to the Treaty, they will provide or support immediate assistance, in accordance with the Charter, to any non-nuclear-weapon State Party to the Treaty which is a victim of an act or an object of a threat of aggression in which nuclear weapons are used.

18. The Conference reiterates its conviction that, in the interest of promoting the objectives of the Treaty, including the strengthening of the security of non-nuclear-weapon States Parties, all States, both nuclear-weapon and non-nuclear-weapon States, should refrain, in accordance with the Charter of the United Nations, from the threat or the use of force in relations between States, involving either nuclear or non-nuclear weapons.

19. The Conference recalls that the Tenth Special Session of the General Assembly in paragraph 59 of the Final Document took note of the declarations made by the nuclear-weapon States regarding the assurance of non-nuclear-weapon States against the use or threat of use of nuclear weapons and urged them to pursue efforts to conclude, as appropriate, effective arrangements to assure non-nuclear-weapon States against the use or threat of use of nuclear weapons.

20. Being aware of the consultations and negotiations on effective international arrangements to assure non-nuclear-weapon States against the use or threat of use of nuclear weapons, which have been under way in the Conference on Disarmament for several years, the Conference regrets that the search for a common approach which could be included in an international legally binding instrument, has been unsuccessful. The Conference takes note of the repeatedly expressed intention of the Conference on Disarmament to continue to explore ways and means to overcome the difficulties encountered in its work and to carry out negotiations on the question of effective international arrangements to assure non-nuclear-weapon States against the use or threat of use of nuclear weapons. In this connection, the Conference calls upon all States, particularly the nuclear-weapon States, to continue the negotiations in the Conference on Disarmament devoted to the search for a common approach

acceptable to all, which could be included in an international instrument of a legally binding character.

Article VIII

The States Party to the Treaty participating in the Conference propose to the Depositary Governments that a fourth Conference to review the operation of the Treaty be convened in 1990.

The Conference accordingly invites States Party to the Treaty which are Members of the United Nations to request the Secretary-General of the United Nations to include the following item in the provisional agenda of the forty-third session of the General Assembly:

"Implementation of the conclusions of the third Review Conference of the Parties to the Treaty on the Non-Proliferation of Nuclear Weapons and establishment of a Preparatory Committee for the fourth Conference."

Article IX

The Conference, having expressed great satisfaction that the overwhelming majority of States have acceded to the Treaty on the Non-Proliferation of Nuclear Weapons and having recognized the urgent need for further ensuring the universality of the Treaty, appeals to all States, particularly the nuclear-weapon States and other States advanced in nuclear technology, which have not yet done so, to adhere to the Treaty at the earliest possible date.

ANNEX II

Declaration by the group of non-aligned and neutral States

The delegations of the States members of the Group of Non-Aligned and Neutral States taking part in the Third Review Conference of the Parties to the Treaty on the Non-Proliferation of Nuclear Weapons submitted to the Conference the following three draft resolutions:

1. Draft resolution on a comprehensive nuclear test ban (NPT/CONF.III/L.1)

2. Draft resolution on a nuclear test ban moratorium (NPT/CONF.III/L.2)

3. Draft resolution on a nuclear-arms freeze (NPT/CONF.III/L.3)

The objective pursued by the first of those three draft resolutions was achieved on the closing day of the Conference thanks to the approval by consensus, for inclusion in paragraph 12 of the Final Declaration of the Conference, of a text in which, with the exception indicated therein, it is unequivocally declared that:

"The Conference ... deeply regretted that a comprehensive multilateral nuclear test-ban treaty banning all nuclear tests by all States in all environments for all time had not been concluded so far and, therefore, called on the nuclear-weapon States Party to the

Treaty to resume trilateral negotiations in 1985 and called on all the nuclear-weapon States to participate in the urgent negotiation and conclusion of such a treaty as a matter of the highest priority in the Conference on Disarmament."

With regard to the other two above-mentioned draft resolutions, the sponsoring delegations wish to place on record that they have decided not to press them to a vote on this occasion for the following reasons: that there was unanimous acceptance for the reproduction of their texts together with this Declaration, immediately following the text of the Final Declaration, and that in paragraphs B-7 and B-9 of the Final Declaration, the Conference explicitly took note of the repeated appeals contained in many resolutions of the United Nations General Assembly, as well as of "similar calls made at this Conference" in connection with a moratorium on nuclear weapons testing and a quantitative and qualitative freeze of all nuclear weapons, respectively.

GROUP OF NON-ALIGNED AND NEUTRAL STATES

Draft resolution on a nuclear test ban moratorium

(Document NPT/CONF.III/L.2)

The Third Review Conference of the Parties to the Treaty on the Non-Proliferation of Nuclear Weapons,

Recalling that article VI of the Treaty on the Non-Proliferation of Nuclear Weapons contains an undertaking by each of the Parties "to pursue negotiations in good faith on effective measures relating to cessation of the nuclear arms race at an early date",

Considering that the cessation of all nuclear weapon tests would constitute a most important and effective measure for the qualitative cessation of the nuclear arms race,

Considering further that a moratorium on nuclear test explosions, as a provisional measure, has been called for by the General Assembly of the United Nations at each of its last five sessions,

Calls upon the three Depositary States of the Treaty on the Non-Proliferation of Nuclear Weapons to institute, as a provisional measure, an immediate moratorium on all nuclear weapon tests.

GROUP OF NON-ALIGNED AND NEUTRAL STATES

Draft resolution on a nuclear-arms freeze

(Document NPT/CONF.III/L.3)

The Third Review Conference of the Parties to the Treaty on the Non-Proliferation of Nuclear Weapons,

Recalling that Article VI of the Treaty on the Non-Proliferation of Nuclear Weapons contains an undertak-

ing by each of the Parties "to pursue negotiations in good faith on effective measures relating to cessation of the nuclear-arms race at an early date and to nuclear disarmament",

Considering that a nuclear-arms freeze, while not an end in itself, would constitute the most effective first step for a cessation of the nuclear-arms race,

Calls on the three Depositary States of the Treaty on the Non-Proliferation of Nuclear Weapons:

1. To agree on a complete freeze on the testing, production and deployment of all nuclear weapons and their delivery vehicles;

2. To begin negotiations for substantial reductions of their existing stockpiles of nuclear weapons and delivery vehicles.

Statement by the Representative of the Islamic Republic of Iran at the 16th plenary meeting of the Third Review Conference of the Parties to the Treaty on the Non-Proliferation of Nuclear Weapons [*]

Mr. President, as you are probably informed, the peaceful nuclear facility of Bushehr has been subjected three times to military attack, twice in 1985 and once in 1984. The attacks have been deliberate in nature in that there are no militarily significant objectives to be gained from attacking the area or its surroundings. As a result of the attack that was carried out in February 1985 against the Bushehr nuclear power plant with two missiles, one of the site's personnel was killed within the boundary of the plant and material damage was caused to the plant. The third attack on the plant, the second in 1985, occurred in the month of March, causing much more extensive damage than previously inflicted. This time damage was inflicted on the plant's operating diesel generator house and the concrete structures of the reactor building of the plant. Each attack was appropriately reported to the Director-General of IAEA. In response to the attack carried out on 4 March 1985 he declared in his communication dated 8 March 1985 that "I want to express my deep regret at the serious material losses which you have reported to me". The Director-General also pointed out that "I continue to concur with the view expressed in General Conference resolution 407 that all armed attacks against nuclear installations devoted to peaceful purposes should be explicitly prohibited".

Mr. President, in the context of the recent attacks against peaceful nuclear facilities I also find it appropriate to refer to the summary record of the statement made on

[*] This statement is attached pursuant to the agreement of the Conference at its 16th plenary meeting on 21 September 1985 (see *Review Conference of the Parties to the Treaty—Nuclear Weapons, Final Documents, Part 1 (1985)*, "I. Organization and Work of the Conference", paragraph 36).

19 February 1985 in the General Conference of IAEA: "One of the most serious problems facing the Agency in recent years had been the threat of armed attack on peaceful nuclear facilities". In another part of this quotation, another part of this summary record, the Director-General says: "In view of proposals to construct nuclear-power reactors in several countries of the Middle East, those countries and indeed the world at large would naturally require without delay firm assurance that such peaceful facilities would be immune from attack".

Mr. President, the delegation of the Islamic Republic of Iran made a very modest proposal with regard to attacks against its peaceful nuclear facilities in Bushehr and in Teheran. The facility in Teheran is a safeguarded facility, I should point out. We proposed a modest formulation in which the Conference strongly deplored attacks against peaceful facilities in Iran.

Then, in Committee III, we had a proposal in this regard by the Chairman of the Committee, Ambassador Imai, for whom we have much respect and admiration. This proposal is reflected in paragraph 14 (d) of document NPT/CONF.III/61. It reads that "the Conference notes that the Islamic Republic of Iran states its concern regarding attacks on its nuclear facilities".

Mr. President, we decided to go along with this formulation although it is indeed too objective for our real concerns. It is a very objective proposal reflected in document NPT/CONF.III/61 and in the report of Committee III, and we decided to accept this in order to facilitate the work of the Conference and in order to cooperate with the Chairman of Committee III and with the Drafting Committee and the President of the Conference.

Mr. President, with this formulation we can go along and we can have consensus with the whole report of the Conference, and without it we regret that we cannot go along with the process of consensus in this Conference. Of course, we are ready to hear proposals which are in a way reflective of the concerns of the Islamic Republic of Iran in an appropriate manner, and in this regard we have been making consultations with you and we very much appreciate your assistance and your cooperation in this regard.

At this point I wish to express our thanks to you and wait for a solution that you might propose to this problem.

Statement by the Representative of Iraq at the 16th plenary meeting of the Third Review Conference of the Parties to the Treaty on the Non-Proliferation of Nuclear Weapons*

Let me first say that the distinguished delegate of Iran has referred to the report submitted to the Directory-General of the Agency in regard to attacks on Bushehr. In that report specific mention of Iraq was made, and this is why I am intervening now.

Mr. President, it is to our deep regret that this Review Conference has meant nothing for the Iranian delegation except to offer an opportunity for a propaganda barrage and fabrications against my country.

Everyone knows there is a war between Iraq and Iran, and everyone knows that this war has continued now for over five years. Any constructive intervention here should be with a view to stopping that war. We know that the war is continuing because Security Council resolutions on this matter have been disregarded, disrespected, and not carried out by the other party to the war.

Neither has that party responded to the many efforts taken by so many international forums as the Islamic Conference, the Non-Aligned Movement, etc.

Now to come to the specific question of Bushehr. First of all, I would like to make clear to the Conference that Bushehr is a war zone declared by Iraq. It is a port where these installations are located. Nevertheless, military authorities in Iraq have once again denied emphatically that any deliberate attack on that construction site has taken place. And that was submitted in a letter to the Director-General of the International Atomic Energy Agency.

These alleged attacks were reported first on 19 April 1984. Iran requested an urgent meeting of the Board of Governors. However, the Director-General found no reason to do so. Again, in June 1984, Iran requested to include an item on the agenda of the Board of Governors to consider that, but the Board refused to do so because there was no evidence of such an attack.

Now the report referred to by the delegate of Iran that was given to the General Conference of IAEA in 1984 was a direct response by the Director-General to resolution 409 adopted in 1983 by the General Conference in regard to the Israeli attack on the Iraqi peaceful nuclear facilities, and not to other matters.

Mr. President, Bushehr site contains no nuclear material, has no facility attachment negotiated with IAEA and does not qualify to be a nuclear facility. These are the words of the Director-General of IAEA.

Under such circumstances our Conference cannot take into account considerations arising from disputes, and for that matter armed conflicts, between two States. Our Conference is not the place where the war should be discussed. There are other fora, namely the Security

* This statement is attached pursuant to the agreement of the Conference at its 16th plenary meeting on 21 September 1985 (see *Review Conference of the Parties to the Treaty—Nuclear Weapons, Final Documents, Part 1 (1985)*, "I. Organization and Work of the Conference", paragraph 36).

Council of the United Nations, or the General Assembly, where one should go.

And one last remark, Mr. President. Every time the question of the Israeli attack comes into the discussion, Iran is quick to level allegations against Iraq in the same spirit. We will not be pressured by that. Our position will stay firm and we will never cease to have our points of view well recognized on the Israeli aggression.

Document 36

Message from the Secretary-General of the United Nations to the Fourth NPT Review Conference

NPT/CONF.IV/SR.1, 28 August 1990

The close of the 1980s has heralded an end to the cold war and to the escalating arms race between the major Powers that prevailed for 45 years after the Second World War.

The momentous changes in the world, particularly in East-West relationships, have diminished the threat of nuclear confrontation and made it possible to initiate and pursue a process of real reduction in nuclear weapons. The first agreement for actual reductions in nuclear weapons, the Treaty between the United States and the Soviet Union on the Elimination of their Intermediate Range and Shorter-Range Missiles, was signed in 1987. The international community has also welcomed the agreement in June 1990 between the USSR and the United States on the framework of a START treaty on the reduction of strategic arms, and looks forward with keen anticipation to the completion of that agreement and to its full implementation.

The entire international community has long been convinced that a major nuclear war would be catastrophic for life on this planet. In the spirit of this conviction, the nuclear-weapon Powers have demonstrated, especially during the last decade, their increased determination to avoid a nuclear conflict. Now, negotiations to reduce nuclear arms have been supplemented by a reassessment of the military doctrines of the two major armed alliances. As a consequence, the arms race and military confrontation between them are giving way to disarmament agreements and confidence-building measures. There have also been important steps toward a widely anticipated agreement on conventional forces in Europe and intensive work on the completion of a chemical weapons convention.

While these positive developments in international relations must be sustained, there is a long road before us. Further substantive measures of nuclear disarmament remain a priority for the international community and must be realized.

In this wider process of nuclear arms limitation, the non-proliferation regime has played and will continue to play a critical role. The nuclear non-proliferation Treaty is central to this regime. Generally recognized as a landmark Treaty, it is the international arms limitation instrument most widely observed. No States have withdrawn from the non-proliferation Treaty and no party has been found to be violating its provisions.

It should be noted, however, that the Treaty imposes asymmetrical obligations on its two groups of States Parties, the nuclear-weapon States and the non-nuclear-weapon States. In such circumstances, it is of the utmost importance that all its parties should discharge their responsibilities in good faith and to the full. This commitment calls for, among other elements, clear assurances about the non-use of nuclear weapons against non-nuclear-weapon States and for energetic endeavours to end all test explosions of nuclear weapons for all time. At the same time, the right of States to develop nuclear technology for economic benefit must be both assured and reconciled with the overriding need to prevent the further spread of nuclear weapons.

Indeed, concern about nuclear weapons proliferation remains acute, particularly in the light of technological developments which could facilitate the development of a nuclear-weapon capability by additional States. Therefore the strict observance of the nuclear non-proliferation regime is of fundamental importance. Wider participation in the international non-proliferation regime is equally vital. This regime would also be strengthened if States Parties to the NPT that have not already done so concluded the requisite safeguard agreements with IAEA.

This Fourth Review Conference is the last one before the parties to the non-proliferation Treaty decide in 1995 "whether the Treaty shall continue in force indefinitely, or shall be extended for an additional fixed period or periods". Thus, this Conference will do much to determine the future and success of non-proliferation. Your review of the Non-Proliferation Treaty must, therefore, in particular provide a strong impetus and effective support to global and regional efforts to implement fully the Treaty's objectives. I send you my best wishes for every success in your work, whose consequences can affect the whole world.

Document 37

Statement by the Director General of the IAEA at the Fourth NPT Review Conference

Not issued as a United Nations document

This fourth review conference of the Non-Proliferation Treaty is taking place at a moment of dangerous confrontation in a strategic region of the world. Although the attention of governments is necessarily focused on the daily developments of this situation, they must give full consideration to the central topic that is before the Conference, namely how the world is to ensure that nuclear weapons are not acquired by further States, and to the subjects which are closely linked to this aim: the efforts to achieve nuclear disarmament and the transfer of peaceful nuclear technology.

The present conflict illustrates starkly that a region of great wealth in human resources and oil may be crippled in its legitimate development efforts by arms races and armed conflict, unless mutual confidence and stability are built up by accommodation, peaceful resolution of conflict, cooperation and verified arms control.

The Non-Proliferation Treaty, committing the parties to non-acquisition of nuclear weapons and to disarmament efforts, is already rendering vital service in many regions of the world to provide confidence and stability. Its shortcomings reside chiefly in its not having succeeded so far in fulfilling its aspiration for universality and its aspiration for nuclear disarmament. In both these respects intense efforts must be made between now and the crucial NPT conference of 1995 in accordance with Articles I, II and VI of the Treaty. The more successful these efforts are, the wider the sharing of peaceful nuclear techniques should become under Article IV of the Treaty.

These weeks must be used for the purpose for which the Conference was convoked, namely to examine how the Treaty can help us on a worldwide basis to control the destructive forces of fission—the weapons—and to harness nuclear energy for safe peaceful uses and development. Since the Third Review Conference in 1985 the international scene has undergone tremendous change.

On the negative side we must note that the threats to the global environment have dramatically increased. These threats require action to stabilize the world's population, to channel more resources to development, to reduce our reliance on fossil fuels and to expand the role of sources of energy which do not threaten our environment—including nuclear power.

On the positive side we note that the risk of military confrontation between East and West is currently giving way to the opportunity for expanded cooperation, includ-

ing peaceful nuclear cooperation. Drastically reduced stockpiles of nuclear weapons and dramatically increased international cooperation to achieve uniformly high levels of nuclear power safety are realistic aims today. Both the positive and the negative factors which I have mentioned are of relevance in reviewing the NPT.

The frustration which many parties to the NPT have felt about years of very modest results in disarmament negotiations should give way to a hope that the INF agreement, a START agreement and a CFE agreement will signal the dawn of a peaceful era, an era in which large resources, which have been locked in arms production, may be released for development and measures to protect the global environment. This should serve to consolidate commitment to the Treaty.

Several States non-parties to the NPT have explained their non-adherence by referring to the different obligations of nuclear-weapon States (NWS) and non-nuclear-weapon States (NNWS) under the treaty—the NWS pledging only negotiations on disarmament, while NNWS committed themselves concretely not to acquire nuclear weapons. As the disarmament negotiations begin to bear fruit, these objections to adherence should be correspondingly reduced.

Potentially of equally great importance for adherence to the NPT is perhaps that nuclear weapons are beginning to look obsolescent. As today's conflict in the Middle East reminds us, it is certainly too early to dream about the emergence of a well-organized international community, invariably using peaceful means to settle disputes. However, the philosophy of suicide pacts—mutually assured destruction—seems to be giving way to a realization that nuclear weapons offer no solutions to security and that accommodation, resolution of regional conflicts and cooperation today offer the only way to resolve differences, especially between great powers. When this realization becomes universal, commitments to non-proliferation and disarmament might also become universal.

This line of reasoning attributes special persuasive value to those nuclear disarmament measures that are now underway and those, like a complete test ban and a cut-off of the production of fissionable material for nuclear weapons, which imply an abandonment of the qualitative and quantitative nuclear arms race.

I should add that positive results of the active cooperation between East and West to help defuse regional conflicts and bring about *détente* may be equally important for non-proliferation, as a peaceful climate lessens interest in nuclear weapons.

The International Atomic Energy Agency has been given some very special, very novel and very central roles under the Non-Proliferation Treaty—in particular the implementation of safeguards. It also serves as a central instrument for the transfer of knowledge and know-how for the safe utilization of nuclear energy.

I shall first address the specific role of IAEA safeguards.

The IAEA safeguards system

IAEA safeguards have come a long way—both quantitatively and qualitatively—since they were first established. At the time of the Agency's inception, on-site inspection by an international organization was a somewhat revolutionary measure and evoked mixed feelings: fears that it would be burdensome for the operators of nuclear installations; fears that commercial or industrial secrets might be divulged; fears of a new age of international supervision. It would be wrong to say that all reservations have dissipated. Some remain and some new difficulties have been encountered. I shall discuss these matters, but I want to start by saying that on the whole the safeguards system has grown strong, has become consolidated and mature. It is respected and recognized as impartial and it is accepted by all States—nuclear-weapon States and non-nuclear-weapon States alike, NPT-parties and non-NPT-parties alike. Moreover, as the paper prepared for this Conference by the Uranium Institute makes clear, the nuclear industry realizes that nuclear trade in today's world would be severely disrupted if the safeguards and the confidence provided by them were to disappear.

The fear that safeguards would impede nuclear research and development have been laid to rest, although at times some concern is still voiced in a small number of States about the cost and burden of safeguards and about the maintenance of commercial and industrial confidentiality.

Throughout the years of operation of the system the Agency's Director General has been able to report every year that he considered it reasonable to conclude that the nuclear material under Agency safeguards had remained in peaceful nuclear activities or was otherwise adequately accounted for. This is encouraging but hardly surprising as the States have accepted and invited the safeguards in order to create confidence in their commitment to non-proliferation.

The background paper submitted to this Conference by the IAEA on Article III of the NPT provides a review of our experience to date in operating safeguards. Let me just highlight some basic data, identify some problems

and—lastly—make some comments on potential future uses of the system.

First, safeguards agreements are in force with 85 out of the 136 non-nuclear-weapon States Parties to the NPT. Negotiations have been underway for some time with the Democratic People's Republic of Korea for an NPT-safeguards agreement. The latest round of talks was ended recently, regrettably without a conclusion satisfactory to all concerned. It has been agreed, however, that contacts will continue and that further efforts will be made to find a satisfactory outcome leading to the conclusion of a safeguards agreement between the Democratic People's Republic of Korea and the IAEA. Periodic reminders are sent to all NPT-States that have outstanding obligations to conclude agreements. The Secretariat is at all times ready to discuss agreements with these States.

Over the past twenty years the number of facilities under inspection has grown from 156 to over 900. In 1970 there were no enrichment plants and only one reprocessing plant under safeguards; today there are five enrichment plants and five reprocessing plants under safeguards. In 1970 there was one small fuel manufacturing plant under safeguards; today there are 43. In the five-year period under review, extensive efforts have been devoted to establishing effective safeguards arrangements at plutonium fuel manufacturing plants. One such plant came into operation during the past five years in Japan.

With technical and financial support from several Member States and advice from the Standing Advisory Group on Safeguards Implementation (SAGSI) a number of key improvements have been made since the last NPT Review Conference. New technical criteria have been developed that will serve as a basis for safeguards implementation and evaluation. These criteria will initially be applied from the beginning of 1991 through 1995.

Improvements in the quality of safeguards and safeguards implementation have resulted from modifications in the organization of the Safeguards Department. Our offices in Toronto and Tokyo have been upgraded to Regional Offices, permitting increased efficiency in the utilization of our inspection resources and improved effectiveness of the safeguards.

The question of an optimal utilization of resources is of particular significance when, as now, expanded duties of safeguarding must be reconciled with zero real growth budgets. For maximum efficiency in the management of safeguards the efforts on the part of the Agency must be matched by maximum cooperation on the part of Member States. Since safeguards are essentially an IAEA service of impartial verification which is also in the interest of the verified parties, it would be natural to expect an attitude facilitating the service. This is normally the case but objections are sometimes raised in one country or another to the use of some equipment or some new method. A better utilization of Agency resources could also be attained if less effort had to be spent in the designation and acceptance of inspectors. Since 1988 a simplified procedure has been used by 22 States on a voluntary basis, but ceilings on the number of inspectors and restrictions placed by some countries on whole categories of individuals still complicate the organization of inspection teams and travel arrangements.

The cautious acceptance of on-site inspection by States was understandable when safeguards were first introduced. Today when such inspection is seen as a normal element in agreements on disarmament, arms control and confidence building measures, governments should examine whether they could not adopt a more relaxed attitude to impartial international inspection. Ideally, the acceptance of safeguards should be coupled with the acceptance of an inspector's passport issued for inspection trips and without requiring a visa.

The need for budgetary restraints has prompted various ideas for savings. It has been suggested, for instance, that greater inspection emphasis should be placed on bulk handling facilities than now, and less emphasis on light water reactors. It might perhaps be examined in the future, e.g. in the context of some major expansion of safeguards, whether some of the suggestions made could be acted upon without loss of safeguards credibility. However, the present moment would not be well chosen for any major modification which could be perceived as a reduction in the effectiveness of safeguards for the sake of economy. Rather this is the time to underpin safeguards by increased resources to sustain their reliability, resilience and responsiveness to new challenges. The IAEA safeguards are the world's first and largest on-site inspection system. The continued success and viability of the system is of vital importance for further reliance upon international verification. I respectfully submit it is unwise to impose severe budgetary restraints on it.

Safeguards are a confidence-building measure. They must therefore be of a quality that justifies and inspires confidence. The annual Safeguards Implementation Report (SIR) is a frank evaluation which allows member governments to assess the quality of the safeguards system. The format and style of this report have recently been updated and simplified to increase transparence. It is perhaps paradoxical that this report, which is an important factor in establishing member governments' confidence in the system, remains a restricted document—not available to the public. Misinterpretations—accidental or deliberate—occur when, as has happened, the report leaks and figures are taken out of context or quoted without adequate explanations.

I should like to conclude my discussion of IAEA safeguards with some comments on the nuclear-weapon States' voluntary offers to accept safeguards. All the declared nuclear-weapon States have made such offers. Those of the United States and the United Kingdom have regard to all nuclear installations in the peaceful sector, while those of France, the Soviet Union and China have regard to identified installations in that sector. There is a body of opinion holding that inspections under these offers are not very meaningful. The function of safeguards, it is pointed out, is to give confidence about the non-nuclear-weapon status of the country inviting inspection. Safeguards in nuclear-weapon States can obviously not have this function. Yet, in the unanimous view of the Third NPT Review Conference the Agency should make wider use of the voluntary offers and reference was made to the principle that all peaceful nuclear installations in all States should be under safeguards. Regrettably no expansion of safeguards in NWS has been possible under current budgetary constraints.

In my view, inspection in nuclear-weapon States is valuable for several reasons. It evidently does not remove the important differences in obligations between NWS and NNWS under the NPT, but the dichotomy between the large number of closely inspected NNWS on the one hand, and a small number of NWS, otherwise exempt from all inspection, on the other, is softened somewhat. States possessing nuclear weapons are not "rewarded" by having their nuclear installations exempt from the duty of continuous accounting and periodic visits of inspectors. Furthermore, safeguards under the voluntary offers accustom NWS to international on-site inspection and gives them a first-hand experience of it. Safeguards also gives these and other States, as a by-product, a useful external check on the accuracy of the national nuclear material accounting and control system. For the IAEA, inspection in NWS has provided inspectors with practical experience in safeguarding types of installations which have later come under safeguards in other countries.

As yet the nuclear disarmament measures which have been taken have not had any impact on the operation of safeguards in NWS. If, as a result of disarmament measures, however, enriched uranium or plutonium were to be moved from the military to the peaceful sector, assurances that this material stays in the peaceful cycle could be provided by Agency safeguards. Perhaps the NWS could lead the way to a system of international plutonium storage. Such a storage is contemplated in the IAEA Statute and has already been intensely discussed for surplus plutonium originating from peaceful utilization of nuclear energy.

In my view, it would be desirable that fissionable material recovered through nuclear disarmament measures be used as far as possible as safeguarded fuel for electricity generation. The world would undoubtedly feel more comfortable if this material were burnt up than if it were stored without time limit and were theoretically available for the production of new weapons. I hope that in their further negotiations, the NWS will consider the potential use of safeguards on material or installations which are moved into the peaceful nuclear sector, either under present or expanded voluntary offers.

That NPT-type safeguards currently predominate does not mean that other types could not be worked out, consistently with the Agency's Statute, to respond to special requirements that may arise in a disarmament context. The same would be true in other contexts as well, e.g. nuclear-weapon-free zones. The main components of any safeguards regime will undoubtedly be the same, but special needs may call for specialized solutions, such as randomized inspection or permanently stationed inspectors.

Promotion of the use of nuclear energy
I turn now to the IAEA's role in promoting "the further development of the application of nuclear energy for peaceful purposes" and "the fullest possible exchange of equipment, materials and scientific and technological information for the peaceful uses of nuclear energy." Although the euphoria of the early years of the "Atoms for Peace" programme has dissipated, there remain very positive results to register from the promotional activities undertaken, *inter alia*, through the IAEA, consistent with Article IV of the NPT.

Thanks to the substantial increase in IAEA funds for technical assistance and cooperation, these activities have grown very much during the years now under review. The benefits of the peaceful uses of nuclear energy are effectively being made available internationally. This is not the moment for a detailed account. Let me refer you to the Agency's report on Article IV and its Report to the 1987 UN Conference for the Promotion of International Co-operation in the Peaceful Uses of Nuclear Energy (PUNE), which provide a comprehensive picture of the situation at that time. I should nevertheless like to highlight a few points.

The first is the encouraging observation that whether we look at the use of nuclear techniques in the field of agriculture, e.g. mutation breeding, or in the field of industry, e.g. non-destructive testing, or in the field of medicine, e.g. radiation treatment of cancer, the use of these techniques, with their attendant benefits, are steadily advancing.

A current dramatic case which warrants specific mention relates to the use of the sterile insect technique to combat the New World Screwworm infestation which has occurred in Northern Africa and which could have tragic consequences unless this large project succeeds.

I should also stress that reliance on regional mechanisms for the dissemination of nuclear techniques is increasing. The Regional Co-operation Agreement in Asia (RCA) which has long been recognized as having very high practical value, not least in the field of industry, has been followed by the Agreement on Regional Co-operation in Latin America (ARCAL) and, recently, by the African Regional Agreement (AFRA). All will require effective governmental commitment in their respective regions. Supplementary resources from the outside are also vitally needed.

With the steady growth in the use of nuclear techniques and radiation sources in developing countries, it is natural that the IAEA is expanding its cooperation with these countries in the fields of safety and waste disposal. With few exceptions the introduction of non-power nuclear techniques has been well received by the public and experts alike. However, this could change if safety and waste are not handled responsibly. Moreover, public attitudes apart, any responsible dissemination of a new technique requires such attention as an integral part of the technique.

A few years ago African States sounded an alarm that hazardous wastes were being dumped on their territories. Such practices would, of course, be condemnable. I am pleased to tell you that no case was found in which any nuclear waste had been dumped in Africa. A Code of Practice has been worked out in the IAEA for International Transboundary Movement of Radioactive Waste. The Code establishes very strict rules for any such movements. Regulatory restrictions—national and international—are not enough, however. Positive action is also needed to establish suitable repositories for nuclear waste that arises in developing countries, e.g. from hospitals. Several accidents that have occurred in the last few years underline the urgency of such action and the IAEA is giving it high priority, *inter alia*, through expert missions.

A similar high priority is given to assistance in the elaboration of nuclear safety regulations and the establishment of authorities responsible for their supervision. Many expert missions are sent for this purpose.

The use of nuclear energy for electricity generation is potentially of tremendous importance for developing countries. The example of the Republic of Korea, in which 50% of the electricity is generated by nuclear power, shows how a rapidly industrializing developing country can benefit from reliance on nuclear power. By and large, however, these countries have been slow to make use of nuclear power.

Following a recommendation by the Third NPT

Review Conference, the IAEA set up an expert working group to examine the problems facing developing countries wishing to use nuclear power. As was expected, the financing of very large and capital intensive projects in countries having vast investment needs was identified as a major problem. However, other bottlenecks relating to the need for industrial infrastructure, regulatory system and trained manpower were found to be almost as important.

On the question of nuclear power for developing countries, some factors are the same today as in 1985, but other factors are new. First, following the Chernobyl accident in 1986, we have been living with the worldwide psychological impact of this accident, as well as—indeed—the material impact of it, mainly in the Soviet Union. Second, although only a few advanced industrialized countries have chosen to abstain from the use of nuclear power, there has occurred a conspicuous stagnation in the global growth of nuclear power, partly because of a limited need for additional electricity in many industrialized countries, but also because of public reluctance in many of these countries to accept a further expansion of nuclear power. In this situation it is not surprising that several developing countries, although foreseeing sharply increased needs for more electricity, hesitate to turn to an introduction or expansion of nuclear power.

There is another factor, however, which has come sharply into focus since 1985, namely the fear that even the present level of use of coal, oil and gas threatens to raise the temperature of the world's atmosphere. While the emissions of sulphur dioxide (SO_2) and nitrogen oxides (NO_x) from the burning of fossil fuels can, at a cost, be drastically reduced through technical means to avoid further destruction of forests and lakes, there is no economically viable way to avoid carbon dioxide (CO_2) emissions from such processes. This simple fact is placing the world in a dilemma: how to generate more electricity while reducing the CO_2 emissions to the atmosphere. Conservation and greater reliance on renewable sources of energy alone are insufficient to answer this formidable problem. Greater use of nuclear power is not a panacea, but it is hard to believe that this significant and technically proven CO_2-free option can be ignored.

For the developing countries this perspective must be closely analysed. It may matter if China, already the world's largest coal consumer, goes through with plans to double this coal use by the year 2000 or is enabled to step up its reliance on nuclear power. It may matter if India and Pakistan, presently not parties to the NPT, but advanced in nuclear techniques, can make much greater use of these techniques to cover their energy needs or may be driven to a greater use of fossil fuels. It may matter if rapidly developing countries like Indonesia and Thailand turn to more fossil energy rather than to nuclear energy. The same is also true of a country like Egypt and of several Latin American countries, including the non-NPT-States, Argentina and Brazil. I need not add that it will matter if new power plants in industrialized countries are fossil-fuelled or nuclear.

Interest in the nuclear power option will inevitably increase if, as seems likely, the scientific evidence of the greenhouse effect mounts. Political events giving rise to uncertainty about oil or gas supplies will also increase awareness that nuclear power, with the small volumes of fuel that it requires and that can be stored for long periods of operation, improves energy independence.

A renewed interest in nuclear power will focus on the questions whether the nuclear technology can be made so safe that the public is convinced that accidents involving any significant releases of radioactivity can be practically ruled out and that high-level waste is being so safely isolated that any significant releases can be practically ruled out.

There is promising technological activity on both of these crucial matters. Already, much improved nuclear power plant designs exist which are developments of the current dominant types of reactors. There is, furthermore, an ambition to build smaller—hopefully cheaper—power reactors of simpler design, which would be easier to operate and rely more on passive safety. Several designs of this nature are being developed and raise hopes for the future—not least for a moderate-sized and moderate-priced, CO_2-free source of electricity of interest for developing countries. Universal adherence to the non-proliferation regime would facilitate worldwide dissemination of such new technology. Such dissemination, in turn, would fulfil the atoms for peace bargain, on which the NPT is built.

I should like to conclude by respectfully submitting that when this Conference looks forward to the crucial date of 1995, three interlinked needs should be kept in mind:

The need for universal adherence to the non-proliferation regime and for drastic global disarmament, including nuclear disarmament;

The need for an increased transfer of nuclear technology, including simpler and more passively safe nuclear power plants, to promote development; and

The need for better protection of the environment, including the need to counteract global warming and acid rain and the relevance of the nuclear power option to help achieve this.

The present moment is overshadowed by a dangerous confrontation in a strategic region. Conflicts remain in some other parts of the world, too. However, a new climate of cooperation gives us hope that many difficult regional disputes will be alleviated or disappear and that very substantial global disarmament will occur. It also gives us hope that more and better use will be made of the international institutions, the United Nations, the specialized agencies and the IAEA, which are indispensable instruments through which governments must tackle many global problems. Is it too much to hope that in such a climate universal adherence to the non-proliferation regime might become a reality? With such adherence, the transfer of the nuclear power technology of the 90s, hopefully satisfying even the present sceptics of nuclear power, could be promoted on a universal basis and help development. All States could benefit. And global environment would benefit.

Document 38

Statement by the President of the Security Council on behalf of the members of the Council on the responsibility of the Security Council in the maintenance of international peace and security (excerpt)

S/23500, 31 January 1992

At the conclusion of the 3046th meeting of the Security Council, held at the level of Heads of State and Government on 31 January 1992 in connection with the item entitled "The responsibility of the Security Council in the maintenance of international peace and security", the President of the Security Council made the following statement on behalf of the members of the Council.

"The members of the Security Council have authorized me to make the following statement· on their behalf.

"The Security Council met at the Headquarters of the United Nations in New York on 31 January 1992, for the first time at the level of Heads of State and Government. The members of the Council considered, within the framework of their commitment to the United Nations Charter, 'The responsibility of the Security Council in the maintenance of international peace and security'.

" . . .

"*Disarmament, arms control and weapons of mass destruction*

"The members of the Council, while fully conscious of the responsibilities of other organs of the United Nations in the fields of disarmament, arms control and non-proliferation, reaffirm the crucial contribution which progress in these areas can make to the maintenance of international peace and security. They express their commitment to take concrete steps to enhance the effectiveness of the United Nations in these areas.

"The members of the Council underline the need for all Member States to fulfil their obligations in relation to arms control and disarmament; to prevent the proliferation in all its aspects of all weapons of mass destruction; to avoid excessive and destabilizing accumulations and transfers of arms; and to resolve peacefully in accordance with the Charter any problems concerning these matters threatening or disrupting the maintenance of regional and global stability. They emphasize the importance of the early ratification and implementation by the States concerned of all international and regional arms control arrangements, especially the START and CFE Treaties.

"The proliferation of all weapons of mass destruction constitutes a threat to international peace and security. The members of the Council commit themselves to working to prevent the spread of technology related to the research for or production of such weapons and to take appropriate action to that end.

"On nuclear proliferation, they note the importance of the decision of many countries to adhere to the Non-Proliferation Treaty and emphasize the integral role in the implementation of that Treaty of fully effective IAEA safeguards, as well as the importance of effective export controls. The members of the Council will take appropriate measures in the case of any violations notified to them by the IAEA.

" . . . "

Document 39

Guidelines for transfers of nuclear-related dual-use equipment, material and related technology (Warsaw Guidelines), Warsaw, 3 April 1992

INFCIRC/254/Rev.1/Part 2, July 1992

OBJECTIVE

1. With the objective of averting the proliferation of nuclear weapons, suppliers have had under consideration procedures in relation to the transfer of certain equipment, material, and related technology that could make a major contribution to a "nuclear explosive activity" or an "unsafeguarded nuclear fuel-cycle activity". In this connection, suppliers have agreed on the following principles, common definitions, and an export control list of equipment, material, and related technology. The Guidelines are not designed to impede international cooperation as long as such cooperation will not contribute to a nuclear explosive activity or an unsafeguarded nuclear fuel-cycle activity. Suppliers intend to implement the Guidelines in accordance with national legislation and relevant international commitments.

BASIC PRINCIPLE

2. Suppliers should not authorize transfers of equipment, material, or related technology identified in the Annex:

—for use in a non-nuclear-weapon State in a nuclear explosive activity or an unsafeguarded nuclear fuel cycle activity, or

—in general, when there is an unacceptable risk of diversion to such an activity, or when the transfers are contrary to the objective of averting the proliferation of nuclear weapons.

EXPLANATION OF TERMS

3. (a) "Nuclear explosive activity" includes research on or development, design, manufacture, construction, testing or maintenance of any nuclear explosive device or components or subsystems of such a device.

(b) "Unsafeguarded nuclear fuel-cycle activity" includes research on or development, design, manufacture, construction, operation or maintenance of any reactor, critical facility, conversion plant, fabrication plant, reprocessing plant, plant for the separation of isotopes of source or special fissionable material, or separate storage installation, where there is no obligation to accept International Atomic Energy Agency (IAEA) safeguards at the relevant facility or installation, existing or future, when it contains any source or special fissionable material; or of any heavy water production plant where there is no obligation to accept IAEA safeguards on any nuclear material produced by or used in connection with any heavy water produced therefrom; or where any such obligation is not met.

ESTABLISHMENT OF EXPORT LICENSING PROCEDURES

4. Suppliers should establish export licensing procedures for the transfer of equipment, material, and related technology identified in the Annex. These procedures should include enforcement measures for violations. In considering whether to authorize such transfers, suppliers should exercise prudence in order to carry out the Basic Principle and should take relevant factors into account, including:

(a) Whether the recipient State is a party to the Nuclear Non-Proliferation Treaty (NPT) or to the Treaty for the Prohibition of Nuclear Weapons in Latin America (Treaty of Tlatelolco), or to a similar international legally-binding nuclear non-proliferation agreement, and has an IAEA safeguards agreement in force applicable to all its peaceful nuclear activities;

(b) Whether any recipient State that is not party to the NPT, Treaty of Tlatelolco, or a similar international legally-binding nuclear non-proliferation agreement has any facilities or installations listed in paragraph 3(b) above that are operational or being designed or constructed that are not, or will not be, subject to IAEA safeguards;

(c) Whether the equipment, material, or related technology to be transferred is appropriate for the stated end-use and whether that stated end-use is appropriate for the end-user;

(d) Whether the equipment, material, or related technology to be transferred is to be used in research on or development, design, manufacture, construction, operation, or maintenance of any reprocessing or enrichment facility;

(e) Whether governmental actions, statements, and policies of the recipient State are supportive of nuclear non-proliferation and whether the recipient State is in compliance with its international obligations in the field of non-proliferation;

(f) Whether the recipients have been engaged in clandestine or illegal procurement activities; and

(g) Whether a transfer has not been authorized to the end-user or whether the end-user has diverted for purposes inconsistent with the Guidelines any transfer previously authorized.

CONDITIONS FOR TRANSFERS

5. In the process of determining that the transfer will not pose any unacceptable risk of diversion, in accordance with the Basic Principle and to meet the objectives of the Guidelines, the supplier should obtain, before authorizing the transfer and in a manner consistent with its national law and practices, the following:

(a) a statement from the end-user specifying the uses and end-use locations of the proposed transfers; and

(b) an assurance explicitly stating that the proposed transfer or any replica thereof will not be used in any nuclear explosive activity or unsafeguarded nuclear fuel-cycle activity.

CONSENT RIGHTS OVER RETRANSFERS

6. Before authorizing the transfer of equipment, material, or related technology identified in the Annex to a country not adhering to the Guidelines, suppliers should obtain assurances that their consent will be secured, in a manner consistent with their national law and practices, prior to any retransfer to a third country of the equipment, material, or related technology, or any replica thereof.

CONCLUDING PROVISIONS

7. The supplier reserves to itself discretion as to the application of the Guidelines to other items of significance in addition to those identified in the Annex, and as to the application of other conditions for transfer that it may consider necessary in addition to those provided for in paragraph 5 of the Guidelines.

8. In furtherance of the effective implementation of the Guidelines, suppliers should, as necessary and appropriate, exchange relevant information and consult with other States adhering to the Guidelines.

9. In the interest of international peace and security, the adherence of all States to the Guidelines would be welcome.

Document 40

Report of the Secretary-General entitled "New dimensions of arms regulation and disarmament in the post-cold war era" (excerpt)

A/C.1/47/7, 27 October 1992

A. Weapons of mass destruction

21. Traditionally, this category of capability has been of paramount concern, and remains so today. Over the years, the thrust of diplomacy has been to reduce and, wherever possible, to eliminate these weapons; to curb their proliferation among States; and to preclude their deployment in certain international domains, such as outer space, the seabed and Antarctica.

22. At long last, we are on the verge of historic accomplishments. The process of nuclear disarmament is gathering momentum, at least as it relates to the United States and the States of the former Soviet Union. By the end of this decade, the multiple-warhead intercontinental ballistic missile (ICBM) may be a thing of the past, and the category of tactical nuclear weapons will be sharply reduced, if not totally eliminated. The scope of nuclear-weapon limitations agreed to by these two major nations is absolutely striking, as is evident from simple statistics. The 1991 START Treaty* will reduce the total number of long-range nuclear warheads in the United States arsenals to some 8,550, compared with 12,640 in 1990. The Russian Federation will retain some 6,160 warheads, compared with the 11,000 held by the former Soviet Union in 1990. The agreement reached last June between the two sides, when translated into treaty language, could by the end of this century leave the United States with as few as 3,500 and the Russian Federation with as few as 3,000 warheads. This would represent a reduction of approximately 70 per cent over the next decade.

23. Now that reductions are occurring, a number of questions assume greater importance: How could envisioned cuts lead to even further reductions? When will the negotiating process be enlarged to include other nuclear-weapon States? And will the parties, having already sharply curtailed their qualitative improvement programmes, finally agree to halt nuclear testing completely?

24. The international community can aim for no less a goal than the complete elimination of nuclear weapons. Achieving this goal may take some time. Nuclear technology cannot be disinvented; and there are a host of difficult questions—including issues of stability and veri-

---

* Treaty between the United States of America and the Union of Soviet Socialist Republics on the Reduction and Limitation of Strategic Offensive Arms, signed on 31 July 1991.

fication—which must be weighed carefully. It is my belief, nevertheless, that the full array of hazards posed to humanity by these weapons cannot be adequately dealt with until we have crossed the threshold of the post-nuclear-weapon age.

25. In this context, a comprehensive ban on nuclear testing would be a significant step leading to the goal of the elimination of all nuclear weapons. The seriousness of purpose demonstrated by the two major Powers as they continue to reduce their nuclear arsenals drastically, and the ongoing efforts by the international community to prevent the proliferation of nuclear weapons, can best be matched by embracing the associated measure of halting the qualitative improvement of nuclear weapons through a cessation of nuclear testing. The annual number of tests carried out in the last several years indicates a most welcome downward trend. In only two years, from 1987 to 1989, the number of tests dropped from 47 to 27. This was followed by further reductions to 18 tests in 1990 and 14 in 1992. I strongly welcome the current moratoria put into effect by some nuclear-weapon States. Gradual and significant reductions in the number and yield of tests are options which should be encouraged in a progressive move towards a total ban on nuclear testing.

26. Fortunately, with respect to chemical arms, the international community is on the verge of just such an achievement. We have before us the long-awaited draft Convention on a Comprehensive Prohibition of Chemical Weapons which has been completed by the Conference on Disarmament. I am aware of the fact that certain aspects of this Convention are not as every State would like. On the whole, however, I believe that this agreement deserves your support. As there are today some 20 States that possess or seek to acquire a chemical weapons capability, this Convention, along with universal adherence to the Convention banning biological weapons, is an indis-pensable element in global efforts to deal effectively with weapons of mass destruction.

B. Proliferation control

27. Current international trends should help immeasurably in achieving a priority which is of growing importance to the global community—the non-proliferation of weapons. At a moment when substantial disarmament is finally beginning to occur, there can be no justification for any State, anywhere, to acquire the tools and technologies of mass destruction. This judgement, I believe, is widely shared by States. It was articulated clearly at the Security Council Summit last January, when the Council declared that the proliferation of nuclear, and indeed all weapons of mass destruction, constituted a threat to international peace and security. The question is how to turn the logic of non-proliferation into concerted action.

28. In the nuclear realm the Non-Proliferation Treaty continues to provide an indispensable framework for our global non-proliferation efforts. All of us know all too well that the Treaty has its contentious aspects. And yet the broad adherence, which now includes all the nuclear-weapon States, emphasizes its fundamental validity. It is clear, however that verification and safeguards arrangements for the Treaty need to be strengthened. When the Treaty itself comes up for extension in 1995, it should be extended indefinitely and unconditionally. *All States should adhere to the Treaty.*

29. Over the longer term, it is my hope that we may achieve more equitable and comprehensive approaches to responsible proliferation control, not only of weapons but also of long-range delivery systems and dual-use technologies. To be fully effective, such controls must be balanced and fair; they must not unduly hamper the peaceful uses of science and technology; and they should not divide the world into the invidious categories of "haves" and "have-nots".

Document 41

Guidelines for nuclear transfers (Revision of NSG London Guidelines of 1977), Lucerne, Switzerland, 1 April 1993

INFCIRC/254/Rev.1/Part 1/Mod.1, July 1993

1. The following fundamental principles for safeguards and export controls should apply to nuclear transfers to any non-nuclear-weapon State for peaceful purposes. In this connection, suppliers have defined an export trigger list and agreed on common criteria for technology transfers.

Prohibition on nuclear explosives

2. Suppliers should authorize transfer of items identified in the trigger list only upon formal governmental assurances from recipients explicitly excluding uses which would result in any nuclear explosive device.

Physical protection

3. (a) All nuclear materials and facilities identified by the agreed trigger list should be placed under effective physical protection to prevent unauthorized use and handling. The levels of physical protection to be ensured in relation to the type of materials, equipment and facilities, have been agreed by suppliers, taking account of international recommendations.

(b) The implementation of measures of physical protection in the recipient country is the responsibility of the Government of that country. However, in order to implement the terms agreed upon amongst suppliers, the levels of physical protection on which these measures have to be based should be the subject of an agreement between supplier and recipient.

(c) In each case special arrangements should be made for a clear definition of responsibilities for the transport of trigger list items.

Safeguards

4. (a) Suppliers should transfer trigger list items to a non-nuclear-weapon State only when the receiving State has brought into force an agreement with the IAEA requiring the application of safeguards on all source and special fissionable material in its current and future peaceful activities.

(b) Transfers covered by paragraph 4 (a) to a non-nuclear-weapon State without such a safeguards agreement should be authorized only in exceptional cases when they are deemed essential for the safe operation of existing facilities and if safeguards are applied to those facilities. Suppliers should inform and, if appropriate, consult in the event that they intend to authorize or to deny such transfers.

(c) The policy referred to in paragraph 4 (a) and 4 (b) does not apply to agreements or contracts drawn up on or prior to April 3, 1992. In case of countries that have adhered or will adhere to INFCIRC/254/Rev.1/Part 1 later than April 3, 1992, the policy only applies to agreements (to be) drawn up after their date of adherence.

(d) Under agreements to which the policy referred to in paragraph 4 (a) does not apply (see paragraphs 4 (b) and (c)) suppliers should transfer trigger list items only when covered by IAEA safeguards with duration and coverage provisions in conformity with IAEA doc. GOV/1621. However, suppliers undertake to strive for the earliest possible implementation of the policy referred to in paragraph 4 (a) under such agreements.

(e) Suppliers reserve the right to apply additional conditions of supply as a matter of national policy.

5. Suppliers will jointly reconsider their common safeguards requirements, whenever appropriate.

Safeguards triggered by the transfer of certain technology

6. (a) The requirements of paragraphs 2, 3 and 4 above should also apply to facilities for reprocessing, enrichment, or heavy-water production, utilizing technology directly transferred by the supplier or derived from transferred facilities, or major critical components thereof.

(b) The transfer of such facilities, or major critical components thereof, or related technology, should require an undertaking (1) that IAEA safeguards apply to any facilities of the same type (i.e. if the design, construction or operating processes are based on the same or similar physical or chemical processes, as defined in the trigger list) constructed during an agreed period in the recipient country and (2) that there should at all times be in effect a safeguards agreement permitting the IAEA to apply Agency safeguards with respect to such facilities identified by the recipient, or by the supplier in consultation with the recipient, as using transferred technology.

Special controls on sensitive exports

7. Suppliers should exercise restraint in the transfer of sensitive facilities, technology and weapons-usable materials. If enrichment or reprocessing facilities, equipment or technology are to be transferred, suppliers should encourage recipients to accept, as an alternative to national plants, supplier involvement and/or other appropriate multinational participation in resulting facilities. Suppliers should also promote international (including IAEA) activities concerned with multinational regional fuel cycle centres.

Special controls on export of enrichment facilities, equipment and technology

8. For a transfer of an enrichment facility, or technology therefor, the recipient nation should agree that neither the transferred facility, nor any facility based on such technology, will be designed or operated for the production of greater than 20% enriched uranium without the consent of the supplier nation, of which the IAEA should be advised.

Controls on supplied or derived weapons-usable material

9. Suppliers recognize the importance, in order to advance the objectives of these guidelines and to provide opportunities further to reduce the risks of proliferation, of including in agreements on supply of nuclear materials or of facilities which produce weapons-usable material, provisions calling for mutual agreement between the supplier and the recipient on arrangements for reprocessing, storage, alteration, use, transfer or retransfer of any weapons-usable material involved. Suppliers should en-

deavour to include such provisions whenever appropriate and practicable.

Controls on retransfer

10. (a) Suppliers should transfer trigger list items, including technology defined under paragraph 6, only upon the recipient's assurance that in the case of:

(1) retransfer of such items, or

(2) transfer of trigger list items derived from facilities originally transferred by the supplier, or with the help of equipment or technology originally transferred by the supplier,

the recipient of the retransfer or transfer will have provided the same assurances as those required by the supplier for the original transfer.

(b) In addition the supplier's consent should be required for: (1) any retransfer of the facilities, major critical components, or technology described in paragraph 6; (2) any transfer of facilities or major critical components derived from those items; (3) any retransfer of heavy water or weapons-usable material.

SUPPORTING ACTIVITIES

Physical security

11. Suppliers should promote international cooperation on the exchange of physical security information, protection of nuclear materials in transit, and recovery of stolen nuclear materials and equipment.

Support for effective IAEA safeguards

12. Suppliers should make special efforts in support of effective implementation of IAEA safeguards. Suppliers should also support the Agency's efforts to assist Member States in the improvement of their national systems of accounting and control of nuclear material and to increase the technical effectiveness of safeguards.

Similarly, they should make every effort to support the IAEA in increasing further the adequacy of safeguards in the light of technical developments and the rapidly growing number of nuclear facilities, and to support appropriate initiatives aimed at improving the effectiveness of IAEA safeguards.

Sensitive plant design features

13. Suppliers should encourage the designers and makers of sensitive equipment to construct it in such a way as to facilitate the application of safeguards.

Consultations

14. (a) Suppliers should maintain contact and consult through regular channels on matters connected with the implementation of these guidelines.

(b) Suppliers should consult, as each deems appropriate, with other Governments concerned on specific sensitive cases, to ensure that any transfer does not contribute to risks of conflict or instability.

(c) In the event that one or more suppliers believe that there has been a violation of supplier/recipient understandings resulting from these guidelines, particularly in the case of an explosion of a nuclear device, or illegal termination or violation of IAEA safeguards by a recipient, suppliers should consult promptly through diplomatic channels in order to determine and assess the reality and extent of the alleged violation.

Pending the early outcome of such consultations, suppliers will not act in a manner that could prejudice any measure that may be adopted by other suppliers concerning their current contacts with that recipient.

Upon the findings of such consultations, the suppliers, bearing in mind Article XII of the IAEA Statute, should agree on an appropriate response and possible action which could include the termination of nuclear transfers to that recipient.

15. In considering transfers, each supplier should exercise prudence having regard to all the circumstances of each case, including any risk that technology transfers not covered by paragraph 6, or subsequent retransfers, might result in unsafeguarded nuclear materials.

16. Unanimous consent is required for any changes in these guidelines, including any which might result from the reconsideration mentioned in paragraph 5.

Document 42

Declaration of the Russian Federation on unilateral security assurances

CD/PV.661, 17 August 1993

The Russian Federation will not use nuclear weapons against any non-nuclear-weapon State Party to the Treaty on the Non-Proliferation of Nuclear Weapons, except in the event of an attack on the Russian Federation, its territory, armed forces or allies conducted by a State of this kind that is linked by an agreement of association with a nuclear-weapon State or that acts together with, or with the support of a nuclear-weapon State in carrying out such an attack.

Document 43

Message of the Secretary-General to the General Conference of the IAEA in Vienna

UN Press Release SG/SM/5113, 27 September 1993

This General Conference meeting of the International Atomic Energy Agency convenes at an important time for the Agency and for the international community as a whole. I regret that my duties at the plenary session of the General Assembly prevent my travelling to Vienna at this time, but I am pleased, nonetheless, to have this opportunity to reflect with you on some of the most important of the challenges that now face the IAEA and the wider international community.

As the new challenges of the post–cold war era begin to emerge with greater clarity, the time has now come for the integration of disarmament and non-proliferation issues into a broader international agenda. Peace, development, and security are closely linked. Non-proliferation and disarmament are integral to development and progress, and central to international peace. But non-proliferation and disarmament can only be achieved in conjunction with other issues—political, economic, and social.

The structure of international relations and the nature of international priorities have changed dramatically. During the cold war, international relations were defined by the political dynamics of superpower competition. States everywhere learned to calculate their interests and seek security in the context of this global bipolar competition.

The end of the cold war has brought new possibilities of cooperation. Political understanding, economic cooperation, and social dialogue have supplanted geopolitical rivalries. In Europe, in the Middle East, in Africa, in Asia, and throughout the world, the results are concrete and tangible.

The end of the cold war has also revealed a dark side. Freed from the constraints of the cold war, long suppressed ethnic, religious, and factional rivalries have burst forth into violent and open conflict. Ultra-nationalism and micro-nationalism threaten to splinter many States into fragments. The relatively weak have again become the prey of the relatively strong. Unable to sustain cold war expenditures in the absence of cold war subsidies, a few States have simply ceased to function.

These are the new challenges of the post-cold war era. To address these challenges, a new conceptual framework for security is needed. The outlines of such a framework have already begun to take shape. The essential components are three. *First*, to ensure our survival as a species, we must stop the competition in weapons of mass destruction. *Second*, to avoid conflicts based on misperceptions and mistrust, we must promote transparency in armaments and other confidence-building measures. *Third*, to deter potential aggressors we must exhibit a greater collective determination to oppose aggression.

In the context of non-proliferation and disarmament, the end of the cold war has had a dramatic effect. A decade ago military expenditures worldwide were rising dramatically and the nuclear arms race was preparing to spread to outer space. There was widespread public apprehension and justified alarm over the seemingly relentless build-up in both nuclear and conventional military forces.

Much has changed. Impressive cuts have been made in strategic and nuclear arsenals. With the signing of the new strategic arms reduction treaty (START-2) the next decade promises to see a 70 per cent reduction in the number of nuclear warheads in the world. The elimination of ground-based multiple warhead missiles has substantially defused the nuclear arms race by removing the fear of a nuclear first strike. The United States and the Russian Federation have concluded 16 bilateral agreements providing for greater transparency and greater security.

The new bilateral spirit of cooperation between the United States and Russia has encouraged and facilitated multilateral cooperation on a global scale. Significant progress has been achieved. Worldwide nuclear tests have declined dramatically, and negotiations towards the completion of a Nuclear Test Ban Treaty have been given new life. The convention on the prohibition of the development, stockpiling, and use of chemical weapons is at long last in effect. A register for conventional arms—intended to increase transparency and build confidence—is now in operation.

For the IAEA, in particular, these developments have had profound ramifications. A new level of cooperation is now possible, and in evidence. Not unexpectedly however, new threats and new challenges have also arisen.

The world remains a dangerous place. As superpower disarmament has gathered momentum, international concern has turned anxiously towards ensuring the non-proliferation of nuclear, chemical, and biological weapons of mass destruction. I have said before, and I say to you again today, that at a moment when substantial disarmament is finally beginning to occur, there can be no justification for any State, anywhere, to acquire the tools and technologies of mass destruction.

In the nuclear realm, the non-proliferation treaty continues to provide an indispensable framework for our global non-proliferation efforts. The treaty now enjoys the adherence of 160 States. All five nuclear-weapon States are now parties to the treaty.

The international community must remain steadfast in insisting upon adherence to and compliance with the terms of this treaty. Iraq's secret and extensive efforts to develop nuclear weapons must serve as a warning against complacency, and as an indication of the resolve that the international community will be required to show if the perils of nuclear proliferation are to be avoided. The Democratic People's Republic of Korea's threat to withdraw from the non-proliferation treaty, and its refusal to fully comply with its obligations under the treaty provide further warning. Vigilance, determination, and perseverance will continue to be needed.

Maintaining the credibility of IAEA safeguards and guaranteeing the full implementation of the non-proliferation treaty is vital. Our collective experience in dealing with the challenges posed by Iraq and the Democratic People's Republic of Korea demonstrates the importance

of strong international backing, including when necessary, the active involvement of the Security Council. Preventing the proliferation of nuclear weapons depends upon this. Success is necessary. Failure would have far-reaching consequences—potentially setting off a chain reaction in the proliferation of these and other dangerous weapons of mass destruction.

The recent confrontations in which the Agency has played a role also clearly demonstrate that the provisions of the non-proliferation treaty should be strengthened. Verification and safeguard arrangements must be improved. I appreciate and fully support the actions taken by the Director General and the Board of the IAEA to strengthen reporting requirements and to conduct special inspections of undeclared facilities in order to reinforce the safeguards system. Individually and collectively, using every means at our disposal, we must ensure that all States adhere to the Non-Proliferation Treaty.

Further progress in this and other areas is still necessary. Three unfinished items remain high on the international security agenda. First, it is of vital importance that the Non-Proliferation Treaty be extended indefinitely and unconditionally when it comes up for review in 1995. Second, the de facto moratoria on nuclear testing by nuclear-weapon States must be maintained and a comprehensive nuclear test ban treaty concluded at an early date. Third, with the momentum gained from the reduction in nuclear arsenals, we must now work towards a complete cut-off in the production of fissile material for weapons purposes.

The opportunity to make substantial progress is now before us. We must not let it slip through our grasp.

*   *   *

Traditional concerns over disarmament and non-proliferation rightly remain central to the IAEA's mission, but increased attention is also being paid to other aspects of the Agency's international mandate—including such vital issues as ensuring the safe storage and disposal of fissile materials, enhancing the safety of nuclear power plants, and addressing the consequences of past nuclear practices.

Ensuring the safety and security of fissile materials recovered from dismantled warheads poses an important challenge for the Agency. International supervision of the storage of such materials is an important aspect of confidence-building and nuclear transparency. It is essential that newly independent States immediately commit themselves to legally binding non-proliferation undertakings, and that there be full transparency in the trade and storage of plutonium and highly enriched uranium.

Concerns about the safety and security of fissile materials are also related to concerns about ensuring the safety of nuclear power plants—an issue that has received wide international attention in the past year. Countries operating outdated plants, as well as their neighbours, are anxious that the IAEA provide necessary advice and support.

The need for specific attention to be given to the safe operation of Soviet-designed reactors has been widely noted. I hope that the International Safety Convention, presently being circulated among Member States, will soon be adopted. The Convention will serve as the basic international frame of reference for safety and review procedures of nuclear plants. Its implementation would be an important and positive step forward.

In keeping with resolutions of the General Assembly and the Economic and Social Council, there has been continued close collaboration between the United Nations and the IAEA to alleviate the consequences of the Chernobyl accident. In June, I was in Kiev and experienced first hand the concerns of the people there about the long-term effects of the nuclear accident. It is important that we work together to accurately assess the damage, prevent further harm, and alleviate suffering.

I am pleased to note that progress is being made in addressing the consequences of the disaster. The UN Trust Fund for Chernobyl funded the application of an innovative technique proven by IAEA and FAO to cut caesium levels substantially in milk and meat. The IAEA and the United Nations Development Programme have undertaken a joint initiative to strengthen national institutions for radiation protection and nuclear safety in the republics of the former Soviet Union. And tangible financial support is now being provided for safety system improvements and for alternative energy mixes.

Cooperation is essential. Together we must work to make things better. We have a duty to all to ensure that the world never again has to face the terrible spectre of a nuclear Chernobyl.

* * *

The Chernobyl disaster underscores the importance of ensuring that all of our energy production techniques—nuclear and non-nuclear—are safe, responsible, and sustainable.

The United Nations Conference on Environment and Development (UNCED) in Rio de Janeiro focused the world's attention on the need to husband resources and minimize waste in order to preserve our fragile ecosystem and provide a better life for all peoples around the world. Safe, abundant, and sustainable sources of energy are required.

Nuclear science has made many valuable contributions to modern life, in industry, in agriculture, in medicine, and in other areas as well. But if nuclear power is to be a truly viable global option, the IAEA must help to ensure that nuclear energy can be safely produced in accordance with international standards, that nuclear wastes can be securely disposed of, and that sufficient safeguards can be developed so as to minimize the risk that commercial technologies will be turned to military uses.

These are difficult challenges, but they are challenges that we must all face together. I wish you a productive and successful General Conference as you address the many issues before you, and I offer you my strong support as together we face the difficult challenges that lie ahead.

Document 44

Statement of the Secretary-General before the Advisory Board on Disarmament Matters (excerpt), Geneva, 12 January 1994

The Disarmament Agenda of the International Community in 1994 and Beyond: Statements of the Secretary-General. Published by the Centre for Disarmament Affairs, April 1994

Another field where progress is vital is nuclear proliferation. As we prepare for the Conference of the Parties to the Nuclear Non-Proliferation Treaty, the creation of a climate of confidence will be vital. Measures need to be taken now to create that climate.

A continuing moratorium on nuclear testing would greatly assist. A follow-up to the idea of a "cutoff" in the production of fissionable materials would also be helpful.

Universal adherence to the NPT must be our goal.

The nuclear safeguards of the IAEA must be further strengthened. The agreement between Argentina and Brazil and the IAEA is a good step forward. I strongly support the plans for a nuclear-weapon-free zone in Africa. I urge interested parties to tackle the establishment of such a zone in the Middle East with an open mind and greater courage and imagination.

Incentives for non-nuclear-weapon States to take the path of nuclear proliferation must be removed. Transgressors must be given to understand that it is in their best interest to return to compliance. Clarity of vision, and firmness of resolve, will be required.

At its historic session on 31 January 1992, the Security Council declared that "proliferation of all weapons of mass destruction constitutes a threat to international peace and security". Members of the Security Council committed themselves to work "to prevent the spread of technology related to the research for or production of such weapons [of mass destruction], and to take appropriate action to that end".

In *New Dimensions*, I continued that theme. I stated that "the question is how to turn the logic of non-proliferation into concerted action".

Last month, I visited North-East Asia, where there is a real concern about nuclear proliferation. I was pleased to note that the Republic of Korea and the Democratic People's Republic of Korea have signed an agreement on the de-nuclearization of the Korean peninsula. I reiterated to the Government of the Democratic People's Republic of Korea my view of the seriousness with which the international community would view a withdrawal of the Democratic People's Republic of Korea from the NPT. I repeat my call to the interested parties to resolve, through negotiations, the remaining difficulties.

The goal must be international inspection of nuclear facilities in all the Member States of the United Nations.

In this connection, the decision by Ukraine to accede to the NPT and to negotiate the process of dismantling all nuclear weapons on its territory was an important step. The agreement, when signed, will strengthen international peace and security.

I would welcome your views on the question of access to new technology. During the cold war, the developed countries restricted access to dual-purpose technologies with a possible military application. The Security Council endorsed this approach. Yet not all Member States are convinced of its validity.

Progress is needed in this field too. I hope that multilateral negotiations on this subject can begin soon. Our aim must be the eventual replacement of the existing export-control regimes by arrangements more satisfactory to the importers. Is there scope for a limited verification regime in this sphere, perhaps similar to the IAEA? To be effective, such a regime would have to depend on an agreement by recipients on limited use, as well as on verification. Are suppliers ready to be more flexible?

Meanwhile, is there scope for improvements to existing supplier regimes? Can the best aspects of each regime be brought together? And, finally, what should be the role of the United Nations?

Document 45

List of States parties to the NPT which had not concluded the required safeguards agreement with the IAEA

NPT/CONF.1995/PC III/7, 1 July 1994

Status as at 1 July 1994

Non-nuclear-weapon States party to NPT without safeguards agreement in force [a] (1)	Date of ratification, accession or succession to NPT (2)	Status of negotiation (3)	Date agreement should enter into force (4)
Albania [b]	12 September 1990		12 March 1992
Antigua and Barbuda [c]	1 November 1981	Signed 1 February 1990	1 May 1983
Azerbaijan	22 September 1992		22 March 1994
Bahamas	10 July 1973		10 January 1975
Bahrain	3 November 1988		3 May 1990
Barbados	21 February 1980		21 August 1981
Belarus	22 July 1993		22 January 1995
Belize	9 August 1985	Signed 13 August 1992	9 February 1987

Non-nuclear-weapon States party to NPT without safeguards agreement in force [a] (1)	Date of ratification, accession or succession to NPT (2)	Status of negotiation (3)	Date agreement should enter into force (4)
Benin	31 October 1972		30 April 1974
Bolivia [c]	26 May 1970	Signed 23 August 1974	5 March 1972
Botswana	28 April 1969		5 March 1972
Burkina Faso	3 March 1970		5 March 1972
Burundi	19 March 1971		19 September 1972
Cambodia	2 June 1972		2 December 1973
Cameroon	8 January 1969	Signed 21 May 1992	5 March 1972
Cape Verde	24 October 1979		24 April 1981
Central African Republic	25 October 1970		25 April 1972
Chad	10 March 1971		10 September 1972
Colombia [d]	8 April 1986		8 October 1987
Congo	23 October 1978		23 April 1980
Dominica	10 August 1984		10 February 1986
Equatorial Guinea	1 November 1984	Approved 13 June 1986	1 May 1986
Estonia	31 January 1992	Approved 24 February 1992	31 July 1993
Gabon	19 February 1974	Signed 3 December 1979	19 August 1975
Georgia	7 March 1994		7 September 1995
Grenada	19 August 1974		19 February 1976
Guinea	29 April 1985		29 October 1986
Guinea-Bissau	20 August 1976		20 February 1978
Guyana	19 October 1993		19 April 1995
Haiti [c]	2 June 1970	Signed 6 January 1975	2 June 1972
Kenya	11 June 1970		11 June 1972
Kuwait	17 November 1989		17 May 1991
Lao People's Democratic Rep.	20 February 1970	Signed 22 November 1991	5 March 1972
Liberia	5 March 1970		5 March 1972
Mali	10 February 1970		5 March 1972
Mauritania	26 October 1993		26 April 1995
Mozambique	4 September 1990		4 March 1992
Myanmar	2 December 1992		2 June 1994
Namibia	2 October 1992		7 April 1994
Niger	9 October 1992		9 April 1994
Panama [c, d]	13 January 1977	Signed 22 December 1988	13 July 1978
Qatar	3 April 1989		3 October 1990
Rwanda	20 May 1975		20 November 1976
St. Kitts and Nevis	22 March 1993		22 September 1994
San Marino	10 August 1970	Approved 23 February 1977	5 March 1972
Sao Tome and Principe	20 July 1983		20 January 1985
Saudi Arabia	3 October 1988		3 April 1990
Seychelles	12 March 1985		12 September 1986
Sierra Leone	26 February 1975	Signed 10 November 1977	26 August 1976
Somalia	5 March 1970		5 March 1972

Non-nuclear-weapon States party to NPT without safeguards agreement in force [a] (1)	Date of ratification, accession or succession to NPT (2)	Status of negotiation (3)	Date agreement should enter into force (4)
Togo	26 February 1970	Signed 29 November 1990	5 March 1972
Uganda	20 October 1982		20 April 1984
United Republic of Tanzania	7 June 1991	Signed 26 August 1992	7 December 1992
Uzbekistan	7 May 1992	Approved 21 February 1994	7 November 1993
Yemen	1 June 1979		1 December 1980
Zambia	15 May 1991	Approved 8 June 1994	15 November 1992
Zimbabwe	26 September 1991		26 March 1993

a/ The information reproduced in columns (1) and (2) was provided to the Agency by the depositary Governments of NPT, and an entry in column (1) does not imply the expression of any opinion on the part of the Secretariat concerning the legal status of any country or territory or of its authorities, or concerning the delimitation of its frontiers. The table does not contain information relating to the participation of Taiwan, Province of China, in the NPT.

b/ A comprehensive safeguards agreement not in connection with the NPT is in force with this State.

c/ The relevant safeguards agreement refers to both the NPT and the Treaty of Tlatelolco.

d/ A comprehensive safeguards agreement pursuant to the Treaty of Tlatelolco is in force with this State.

Document 46

Situation with respect to the conclusion of safeguards agreements between the IAEA and non-nuclear-weapon States parties to the NPT

NPT/CONF.1995/PC III/7, 1 July 1994

Status as at 1 July 1994

NNWS which have signed, ratified, acceded to or succeed to NPT [a] (1)	Date of ratification, accession or succession [a] (2)	Safeguards agreement with the Agency (3)	INFCIRC (4)
Afghanistan	4 February 1970	In force: 20 February 1978	257
Albania	12 September 1990		
Antigua and Barbuda [b]	1 November 1981	Signed: 1 February 1990	. . .
Armenia	15 July 1993	In force: 6 May 1994	. . .
Australia	23 January 1973	In force: 10 July 1974	217
Austria	27 June 1969	In force: 23 July 1972	156
Azerbaijan	22 September 1992		
Bahamas	10 July 1973		
Bahrain	3 November 1988		
Bangladesh	27 September 1979	In force: 11 June 1982	301
Barbados	21 February 1980		
Belarus	22 July 1993		
Belgium	2 May 1975	In force: 21 February 1977	193

NNWS which have signed, ratified, acceded to or succeed to NPT [a] (1)	Date of ratification, accession or succession [a] (2)	Safeguards agreement with the Agency (3)	INFCIRC (4)
Belize	9 August 1985	Signed: 13 August 1992	. . .
Benin	31 October 1972		
Bhutan	23 May 1985	In force: 24 October 1989	371
Bolivia [b]	26 May 1970	Signed: 23 August 1974	. . .
Botswana	28 April 1969		
Brunei Darussalam	25 March 1985	In force: 4 November 1987	365
Bulgaria	5 September 1969	In force: 29 February 1972	178
Burkina Faso	3 March 1970		
Burundi	19 March 1971		
Cambodia	2 June 1972		
Cameroon	8 January 1969	Signed: 21 May 1992	. . .
Canada	8 January 1969	In force: 21 February 1972	164
Cape Verde	24 October 1979		
Central African Republic	25 October 1970		
Chad	10 March 1971		
Colombia	8 April 1986		
Congo	23 October 1978		
Costa Rica [b]	3 March 1970	In force: 22 November 1979	278
Côte d'Ivoire	6 March 1973	In force: 8 September 1983	309
Croatia [c]	29 June 1992	Approved: 8 June 1994	. . .
Cyprus	10 February 1970	In force: 26 January 1973	189
Czech Republic [d]	1 January 1993	In force: 3 March 1972	173
Dem. People's Rep. of Korea	12 December 1985	In force: 10 April 1992	403
Denmark [e]	3 January 1969	In force: 21 February 1977	193
Dominica	10 August 1984		
Dominican Republic [b]	24 July 1971	In force: 11 October 1973	201
Ecuador [b]	7 March 1969	In force: 10 March 1975	231
Egypt	26 February 1981	In force: 30 June 1982	302
El Salvador [b]	11 July 1972	In force: 22 April 1975	232
Equatorial Guinea	1 November 1984	Approved: 13 June 1986	. . .
Estonia	31 January 1992	Approved: 24 February 1992	. . .
Ethiopia	5 February 1970	In force: 2 December 1977	261
Fiji	14 July 1972	In force: 22 March 1973	192
Finland	5 February 1969	In force: 9 February 1972	155
Gabon	19 February 1974	Signed: 3 December 1979	. . .
Gambia	12 May 1975	In force: 8 August 1978	277
Georgia	7 March 1994		
Germany [f]	2 May 1975	In force: 21 February 1977	193
Ghana	5 May 1970	In force: 17 February 1975	226
Greece [g]	11 March 1970	Accession: 17 December 1981	193
Grenada	19 August 1974		
Guatemala [b]	22 September 1970	In force: 1 February 1982	299
Guinea	29 April 1985		

NNWS which have signed, ratified, acceded to or succeed to NPT [a] (1)	Date of ratification, accession or succession [a] (2)	Safeguards agreement with the Agency (3)	INFCIRC (4)
Guinea-Bissau	20 August 1976		
Guyana	19 October 1993		
Haiti [b]	2 June 1970	Signed: 6 January 1975	. . .
Holy See	25 February 1971	In force: 1 August 1972	187
Honduras [b]	16 May 1973	In force: 18 April 1975	235
Hungary	27 May 1969	In force: 30 March 1972	174
Iceland	18 July 1969	In force: 16 October 1974	215
Indonesia	12 July 1979	In force: 14 July 1980	283
Iran (Islamic Republic of)	2 February 1970	In force: 15 May 1974	214
Iraq	29 October 1969	In force: 29 February 1972	172
Ireland	1 July 1968	In force: 21 February 1977	193
Italy	2 May 1975	In force: 21 February 1977	193
Jamaica [b]	5 March 1970	In force: 6 November 1978	265
Japan	8 June 1976	In force: 2 December 1977	255
Jordan	11 February 1970	In force: 21 February 1978	258
Kazakhstan	14 February 1994	Signed: 26 July 1994	. . .
Kenya	11 June 1970		
Kiribati	18 April 1985	In force: 19 December 1990	390
Kuwait	17 November 1989		
Lao People's Dem. Republic	20 February 1970	Signed: 22 November 1991	. . .
Latvia	31 January 1992	In force: 21 December 1993	434
Lebanon	15 July 1970	In force: 5 March 1973	191
Lesotho	20 May 1970	In force: 12 June 1973	199
Liberia	5 March 1970		
Libyan Arab Jamahiriya	26 May 1975	In force: 8 July 1980	282
Liechtenstein	20 April 1978	In force: 4 October 1979	275
Lithuania	23 September 1991	In force: 15 October 1992	413
Luxembourg	2 May 1975	In force: 21 February 1977	193
Madagascar	8 October 1970	In force: 14 June 1973	200
Malawi	18 February 1986	In force: 3 August 1992	409
Malaysia	5 March 1970	In force: 29 February 1972	182
Maldives	7 April 1970.	In force: 2 October 1977	253
Mali	10 February 1970		
Malta	6 February 1970	In force: 13 November 1990	387
Mauritania	26 October 1993		
Mauritius	25 April 1969	In force: 31 January 1973	190
Mexico [b]	21 January 1969	In force: 14 September 1973	197
Mongolia	14 May 1969	In force: 5 September 1972	188
Morocco	27 November 1970	In force: 18 February 1975	228
Mozambique	4 September 1990		
Myanmar	2 December 1992		
Namibia	2 October 1992		
Nauru	7 June 1982	In force: 13 April 1984	317

NNWS which have signed, ratified, acceded to or succeed to NPT [a] (1)	Date of ratification, accession or succession [a] (2)	Safeguards agreement with the Agency (3)	INFCIRC (4)
Nepal	5 January 1970	In force: 22 June 1972	186
Netherlands [b]	2 May 1975	In force: 21 February 1977	193
New Zealand	10 September 1969	In force: 29 February 1972	185
Nicaragua [b]	6 March 1973	In force: 29 December 1976	246
Niger	9 October 1992		
Nigeria	27 September 1968	In force: 29 February 1988	358
Norway	5 February 1969	In force: 1 March 1972	177
Panama	13 January 1977	Signed: 22 December 1988	...
Papua New Guinea	25 January 1982	In force: 13 October 1983	312
Paraguay [b]	4 February 1970	In force: 20 March 1979	279
Peru [b]	3 March 1970	In force: 1 August 1979	273
Philippines	5 October 1972	In force: 16 October 1974	216
Poland	12 June 1969	In force: 11 October 1972	179
Portugal [i]	15 December 1977	Accession: 1 July 1986	193
Qatar	3 April 1989		
Republic of Korea	23 April 1975	In force: 14 November 1975	236
Romania	4 February 1970	In force: 27 October 1972	180
Rwanda	20 May 1975		
St. Kitts and Nevis	22 March 1993		
St. Lucia	28 December 1979	In force: 2 February 1990	379
St. Vincent and the Grenadines	6 November 1984	In force: 8 January 1992	400
Samoa	17 March 1975	In force: 22 January 1979	268
San Marino	10 August 1970	Approved: 23 February 1977	...
Sao Tome and Principe	20 July 1983		
Saudi Arabia	3 October 1988		
Senegal	17 December 1970	In force: 14 January 1980	276
Seychelles	12 March 1985		
Sierra Leone	26 February 1975	Signed: 10 November 1977	...
Singapore	10 March 1976	In force: 18 October 1977	259
Slovakia [j]	1 January 1993	In force: 3 March 1972	173
Slovenia [k]	7 April 1992	Approved: 8 June 1994	...
Solomon Islands	17 June 1981	In force: 17 June 1993	420
Somalia	5 March 1970		
South Africa	10 July 1991	In force: 16 September 1991	394
Spain	5 November 1987	Accession: 5 April 1989	193
Sri Lanka	5 March 1979	In force: 6 August 1984	320
Sudan	31 October 1973	In force: 7 January 1977	245
Suriname [b]	30 June 1976	In force: 2 February 1979	269
Swaziland	11 December 1969	In force: 28 July 1975	227
Sweden	9 January 1970	In force: 14 April 1975	234
Switzerland	9 March 1977	In force: 6 September 1978	264
Syrian Arab Republic	24 September 1969	In force: 18 May 1992	407
Thailand	7 December 1972	In force: 16 May 1974	241

NNWS which have signed, ratified, acceded to or succeed to NPT [a] (1)	Date of ratification, accession or succession [a] (2)	Safeguards agreement with the Agency (3)	INFCIRC (4)
Togo	26 February 1970	Signed: 29 November 1990	. . .
Tonga	7 July 1971	In force: 18 November 1993	426
Trinidad and Tobago [b]	30 October 1986	In force: 4 November 1992	414
Tunisia	26 February 1970	In force: 13 March 1990	381
Turkey	17 April 1980	In force: 1 September 1981	295
Tuvalu	19 January 1979	In force: 15 March 1991	391
Uganda	20 October 1982		
United Republic of Tanzania	7 June 1991	Signed: 26 August 1992	. . .
Uruguay [b]	31 August 1970	In force: 17 September 1976	157
Uzbekistan	7 May 1992	Approved: 21 February 1994	. . .
Venezuela [b]	26 September 1975	In force: 11 March 1982	300
Viet Nam	14 June 1982	In force: 23 February 1990	376
Yemen	1 June 1979		
Yugoslavia (Serbia and Montenegro) Federal Republic of [l]	3 March 1970	In force: 28 December 1973	204
Zaire	4 August 1970	In force: 9 November 1972	183
Zambia	15 May 1991	Approved: 8 June 1994	. . .
Zimbabwe	26 September 1991		

a/ The information reproduced in columns (1) and (2) was provided to the Agency by depositary Governments of NPT, and an entry in column (1) does not imply the expression of any opinion on the part of the Secretariat concerning the legal status of any country or territory or of its authorities, or concerning the delimitation of its frontiers. The table does not contain information relating to the participation of Taiwan, Province of China in NPT.

b/ The relevant safeguards agreement refers to both NPT and the Tlatelolco Treaty.

c/ The NPT safeguards agreement concluded with the Socialist Federal Republic of Yugoslavia (INFCIRC/204), which entered into force on 28 December 1973, continues to be applied in Croatia to the extent relevant to the territory of Croatia.

d/ The NPT safeguards agreement concluded with the Czechoslovak Socialist Republic (INFCIRC/173), which entered into force on 3 March 1972, continues to be applied in the Czech Republic to the extent relevant to the territory of the Czech Republic.

e/ The NPT safeguards agreement with Denmark (INFCIRC/176), in force since 1 March 1972, has been replaced by the agreement of 5 April 1973 between the non-nuclear-weapon States of EURATOM, EURATOM and the Agency (INFCIRC/193) but still applies to the Faroe Islands. Upon Greenland's secession from EURATOM as of 31 January 1985, the Agreement between the Agency and Denmark (INFCIRC/176) re-entered into force for Greenland.

f/ The safeguards agreement of 7 March 1972 concluded with the German Democratic Republic (INFCIRC/181) is no longer in force with effect from 3 October 1990 on which date the German Democratic Republic acceded to the Federal Republic of Germany.

g/ The application of Agency safeguards in Greece under the agreement INFCIRC/166, provisionally in force since 1 March 1972, was suspended on 17 December 1981, at which date Greece acceded to the agreement of 5 April 1973 (INFCIRC/193) between the non-nuclear-weapon States of EURATOM, EURATOM and the Agency.

h/ An agreement had also been concluded in respect of the Netherlands Antilles (INFCIRC/229). This agreement entered into force on 5 June 1975.

i/ The NPT safeguards agreement with Portugal (INFCIRC/272), in force since 14 June 1979, was suspended on 1 July 1986, on which date Portugal acceded to the agreement between the non-nuclear-weapon States of EURATOM, EURATOM and the Agency of 5 April 1973 (INFCIRC/193).

j/ The NPT safeguards agreement concluded with the Czechoslovak Socialist Republic (INFCIRC/173), which entered into force on 3 March 1972, continues to be applied in Slovakia to the extent relevant to the territory of Slovakia.

k/ The NPT safeguards agreement concluded with the Socialist Federal Republic of Yugoslavia (INFCIRC/204), which entered into force on 28 December 1973, continues to be applied in Slovenia to the extent relevant to the territory of Slovenia.

l/ The NPT safeguards agreement concluded with the Socialist Federal Republic of Yugoslavia (INFCIRC/204), which entered into force on 28 December 1973, continues to be applied in the Federal Republic of Yugoslavia (Serbia and Montenegro) to the extent relevant to the territory of the Federal Republic of Yugoslavia (Serbia and Montenegro).

Document 47

Statement of the Secretary-General in the First Committee of the General Assembly (excerpts)

A/C.1/49/PV.3, New York, 17 October 1994

...

At its Summit meeting in January 1992, the Security Council declared that the proliferation of weapons of mass destruction constitutes a threat to international security. This declaration has reinforced the resolve of the international community. It has strengthened our commitment to adhere to the global norms enshrined in existing treaties.

...

With 165 signatories, the Nuclear Non-Proliferation Treaty (NPT) is one of today's global arrangements with the largest number of participants. For the vast majority of the international community, it is the primary normative foundation for the non-proliferation of nuclear weapons. I call upon all Member States to support the indefinite and unconditional extension of the NPT at the forthcoming Review Conference in 1995. This will not only strengthen its effective implementation but also speed progress towards the goal of eliminating all nuclear weapons. I look forward to new accessions to the treaty so that it may become truly universal in acceptance and in practice.

Still more global measures are required, however. I am concerned that negotiations on the comprehensive nuclear-test ban have not progressed as smoothly as I had hoped. I am encouraged by the text of the draft treaty produced by the Conference on Disarmament, but important issues remain unresolved. I strongly urge the participants in these negotiations to work towards a consensus. An early conclusion of a test-ban treaty is fundamental to real progress in nuclear disarmament and to the security of the non-nuclear-weapon States.

Also required is a treaty banning the further production of fissile material for nuclear weapons and other nuclear explosive devices. Intentions to create such a treaty have been clearly stated, but negotiations on such a treaty have yet to start. We must not allow technical and procedural difficulties to delay negotiations for ever. Now is the time to overcome them. Now is the time to act.

With the START, we have seen definitive and positive trends for quantitative reduction of nuclear weapons. I suggest today that we must now seek to curb qualitative development of such weapons. I believe that a comprehensive test-ban treaty and a treaty on the non-

production of fissile material, are the most tangible means to that end.

I would also like to stress that there is an urgent need for a binding global agreement on security assurances.

As I have mentioned, in the last few years unprecedented strides have been made in actual nuclear disarmament. The United States and the Russian Federation have indicated their intention to expedite the implementation of the Strategic Arms Reduction Treaties (START), with regard to reductions of strategic nuclear weapons. Other nuclear-weapon States have indicated a willingness to make their own contribution to this process. Within this context, the non-nuclear-weapon States demand—rightly, in my view—stronger international and legally binding security assurances.

I firmly believe that there should be no delay in making such assurances. Especially to those States that have pledged to renounce fully and unconditionally the possession and acquisition of nuclear weapons, security assurances must be granted. The nuclear-weapon States must take the lead in making positive moves towards a binding global agreement on this issue.

All these efforts form a global web of protection against weapons of mass destruction, but they can be successful only with the full commitment and practical participation of all Member States. In my recent meetings with Heads of State and Ministers I have stressed the importance of developing new approaches consistent with the present political and security environment. Such approaches are needed, for instance, to provide greater support for the Security Council in its responsibilities concerning weapons of mass destruction.

New approaches are also needed to provide better support to the work of organizations such as the International Atomic Energy Agency (IAEA). The Agency's current initiatives deal with the problem of the security of nuclear materials; they deserve the full support of all Member States. I am in close contact with Mr. Hans Blix, the Director General of the Vienna Agency, on this subject as well as on that of nuclear proliferation in general. Tomorrow, I will meet with him to discuss these issues in further detail. My aim is to ensure the closest possible cooperation between our two offices and to build the necessary political support for the Agency's efforts in these areas.

...

Treaties, agreements and regimes give cooperative security arrangements a legal or political foundation, but they must also be built upon firm economic, scientific and technological realities. Accords will be durable and effective so long as they integrate all of these components.

Thus non-proliferation regimes based on denial alone will not be effective in the long run. To succeed, non-proliferation regimes must be coupled with the transfer of technology for peaceful and legitimate purposes.

...

Document 48

List of States parties to the NPT

Not issued as a United Nations document

(as of 31 January 1995)

1. Afghanistan
2. Albania
3. Algeria
4. Antigua and Barbuda
5. Armenia
6. Australia
7. Austria
8. Azerbaijan
9. Bahamas
10. Bahrain
11. Bangladesh
12. Barbados
13. Belarus
14. Belgium
15. Belize
16. Benin
17. Bhutan
18. Bolivia
19. Bosnia and Herzegovina
20. Botswana
21. Brunei Darussalam
22. Bulgaria
23. Burkina Faso
24. Burundi
25. Cambodia
26. Cameroon
27. Canada
28. Cape Verde
29. Central African Republic
30. Chad
31. China
32. Colombia
33. Congo
34. Costa Rica
35. Côte d'Ivoire
36. Croatia
37. Cyprus
38. Czech Republic
39. Democratic People's Republic of Korea
40. Denmark
41. Dominica
42. Dominican Republic
43. Ecuador
44. Egypt
45. El Salvador
46. Equatorial Guinea
47. Estonia
48. Ethiopia
49. Fiji
50. Finland
51. France
52. Gabon
53. Gambia
54. Georgia
55. Germany
56. Ghana
57. Greece
58. Grenada
59. Guatemala
60. Guinea
61. Guinea-Bissau
62. Guyana
63. Haiti
64. Holy See
65. Honduras
66. Hungary
67. Iceland
68. Indonesia
69. Iran (Islamic Republic of)
70. Iraq
71. Ireland
72. Italy
73. Jamaica
74. Japan
75. Jordan
76. Kazakhstan
77. Kenya

78.	Kiribati	126.	Saint Kitts and Nevis
79.	Kuwait	127.	Saint Lucia
80.	Kyrgyzstan	128.	Saint Vincent and the Grenadines
81.	Lao People's Democratic Republic	129.	Samoa
82.	Latvia	130.	San Marino
83.	Lebanon	131.	Sao Tome and Principe
84.	Lesotho	132.	Saudi Arabia
85.	Liberia	133.	Senegal
86.	Libyan Arab Jamahiriya	134.	Seychelles
87.	Liechtenstein	135.	Sierra Leone
88.	Lithuania	136.	Singapore
89.	Luxembourg	137.	Slovakia
90.	Madagascar	138.	Slovenia
91.	Malawi	139.	Solomon Islands
92.	Malaysia	140.	Somalia
93.	Maldives	141.	South Africa
94.	Mali	142.	Spain
95.	Malta	143.	Sri Lanka
96.	Marshall Islands	144.	Sudan
97.	Mauritania	145.	Suriname
98.	Mauritius	146.	Swaziland
99.	Mexico	147.	Sweden
100.	Mongolia	148.	Switzerland
101.	Morocco	149.	Syrian Arab Republic
102.	Mozambique	150.	Thailand
103.	Myanmar	151.	Togo
104.	Namibia	152.	Tonga
105.	Nauru	153.	Trinidad and Tobago
106.	Nepal	154.	Tunisia
107.	Netherlands	155.	Turkey
108.	New Zealand	156.	Turkmenistan
109.	Nicaragua	157.	Tuvalu
110.	Niger	158.	Uganda
111.	Nigeria	159.	Ukraine
112.	Norway	160.	United Kingdom of Great Britain and Northern Ireland
113.	Panama	161.	United Republic of Tanzania
114.	Papua New Guinea	162.	United States of America
115.	Paraguay	163.	Uruguay
116.	Peru	164.	Uzbekistan
117.	Philippines	165.	Venezuela
118.	Poland	166.	Viet Nam
119.	Portugal	167.	Yemen
120.	Qatar	168.	Yugoslavia
121.	Republic of Korea	169.	Zaire
122.	Republic of Moldova	170.	Zambia
123.	Romania	171.	Zimbabwe
124.	Russian Federation		
125.	Rwanda		

Document 49

Nuclear fuel cycle

Not issued as a United Nations document 1/

Evolution of the nuclear fuel cycle

The concept of a nuclear fuel cycle is an old one, almost dating back to the conception of controlled nuclear fission to generate electricity. At the time of the development of the first nuclear power plants, it was generally taken for granted that fuel from power reactors would be reprocessed and that the recovered uranium and plutonium would be recycled.

In those days, uranium ore was a scarce and expensive commodity and it was naturally assumed that economically available supplies would not meet the demands required by a widespread use of nuclear power. Consequently, the extraction of all the potential energy content of uranium, not just from uranium-235, seemed to be essential. Such a complete exploitation of uranium resources requires reprocessing of the spent fuel and the extraction of plutonium for burning in specially designed "fast" reactors. The approach became more attractive with the concept of fast breeder reactors, which could produce more fuel than they consumed. For such reasons, many countries during the 1960s attached high priority to the development of fast reactors, and it was anticipated that they would be widely deployed in the 1980s.

Until the early 1970s then, the nuclear fuel cycle was pictured as an orderly sequence of processes. It began with uranium mining, milling, and conversion, was followed by fuel enrichment, fuel fabrication, and power generation, and was finally completed by reprocessing, recycling of plutonium and uranium to fast reactors, and final disposal of waste streams from reprocessing plants. In essence, closure of the fuel cycle meant the effective use of plutonium generated in thermal reactors to fuel fast breeder reactors.

Why the concept has been modified

The situation has changed dramatically during the last 20 years. No closed fuel cycle of the type originally envisaged to be operational in the 1980s exists today. Although the closure of the nuclear fuel cycle has been experimentally demonstrated in France, Japan, the Russian Federation and the United Kingdom, it has not been demonstrated yet on a commercial scale.

Current thinking is divided into two schools. One believes that plutonium as an energy source has no economic value and spent fuel should be disposed of in a safe way (the "once-through" option). The other essentially adheres to the traditional nuclear fuel cycle (closed cycle option). The difference of opinions stems mainly from the predictions of nuclear electricity growth and the predicted availability of economical supplies of uranium, although it is coloured by political and environmental issues as well.

It should be noted that plutonium can be used in fast reactors for more efficient energy production, with the added advantage that the inventory of transplutonium elements inherent in the once-through option can be reduced. In the closed cycle option, the burning of plutonium in the form of mixed-oxide (MOX) fuels in light-water reactors (LWRs) is only a temporary expedient until fast reactors are available.

The future of nuclear fuel cycle options

At the present time, the two options for the nuclear fuel cycle are hotly debated by their proponents. It seems that the once-through option combines pessimistic predictions about the future of nuclear energy with optimistic predictions about the availability of economical uranium resources. In our view, however, this option has an inherent problem. The spent fuel, or vitrified plutonium mixed with fission products, that is disposed of in geological repositories will become potential plutonium mines after thousands of years. This is because most of the fission products will decay more rapidly than plutonium.

The closed fuel cycle option is supported by the long-term outlook for nuclear energy. It is estimated that the world population of 5.5 billion will increase yearly at the rate of 100 million. By the year 2010, it has been estimated that about four times as much electrical energy as is currently consumed will be needed. Such a drastic increase cannot be supplied without jeopardizing the environment unless there is a greater commitment to nuclear energy. Also, it is likely that stronger commercial competition in reprocessing and MOX fuel fabrication will develop over the next 20 years, resulting in substantial price reductions. With the inevitable price escalation of uranium, there will be more justification on economic grounds for using plutonium to fuel fast reactors, and thus for closing the fuel cycle.

Nevertheless, the closed fuel cycle option has several attendant difficulties. Among the most important may be

1/ This document is an excerpt from an article entitled "Nuclear fuel cycles: Adjusting to new realities" by B. A. Semenov and N. Oi, published in the *IAEA Bulletin*, 3/1993, and is reproduced here with the permission of the IAEA.

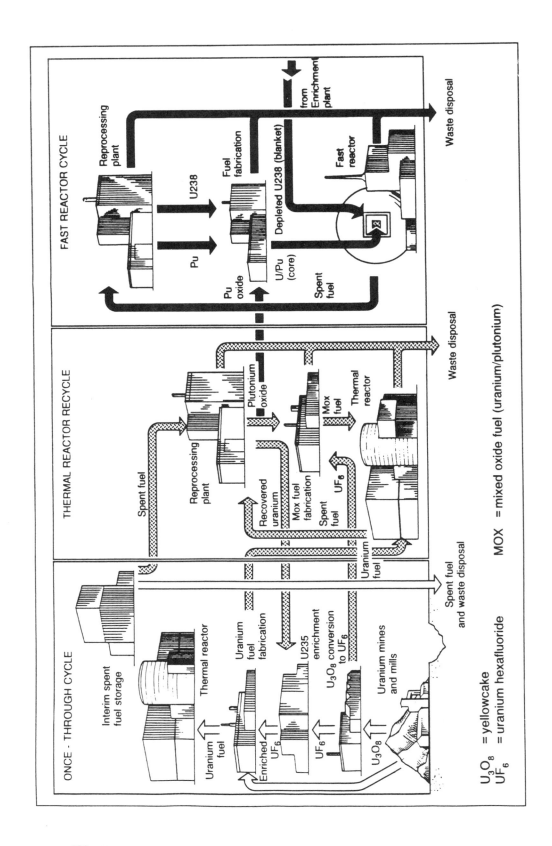

FAST REACTOR CYCLE

Reprocessing plant

U238

Pu

Fuel fabrication

Pu oxide

Depleted U238 (blanket)

U/Pu (core)

from Enrichment plant

Fast reactor

Spent fuel

Waste disposal

THERMAL REACTOR RECYCLE

Spent fuel

Reprocessing plant

Plutonium oxide

Recovered uranium

Mox fuel fabrication

Spent fuel

Mox fuel

UF₆

Thermal reactor

Waste disposal

Uranium fuel

ONCE - THROUGH CYCLE

Interim spent fuel storage

Thermal reactor

Uranium fuel fabrication

Uranium fuel

Enriched UF₆

U235 enrichment

UF₆

U₃O₈ conversion to UF₆

Uranium mines and mills

U₃O₈

Spent fuel and waste disposal

U_3O_8 = yellowcake
UF_6 = uranium hexafluoride

MOX = mixed oxide fuel (uranium/plutonium)

national policies and regulations governing licensing and their effect on the economics of future fast reactors. Detailed regulatory considerations developed over decades for current water reactors undoubtedly will be adapted to fast reactors. This would cause long delays and impose heavy economic burdens.

Some modifications to the two basic fuel-cycle options can be considered. One is to proceed to extra-high burnup levels of fuels in present light-water reactors to produce plutonium of isotopic composition that is easier to verify and safeguard. Another is to revisit the thorium/uranium cycle that is free of the stigma associated with plutonium.

The future development of the nuclear fuel cycle will probably differ from one country to another. Those who can afford expensive natural resources may decide for political and other reasons to curtail their nuclear energy programmes and adopt the once-through option. Others will surely expand their nuclear programmes and strive to implement the closed cycle option. It may take another 20 years to visualize how the trend will take shape.

Nuclear fuel cycles

Three different types of fuel cycle are commonly identified for nuclear power generation, depending on whether fuel is recycled and on the type of reactor used for electricity production.

- The "once-through" fuel cycle. In this cycle, the spent fuel is not reprocessed but kept in storage until it is eventually disposed of as waste.

- The thermal reactor cycle. In this cycle, the spent fuel is reprocessed and the uranium and plutonium are separated from the fission products. Both the uranium and the plutonium can be recycled in new fuel elements. It also is possible to recycle only the uranium and to store the plutonium, and vice versa.

- The fast breeder reactor cycle. In this cycle, the spent fuel is similarly reprocessed and the uranium and plutonium fabricated into new fuel elements. However, they are recycled to fast breeder reactors, in which there is a central core of uranium/plutonium fuel surrounded by a blanket of depleted uranium (uranium from which most of the uranium-235 atoms have been removed during the process of enrichment) or to burner reactors. This depleted uranium consists mostly of uranium-238 atoms, some of which are converted to plutonium during irradiation. By suitable operation, fast breeder reactors thus can produce slightly more fuel than they consume, hence the name "breeder".

V   Subject index to documents

[This subject index to the documents reproduced in this book should be used in conjunction with the index on pages 197-199. A complete listing of the documents indexed below appears on pages 39-42.]

A

Accessions.
> *See:* Signatures, accessions, ratifications.

Africa—Nuclear-weapon-free zone.
– Document 44

Agency for the Prohibition of Nuclear Weapons in Latin America and the Caribbean.
– Document 9

Aggression.
– Document 12
> *See also:* International security.

Armaments race.
> *See:* Arms race.

Armed incidents.
– Documents 34-35

Arms control.
> *See:* Arms limitation.

Arms limitation.
– Documents 25, 38
> *See also:* Arms race. Disarmament agreements. Nuclear freeze. Nuclear non-proliferation.

Arms race.
– Document 25
> *See also:* Arms limitation. Arms transfers. Disarmament. Military expenditures. Nuclear arms race.

Arms sales.
> *See:* Arms transfers.

Arms transfers.
– Document 38
> *See also:* Arms race.

Atomic energy.
> *See:* Nuclear energy.

Atomic energy research.
> *See:* Nuclear research.

Atomic weapons
> See: Nuclear weapons.

B

Bacteriological weapons.
> *See:* Biological weapons.

Biological weapons.
– Document 40
> *See also:* Chemical weapons.

C

Caribbean region—Nuclear-weapon-free zone.
– Documents 9, 28

Charter of the United Nations (1945).
– Document 25

Chemical weapons.
– Document 40
> *See also:* Biological weapons.

Chernobyl (Ukraine)—Nuclear accidents.
– Document 43

China—Security assurances.
– Documents 22, 29

Collective security.
> *See:* International security.

Comprehensive Nuclear Test-ban Treaty (Draft).
– Documents 35, 40, 47

Confidence-building measures.
– Documents 25, 33-34, 36, 43
> *See also:* Disarmament. Dispute settlement. Verification.

Conflict prevention.
> *See:* War prevention.

Conflict resolution.
> *See:* Dispute settlement.

Consultations.
– Documents 10, 32, 41
> *See also:* Dispute settlement.

Convention on the Prohibition of the Development, Production and Stockpiling of Bacteriological (Biological) and Toxin Weapons and on Their Destruction (1972).
– Documents 25, 40

Convention on the Prohibition of the Development, Production, Stockpiling and Use of Chemical Weapons and Their Destruction (1993).
– Document 40

Conventional weapons.
– Document 25

Conventions.
> *See:* Treaties.

D

Declarations.
– Documents 18, 25, 35

Deep seabed.
> *See:* Seabed.

Deterrence.
– Document 6

Development-disarmament link.
> *See:* Disarmament-development link.

Disarmament.
– Documents 5, 25, 38
> *See also:* Arms limitation. Arms race. Confidence-building measures. Disarmament agreements. Disarmament negotiations. Disarmament-development link. International security. Nuclear disarmament. Regional disarmament. Verification. War prevention.

Disarmament agreements.
– Documents 1-12, 14-18, 23, 25, 28, 33-36, 38-40, 43, 45-48
> *See also:* Arms limitation. Disarmament. Disarmament negotiations. On-site inspection. Regional disarmament.

Disarmament negotiations.
– Documents 5, 7-8, 10-11, 14, 16, 18, 25, 27, 33, 35, 40, 44, 47
> *See also:* Disarmament. Disarmament agreements.

Disarmament-development link.
– Document 25
> *See also:* Disarmament. Military expenditures.

Dispute settlement.
– Documents 15, 25, 38
> *See also:* Confidence-building measures. Consultations. War prevention.

Documents.
– Document 8
> *See also:* Maps. Report preparation.

E

Eastern Europe.
> *See also:* Russian Federation. Ukraine.

Environmental protecion.
– Document 43

Equipment and supplies.
– Documents 39, 41

Explosives.
– Documents 28, 32, 35

F

Fast reactors.
– Document 49

Final Declaration of the First Review Conference of the Parties to the Treaty on the Non-Proliferation of Nuclear Weapons (1975).
– Document 18

Final Declaration of the States Party to the Treaty on the Non-Proliferation of Nuclear Weapons (1985).
– Document 35

Fissionable materials.
– Documents 6, 16-17, 19, 37, 39, 41, 43, 47

France—Security assurances.
– Documents 20, 24, 30

G

Guidelines.
– Documents 19, 39, 41

I

IAEA.
> *See:* International Atomic Energy Agency.

Information exchange.
– Documents 32, 43
> *See also:* Scientific cooperation. Technology transfer.

International agreements.
> *See:* Treaties.

International Atomic Energy Agency
– Documents 9, 13, 15-19, 27-28, 32, 34-39, 41, 43-47

International Atomic Energy Agency. Director General.
– Documents 17, 28, 34, 37

International Atomic Energy Agency. General Conference.
– Document 43

International instruments.
– Document 34
  See also: Declarations. Treaties.

International obligations.
– Documents 6, 12, 16, 18
  See also: Obligations. Treaties.

International security.
– Documents 25, 38
  See also: Aggression. Disarmament. Security assurances. War prevention.

Iraq—Armed incidents.
– Document 35

Iraq—Nuclear facilities.
– Document 35

K

Korean peninsula—Nuclear-weapon-free zone.
– Document 44

L

Latin America—Nuclear-weapon-free zone.
– Documents 9, 28

Liability for nuclear damages.
– Document 15

M

Maps.
– Document 32
  See also: Documents.

Middle East—Nuclear-weapon-free zone.
– Document 44

Military applications.
– Document 44

Military expenditures.
– Document 25
  See also: Arms race. Disarmament-development link.

Military technology.
– Document 38

N

Negative security assurances.
  See: Security assurances.

New technologies.
– Document 44
  See also: Research and development.

Non-first-use policy.
– Documents 21-22, 29, 31
  See also: Nuclear war. Nuclear weapons.

Non-nuclear-weapon States.
– Documents 2-6, 8, 11-12, 14-16, 18-30, 33, 35-37, 41-42, 44-47
  See also: Nuclear weapon States. Nuclear weapons. Nuclear-weapon-free zones. Security assurances.

Nuclear accidents.
– Document 43

Nuclear arms race.
– Documents 11, 18, 25, 33

Nuclear disarmament.
– Documents 1-6, 11, 14, 16, 18, 25, 27-28, 33-37

Nuclear energy.
– Documents 14, 16-18, 28, 35, 37, 49

Nuclear engineering.
  See: Nuclear technology.

Nuclear explosions.
  See: Peaceful nuclear explosions.

Nuclear facilities.
– Documents 13, 15-19, 34-35, 37, 39, 41, 44
  See also: On-site inspection.

Nuclear freeze.
– Document 35

Nuclear fuel cycle.
– Documents 27, 35, 49
  See also: Plutonium.

Nuclear fuel reprocessing.
– Document 49

Nuclear fuels.
– Documents 17, 19, 39
  See also: Plutonium. Uranium.

Nuclear installations.
  See: Nuclear facilities.

Nuclear materials.
– Documents 13, 15-19, 28, 35, 39, 41, 47
  See also: Fissionable materials.

Nuclear moratorium.
See: Nuclear freeze.

Nuclear non-proliferation.
– Documents 5-8, 10-12, 14-18, 21, 23, 25-28, 33-40, 43-48
    See also: Arms limitation.

Nuclear power.
– Documents 17, 34, 37

Nuclear power plants.
– Document 6, 13, 28, 43

Nuclear reactor sites.
    See: Nuclear facilities.

Nuclear reactors.
– Documents 6, 13, 17, 19, 34, 49
    See also: Fast reactors. Peaceful nuclear explosions.

Nuclear research.
– Document 17

Nuclear safeguards.
– Documents 13-19, 27-28, 32, 34-35, 37-39, 41, 43-46

Nuclear safety.
– Document 43

Nuclear technology.
– Documents 18-19, 27, 34-37, 39, 41

Nuclear tests.
    See: Nuclear weapon tests.

Nuclear war.
– Documents 25, 33, 36

Nuclear warfare.
    See: Nuclear war.

Nuclear weapon States.
– Documents 2-5, 8, 11-12, 20-27, 29-31, 33, 35-37, 40, 42, 47
    See also: Security assurances.

Nuclear weapon tests.
– Documents 3, 18, 27-28, 32, 35, 40, 43, 47
    See also: Comprehensive Nuclear Test-Ban Treaty (Draft). Peaceful nuclear explosions.

Nuclear weapons.
– Documents 1, 4, 6, 25, 32, 44
    See also: Security assurances.

Nuclear-weapon-free zones.
– Documents 9, 18, 20, 22, 24-25, 28-29, 32, 35, 44

O

Obligations.
– Document 5
    See also: International obligations.

Oceania—Maps.
– Document 32

Oceania—Nuclear-weapon-free zone.
– Document 32

Offshore nuclear power plants.
    See: Nuclear power plants.

On-site inspection.
– Documents 13, 15, 17, 34, 37, 44
    See also: Disarmament agreements. Nuclear facilities.

Outer space.
– Document 25

P

Pacific islands.
    See: Oceania.

Peaceful nuclear explosions.
– Documents 14, 16
    See also: Nuclear reactors. Nuclear weapon tests.

Peaceful settlement of disputes.
    See: Dispute settlement.

Plutonium.
– Documents 6, 49
    See also: Nuclear fuel cycle.

Privileges and immunities.
– Document 15

Protocol for the Prohibition of the Use in War of Asphyxiating, Poisonous or Other Gases, and of Bacteriological Methods of Warfare (1925).
– Document 25

R

Radiation protection.
– Document 43

Radioactive waste management.
– Documents 32, 34, 43

Radiological protection.
    See: Radiation protection.

Regional disarmament.
– Document 5
    See also: Disarmament agreements.

Report preparation.
– Documents 3, 5, 8, 10-11
    See also: Documents.

Research and development.
– Documents 14, 35
    See also: New technologies.

Review Conference of the Parties to the Treaty on the Non-Proliferation of Nuclear Weapons (1st : 1975 : Geneva).
– Documents 16-18

Review Conference of the Parties to the Treaty on the Non-Proliferation of Nuclear Weapons (2nd : 1980 : Geneva).
– Documents 18, 27, 28

Review Conference of the Parties to the Treaty on the Non-Proliferation of Nuclear Weapons (3rd : 1985 : Geneva).
– Documents 33-35

Review Conference of the Parties to the Treaty on the Non-Proliferation of Nuclear Weapons (4th : 1990 : Geneva).
– Documents 36-37

Russian Federation—Disarmament agreements.
– Document 40

Russian Federation—Security assurances.
– Document 42

Russian Federation—Strategic nuclear weapon systems.
– Document 40

S

Scientific cooperation.
– Documents 16, 18
    See also: Information exchange. Technical cooperation.

Seabed.
– Document 25

Security assurances.
– Documents 8, 12, 14, 16, 18, 20-27, 29-31, 35-36, 42, 47
    See also: International security. Non-nuclear-weapon States. Nuclear weapon States. Nuclear weapons.

Signatures, accessions, ratifications.
– Documents 9, 11, 16, 25, 28, 32, 40, 45-46, 48
    See also: Treaties.

South Pacific islands.
    See: Oceania.

South Pacific Nuclear Free Zone Treaty (1985).
– Document 32

South Pacific Nuclear Free Zone Treaty (1985). Protocols, etc., 1986 Aug. 8 (Protocol 1, Protocol 2 and Protocol 3).
– Document 32

Strategic nuclear weapon systems.
– Documents 27, 40

T

Technical cooperation.
– Documents 16, 18, 34-35
    See also: Scientific cooperation.

Technology transfer.
– Documents 2, 4, 19, 34, 37-39, 41
    See also: Information exchange.

Treaties.
– Documents 9, 11, 32
    See also: Disarmament agreements. International obligations. Signatures, accessions, ratifications. Verification.

Treaty Between the United States of America and the Union of Soviet Socialist Republics on the Reduction and the Limitation of Strategic Offensive Arms (1991).
– Document 40

Treaty for the Prohibition of Nuclear Weapons in Latin America and the Caribbean (1967).
– Documents 9, 25, 28

Treaty for the Prohibition of Nuclear Weapons in Latin America and the Caribbean (1967). Protocols, etc., 1967 Feb. 14 (Protocol I and Protocol II).
– Document 9

Treaty on Principles Governing the Activities of States in the Exploration and Use of Outer Space, including the Moon and Other Celestial Bodies (1966).
– Document 25

Treaty on the Non-Proliferation of Nuclear Weapons (1968).
– Documents 11-12, 14-18, 23, 25, 27-28, 33-40, 42-48

U

UK.
>See: United Kingdom.

Ukraine—Nuclear accidents.
– Document 43

Ukraine—Nuclear weapons.
– Document 44

Ukrainian SSR.
>See: Ukraine.

UN.
– Document 38

UN. Advisory Board on Disarmament Matters.
– Document 44

UN. Conference of the Committee on Disarmament.
– Documents 5, 8, 10-11, 16

UN. Disarmament Commission.
– Documents 1, 3

UN. Disarmament Commission (1962 : New York).
– Document 3

UN. Eighteen-Nation Committee on Disarmament.
– Documents 5-6

UN. General Assembly. 1st Committee.
– Documents 5, 8

UN. General Assembly (10th Special Sess. : 1978).
– Document 25

UN. General Assembly (22nd Sess. : 1967-1968)—Agenda.
– Document 10

UN. General Assembly (49th Sess. : 1994-1995). 1st Committee.
– Document 47

UN. Secretary-General.
– Documents 5, 6, 14, 16, 27, 33, 36, 40, 43-44, 47

UN. Security Council.
– Document 38

UN. Security Council. Summit Meeting (1992 : New York).
– Document 38

UN. Ten-Nation Committee On Disarmament.
– Document 1

Underground nuclear explosions.
>See: Nuclear weapon tests. Peaceful nuclear explosions.

Union of Soviet Socialist Republics.
>See: Russian Federation. Ukraine.

Union of Soviet Socialist Republics—Disarmament agreements.
– Documents 36, 40

Union of Soviet Socialist Republics—Security assurances.
– Documents 21, 31

Union of Soviet Socialist Republics—Strategic nuclear weapon systems.
– Document 40

United Kingdom—Security assurances.
– Document 23

United States—Disarmament agreements.
– Documents 36, 40

United States—Security assurances.
– Document 26

United States—Strategic nuclear weapon systems.
– Document 40

Uranium.
– Document 49

USA.
>See: United States.

USSR.
>See: Union of Soviet Socialist Republics.

V

Verification.
– Documents 1, 9, 15, 18, 25, 32, 34, 37, 43-44
>See also: Confidence-building measures. Disarmament. On-site inspection. Treaties.

Verification measures.
>See: Verification.

W

War prevention.
– Documents 25, 33, 36
>See also: Disarmament. Dispute settlement. International security.

Weapons deployment.
– Documents 18, 35

Weapons of mass destruction.
– Documents 25, 38, 40, 44, 47
>See also: Biological weapons. Chemical weapons. Nuclear weapons.

VI Index

[The numbers following the entries refer to paragraph numbers in the text.]

A

ABACC
  see Brazilian-Argentine Agency for Accounting and Control of Nuclear Materials
Ad Hoc Committee on a Nuclear Test Ban 83
Ad Hoc Committee on Effective International Arrangements to Assure Non-Nuclear-Weapon States Against the Use or Threat of Use of Nuclear Weapons 62
Ad Hoc Group of Scientific Experts 81
Africa
  nuclear-weapon-free zones 21, 69
Agency for the Prohibition of Nuclear Weapons in Latin America and the Caribbean 41, 67
Aggression 60
Agreement Governing the Activities of States on the Moon and Other Celestial Bodies 72
Amendment Conference 82
Antarctic Treaty 70
Atmosphere
  nuclear tests 75-76

B

Ballistic missiles 19, 86
Belarus
  accession to NPT 20, 88
Bilateral agreements 86-90
Brazilian-Argentine Agency for Accounting and Control of Nuclear Materials 41

C

China
  security assurances 61a

Comprehensive test ban 79-83
Conference on the Discontinuance of Nuclear Weapon Tests 80
Confidence-building measures 23-24, 41
  see also Nuclear-weapon-free zones; Verification
Convention on the Physical Protection of Nuclear Material 50
Cruise missiles 19, 86

D

Delivery systems 55-56
Demilitarized zones
  see also Nuclear-weapon-free zones
  Antarctica 70
  Moon 72
Democratic People's Republic of Korea
  compliance with NPT 32, 34
Disarmament
  see General and complete disarmament; Nuclear disarmament
Dual-use technology 54

E

Environment
  & nuclear tests 76
European Atomic Energy Community 41
Export licences
  information exchange 52, 54
Export restrictions 37, 51-58
Extension Conference of the NPT 29

F

Fissionable materials 25
  export restrictions 51-52
France
  security assurances 61b

G

General and complete disarmament 27, 97

I

IAEA
  see International Atomic Energy Agency
India
  nuclear explosions 30
INF Treaty 19, 86
International Atomic Energy Agency 24, 33-34, 42-47, 94
  INFCIRC/66/Rev.2 46
  INFCIRC/153 46
  terms of reference 42-43
International Atomic Energy Agency. Director General 28
International Convention on Nuclear Safety 48-49
Iraq
  compliance with NPT 32-33

K

Kazakhstan
  accession to NPT 20, 88

L

Latin America
  nuclear-weapon-free zone 21, 65-67
Lisbon Protocol 88
London Guidelines for Nuclear Transfers 53

M

Missile Technology Control Regime 55-56
Missiles
  see also Ballistic missiles; Cruise missiles
  export restrictions 55-56
Moon Agreement 72

N

Negative security assurances 61
  definition 59

197

United Nations publications of related interest

The following UN publications may be obtained from the addresses indicated below, or at your local distributor:

An Agenda for Peace
Second edition, 1995
By Boutros Boutros-Ghali,
Secretary-General of the United Nations
E.95.I.15 92-1-100555-8 155 pp.

An Agenda for Development
By Boutros Boutros-Ghali,
Secretary-General of the United Nations
E.95.I.16 92-1-100556-6 132 pp.

Building Peace and Development, 1994
Annual Report of the Work of the Organization
By Boutros Boutros-Ghali,
Secretary-General of the United Nations
E.95.I.3 92-1-100541-8 299pp.

New Dimensions of Arms Regulation snd
Disarmament in the Post–Cold War Era
By Boutros Boutros-Ghali,
Secretary-General of the United Nations
E.93.IX.8 92-1-142192-6 53pp. $9.95

Basic Facts About the United Nations
E.93.I.2 92-1-100499-3 290pp. $5.00

Demographic Yearbook, Vol. 44
B.94.XIII.1 92-1-051083-6 1992 823pp.
$125.00

Disarmament—New Realities:
Disarmament, Peace-Building and Global
Security
E.93.IX.14 92-1-142199-3 397pp. $35.00

United Nations Disarmament Yearbook, Vol. 18
E.94.IX.1 92-1-142204-3 1993 419pp.
$50.00

Statistical Yearbook, 39th Edition
B.94.XVII.1 H 92-1-061159-4 1992/93
1,174pp. $110.00

Women: Challenges to the Year 2000
E.91.I.21 92-1-100458-6 96pp. $12.95

World Economic and Social Survey 1994
E.94.II.C.1 92-1-109128-4 308pp. $55.00

World Investment Report 1994—
Transnational Corporations, Employment
and the Work Place
E.94.II.A.14 92-1-104435-9 446pp.
$45.00

Yearbook of the United Nations, Vol. 47
E.94.I.1 0-7923-3077-3 1993 1,428pp.
$150.00

The United Nations Blue Books Series
The United Nations and Apartheid, 1948-1994
E.95.I.7 (Soft) 92-1-100546-9 565 pp. $29.95

The United Nations and Cambodia, 1991-1995
E.95.I.9 (Soft) 92-1-100548-5 352 pp. $29.95

United Nations Publications
2 United Nations Plaza, Room DC2-853
New York, NY 10017
United States of America

United Nations Publications
Sales Office and Bookshop
CH-1211 Geneva 10
Switzerland

Typeset by the Copy Preparation and Proofreading Section
Printed on recycled paper by the United Nations Reproduction Section